HISTORY WILL PROVE US RIGHT

HISTORY WILL

PROVE US RIGHT

*Inside the Warren Commission Report
on the Assassination of John F. Kennedy*

HOWARD P. WILLENS

The Overlook Press
New York, NY

This edition first published in hardcover in the United States in 2013 by
The Overlook Press, Peter Mayer Publishers, Inc.

141 Wooster Street
New York, NY 10012
www.overlookpress.com
For bulk and special sales, please contact sales@overlookny.com
or write us at the above address.

Cataloging-in-Publication Data is available from the Library of Congress

Book design and typeformatting by Bernard Schleifer
Manufactured in the United States of America
ISBN: 978-1-4683-0755-9
10 9 8 7 6 5 4 3 2 1

To my colleagues on the staff of the Warren Commission
who knew that Truth was their only client

CONTENTS

■

INTRODUCTION

■

UNDER CLEAR SKIES IN DALLAS ON NOVEMBER 22, 1963, THE PRESIDENTIAL motorcade moved slowly through the streets to a luncheon event, where President John F. Kennedy was set to speak. The day before, President Kennedy had flown to San Antonio, where Vice President Lyndon B. Johnson had joined the party and the president had dedicated new research facilities at the US Air Force School of Aerospace Medicine. After a dinner in Houston honoring Albert Thomas of the US House of Representatives, the president flew to Fort Worth, where he spoke at a large breakfast meeting the next morning before flying to Dallas. After his luncheon speech in Dallas, President Kennedy's itinerary continued with a flight to Austin to attend a reception and speak at a Democratic fund-raising dinner, followed by a weekend stay at Johnson's Texas ranch.

So far, the trip to Texas had been very successful—personally and politically—as the president was seen in the various roles expected of our presidents—chief executive, party leader, and (on this occasion) a prospective candidate for reelection in 1964. President Kennedy and his wife had been greeted with great enthusiasm and warmth by the Texas crowds at his earlier stops, and it was hoped that the Dallas motorcade would provide further evidence of his personal popularity in a city that had rejected him in the 1960 election.

Dallas police motorcycles led the motorcade, followed by a pilot car manned by Dallas policemen about a quarter of a mile ahead of the main participants in the motorcade. Then came more motorcycles and an unmarked police car described as a "rolling command car" driven by Chief of Police Jesse E. Curry, and occupied by Secret Service agents Forrest V. Sorrels and Winston G. Lawson and by Dallas County Sheriff J. E. Decker. The presidential limousine followed, driven by Secret Service agent William R. Greer with agent Roy H. Kellerman in the front seat with him. President Kennedy rode on the right-hand side of the rear seat, with Mrs. Kennedy on his left. Texas Governor John B. Connally occupied the right jump seat in front of the president, and Mrs.

Connally was in the left jump seat. Four police motorcycles flanked the rear of the presidential car, and a follow-up car occupied by eight Secret Service agents was close behind. Next came the vice-presidential car in which Johnson sat on the right-hand side of the rear seat, Senator Ralph W. Yarborough sat on the left-hand side, and the vice president's wife, Claudia Alta ("Lady Bird") Johnson, sat between them. The motorcade concluded with a vice-presidential follow-up car, and several cars and buses for other local and federal dignitaries, White House staff, the press, and photographers.

The path of the motorcade through the streets of Dallas had been publicized in the local papers starting on November 19. As the motorcade went through residential neighborhoods on the way from the airport to Main Street in downtown Dallas, the reception was more enthusiastic and favorable than the president's political advisers could have hoped for. Twice at the president's request, the motorcade stopped to let the president get out to personally greet well-wishers in the friendly crowds.

After leaving Main Street, the motorcade had to turn right on Houston Street and, a block later, turn left on Elm Street to proceed toward a railroad overpass on the way to the luncheon site. As the president's limousine turned left onto Elm Street, the Texas School Book Depository was on the president's right and he waved to the crowd assembled there. His vehicle was now entering Dealey Plaza, an attractively landscaped triangle of about three acres, where hundreds of spectators had located themselves on both sides of Elm Street, hoping for the best possible view. Amateur photographers had their cameras focused and ready to capture a picture of the glamorous couple; children perched on sturdy shoulders to get a better view; and everyone waved enthusiastically at the slow-moving vehicle. President Kennedy, his wife, and all the politicians in the motorcade smiled and waved back at the spectators.

Moments later, shots were heard and the president's hands moved to his neck. A split second passed, then another bullet struck President Kennedy in his head, causing a massive wound. He fell sideways into his wife's lap. The motorcade rushed to Parkland Hospital, where the doctors tried to preserve his life, but the effort was futile. A short time later, President Kennedy was declared dead.

Federal and local law enforcement officials responded immediately. Within hours, a suspect, Lee Harvey Oswald, was apprehended after killing a Dallas police officer who was cruising alone in his patrol car in downtown Dallas on orders from headquarters. Oswald had recently begun work at the Texas School Book Depository and was seen leaving the building after the shooting of the president. Rumors, suspicions, and conspiratorial allegations multiplied with every hour. Two days later, Jack Ruby, a nightclub owner in Dallas, killed Oswald in the basement of the city's municipal building when Oswald was being transferred from police headquarters there to a more secure county jail. This event—witnessed on television by millions of people around the world— led to new suspicions about the motives of both Oswald and Ruby, and whether either was engaged in a conspiracy fostered by the Soviet Union, Cuba, organized crime, Teamsters Union, right-wing interests in Texas, Cuban exiles in the United States, or some US government agency. At President Johnson's direction, the Federal Bureau of Investigation took charge of the investigation.

As a lawyer in the Justice Department's criminal division, I needed to follow these developments intensely—among other reasons because the department might be called upon to play an active role in the prosecution of these crimes. But faced with the prospect of competing Texas and congressional investigations, President Johnson decided otherwise. He appointed a commission headed by Chief Justice Earl Warren to conduct a thorough investigation of these events and report its findings to him and the American people.

A few weeks later, my boss at the Justice Department called me into his office to tell me that the deputy attorney general had volunteered my services to help the commission get up and running. I did not know that what sounded like a short temporary assignment would evolve into a nine-month marathon investigation and supervision of the preparation of a 469-page report with 410 pages of appendices, supported by twenty-six volumes of exhibits and other materials. I also had no way of knowing that this report and its authors would become the object of challenge, hostility, suspicion, ridicule, and scorn, or that seemingly endless conspiracy theories would dominate the debate about President Kennedy's assassination for decades to come.

After the Warren Commission report was published, one of the commission lawyers complained to Chief Justice Warren about the widespread unfair criticism of our work. Warren urged the lawyer not to worry, because "history will prove us right." I am writing this book because Chief Justice Warren turned out to be prescient. In the nearly fifty years since the report was published in 1964, not one fact has emerged that undercuts the main conclusions of the commission that Oswald was the assassin and that there is no credible evidence that either he or Ruby was part of a larger conspiracy.

I kept detailed notes about my work on the Warren Commission staff, a journal born by chance. A Defense Department historian was assigned to the commission to provide some historical perspective for our work. At his first meeting with the commission staff, he suggested that keeping some form of diary might be useful for future historians. I decided to follow his advice and from then on, at irregular intervals, summarized what I had done, the problems we had faced, how we were conducting the investigation, and our progress in preparing the report. I have quoted extensively from my journal in this book.

This book explains what I saw and did as a member of the Warren Commission staff and why I firmly believe the criticism of our work is seriously misguided. My journal and boxes of documents resided undisturbed in my attic after I put them away in 1965; at one point a visiting mouse apparently nibbled around the edges of some pages. In recent years, my wife and children have urged me to explain my journal, put its entries in context, and evaluate this unique assignment after the passage of nearly fifty years. I still regard my work on the Warren Commission as the most intense—and important—professional assignment I ever had. I know that all of my colleagues on the commission staff feel the same way.

The fiftieth anniversary of President Kennedy's assassination provides an opportunity to revisit the report in light of all that has happened since then. This includes the several congressional investigations that exposed the failures of federal agencies to honor President Johnson's mandate to assist the commission fully in the performance of its solemn task. I was witness to the thoroughness, seriousness, and integrity with which the Warren Commission approached its task. I saw every day the intellectual effort and devotion to finding the truth exhibited by every member of the commission staff. This book explains how the commission members and staff fulfilled their responsibilities to investigate the assassination and to prepare a fair and complete report of what they found.

I dedicate this work to my colleagues, who brought their great talents, varied political orientations, and contrasting personalities to a historic assignment. I hope this book will contribute to a renewed and more reasoned discussion of the Warren Commission's findings.

CHAPTER 1

DECEMBER 1963: THE NATION RESPONDS
■

O N THE AFTERNOON OF DECEMBER 17, 1963, I TRIED TO SIT UP STRAIGHT and look respectfully across a large desk at the chief justice of the United States, Earl Warren, who had been appointed the chairman of the presidential commission to investigate the assassination of President Kennedy. A thirty-two-year-old Justice Department lawyer, I had been "volunteered" by Deputy Attorney General Nicholas Katzenbach to assist the chief justice in getting the commission under way. The chief justice explained how he had reluctantly accepted President Johnson's request to lead the commission and the importance of the commission's work. He was a handsome man—with blue eyes, broad shoulders, and a thicket of white hair—who looked me in the eye as he spoke with the calm assurance of the accomplished politician that he was. I certainly was intimidated. When he asked me to serve in a liaison capacity with the commission, I said I was available to do anything he wanted.

When I returned to the department, I told my boss, Assistant Attorney General Herbert J. ("Jack") Miller, about the meeting with Chief Justice Warren. Miller was the head of the criminal division, and I was one of his two deputies. He and I had learned of the assassination after a late lunch together on November 22. Washington was chilly that day, but sunny. Finished with our customary hamburgers at a nearby restaurant, we headed back to the department a few blocks away, across Pennsylvania Avenue. As we approached the stoplight at Pennsylvania, we were surprised to see a young lawyer from our division rushing toward us and shouting. The words hit like blows to the chest: "The president has been shot."

Jack and I nearly ran the rest of the way to the department. Inside, Jack hurried to the attorney general's office, where he told me later that he had found Robert Kennedy's secretary in tears. I joined the group of criminal division lawyers milling in the halls of the division and listening to a radio in the reception area outside of Jack's office. About thirty minutes later, we learned that the president was dead. Within an hour or so, reports confirmed that a suspect had been apprehended by the Dallas police.

■ Hoover and the FBI Take the Lead

J. Edgar Hoover, the director of the Federal Bureau of Investigation since 1935, wanted the FBI to have complete control of the investigation of the Kennedy assassination. Although there was no federal law making the assassination of the president a crime, President Lyndon Johnson announced to the public that he had instructed the FBI to take charge and to report directly to him. He commanded that all other federal agencies, including the CIA and the Secret Service, cooperate with the FBI. The decision whether there was any way to prosecute the killing of Kennedy and the murder of Oswald by Ruby under existing federal laws would be made by the Department of Justice. At the same time, the two murders were under investigation by the Dallas Police Department for possible prosecution in the local Dallas court. The Texas attorney general initiated the creation of a special court of inquiry under Texas law to conduct an independent investigation at the state level. Several congressional leaders were eager to undertake investigations of the assassination and, in particular, the failure of the Secret Service to protect the president.

Many important facts became known almost immediately. President Kennedy and Governor Connally were hit by shots fired at the presidential motorcade after it had turned onto Elm Street and passed the Texas School Book Depository. Three shots were fired in rapid succession. The vehicle took the president immediately to Parkland Hospital, about four miles away. The doctors there found an extensive wound in the president's head and a small wound approximately one-fourth inch in diameter in the lower third of his neck. In an effort to facilitate his breathing, the doctors performed a tracheotomy by enlarging the throat wound and inserting a tube. They never turned the president over for an examination of his back. At about 1 P.M., some thirty minutes after the shooting, all heart activity ceased and a priest administered last rites. President Kennedy was dead.[1]

Local police and Secret Service officials at the assassination scene went into action quickly. They interviewed witnesses who recounted seeing a rifle firing from the southeast corner window on the sixth floor of the depository. One witness described the man he saw firing from the building, and police broadcast this description of the suspected assassin over the police radio at 12:45 P.M. Other witnesses reported that after the shots were fired, they had seen Lee Harvey Oswald, a new employee at the depository, walking toward the front of the building where an elevator and a short flight of stairs led to the main entrance of the building on the first floor.[2]

About forty-five minutes after the assassination, J. D. Tippit, a Dallas police officer on patrol, spotted a man on the street who met the general description of the suspected assassin. Tippit pulled his patrol car up to this man, who responded by walking over to the passenger side of Tippit's car. Tippit got out and started to walk around the front of his car, when the man drew a revolver and fired four shots into Tippit, killing him instantly. Some eyewitnesses saw the killing and others observed the gunman leave the scene and enter a movie theater several blocks away without buying a ticket. They called the Dallas police and within minutes officers swarmed to the theater. When police approached the man in the theater, he drew a gun and struck one of them. After a struggle, the police officers subdued the man, arrested him, and hustled him to police headquarters. They arrived there at about 2 P.M. The man was Lee Harvey Oswald.[3]

Meanwhile, having learned of Kennedy's death at Parkland Hospital, Vice President Lyndon B. Johnson and his wife, Lady Bird, left under guard for the airport. Although Johnson became president immediately upon Kennedy's death, he wanted the formal swearing-in ceremony to take place as soon as possible. He called the president's brother, Robert Kennedy, in part to satisfy himself that the attorney general did not oppose a prompt swearing-in, but also to obtain the precise language of the oath to be administered. Deputy Attorney General Katzenbach subsequently dictated to Johnson's secretary the thirty-seven-word oath of office contained in the Constitution. Johnson also insisted that Mrs. John F. Kennedy participate in the swearing-in ceremony and return to Washington on the presidential plane with him. He believed that no single gesture "would do more to demonstrate continuity and stability" in the United States after the assassination "than the attendance at his swearing-in ceremony of the late President's widow." At 2:38 P.M., Mrs. John F. Kennedy, in her bloodstained pink suit, was standing at Johnson's side as he was sworn in as the thirty-sixth president of the United States by Federal District Court Judge Sarah T. Hughes.[4]

When the plane arrived in Washington, DC, a police-escorted ambulance took Kennedy's body to the National Naval Medical Center in Bethesda, Maryland. The doctors there performed the autopsy. They examined the massive head wound observed at Parkland and the one in the front of the neck, which had been enlarged by the Parkland doctors when they performed the tracheotomy. The autopsy report described both of these as being "presumably" exit wounds. The doctors in Bethesda also noticed two wounds missed at Parkland: a small wound of entry in the rear of the president's skull and another wound of entry near the base of the back of the neck. The autopsy report described the bullets that struck the president as having been fired "from a point behind and somewhat above the level of the deceased."[5]

The confusion at the assassination scene and the many conflicting versions from eyewitnesses and local officials about what had happened immediately raised questions regarding the number, identity, and location of the likely assassin or assassins. Reporters from around the world descended on Dallas to pursue any and all details about the assassination and quickly published any newly acquired information regardless of source or credibility. Some witnesses as well as commentators who saw films of the motorcade alleged that one or more shots had been fired from the president's front because of the backward motion of his head after being hit. In addition, one of the Parkland Hospital doctors had speculated about the president's wounds, in response to press inquiries, in a way that contributed to public confusion about the direction of the shots.

After Oswald was apprehended, snippets of information about his background—defection to the Soviet Union in 1959, his effort to renounce his American citizenship, his return to the United States in 1962 with a Soviet wife and young daughter, and his pro-Cuba activities—raised immediate suspicions of possible foreign involvement in the assassination. The most pressing questions about him in the first few hours concerned logistics: How had he been able to recently get a job at a location on the motorcade route, how had he acquired a rifle and secreted it in the book depository, and how had he planned to escape?

A day after the assassination, Hoover produced a five-page memorandum for the attorney general, the deputy attorney general, and Jack Miller as head of the criminal division. The FBI named Oswald as the assassin, identified the depository as the location where he fired the shots, and described the rifle and other physical evidence found at the scene. Their report also gave us some quickly gathered information regarding Oswald's defection to Russia in 1959, his return to the United States in 1962, his trip to Mexico in 1963 in an effort to go to Cuba, and his activities for the Fair Play for Cuba Committee.

Immediately after the assassination, Katzenbach essentially became the "acting" attorney general to whom the new president and Congress looked for guidance in coping with this tragedy. The grief-stricken Robert Kennedy had personal and family responsibilities that limited his role at the Justice Department for several weeks after the assassination. A former Rhodes Scholar and a professor of law at Yale, Katzenbach had come to the department as the

assistant attorney general in charge of the office of legal counsel on the recommendation of Byron "Whizzer" White, who was then Kennedy's deputy
attorney general. When White was elevated to the Supreme Court in 1962,
Katzenbach became the new deputy.

Nick Katzenbach was a truly remarkable man. Several inches over six
feet, with a large frame and head, he always stood out in a crowd. He left
Princeton to join the Air Force during World War II, and after his plane crashed
was a prisoner of war for some two years. He escaped more than once, but was
recaptured each time. During his imprisonment he read an estimated four hundred books, and based on this self-education, persuaded the Princeton faculty
to award him his degree after passing the required tests. At the Justice Department, he consistently addressed problems in a thoughtful manner, with considerable patience, and an unusual readiness to listen carefully to everyone,
regardless of age, title, or political affiliation.

Within hours of the assassination, rumors began to circulate in the United
States and abroad that Oswald was selected as the triggerman in an assassination plot engineered by right-wing extremists in the United States. During his
short term in office, Kennedy had initiated liberal programs that challenged
the established practices of some of the largest corporations in the country, and
many were outspoken in their opposition to his administration. Commentators
all over the world reported that the assassination had been the work of
Kennedy's most violent political opponents. In the following months we would
learn that the Soviet government had originated this rumor. The CIA found
that Radio Moscow was the first news service in the world to suggest that ultra-
rightists in the United States were responsible for the president's death. Eastern
European radio stations fell into line, and the story began to spread.[vi]

Two days after the assassination, another unthinkable act occurred.
Jack Ruby, the manager of a small Dallas nightclub, slipped into the basement of police headquarters as officers were transferring Oswald to a more
secure county jail. Even though there had been threats against Oswald's life,
the basement was crowded with news reporters and curious bystanders anxious to get a look at the accused assassin. As Oswald emerged from the jail
office with detectives on either side of him, Ruby darted out from Oswald's
left and fired one shot into his stomach. A television camera caught the entire event. Oswald was immediately taken to Parkland Hospital, where he
never regained consciousness, and was declared dead less than two hours
after he was shot. In custody, Ruby denied that his action was in any way
connected with a conspiracy to assassinate Kennedy. He claimed "that he

had killed Oswald in a temporary fit of depression and rage over the president's death."[7]

Oswald's murder immediately spawned countless new conspiracy theories based on the proposition that Oswald had been "silenced" to protect the true architects of the assassination. It also supported a spreading popular belief that law enforcement officials were complicit in the president's killing. How could Ruby have been allowed to enter the basement just minutes before Oswald came into the room? It seemed inconceivable that this was a chance occurrence rather than a planned conspiracy in which Ruby got help from Dallas police officers, and perhaps from the same groups that had assisted Oswald in the assassination.

Ruby's criminal record and reported associations with the underworld prompted suspicions of a connection among Ruby, Oswald, and organized crime. Most versions of this allegation rested on speculation that Ruby and the Dallas police conspired to kill Oswald. The *Washington Post* reported that in Europe, rumors circulated that the assassination had been instigated by those challenged by the president and his brother, such as the Teamsters Union, the Mafia, or Texas oil interests. Writing in *Paris Match* in December, a leading European commentator pointed out that "while most Americans seemed to accept 'FBI leaks' that Oswald was a loner, Europeans rejected the claim 'almost universally.'" He added that "they *absolutely* [his italics] do not believe the 'laughable' story that Ruby—a gangster—acted out of patriotic indignation."[8]

Hoover urgently wanted his report to reassure the president that there was no conspiracy. The day after Ruby killed Oswald, the FBI supplied additional information regarding both Oswald and Ruby. Although the FBI is a branch of the Justice Department and therefore subordinate to the attorney general, the reality was that for decades Hoover had run the agency as his own independent fiefdom. Consistent with this practice, those of us in the department remained in the dark about the FBI's continued investigation of these crimes and the timing of its report.[9]

On November 26, Hoover talked with Katzenbach about the upcoming FBI report and later told his associates that Katzenbach believed the report should "settle the dust, insofar as Oswald and his activities are concerned, both from the standpoint that he is the man who assassinated the president and relative to Oswald himself and his activities and background." As I would later learn, Hoover's version of facts and reports of conversations were often unreliable. Hoover wanted the FBI report to address definitively "all allegations and angles" relating to possible conspiracies and had established a target date of November 29 for delivery of the report to President Johnson. Several years later, it emerged that at least one of his assistant directors cautioned about trying to attain that goal because of the "literally hundreds of allegations regarding the activities of Oswald and Ruby" that needed to be investigated.[10]

■ The Criminal Division Undertakes Its Own Effort

We lawyers in the Department of Justice were just as susceptible as the rest of the nation to the emotions prompted by these extraordinary events. But we had an additional perspective as well—resulting from the fact that our attorney general was the brother of President Kennedy. The career lawyers in the department—those who had not come with the new administration—may have greeted Robert Kennedy's appointment with some apprehension because of his youth and relationship to the president. But for me and other new appointees in the department, no reservations diluted our enthusiasm. We relished the opportunity to work with him and embraced the energy and commitment that he brought to the department. By 1963, the attorney general commanded intense loyalty from the lawyers and staff. We realized immediately that President Kennedy's death marked the end of this unique experience under our attorney general.

I returned to my office at the department on Saturday, November 23, the day after the assassination. I was surprised by the empty, silent corridor of the Justice Department's second floor, which housed the criminal division. All the offices were dark. The only person I ran into was a *Wall Street Journal* reporter who, in those days before security guards, was free to enter the department whenever the doors were open. "Do you think things are going to be different at the department after the assassination of the attorney general's brother?" he asked me. I recall only that my response reflected my exasperation and impatience with the question. Everyone knew that the department's singular prominence within the Kennedy administration was because the attorney general and president were brothers.

Whatever Hoover's plans, Jack Miller didn't intend to stay on the sidelines. He recognized that the FBI was not going to seek any input from the criminal division's lawyers or share the results of its ongoing investigation with us. He directed several of the most experienced lawyers in the division to canvass their contacts in law enforcement agencies and to start thinking about how to organize a comprehensive investigation of the assassination. For several days after the assassination, it was unclear whether the federal government had the authority to initiate a prosecution based on the facts being developed by the FBI. If so, Miller's division would be taking the lead within the department and he wanted to be prepared to propose a course of action to Katzenbach. Within a few days of the assassination, the division's lawyers produced a detailed outline of a proposed report that would address the factual and legal issues with respect to the assassination and Ruby's killing of Oswald under the applicable federal civil rights laws. Based on this work, Miller went to Katzenbach on November 27 with a detailed proposal for action.[11]

Jack Miller had energy and enthusiasm to spare. He was not tall, but had a large, muscular frame with noticeable biceps and a taut stomach, the results of his hobby of splitting wood by hand with an axe. The wood splitting happened at his home in Potomac, Maryland, where he had acreage enough for his wife to raise racehorses. Jack often said that racehorses were one of the most efficient means of disposing of excess wealth. Although born of Swedish and German stock and raised in Minnesota, Jack was as gregarious—with his big smile, hearty handshake, loud laughter, and terrible puns—as the Irish American friends that congregated around him. As a lawyer, he was very careful, and insistent on doing his own research; he was an effective advocate in court or conference, a truly creative lawyer, and unafraid of making the difficult judgments that came his way.

I had been at the Justice Department for a little more than two and a half years at this point. It was customary then for each assistant attorney general in charge of a division to have two deputies—one typically a career department attorney and the other someone brought in from the private sector. I was Jack Miller's "second" deputy. I had worked for Miller at a Washington law firm, which I joined after graduating from Yale Law School and serving two years in the Army. Jack and I had represented a board of monitors appointed by a federal court to enforce new policies and practices aimed at eliminating corruption in Jimmy Hoffa's Teamsters Union. It was in connection with this assignment that Miller came to the attention of Robert Kennedy, who was then working for a Senate committee investigating labor racketeering.

Miller was a committed Republican and his appointment to head the criminal division in this Democratic administration was an exceptional departure from previous administrations. After Miller left the law firm in February 1961 for the Justice Department, I pestered him repeatedly to let me join him at the department. It was one of those unique opportunities for public service that had brought me to Washington, rather than Chicago, where I had grown up. Like countless others, I was excited by President Kennedy's election and his call to public service. Miller finally relented and, after obtaining my security clearance, I joined the division in May 1961.

Under Robert Kennedy, the criminal division's lawyers increased from about 90 in 1961 to an anticipated 150 in 1964, primarily due to the new emphasis on organized crime and labor racketeering. Jack Miller depended on the division's first assistant, Bill Foley, and me (as executive or second assistant) to review the steady flow of memoranda, correspondence, legislative proposals, and recommendations for prosecution and to advise which required his personal attention. Relations with the more than ninety appointed US attorneys around the country, especially where important cases were involved, almost always required the assistant attorney general's attention. Each evening we prepared a report for Miller on the most important developments of the day, which he then delivered personally to the attorney general. In addition, he regularly asked me to work on special projects, which on occasion required independent research and analysis, coordination with other federal agencies, working with a team of lawyers investigating a potential case, or preparing a memorandum for the attorney general or the White House on matters with political implications.

In my role as Jack's general factotum after the assassination, I tried to coordinate what we knew about the assassination and to help plan an appropriate department response. Other agencies in the federal government were quick to provide information possibly relevant to the investigation. Thomas Ehrlich, a lawyer friend in the State Department, sent us files on Oswald's departure to (and return from) the Soviet Union, as well as a chronological summary of State's information relating to Oswald and his military record. The Intelligence Office at the Internal Revenue Service gave us information regarding its interest in Jack Ruby's brother Earl, who was living in Detroit. The internal security division within the Justice Department quickly gathered information from the Immigration and Naturalization Service (then a part of the department) on Oswald's background and his promoting of the Fair Play for Cuba Committee, whose materials Oswald was distributing in New Orleans in August, three months before the assassination, when he was arrested for disturbing the peace.[12]

By November 25, federal officials, as well as media commentators, were expressing alarm about the detailed, often conflicting, and potentially prejudicial reports originating from the Dallas Police Department and the local Dallas prosecutor. Katzenbach took his concerns to Bill Moyers, who was our go-to person in the White House. Referring to some of the statements made by the Dallas police, Katzenbach's memo for Moyers pointed out that "the matter has been handled thus far with neither dignity nor conviction. Facts have been mixed with rumor and speculation. We can scarcely let the world see us totally in the image of the Dallas police when our President is murdered." He suggested "making public as soon as possible a complete and thorough FBI report on Oswald and the assassination," although he knew that the FBI report would likely contain facts inconsistent with statements by Dallas police officials.[13]

Katzenbach asked Miller to go to Dallas to get a better idea of what the Texas authorities were doing and saying. It also provided an opportunity for Jack to learn more about the FBI investigation being conducted there. Miller flew down to Dallas in a government Lear jet, putting on radio earphones as the plane approached the airport to discuss with Harold Barefoot Sanders, the US attorney for the Northern District of Texas, how best to avoid the "absolute mob scene of reporters at the main terminal." Sanders and Jack Miller were a perfect match. Both lacked pretension, had an easygoing manner, and were decisive and confident in their decision making. Having successfully avoided the crowd by landing far from the main terminal, Miller went to Sanders' office in Dallas where they decided that their principal objective was to get the local prosecutor off of television news programs in order to reduce the flow of potentially prejudicial publicity. With this objective in mind, they met with Dallas District Attorney Henry Wade that evening and tried to persuade him not to make any further statements about the case to the media.[14]

A day or so later, Miller was preparing to return to Washington when Katzenbach called to report that the Texas attorney general was about to announce in Austin the formation of a Texas court of inquiry to investigate the assassination, which he would claim had the blessing of the White House. Later, Jack would remember: "Nick and I discussed what a lousy idea it was for Lyndon Johnson's home state to conduct an inquiry into that assassination, but that was one of those brainless things that happen, I guess." Nonetheless, he had his "marching orders" to drive to Austin to deal with the situation, and he and Sanders set out with Sanders driving. As Miller recalled the drive: "I remember both Barefoot and I had quit smoking. He had an old Oldsmobile, and we were barreling along the road about a hundred miles an hour, and he said I can't stand it, and I said neither can I. He slammed the brakes on, and we went and both bought two packs of cigarettes. We were puffing like mad all the way trying to figure out what to do."[15]

Miller and Sanders managed to get to Texas Attorney General Waggoner Carr and some of his aides before his press conference. They pointed out some of the difficulties with conducting any kind of inquiry in Texas and tried to persuade Carr not to initiate such an investigation. Carr decided to go ahead anyway. Miller told Carr that, if asked at the press conference about the Justice Department's view on the matter, he would say that the department would cooperate with the Texas investigation but would go ahead and conduct its own investigation—and he did. When a reporter asked Carr if the White House had approved this Texas investigation, he said that it had and mentioned Abe Fortas as one of the persons who had given the go-ahead. Abraham ("Abe") Fortas, a partner in a prominent Washington law firm, was a key adviser to President Johnson going back to 1948, when he represented Johnson in a legal dispute over a congressional primary election in Texas, which Johnson ultimately won.[16]

■ President Johnson Appoints a Commission

Katzenbach was well aware of the likely criminal prosecutions and proposed court of inquiry in Texas and possible congressional investigations in Washington. He suggested to Moyers the alternative of a presidential commission to examine the evidence and announce its conclusions. He appears to have been among the first to do so. He told Moyers, however, that such an approach had both advantages and disadvantages and that a decision regarding such a commission should wait until after the FBI report was made public. Katzenbach pressed this suggestion because the president could select people of impeccable integrity and distinguished credentials to serve on such a commission, without any connection or obligation to the State of Texas or the federal government. Their sole mission would be to search for the truth and to make that truth public. Such a prestigious commission, he hoped, might persuade other potential investigators to defer their own efforts—at least until they saw the presidential commission's findings.[17]

President Johnson was initially opposed to the idea of appointing a commission, reflecting the views of Hoover and Fortas. Fortas saw no reason to believe that the public would accept the findings of such a commission nor any advantage to the president in getting involved in an investigation of his predecessor's murder. It was a state responsibility, Fortas argued, and should be left to Texas.[18]

Hoover took his objections to Walter Jenkins, one of the president's trusted assistants. In a phone call on November 24, Hoover argued that the investigation should be left to the FBI. After it submitted its report, Johnson could decide which portion to make public. Hoover worried that a presidential commission would disclose the use of sensitive "sources and methods"—namely, CIA telephone intercepts in Mexico City and FBI mail openings in Washington. What would not emerge for some time, though, was that Hoover's most pressing concern was to prevent anyone from criticizing the FBI for not notifying the Secret Service before the Dallas motorcade of Oswald's presence in Dallas, based on the FBI's ongoing investigation of Oswald after his return to the United States in 1962. Late that same day, Johnson called Katzenbach and told him that he wanted the investigation of the assassination to be left to normal legal processes, specifically the FBI report and concurrently a court of inquiry under Texas law. The next morning, Johnson informed Hoover of that decision and asked Hoover for help in persuading the *Washington Post* not to endorse the concept of a presidential commission.[19]

Despite Johnson's wariness of involving himself in the investigation, it became clear that something had to be done. The prospect of four separate investigations (County of Dallas, State of Texas, US Congress, and US Department of Justice) persuaded Fortas and other reluctant presidential advisers to support the creation of a presidential commission. After reconsidering the question in light of these developments, President Johnson agreed and announced the creation of a commission on November 29, 1963, seven days after the assassination. He called Hoover before this decision was made public. Hoover's version of the conversation was that "[t]he President stated he wanted to get by just with my file and my report. I told him I thought it would be very bad to have a rash of investigations. He then indicated the only way to stop it is to appoint a high-level committee to evaluate my report and tell the House and Senate not to go ahead with the investigation." On another occasion, Hoover described the president's decision as "very wise, because I feel that the report of any agency of government investigating what might be some shortcomings on the part of other agencies of government ought to be reviewed by an impartial group such as this [new] commission."[20]

However reluctant he may have been, Johnson's decision to create a commission was both necessary and appropriate. It was the only available mechanism that held out any hope of preventing, or at least delaying, the simultaneous (and inevitably conflicting) investigations by Texas and federal authorities. It also responded to the widespread public demand for a professional and non-political examination of the facts and the various conspiracy allegations that were being so widely publicized around the world—a demand that could not be even partially satisfied by any trial of Oswald or possible conspirators not yet identified. The commission's goal was to report the truth as far as it could be known, not to prosecute a crime.

Hoover's statement highlighted yet another reason for such a commission. It was obvious that the performance of the nation's key investigative

agencies—the FBI, CIA, and Secret Service—in connection with the assassination needed to be critically examined. It was far better that this task be undertaken by a presidential commission than be pursued by Texas authorities
or congressional committees.

The President's Executive Order No. 11130 directed the commission:

> to examine the evidence developed by the Federal Bureau of Investigation
> and any additional evidence that may hereafter come to light or be uncov-
> ered by federal or state authorities; to make such further investigation as
> the Commission finds desirable; to evaluate all the facts and circumstances
> surrounding such assassination; including the subsequent violent death of
> the man charged with the assassination, and to report to me its findings and
> conclusions.

The executive order empowered the commission to prescribe its own
procedures and to employ such personnel as it deemed necessary.[21]

The seven members of the commission illustrated the president's sure
hand at political matters. He selected Earl Warren, the current chief justice of
the US Supreme Court, as chairman. Warren had come up through the ranks
as district attorney in Alameda County, California, and then as state attorney
general, before being elected governor three times. He had been the Republican
Party's vice-presidential nominee in 1948 when Truman upset Dewey. Initially,
Warren was reluctant. He told Katzenbach and Solicitor General Archibald
Cox that all previous such nonjudicial assignments by Supreme Court justices
had been divisive and disruptive of the court.[22]

But Johnson overcame his objections at a meeting later that day. Johnson
told the chief justice about his personal concerns about the assassination and
the need for an objective exploration of the facts and statement of conclusions
that would be respected by the public. Otherwise, he said, "it would always
remain an open wound with ominous potential." The president emphasized to
the chief justice the possible international repercussions and also made a personal appeal, reminding the chief justice of his time as a soldier in World War
I. "There was nothing you could do in that uniform comparable to what you
can do for your country in this hour of trouble," he said. Warren relented.[23]

Four members, constituting a majority of the commission, were drawn
from Congress—Senator Richard Russell, a Democrat from Georgia; Senator
John Sherman Cooper, a Republican from Kentucky; Representative Hale
Boggs, a Democrat and the majority whip, from Louisiana; and Representative

Gerald Ford, a Republican from Michigan. All were experienced politicians aware of the public's expectations for the investigation and the political aspects of any report they might issue.

Johnson was particularly concerned to have Russell on the commission because he was the leader of the states' rights contingent in the Senate. As colleagues in the Senate, the two had shared most views, except those bearing on race. Russell also had long experience in overseeing the CIA, and Johnson had witnessed firsthand Russell's dignified management of the controversial hearings in 1951 over President Truman's firing of General MacArthur. Johnson trusted his judgment. Russell, too, was reluctant to serve; he disapproved of the Warren Court's liberal rulings. However, he felt personal loyalty to the president—and he didn't really have a choice anyway. Johnson had already publicly announced Russell's appointment.[24]

Johnson had asked Robert Kennedy to suggest possible commission members from the private sector. Kennedy proposed Allen W. Dulles, the former CIA director, and John J. McCloy, the former president of the World Bank. President Johnson agreed. Although now in the private sector, both men had many years of experience in government.[25]

Dulles was a corporate lawyer and a partner in a prominent New York law firm. Before World War II, he had served as a diplomat in Europe and wound up in Switzerland during the war, where he directed US intelligence operations. After the war, Dulles became the first civilian to head the CIA, where he remained until 1961, when President Kennedy replaced him and other agency officials after the failed Bay of Pigs operation.

McCloy had been an assistant secretary of war during World War II, a US high commissioner for Germany after the war, and a president of the World Bank. A frequent adviser to many presidents, he also had many contacts in foreign countries. Earlier in his career, during and after World War I, he had developed investigative skills looking into crimes committed by German government agents in the United States—murder, arson, explosions, and sabotage—while this country held to its neutral status in that war.[26]

While the media generally responded well to the selection of commission members, their prestigious stature raised some concerns about the crimes they were to investigate. After commenting that "it would be hard to imagine a more high-powered commission," one reporter suggested that the appointment of such an "ultra-high-level Commission has increased suspicion" and "caused foreign governments to be puzzled and to wonder if there isn't much more in the Oswald-plus-Ruby affair than meets the eye." There was also a sprinkling of concerns about the vagueness of the commission's charter of investigation. The charter was indeed very broad and clearly required an examination of those federal agencies charged with the responsibility of protecting the president. Under its own reading of its charter, however, all the commission could do was report its factual findings and make recommendations to the established institutions of government regarding such matters as prosecutions, new legislation, or agency reforms.[27]

Within the criminal division there was broad approval for the creation of the commission. At this point, we thought it was obvious that the commission should receive a copy of whatever report the FBI had prepared for the president and that the decision of how to handle the report would now rest with the commission. The internal debate at the Justice Department focused on our major concern that the FBI report was necessarily (due to time constraints) only a first effort at determining the facts and answering the endless questions being raised about Oswald, Ruby, and possible conspiracies. We also suspected that the FBI would maintain that it should be the only investigative agency responsible for conducting such further inquiries as the commission thought was necessary. Giving the FBI any such exclusive investigating function would grant Hoover full control over the information flow to the commission and seriously restrict the commission's ability to accomplish its mission.[28]

The FBI delivered its report to the department late on December 5—a week after Hoover's initial target date. I remember "being called to the Deputy's office and asked to take possession of one of the few copies and review it before it went to the White House." I prepared "a short two-page release regarding the finding of the report." The report reflected a prodigious investigative effort conducted by the bureau in less than two weeks. It represented the work of some 150 agents under the direction of Gordon Shanklin, the head of the Dallas field office, who in turn reported to Alexander ("Al") Rosen, the assistant director in charge of the FBI's general investigative division.[29]

The report was seventy-five pages long, supplemented by a thirteen-page index and three volumes of exhibits. Part I described the assassination and identified Oswald as the killer. Part II set forth the evidence "conclusively showing that Oswald did assassinate the President." Part III discussed what the FBI knew about Oswald prior to the assassination and reported the results of the FBI's investigation, after the assassination, of Oswald's background, activities, and associates. The exhibits included the documents relating to Oswald's contacts with the Soviets and the Communist Party. The FBI found no evidence that Oswald was part of a conspiracy to kill the president. Although the scope of the investigation and the documentation in the FBI report were impressive, I immediately noticed some critical errors that required further review. I concluded that this initial report could not be accepted as a complete or authoritative assessment of the facts relating to the assassination.[30]

■ The Commission's First Challenge: Review or Investigate

Hoover staked out a clear position from the outset: if the president had to have this commission, its function should be to receive the FBI's report, review it, ask questions aimed at clarifying its findings, then endorse the report and disband. All of the members of the commission appreciated the difficulties that Hoover might cause if he perceived the commission to be an adversary.

The commission held three meetings before I became a member of its staff—on December 5, 6, and 16. All of the commission meetings were private, and a court reporter transcribed their deliberations. I joined the staff on December 17. My journal reflects what I learned secondhand about these first commission meetings and later meetings as well.[31]

At these early meetings, Katzenbach served as the department's contact with Warren and the commission, which had been quickly labeled the "Warren Commission." Katzenbach attended the first meeting, but the FBI declined to send a representative or to brief Katzenbach about its investigation before he attended. Assistant Director Alan Belmont explained that the FBI had not yet completed its report, which was delivered to the department later that very day. Some people thought Hoover was deliberately insulting Katzenbach and the Warren Commission. Katzenbach viewed it differently. Until Hoover approved and released the report, no FBI representative would be permitted to comment on its contents. Under these circumstances, Katzenbach thought it was reasonable for the FBI not to attend the meeting.[32]

At that first meeting, Katzenbach invited the members to excuse him from their proceedings at any time; he wanted to avoid any appearance of Justice Department interference with the commission's work. He explained the inquiry that Texas planned to initiate and said that the White House had approved that inquiry before the commission had been appointed. He also said he and others in the administration did not regard the Texas investigation as a desirable mechanism for developing the facts relating to the assassination. That was why President Johnson had ultimately agreed to appoint the commission.[33]

Katzenbach told the commission that the Texas lawyers leading the investigation (Robert Storey and Leon Jaworski) would consider postponing their investigation out of deference to the commission. After Katzenbach left the meeting, Warren told the other members that he had learned the previous evening that the Texas lawyers would defer their proceedings so long as there was a suitable level of cooperation by the Warren Commission. The commission was pleased to accept the Texas deferral.[34]

Katzenbach and the commission also discussed a news article from two days earlier that described the purported findings of the not-yet-delivered FBI report. Katzenbach had raised this leak with Hoover and Belmont and both denied that it had come from the FBI. Katzenbach said "with candor to this committee, I can't think of anybody else it could have come from, because I don't know of anybody else that knew that information."[35]

By now a veteran of the department's difficult relations with Hoover, Katzenbach thought the FBI's leaking the story to favored reporters resulted from their resentment about the appointment of the Warren Commission. In later years, he said, "They very much wanted the report to be made public. They very much wanted to get all the credit for it. They very much wanted the center stage. When that was frustrated, I think they took steps of leaking the information. They have done that in many lesser contexts many, many times when I was in the department." Katzenbach offered the commission any Justice Department assistance it wanted, but noted that the commission was now fully in charge of the investigation as directed by the president.[36]

I never thought that the Justice Department abdicated its responsibilities with respect to the investigation of the assassination, as some have suggested. The department certainly had enormous resources—its specialized investigative sections and attorneys, as well as the powers and capabilities of a federal grand jury and the granting of immunity—but I thought that Katzenbach had it right. Initiation of a public investigation by the Department of Justice in the days following the assassination would have destroyed the political accommodation that had been reached with the Texas authorities and congressional committees by the creation of the commission. Any such investigation before the FBI completed its work would have clashed with established department practice and with President Johnson's decision to rely on a commission, rather than the customary federal agencies, to investigate the assassination.

FBI officials were displeased when they heard of the commission meetings in December. Representative Gerald Ford talked confidentially with a senior FBI official in his office on two occasions during the first few weeks of the commission's existence. The official reported both conversations to Hoover. Ford explained years later to a congressional committee that he had a longstanding relationship with Cartha DeLoach (and his predecessor) at the FBI, and that these officials would periodically drop by his congressional office. Ford had some reservations about the chief justice's initial decisions with respect to the commission and was concerned, along with other commission members, that Warren "appeared to be moving in the direction of a one-man Commission." He was especially concerned with the chief justice's strong advocacy in support of a fellow Californian as a potential general counsel and saw a risk that Warren would seek to dominate the commission's work in a way that did not reflect the concerns of the other members. Ford passed on to DeLoach some of these concerns, as well as Katzenbach's suggestion that the FBI probably leaked portions of its anticipated report to members of the press.[37]

Katzenbach's remark about the leak especially offended Hoover. He told his FBI confidants that Katzenbach had lied, and that Katzenbach had leaked the report himself. Hoover added in a handwritten note that Katzenbach's allegation regarding the FBI "showed his true colors." Having bristled under the direction of an attorney general who was a brother of the president, Hoover was not warmly disposed toward Katzenbach. He was looking forward to a day when he regained the independence in running the FBI that he had enjoyed for several decades.[38]

At its second meeting on December 6, the commission approved a letter drafted by Warren to the Texas authorities that set forth the basis for the commission's cooperation in return for the deferral of any Texas court of inquiry. This was a very significant accomplishment by the commission and was due in large measure to the chief justice's political sensitivities and the prestige that he brought to the table in dealing with the Texas officials. Giving the commission both the opportunity and the responsibility for conducting its investigation of the assassination without the confusion and duplication of concurrent Texas (and congressional) inquiries created a clear path forward.[39]

The commission agreed to ask Congress for the subpoena power and the authority to grant immunity to witnesses that it might summon to testify. This was the first step toward a thorough and independent investigation. The subpoena power grants the authority to require a person or organization to appear and provide oral testimony, documents, and physical objects. The authority to grant immunity prevents any state or federal prosecutor from using what a witness says, or the documents that a witness produces, to build a criminal case against that witness. The FBI did not have these investigative powers, which the commission could use to go far beyond what the FBI had produced in its investigation. Both were readily granted by a law enacted on December 13.[40]

At this second meeting, the commission members appointed J. Lee

Rankin as general counsel, but only after rejecting Warren's choice of Warren Olney. There was no discussion among the members of their reasons for rejecting Olney, but his background and close relationship with the chief justice was almost certainly the cause. Looking for someone acceptable to the chief justice (but not so close to him) led the commission members to Rankin, who accepted the offer and came to the commission's next meeting on December 16.[41]

Rankin had attended his home state's University of Nebraska for both undergraduate and law school, and then joined a law firm in Lincoln, Nebraska, where he became a partner, in 1935, and remained for eighteen years. In 1952, he managed the Eisenhower presidential campaign in Nebraska. After Eisenhower appointed Herbert Brownell Jr. of Nebraska as his attorney general in 1953, Brownell had selected his friend and fellow-Nebraskan Rankin to serve as assistant attorney general in charge of the office of legal counsel, the same office that Katzenbach filled a decade later.

Rankin argued against the "separate but equal" doctrine before the Supreme Court in the monumental desegregation case *Brown v. Board of Education*. In 1956, by then the US solicitor general, Rankin became deeply involved in legislative reapportionments cases. He was principally responsible for developing the Justice Department's position that led to the "one person, one vote" doctrine. When Eisenhower's second term ended, Rankin returned to private law practice, this time in New York City. He continued to appear before the Supreme Court, representing the American Civil Liberties Union in *Gideon v. Wainwright*, another significant case, which strengthened the right of an indigent person accused of a crime to have legal counsel at public expense.

Though Rankin was not his first choice, Warren liked Rankin's straightforward Midwestern style and his quiet demeanor. It probably did not detract from the chief justice's view of Rankin's legal skills that he and a majority of the other justices agreed with nearly every position Rankin had advocated before the court. The other commission members—all lawyers—were also suitably impressed.

Like its first two meetings, the third commission meeting was held at the National Archives because the commission had not yet obtained its own space. Warren announced that he and Rankin had secured offices for the commission on the fourth floor of a new Veterans of Foreign Wars building located just a block away from the Supreme Court and close to congressional offices. Warren was enthusiastic about the space—commenting that it was as "clean as a whistle." He also reported that the General Services Administration, the federal government's general manager of buildings and grounds, had supplied an office manager and that the National Archives had provided an archivist to assist the commission.

The commission had a long discussion about the FBI report and its annexes, which the members had received a week earlier. Warren and Russell noted that virtually everything contained in the FBI report had already appeared in the press. One major issue that came up right away was the bureau's preliminary finding regarding the bullets that struck President Kennedy and wounded Governor Connally. The FBI concluded that two bullets had struck the president and a third had wounded Connally. To support this assessment, the FBI relied in part on the initial, but inaccurate, information from Parkland Hospital that the first bullet that hit Kennedy had not exited from his body. As captured in the transcript of the meeting, the members did not react favorably.

> BOGGS: "There is nothing in there about Governor Connally."
> CHAIRMAN: "No."
> COOPER: " And whether or not they found any bullets in him."
> McCLOY: "This bullet business leaves me confused."
> CHAIRMAN: "It's totally inconclusive."
> [...]
> McCLOY: "I think you ought to have the autopsy documents."
> CHAIRMAN: "By all means we ought to have the medical reports."

McCloy reminded members that the FBI had been under considerable pressure to complete the report.[42]

Warren proposed that the commission request all agencies submitting reports to provide the underlying investigative materials on which they were based. He told the members that after reading the FBI report he had the feeling that "unless we had the raw materials that went into the making of this report and had an opportunity to examine those raw materials and make our own appraisal, that any appraisal of this report would be little or nothing." He added that the commission should continue to get such raw materials as they are obtained from the agencies so that it could be kept current regarding ongoing investigations. The commission unanimously approved his motion and followed this practice with respect to all the summary reports submitted by the FBI, CIA, and Secret Service. By emphasizing its need to see the basic investigative materials—the interview reports, the ballistic and other scientific analyses, and key documents—the commission was driving home the message that it alone had the responsibility to evaluate all the evidence and reach its own conclusions.[43]

The commission knew that the initial FBI conclusion that Oswald acted alone was received with great skepticism at home and abroad. Once it became known that Oswald had lived for three years in the Soviet Union and returned to the United States with a Soviet wife, suspicions of possible Soviet involvement gained wide currency. The United States and the Soviet Union had been engaged for more than a decade in a cold war that had worldwide implications. In 1962, the Soviet Union's effort to bring missiles to Cuba provoked a dispute between the two countries that threatened a nuclear confrontation. Fear and apprehension of the Soviet Union was widespread in the United States in 1963 and the possibility that the Soviet Union was behind the assassination of President Kennedy had to be considered. The contention that the assassination resulted from a Communist conspiracy quickly became "the standard propaganda line of the extreme right wing in the United States," with the John Birch Society being its principal advocate.[44]

The possible involvement of Castro's Cuban government also demanded critical analysis. Information about Oswald's activities on behalf of the Fair Play for Cuba Committee and his efforts in Mexico to get a visa to go to Cuba raised questions about his possible connection with Cuban officials. All the commission members were familiar with US policy toward Cuba, and Allen Dulles had detailed information regarding CIA covert programs directed against Cuba during his tenure at the CIA. The Bay of Pigs invasion in April 1961, only a few months after Kennedy became president, had involved a CIA-trained force of Cuban exiles whose objective was to overthrow the Cuban government of Fidel Castro. The Cuban armed forces defeated the invaders within three days, which the anti-Castro exiles blamed on the failure of the United States to produce its promised support. In succeeding years, US policy had remained firmly hostile toward Cuba, but reverted to reliance on covert actions. In September, before the assassination, Castro had made a widely publicized speech in which he suggested that retaliation against the United States might be appropriate if these covert efforts did not cease.

As the commission got organized, these and other conspiratorial possibilities were circulated widely in the press. In addition to the allegations that arose immediately after the assassination, new contentions held that Oswald was not in fact the assassin. For its part, the Soviet Union's propaganda focused on the possibility that Oswald was the dupe of a conspiracy by parties unknown. The Soviet publication *Pravda* on November 28 alluded to a "growing conviction in the United States" that the president had been shot by someone else whom "the Dallas police are carefully protecting." The paper quoted unnamed "specialists" who said that it could be "assumed that the attempt was made not by one person" and that shots were fired from more than one rifle.[45]

Speculation concerning Oswald's innocence increased significantly after the publication of a "defense brief" written by Mark Lane, a thirty-six-year-old New York lawyer with a flair for publicity. In this article, published in the *National Guardian* on December 19, Lane contended that Oswald was not the person with a rifle in the depository and did not kill Patrolman Tippit. He maintained there were two assassins, five shots instead of three, and that the fatal bullets had come from the front. He contended further that the autopsy reports had been altered, witnesses harassed, and statements distorted. After a copy of his "defense brief" was sent to Oswald's mother, she hired him to represent her son and argue before the commission that he had not killed the president.[46]

Lane traveled around the United States to publicize his views about the assassination and his lack of confidence in the newly appointed Warren Commission. His arguments were serialized verbatim in a Soviet news magazine beginning in late December, and an abridged version appeared in the Soviet newspaper *Izvestia* in early January. Within a week, similar summaries were published in Polish and Czech papers. Also in January 1964, a sensational version of the assassination appeared in an Italian neofascist daily, reporting that Texas political and criminal interests hired Ruby to plan the murder of the president. These stories, along with Lane's theories, afforded Soviet propagandists an opportunity to build on their standard line that right-wing extremists had killed Kennedy.[47]

■ Staffing for an Independent Investigation

At the December 16 meeting, Warren raised the question of staffing the commission. He wanted lawyers added and assigned to specific areas of critical importance to the commission's investigation, such as Oswald's life, Ruby's life, the assassination itself, and the relationship among the FBI, CIA, and Secret Service. Rankin suggested that Frank Adams, a former New York police commissioner and distinguished lawyer, was available to assist the commission.[48]

Russell emphasized the need for someone on the staff "with a most skeptical nature, sort of a Devil's Advocate, who would take this FBI report and this CIA report and go through it and analyze every contradiction and every soft spot in it, just as if he were prosecuting them or planning to prosecute." Warren agreed and announced that he had checked out Albert Jenner, one of Chicago's leading trial lawyers, with several people with whom Jenner had worked, including former Supreme Court justice Tom Clark and former secretary of state Dean Acheson. According to them, Jenner "was an indefatigable worker and will never commit himself to the proposition of anything unless he's certain."[49]

The commission agreed to hire those two senior lawyers, and more like them, as well as younger lawyers to work on a full-time basis. The members differed as to whether they could expect lawyers like Adams and Jenner to work full-time for the commission. They left that issue for Rankin to resolve with individual lawyers.

The commission turned back to the FBI report. Members agreed that they should visit Dallas and inspect all aspects of the assassination site. Rankin raised the question whether the commission would need investigative services from outside the federal government. He said that Warren and he had agreed that the commission might need such help under circumstances where a federal agency like the FBI was simply unable to provide a work product that would fully satisfy the commission's needs or, on some technical issues, where a second opinion should be sought from outside of the federal government. Russell, who previously thought that the commission wouldn't need much staff, now recognized that the members might require the independent capability to address issues and that a small commission staff would be needed for this purpose.[50]

The commission had earlier deferred the question whether it should issue a public statement after it had received the FBI report. Before appointing the commission, President Johnson had announced that the FBI report would be made public. Based on their initial review of the FBI report, the commission members did not wish to endorse or reject the bureau's conclusions until the commission itself had examined the underlying materials and conducted the additional investigation necessary. Consequently, after adjournment that day, Warren told reporters that the commission would not be issuing any summary of the FBI report or any statement about it. That struck me as a wise decision. Any endorsement of the report at that early stage of the commission's existence would have thoroughly compromised its mission, in light of the widespread skepticism about the FBI report and the outstanding questions not addressed by it.

Hoover was displeased. He complained to his lieutenants that Warren's insistence on seeing the supporting materials for the report was an insult. He described Warren's comment as "entirely unwarranted" and could have been better phrased "so as not to leave the impression, at least by innuendo, that the FBI had not done a thorough job."[51]

By this time Hoover had told Assistant Director Belmont that he would be "personally responsible for reviewing every piece of paper that went to the Warren Commission" and had designated Inspector James Malley to be the FBI liaison to the commission. Malley was a high-ranking official in the general investigative division of the FBI, which was responsible for handling most of the bureau's criminal investigations, but was entirely separate from the more specialized FBI sections dealing with organized crime, the Soviet Union, and Cuban-related matters. Malley later said that his instruction from Hoover was to provide the commission with whatever assistance it requested.[52]

When Jack Miller called me into his office on the morning of December 17, I had no idea what was on his mind. He told me that Katzenbach had just called and asked whether I was available to assist the Warren Commission. Jack and I did not have a long, or serious, discussion about whether I should take this on. I was excited by the opportunity to participate in this historic assignment. And I think that Jack was pleased that the deputy attorney general had shown this confidence in someone that Jack had brought into the department. I asked Jack whether he could manage the criminal division without my assistance. He laughed and told me to keep in touch.[53]

After getting an "overdue haircut," I called Rankin and made an appointment to see him later that morning. When I visited the VFW building for the first time, Rankin discussed the unique task before the commission and asked if I would be willing to assist. I said that I would and explained some of the work that we had done in the criminal division before the commission was appointed. He asked me to return in the afternoon to be interviewed by Chief Justice Warren.[54]

I had a favorable impression of Rankin at our first meeting. He was in his fifties, slender, of ordinary size, wore glasses, and had light brown hair and blue eyes. He listened with steady attention, never interrupted, and smiled only sparingly. He spoke carefully, with well-modulated tones. He was well aware of the enormous task that he had undertaken, but reflected a quiet confidence that he could do the job if I, and others, helped him. He gave me every indication that he wanted me to come on board and that we would be able to work together as colleagues, despite our differences in age and experience. I did not know much about Rankin at the time, although I knew that his service as solicitor general was much admired among knowledgeable practitioners before the Supreme Court. Lawyers in the department remembered him as having an exceptional intellect, but also great modesty. Tangling with the Supreme Court on a regular basis, which Rankin had done, demands a commanding analytical ability and deft verbal skills. So, there was no doubt that he was up to the task. Another fact stood out: Warren obviously liked him a lot.

During my meeting with the chief justice that afternoon, Warren "indicated that he had decided not to have any government people on the staff of the Commission since it would appear as though they were being influenced by their governmental positions." His concern about government lawyers working for the commission was certainly understandable, and widely shared. This is what led me to believe that he thought I "would serve as a sort of liaison officer," help to get the commission operational, and then return to my day job at the department. I did not raise this subject with Rankin when I returned to his office after my interview with the chief justice. I told Rankin that I could spend one half of each of the next two days at the commission and be ready to work full-time on Friday, December 20.[55]

By this time, the commission had received the FBI's report regarding Ruby and the murder of Oswald. This thirty-page report discussed the killing of Oswald; Ruby's background; the FBI interview of Ruby; Ruby's whereabouts on November 22–24, 1963; his purchase of the gun used to kill Oswald; and Ruby's arrest record. It included two exhibits: a photograph of the shooting and a diagram of the Dallas police headquarters basement. The preface to this report acknowledged its limitations, emphasizing the fact that no records were kept of the police officers or news media representatives who were in the basement at the time of the shooting. It pointed out, however, that the FBI had already interviewed 98 Dallas police officers and was attempting to identify others who would also be interviewed. The FBI reported that it had been able to identify and interview 51 news media representatives, out of an estimated 150 who were in the basement. This Ruby report indicated, as did the Oswald report, that the investigation "will continue until every possible source of pertinent information has been exhausted."[56]

Beginning on December 20, 1963, I devoted the next three weeks to assisting Rankin in getting the commission staffed and organized. He asked that I review all applications we received and prepare recommendations of qualified candidates to fill our younger lawyer slots, reserving the selection of senior lawyers to Warren and himself. We implemented the commission's desire for underlying investigative materials by getting letters out to a long list of federal agencies requesting documents and information about any relationship the agencies might have had with Oswald, his wife Marina, his family, or his associates. I began to prepare an outline of the overall investigation for his consideration, building on the earlier effort by criminal division lawyers. And, as the FBI began to provide the underlying supporting materials, I undertook to review them, however superficially, in an initial effort to determine where they fell within the range of the commission's work, so that they could be duplicated and ready for distribution to our lawyers when they arrived.[57]

The commission worked in circumstances far different from those of today. There were no computers and no Internet. Xerox photocopy machines had become available only very recently. Most copies of documents were prepared using carbon paper. Communication with outside offices was done by telephone, mail, or messengers. Secretaries, almost always women, were indispensable to the lawyers for whom they worked. A secretary maintained the lawyer's calendar and files, arranged meetings and telephone calls, and guarded her lawyer's privacy. Secretaries took dictation from their bosses using shorthand, transcribed their shorthand notes on typewriters making any necessary clarifying changes, waited for the lawyer to make further revisions, and repeated this process until the final written product was approved by the lawyer. Few of the older lawyers could use a typewriter; most of the younger lawyers had perfected this skill at least by the time they got to law school.

Rankin made his next hire for the staff in the midst of all this activity. He recruited Norman Redlich, a professor at New York University Law School, to be his special assistant. Redlich had invited Rankin to attend a summer workshop held at NYU Law School in 1961 for professors of constitutional law, which led to a close friendship. Redlich had grown up in the Bronx and served in the Army in World War II. After the war, he went to Williams College and Yale Law School, graduating from Yale in 1950 with an outstanding record. He worked in a family manufacturing business for ten years while pursuing graduate work in tax law. He began teaching at NYU Law School in 1959.

During the 1950s, Redlich became an articulate opponent of the death penalty and represented death-row inmates on a pro bono basis. He also joined one of many groups opposing the House Committee on Un-American Activities and the excesses of Senator Joseph R. McCarthy. He played an important role in the community effort in Greenwich Village to prevent a major highway from destroying the neighborhood. Redlich was an extraordinarily talented lawyer, a soft-spoken but prodigious worker, and a thoughtful observer of life. During his time at the commission, he invited everyone to speak their mind on the issues and problems they encountered. He was also willing to share his views, so you always knew where you stood with him.

Rankin also recruited two other senior lawyers, Joseph Ball from California and William Coleman from Philadelphia. Ball was a very experienced criminal trial lawyer whose talent for finding the weaknesses in the prosecutor's case against his client would be invaluable as the commission's work proceeded. Coleman had graduated first in his class from Harvard Law School and at a relatively young age achieved national recognition for his success as a corporate lawyer and civil rights advocate. He was the first African American law clerk at the Supreme Court, working for Justice FelixFrankfurter.

In identifying younger lawyers who might be hired, I reviewed a few hundred letters and recommendations that we had received. The easily stated objective was to hire candidates with outstanding credentials and some diversity in residence, legal experience, and political affiliation. It was definitely a mark of the times that all the members of the commission, the general counsel, and all fourteen of the assistant counsels (except Coleman) were white males with very similar backgrounds. The only woman considered as a member of the professional staff was Alfredda Scobey of Atlanta, who was a law assistant in the Georgia Court of Appeals and assisted Senator Russell.

Even after narrowing the candidates down with respect to age and experience, the number was still very large. Getting people on board as soon as possible was essential, and the urgency of the commission's needs shaped my further review of the applications. I thought it was very important that an applicant be well known either to me or to some colleague in Washington on whose judgment I could rely. There was no time for bringing dozens of candidates to Washington for interviews, and I thought we should not rely on the references included in their letters without such interviews. As a result, I basically decided to add candidates by seeking recommendations from some ten to fifteen friends in Washington and elsewhere.

I knew three lawyers personally who had the necessary professional and personal qualifications: David Belin, Arlen Specter, and Sam Stern. So I recruited them.

David Belin had been a few years ahead of me at the University of Michigan, where he also went to law school. At the time of my call in December, Belin had been practicing law in Des Moines, Iowa, for nine years. Belin was, of course, surprised to hear from me. When I asked whether he would consider working for the commission, he quickly said that he would enthusiastically accept an offer if it were extended to him.

Arlen Specter was a classmate of mine at the Yale Law School and was an assistant district attorney in the Philadelphia prosecutor's office. Specter initially turned me down because of his ongoing commitments within the district attorney's office. That evening—New Year's Eve—Specter mentioned my overture to one of his lawyer friends, who urged him to pursue the matter or, alternatively, to recommend him for the job. Specter changed his mind and sent me his résumé.[58]

Sam Stern was a Washington lawyer who had gone to Harvard Law School and served as a law clerk to Chief Justice Warren during the court's 1955–56 term. Stern had written the chief justice after the commission was established to offer his assistance. Stern was now a partner with a newly formed firm in Washington and pleased to hear that he would be considered for a position on the staff.

I continued to review other potential candidates, as well as work on my other assignments, until the end of December. As the year ended, I told Jack Miller that the commission assignment was going to be full-time, and he would see even less of me than he had anticipated. We had taken significant steps to staff the commission and organize its work, but key decisions by Rankin and the commission had to be made in January to implement these proposals.

Throughout the country, holiday celebrations were more solemn than usual, as Americans were still trying to comprehend the events of November and looking to the commission for clarity and certainty. The purveyors of rumors and conspiracy theories took no holiday and the pressure mounted on the commission to get going on its investigation. I knew that 1964 was going to be the most important and challenging year in my brief legal career.

CHAPTER 2

JANUARY 1964: DISTRUST OF THE FBI GROWS

■

OUR PRIORITIES IN EARLY JANUARY WERE QUITE CLEAR. WE NEEDED GOOD lawyers and we needed them quickly. We had to organize the investigation in some sensible fashion. We needed to instruct the lawyers in how to undertake their assignments in a way best designed to meet the commission's needs. Within the first two weeks of the month we had largely achieved these goals.

On January 14, the FBI delivered two supplemental reports to the commission that it believed provided all the answers the investigation required. One report extended the FBI's December report about Oswald and included the laboratory examination of the president's clothing, the paper bag in which Oswald carried his rifle, and the bullet fragments found after the assassination. The other extended its December report covering Ruby's killing of Oswald, reflecting the many interviews of Dallas police officers and reporters who were in the police headquarters basement on the morning of November 24, 1963.

The FBI Oswald report included analysis of the now famous Zapruder film. A Dallas manufacturer of women's clothing named Abraham Zapruder produced one of the most important pieces of evidence in the investigation. When the president's motorcade turned onto Elm Street from Houston Street and entered Dealey Plaza, Zapruder was filming with an eight-millimeter camera, intending to add to the family's collection of home movies. Zapruder focused his camera on the limousine as it passed almost exactly in front of, and slightly below, his position. The Zapruder film captured Kennedy's reaction to the shot that pierced through his throat and the one that struck the back of his head and killed him. Zapruder's film contained approximately twenty-six seconds of footage—perhaps the most scrutinized film in American history.

Zapruder knew immediately the value of his film. He made three copies right away and gave two to the Secret Service. On the morning of November 23, he sold the print rights to *Life* magazine for $150,000. After many years of legal wrangling regarding ownership of the film and its permissible use by the media and others, the US government purchased the film from Zapruder's heirs in 1999 for $16 million. The original version and the two given to the Secret Service are now in the National Archives.

The report on Oswald also provided additional information about his personal history, relatives, associates, finances, affiliations with political groups, forged documents, travel to Mexico, activities in the Soviet Union, and plans to return to the Soviet Union, as well as the murder of Officer Tippit. The FBI pointed out that its agents had interviewed more than two thousand people. Based on these interviews and the physical evidence, the FBI concluded that Oswald was the assassin "although no clear-cut motive has been established." There was no evidence that he was assisted by any other person, group, or government; there was no evidence that he had been recruited or assisted by the Soviet Union intelligence services; and there was "no proof of any prior contact or association between Oswald and his murderer, Jack Leon Ruby." The FBI advised: "Leads are still being covered, and the FBI will continue to check out any additional allegations or information which come to its attention."[1]

In its twenty-four page supplemental report on Ruby, the FBI concluded that its investigation "thus far has not established any connection between Ruby and Oswald or that Ruby conspired with any individual including police officers." The FBI advised: "Investigation is continuing on an expedited basis to exhaust every logical source of pertinent information."[2]

The FBI's supplemental Oswald report did not revisit its earlier conclusion that two bullets struck the president and a third wounded Connally. It reported that the bullet that entered the president's back "had penetrated to a distance of less than a finger length."[3] This was at odds with the conclusions of the autopsy doctors at Bethesda's National Naval Medical Center. After consulting with doctors at Parkland Hospital, the autopsy doctors had concluded as early as November 23 that the bullet entering the president's back had exited through his neck, and the Parkland doctors had agreed.[4]

The failure of the FBI to correct its earlier error on such an important matter created an immediate stir among the lawyers now on board. The FBI had not yet recognized that its conclusion that the first shot hitting the president had not exited from his body was inconsistent with the medical and ballistics evidence. That the FBI would make a mistake wasn't especially astonishing. Based on my own experience with the FBI and comments from veterans in the criminal division, I was aware of the bureau's investigative limitations. The FBI's rivalry with other agencies and its bureaucratic rigidity were well known in Washington, as were Hoover's titanic sensitivities.

Nonetheless, I was amazed by the enormity of this error. This was a serious mistake regarding one of the most critical factual issues in the investigation. The conclusion was founded on the responses to hypothetical questions on November 22 of a Parkland Hospital physician based on his limited knowledge of the president's wounds. Its consequences lasted through the decades, as critics enthusiastically embraced the FBI's misstatement as confirmation that the commission's findings about the president's wounds and the single-bullet theory were false. At the commission, we worried about what other, perhaps less detectable, errors might be found in the FBI reports on the assassination and the murder of Oswald.[5]

■ The Lawyers Get Their Assignments

At the commission's last meeting in December, Warren had sketched out how the staff would investigate the assassination. He envisioned individual lawyers assigned to specific parts of the investigation, such as Oswald's life, Ruby's life, details of the assassination, and aspects of the work of the FBI, CIA, and Secret Service. He expected Rankin to propose an organization based on his comments for the commission to consider.

When I arrived at the commission, I started working on a tentative outline of the commission's investigation. I didn't know what the chief justice had suggested at the commission meeting, but I had with me the criminal division's proposal of how to organize a comprehensive investigation of the assassination. I augmented that draft in light of what I had learned since coming to the commission.

I gave my eleven-page outline to Rankin on December 30. In it, I identified five areas for investigation: (1) the basic facts about the events on November 22; (2) the facts that pointed to Oswald as the assassin; (3) Oswald's background and possible motive; (4) the facts about the murder of Oswald by Ruby; and (5) the security measures that had failed to protect the president. If he approved, I proposed that Rankin submit the draft outline to the commission members.[6] Rankin welcomed the suggestion.

Rankin made one change. He decided to divide the section dealing with Oswald's background and motive into two sections—one dealing with his activities in the United States and the other dealing with his foreign activities, especially his stay in Russia and his trip to Mexico for the stated purpose of returning to the Soviet Union. Rankin submitted the revised outline to Warren, who sent it to the commission members on January 11. Warren told the members that the proposed organization of the commission's investigation was necessarily tentative and encouraged them to "advise Mr. Rankin of any suggestions they wish to make regarding this outline."[7]

Little did Rankin and I realize that our tentative organization of the commission's work—in particular the focus on Oswald as the likely assassin—would be cited for decades as evidence that the commission had prematurely concluded that he was the assassin before any thorough and impartial inquiry had been undertaken. I believed then and now that any effort by the commission to embark on an investigation that ignored the facts implicating Oswald in the killing of the president and Officer Tippit would have smacked of pretense or naïveté that would have thoroughly impeached the commission's credibility. We had to take as a starting point the facts that had been developed (and publicized worldwide) and make clear that the commission's final determinations would not be made until its investigation had been concluded.

By this time, our staff was growing. Earlier in January, Rankin had moved on my recommendations for hiring junior lawyers. In addition to Belin, Specter, and Stern, Rankin invited Burt Griffin and David Slawson to join the staff. Rankin sent telegrams to all five candidates on January 8 and almost immediately received acceptances from each.

Burt Griffin, a Yale Law School graduate, had served as a prosecutor in the United States Attorney's office in Cleveland for a few years before entering private practice. When I described the job, Griffin was very excited by the prospect and assured me he would accept an offer. He told me later he consulted with two of his firm's partners about this possible offer with the Warren Commission. One told him that the job was likely to be very dull; the other worried that it might delay Griffin's development of a client base. His wife, though, shared his enthusiasm about the opportunity.[8]

David Slawson, a Harvard Law School graduate, was working at the law firm in Denver where Supreme Court Justice White had practiced law and was very interested in coming to Washington to work with the commission. I learned later that Slawson had worked closely with White in support of Kennedy's presidential campaign.[9]

The commission issued a press release on January 12 announcing the appointment of Adams, Ball, Coleman, and Jenner as four senior lawyers who would assist Rankin. A fifth, Leon D. Hubert Jr., a former US attorney from New Orleans, would be named the following week. Close observers noticed that the senior lawyers all came from different parts of the country, which was hardly a coincidence. The release also identified the five new junior lawyers, as well as Redlich's appointment as Rankin's special assistant. All of the lawyers were given the status of special government employees, a classification that applied to people who did not work in the federal government for more than 130 days during any period of 365 consecutive days.[10]

On January 13, Rankin and I looked over the results of our rapid hiring for the first time. The quick timetable for choosing our law firm could have resulted in disaster. It was impossible to know if the mix of strong personalities would mesh well. This first meeting marked the start of what would become the largest criminal investigation ever conducted in the United States. Some of our lawyers had criminal law experience; others none. We likely faced considerable difficulty with the FBI. Some lawyers might be able to handle that; others not. Rankin and I each knew personally only a few of our new recruits. The unknowns made up the majority of the faces at this meeting.

The room buzzed with enthusiasm and anticipation. The lawyers sized each other up, probed for mutual acquaintances, and exchanged stories about their experiences. This was a group of very self-confident lawyers, but eager to get to know one another. Rankin stressed the importance of the task and the need for "thoroughness, imagination and speed." He presented an organizational structure that paired one senior lawyer with one junior lawyer in each of the six areas of the investigation.[11]

Rankin gave the lawyers no choice in their assignments, but his manner gave each the impression that he had selected them specifically for their particular area. I began to see what made Rankin so special. He succeeded at every task that life and luck threw his way because he focused relentlessly on substance and refused to make things personal. Some friends said of Katzenbach that he treated old people, young people, and dogs with equal affection and respect. Rankin had that same quality.

Because the commission had already drawn criticism for identifying Oswald as a likely assassin, Rankin and I had agreed that it would be better to assign Ball, a defense lawyer, and Belin, a civil lawyer, to the area dealing with Oswald's involvement, rather than a prosecutor like Specter. Rankin also didn't want Specter and Coleman teamed up because they were both from Philadelphia. Therefore we slotted Specter to investigate the facts relating to the assassination, and we paired him with Adams, the former New York City police commissioner. Rankin tasked Slawson with the investigation of Oswald's foreign contacts and the possibility of a foreign conspiracy, the area that Slawson later said held the most interest for him.[12]

As Rankin handed out the assignments and described the task ahead, I relaxed. The lawyers were enthusiastic about their assignments, eager to get to work, and determined to ferret out whatever conspiracy might have led to the assassination and the murder of Oswald. No one in the room expressed the view that Oswald had acted alone. No one expressed the view that there had been a conspiracy. We all realized the immensity of our task to explain how and why one of the most traumatic events in American history had happened. And we were all honored to have been chosen to participate.

As the lawyers arrived, I handed each a copy of the two FBI reports we'd received in December. I also gave each the pile of raw materials I had identified as most relevant to his area of investigation. Rankin told the lawyers that Norman Redlich, the constitutional law professor from New York, would be working with him on special projects and that I would be providing the coordination among the staff lawyers and with outside agencies and individuals.

I sensed that many of the lawyers were curious about how I came to the commission. I believe that my position as a political appointee at Robert Kennedy's Justice Department provided a sufficient explanation. Having known three of the junior lawyers for years and recommended two others, I think I was accepted as a worthy colleague until and unless I proved to be wholly incompetent or offensive.

There were two other notable additions to the staff. Mel Eisenberg, an associate at a New York law firm, came aboard ostensibly to work with Redlich. As Eisenberg tells the story, Redlich called a tax partner at Eisenberg's firm to check out another possible candidate for the staff, but the partner convinced Redlich to consider Eisenberg instead. Rankin promptly charged Eisenberg with the task of mastering the scientific evidence that should be considered in evaluating the assassination.

At this initial staff meeting, Rankin introduced Charles Shaffer, also from the criminal division, who had appeared at the commission offices in early January offering to assist me on a part-time basis. A former assistant US attorney in New York, Shaffer joined the division in 1961 as a special trial attorney in our labor racketeering unit. I knew he enjoyed the confidence and respect of Jack Miller and Robert Kennedy. I hadn't requested any assistance from the criminal division, but was glad to have his help.[13]

I learned from Shaffer many years later that he had been sent by Robert Kennedy to find out if the commission's investigation turned up any links to the Teamsters Union. This did not surprise me. Kennedy's pursuit of the Teamsters Union had resulted in dozens of convictions of Teamster officials. The department had indicted James Hoffa, the head of the Teamsters Union, in 1963 for attempting to bribe jurors in an earlier case against him. The trial was scheduled for early 1964.[14]

After a few weeks, Rankin, perhaps more sensitive to Shaffer's presence than I was, cornered Shaffer and interrogated him about exactly why he was hanging around. Instead of answering, Shaffer told me that he handed Rankin a slip of paper and told him to call the telephone number on it if he needed any information about Shaffer's responsibilities. The number was Robert Kennedy's private line. Rankin never mentioned this conversation to me. Shaffer stayed for about three months, worked hard, and provided valuable assistance. Once convinced that neither the commission nor the FBI had found any evidence of Teamster involvement, he quietly retreated to his duties at the Justice Department.[15]

If the commission was going to be successful, the effective utilization of the staff was essential. Time was precious. Although we were not given a deadline, everyone understood that the public was impatient for answers. At the January 13 meeting, Rankin asked that each team prepare a comprehensive memorandum setting out the known facts within its area and proposing additional investigation. He emphasized the need to carefully review the reports of the investigative agencies and departments to avoid the embarrassment of asking agencies for information that had already been provided.

During these first few weeks in January, our space in the VFW building acquired the look and sound of a functioning organization. Lawyers and secretaries filled the offices. I was in an office down the hall from Rankin. I sat at one desk and Shaffer another. I had also persuaded my talented criminal division secretary, Adele Lippard, to help me at the commission.

Rankin had three secretaries to support the front office. Julia Eide came with Rankin from his New York office and worked as his personal secretary. Beverly Heckman and Anne Welsh were on loan from government agencies. In early January, Rankin asked his secretaries to provide a copy to "Willens–Chrono" of all his commission correspondence and memoranda. I do not recall any discussion with him about this instruction. I assumed that Rankin wanted me to be familiar with the full scope of the commission's activities so that I could better assist him and advise Justice Department officials about the commission's work.

Rankin encouraged me to perform a managerial role. He always listened to my suggestions, no matter how numerous or irreverent, almost certainly because I represented the department and the attorney general. He had great respect for the Department of Justice, where he had served for eight years during the Eisenhower administration, and he spoke of the deceased president and the Kennedy family with affection.

With a tentative outline of the investigation approved by the commission, and the staff eager to get started, we needed to decide exactly how best to get the information we needed. We did not lack for advice on this score. In these early weeks, Rankin received unsolicited phone calls and letters from members of Congress, Texas officials, and others who weren't shy about making suggestions about how he should run the investigation or pursue speculations that each correspondent thought deserved immediate attention.

In late December 1963, Norman Redlich and I, along with Frank Adams, the first of the senior lawyers to appear, debated how to get the investigation done. We proposed to Rankin a two-pronged approach. Some of the needed investigation would be done by federal agencies. Other parts of the investigation would be done by the commission. Staff members would make an initial assessment whether particular witnesses should be called to testify before the commission. The commission had already decided that Oswald's wife, Marina Oswald, should be one of its first witnesses.[16]

As January progressed, the newly arrived lawyers offered their views on the subject. Everyone agreed we needed a chronological chart setting forth by date and time all the relevant facts disclosed in our investigation. Its preparation would be an arduous assignment, and Rankin agreed with my suggestion that it be prepared by federal agency personnel rather than our lawyers. Two IRS agents appeared promptly to work on this project.

After talking to Warren, Rankin decided that he would retain immediate responsibility for evaluating presidential security arrangements and that Sam Stern, the former Warren clerk, would work with him. I learned later that the chief justice regarded the presidential protection issues as the most important before the commission. It was the only forward-looking area of the commission's assignment. The Secret Service had failed in its responsibility. Something had gone terribly wrong, either with the service's personnel or its procedures, or both. It was essential to find the problems and fix them, but this inquiry presented two sticky problems. First, in order to evaluate the policies and procedures of the Secret Service, we needed the cooperation of the Treasury Department (where the Secret Service was located), and it might well object to our intrusion into their bureaucratic domain. Second, our investigation had to avoid inadvertently making information public that could compromise the safety of future presidents.

The initial press coverage of the commission was favorable. Although the commission had made no public statement regarding its initial decisions, one *Washington Post* reporter apparently had a very good source among the commission members. Early in January, he reported that the commission "is undertaking a far more wide-ranging and independent inquiry than most Washington observers expected." He went on to report that the commission would not be accepting any set of premises, or formulating even tentative conclusions, until it made its own investigation. He said the commission would use "its own counsel and staff to interview sources already questioned by the FBI and the police," conduct its own investigation, and take the testimony of witnesses in Washington.[17]

This reporter thought that the commission's plan to have some public hearings was a bad idea. He suggested that "a better investigation will be conducted if it is held entirely in private until the final report is issued." He supported this position with the argument that had been influential in establishing the commission: "This is not a trial. It is an extra-legal inquiry to obtain and assess evidence in a case which cannot go to trial. It seems to me that it would be misleading and harmful to have the information which the Commission will be collecting coming out piecemeal at periodic public sessions." Reflecting this concern, the commission decided that its hearings would be private unless a witness requested a public hearing. As the inquiry unfolded, only one witness did so.[18]

I had mixed feelings about this news report. The reporter's account of the commission's intentions was accurate and the issue of public hearings was an important one. But I was upset that the reporter had demonstrated easy (and early) access to the commission's deliberations. It didn't bode well for protecting the confidentiality of the commission's actions and discussions in the coming months.

A long and complimentary story by Anthony Lewis in the *New York Times* later in January featured Warren's role in directing the commission. Lewis, the *Times'* Supreme Court reporter, observed that Warren had "an extraordinary reputation abroad" but was a figure of controversy in his own country because of the Supreme Court rulings under his leadership. Lewis cautioned against any commission investigation of the country's "guilt" or state of mind and argued that what the public needed from the commission was "a highly particularized factual analysis completed as swiftly and with as little controversy as possible." Referring to the difficulties encountered by justices who previously accepted such nonjudicial tasks, Lewis concluded: "The potential for divisiveness is surely there in this investigation of an act that the Birch Society has already attributed to a Communist conspiracy and foreign observers to a plot by rightists. And divisiveness is what must be avoided above all. Earl Warren will need all his skill to pilot the inquiry through to a conclusion that removes the cloud from this country's honor and institutions."[19]

The Commission Begins to Shape the Priorities

On January 20, the staff gathered in our large conference room to be welcomed by the chief justice. Everyone showed up. "All the commission lawyers revered him," Specter later observed. "When we were in the same room with Earl Warren, we felt we were in the presence of history."[20]

Warren was relaxed and informal, though he commanded the room. He explained his initial reluctance in serving as chairman. "Previous non-judicial appointments of Supreme Court justices had proved to be divisive and controversial," he said. "It is simply not a good idea." But he told us how President Johnson had equated Warren's service to the country during World War I to this assignment. The president had also expressed his great concern about the international repercussions of the assassination and made a personal and earnest request for his help. Under these circumstances, the chief justice told us that he had no alternative. Warren went on to say that Johnson expected the commission "to find out the whole truth and nothing but the truth." Looking directly at each of us, Warren said, "That is what I intend to do."[21]

The next day, the commission approved the six-part outline for the investigation, which meant that we needed a sixth junior lawyer. A day or two later, I called a former law-firm colleague now teaching at the University of Chicago Law School, and asked for a recommendation. He suggested that we consider Jim Liebeler, a Chicago Law School classmate with a North Dakota farm background who was ready to leave his New York law firm. He cautioned me, however, that Liebeler was very conservative, very outspoken, and very independent-minded—but also very smart.

After Rankin and I interviewed him, Liebeler was hired for the sixth slot. I learned over time that Liebeler was a dedicated Goldwater conservative, a Milton Friedman economics devotee, and a libertarian before Americans had ever heard of Ron Paul.

Now we could fill in the blanks in our organization chart:

Area 1, the facts of the assassination: Frank Adams, the former police commissioner from New York, as the senior lawyer and Arlen Specter, the prosecutor from Philadelphia, as the junior lawyer.

Area 2, Oswald as the assassin: Joe Ball, the criminal defense lawyer from Los Angeles, as the senior lawyer and David Belin, the civil trial lawyer from Iowa, as the junior lawyer.

Area 3, Oswald's domestic US background and possible motives: Bert Jenner, the civil trial lawyer from Chicago, as the senior lawyer and Jim Liebeler, the civil lawyer from New York, as the junior lawyer.

Area 4, Oswald's foreign involvements: Bill Coleman, the corporate lawyer from Philadelphia, as the senior lawyer and David Slawson, the antitrust litigator from Colorado, as the junior lawyer.

Area 5, the murder of Oswald by Ruby: Leon Hubert, the former prosecutor from New Orleans, as the senior lawyer and Burt Griffin, the former prosecutor from Cleveland, as the junior lawyer.

Area 6, the arrangements for presidential protection: staffed only by a junior lawyer, Sam Stern, the corporate lawyer from Washington, DC, but with participation by Rankin, the appellate lawyer from Nebraska and New York.

We already knew that forensic and investigative reports weren't going to be enough to ensure the credibility of the commission's report. Sworn testimony from witnesses with personal knowledge of the facts was crucial. But preparing for and obtaining such testimony was time-consuming. The task had to be divided so that the commission would hear only the highest-priority witnesses while our lawyers interrogated less-central witnesses.

The process of taking testimony under oath necessarily meant that we went back over ground that had been covered through interviews by the FBI or another federal agency. But these agents were not authorized to take testimony under oath recorded by an independent court reporter. The important difference is that only sworn testimony is subject to a perjury charge if the witness lied. We planned to take sworn testimony in two ways: at hearings attended by the members and governed by its procedures and the powers granted by Congress; and in depositions by our lawyers under generally applicable court rules. In both instances, the testimony would be recorded verbatim by an authorized court reporter.

Each team needed to develop strategies for obtaining the necessary testimony. This involved determining which witnesses the commission was prepared to question based on the available investigative record and what investigation was required before other witnesses could be called to testify. Rankin sent a memo to all the lawyers on January 22 expressing a new sense of urgency. The commission wanted a progress report at its next meeting. Rankin asked each team to produce a preliminary, and relatively short, memo containing a statement of objectives and problems in the team's assigned area of investigation based on the materials at hand. He asked that these memos be prepared within the next two days so that they could be considered at a staff meeting on January 24.[22]

Rankin's directives and timetable stimulated much discussion. Staff lawyers would drift into my office to discuss, complain, debate, question, or just generally muse about the task ahead. The same occurred in Redlich's office, just down the hall. The senior trial lawyers, Adams, Ball, Jenner, and Hubert, had done many important trials. They didn't consider themselves to be memo writers; they wanted to get out in the field and have at it with live witnesses.

Others viewed the piles of reports from the FBI and other government agencies as presenting the familiar challenge of mastering the facts before embarking on exploratory depositions. Rankin never wavered in his determination that each team should assess everything that was currently known, from every source, before marching into the field to do further investigating.

At the staff meeting a few days later, Rankin set a deadline of February 10 for the comprehensive memo from each team that would summarize the known facts in its area. Redlich complained it wasn't enough time, citing the voluminous investigative reports from the FBI and other agencies. Redlich had probably read more of these reports than the rest of us because he had been assigned to prepare for Marina Oswald's testimony. He made the point that future critics would not excuse any failings by the commission on the grounds that it hadn't had sufficient time to do the job. Most on the staff agreed. Rankin pushed the target date back to February 18.[23]

Producing long written memos brought the role of the commission's secretaries to the forefront. Some lawyers, accustomed to very high quality personnel in their private law offices, complained to Rankin about the competence of their secretaries. Rankin called McGeorge Bundy, national security adviser, at the White House and, within a day or two, some very competent secretaries appeared at the commission office.[24]

With secretarial reinforcements in place, all six teams submitted preliminary memoranda on time. Because the commission had changed the agenda for its January 27 meeting, Rankin and the rest of us were able to relax somewhat at the January 24 staff meeting. He took the occasion to elaborate on the background of the commission members and to emphasize Warren's commitment to his assignment. Then Rankin addressed us in a more sober mood. In a phrase often repeated during the following months, he said, "Our client is the Truth." "The commission's report will be examined by the entire United States and will be examined for the next fifty years," he said.[25]

About this time we started to feel more pressure from the press. Requests from reporters seemed to arrive daily. Rankin, no stranger to public issues, valued good relations with the press but at the same time let us know he wanted no leaks. He told us that the commission had decided at its January 21 meeting to publicly announce each commission meeting and to issue a press release after the meeting. Apart from this arrangement, no other releases should be made to the press and staff lawyers should issue a firm "no comment" if approached by reporters.[26]

I had some limited experience with the press during my time at the Justice Department. I saw how effectively Robert Kennedy's press secretary Ed

Guthman and his talented deputy Jack Rosenthal dealt with press demands. Even before joining the commission, I had discussed with them whether the commission should hire a public information officer to help with the press. In late December I had recommended to Rankin that we do so. I don't remember whether Rankin agreed, but I learned later that Warren rejected the idea when Katzenbach raised it at the commission's first meeting. Consequently, we fended off the press by ourselves as best we could. I still think the commission should have hired a press specialist. Our experience with an impromptu and damaging statement to the press by the chief justice in early February illustrated the difficulties that might have been avoided.

■ Was Oswald an FBI Informant?

The words of warning about the press had hardly escaped Rankin's lips before Waggoner Carr, the Texas attorney general, called him to pass on a third-hand report that Oswald might have been a paid FBI informant before the assassination. Carr had gotten this information from Henry Wade, the Dallas County district attorney, who in turn had received it from an undisclosed source. The source said that the FBI had paid Oswald at the rate of two hundred dollars per month from some time in 1962 until the assassination. Carr told Rankin that Wade or one of his staff lawyers had mentioned this allegation at a public court hearing in the Ruby case, so the Dallas officials believed that one or more newspaper reporters had the story even if it hadn't yet been published.[27]

Rankin immediately called the chief justice to report this allegation and told me very soon thereafter. Warren and Rankin wanted to go directly to Robert Kennedy to pursue this allegation with Hoover. I got on the phone and called Katzenbach and Jack Miller. They both emphatically vetoed this idea. They said it would be embarrassing for Kennedy, who was, after all, Hoover's boss, and would make his continued administration of the department more difficult. I believed from the beginning that the allegation was improbable, but agreed it required immediate consideration by the full commission.[28]

Warren convened an emergency meeting of the commission the next day, January 22. The members recognized the difficulty in the FBI disproving such an allegation in light of the records, or likely lack of records, at the bureau. In the course of speculating about this allegation and its implications, Rankin told the commission that he suspected that the FBI had jumped the gun by identifying Oswald as the lone assassin before completing its investigation. Rankin emphasized that this was not consistent with his experience with the FBI. Responding to questions from commission members, he said the FBI "would like us to fold up and quit. . . . They found the man. There is nothing more to do. The Commission supports their conclusions, and we can go home and that is the end of it."[29]

The commission decided to ask some key Texas officials to come to Washington. Carr, Wade, assistant district attorney William Alexander, Leon Jaworski, and Robert Storey (former dean of Southern Methodist University Law School) all quickly made their way to Washington to discuss the matter with Rankin. None of the Texas officials knew the origin of the allegation about Oswald. Some had heard that this possibility had surfaced in connection with a dispute in the Ruby criminal case whether the FBI should be compelled to produce certain documents sought by Ruby's attorneys. By this time, the *Nation* had published a story about the possibility that Oswald was an informant not only for the FBI but also for the CIA. Lonnie Hudkins, a reporter for the *Houston Post*, had authored the *Nation* story. It turned out that a similar allegation had been made to the Secret Service in December, but a report from that agency on the allegation did not reach the commission until late in January. That tip also mentioned Hudkins as the source for the allegation.[30]

Commission members debated the merits of two different approaches to the problem. Under the first, the commission would initiate its own investigation, which would necessarily include seeking information from Hudkins, who almost certainly would invoke a reporter's privilege not to disclose his source. Rankin recommended a second approach, which involved his encouraging Hoover to cooperate with the commission in trying to resolve this matter. Rankin intended to urge Hoover to demonstrate by whatever records the bureau had that the allegation was simply not true. But Rankin realized that he would have to alert Hoover to the fact that "the Commission would have to feel free to make such other investigations and take testimony if it found it necessary in order to satisfy the American people" that Oswald was not an undercover agent. After extended discussion, the commission adopted Rankin's approach.[31]

Rankin scheduled an appointment with Hoover for the next afternoon. On the morning of that day, January 28, he received a letter from Hoover brimming with anger. Hoover knew that Texas officials had been in town to discuss the *Nation* piece. He acknowledged that FBI agents had interviewed Oswald three times after his return to the United States and before the assassination. But he issued a flat denial: "Lee Harvey Oswald was never used by this Bureau in an informant capacity. He was never paid any money for furnishing information and he most certainly never was an informant of the FBI. In the event you have any further questions concerning the activities of the FBI in this case, we would appreciate being contacted directly." Hoover made this denial public on January 27, the day before he delivered the letter to Rankin. Rankin was not surprised. He knew Hoover.[32]

Rankin went ahead with his scheduled meeting with Hoover. It was not pleasant. During his eight years in the Justice Department, Rankin's responsibilities as assistant attorney general and solicitor general occasionally had involved him with Hoover. During those years, he recalled that "our relations were warm and cordial and we seemed to have an understanding between each other and cooperation in trying to get the work accomplished that we had before us." The relationship deteriorated during Rankin's service as general counsel to the commission. He described Hoover's attitude toward him then as "quite cold and uncommunicative." Rankin said that "he acted as though he felt that the commission was hostile to him and to the FBI, and he commented upon all the man-hours we were demanding of him and how it was a burden to the FBI in its carrying on its other work." Notwithstanding Hoover's attitude, Rankin made the presentation that had been approved by the commission.[33]

Hoover subsequently sent several letters to Rankin in early February that summarized interviews with people alleged to have information supporting the allegation that Oswald was an FBI informant and provided affidavits in support of the bureau's denial of the allegation. He advised Rankin that Wade stated that he had no information to support this allegation and that Hudkins had refused to supply the name of a Dallas law enforcement official who had made the allegation to him. Hoover also provided his own affidavit, the affidavit of the agent who participated in two of the interviews of Oswald, and nine additional affidavits of bureau personnel "who, because of their assignments, would have been responsible for or cognizant of any attempt to develop Lee Harvey Oswald as an informant of the FBI." All of them denied the allegation.[34]

While investigating this allegation, as we learned more about the FBI's contacts with Oswald, the commission discovered a disturbing lack of candor about those contacts, which damaged the bureau's credibility. For example, Hoover's January 27 letter to Rankin also referred to a report that Oswald had certain information in his address book that related to FBI agent James Hosty—specifically Hosty's name and telephone number—a fact that Redlich had previously discovered from his examination of the address book. Hoover confirmed that the address book did contain this information, which Hosty had provided to Ruth Paine, with whom Marina Oswald was living with her two daughters (one recently born) when he interviewed her on November 1 and 5, 1963, regarding Oswald's whereabouts. The FBI had not previously told us about that fact. Soon thereafter, it became apparent that the FBI intentionally omitted these references to Hosty from its report to the commission dealing with Oswald's address book. We all knew that Hoover personally directed or approved these self-protective moves. We suspected more would come of this, and it soon did.[35]

■ The Commission's Decides to Do Its Own Investigating

Our discovery that the FBI was hiding information, apparently for self-serving reasons, required a decision about the continued use of FBI agents in our investigation. Could the commission work with an agency that proved willing to withhold information from us?

I thought we could handle this problem and, in fact, had no alternative. We had very competent lawyers who would be hard to fool as they became more knowledgeable about the facts. I had seen instances at the Justice Department where department lawyers had some reservations about Hoover's direction of the FBI, but found ways to work around the problem. They used other investigative agencies to cross-check what the FBI told them; they developed their own sources; and they always were aware of the possibility that the FBI was gaming them in some respect. FBI agents out in the field tended to act with fewer "political" motives than their Washington superiors, especially while working closely with department lawyers to prosecute a case successfully.

But we all feared that this instance of deliberately withheld information was not likely to be an isolated event. Our continued use of the FBI did give rise to criticism over the years that we failed to use "independent" investigators not employed by the federal government. Some critics believed that the commission's investigation was already fatally tainted because of its initial reliance on the FBI and other federal agencies. In their view, federal agents could not be relied upon to investigate allegations that their own agencies failed in their responsibilities. In addition, critics claimed that federal agents (and their superiors) would be more susceptible to political pressures within the federal government to ensure that the investigation came to a predetermined conclusion. I understood these concerns, but saw no problem in using federal agencies so long as the commission's ultimate decisions were based on its own extensive record of sworn testimony.

By late January, commission lawyers had identified hundreds of details that had to be checked out, stories that had to be confirmed or rejected, and additional physical evidence that had to be recovered. Only the FBI could muster the resources and manpower to do this work within an acceptable time frame. We had no other comparable pool of trained and experienced investigators in the United States. If the FBI and other federal agencies were barred from assisting the commission, candidates would have to come primarily from state and local police departments, with no assurance of their quality or independence. Many of these law enforcement officials had been employed or trained by the FBI, so they might not be considered "independent" investigators. Even if such candidates were found in suitable numbers, the required security clearances (typically done by the FBI) would have delayed any significant investigation by the commission for several months. I simply didn't see any practical or politically acceptable alternative to using investigators from the FBI, the CIA, and the Secret Service.

The commission members, all of whom had extensive Washington experience, came to the same conclusion, despite reservations about Hoover's trustworthiness. Former commission members Ford and McCloy later emphasized the ability of the commission's staff and its supervision of the federal agencies. Ford noted,

> Although the staff and the Commission utilized the investigative personnel and capabilities of organizations within the Federal establishment, we as a Commission and the staff were never satisfied with what information we got from these Federal organizations. What we did was to use them as a base, and then the staff and the Commission took off from there and handled individually the inquiries, the questions, and any leads that came to the Commission or to the staff.[36]

McCloy supported Ford's position and stated: "It is not true, as has been alleged, that we relied entirely on the agencies of the Government."[37]

Rankin explained later that he had examined the possibilities of using an independent investigative staff. He concluded and reported to the commission "that it would be a long time before we got any such staff put together that could handle all the problems that were involved with the size of the investigation" that we were conducting. Because President Johnson had instructed all government agencies to cooperate fully with the commission, Rankin decided "that it seemed prudent to try to use the intelligence facilities that the Government had at hand."[38]

Redlich and I shared the view that our reliance on an FBI we didn't fully trust meant we would have to work harder and longer to be sure we checked out every fact. We felt the weight of the staff lawyers' distrust of the FBI as they accelerated the pace of investigative requests to check and double-check facts. Rankin had instructed that all such investigative requests should go to me before they went to him for approval. Rankin also felt the burden as he approved the taking of sworn testimony from an ever-growing list of individuals with potentially relevant information.

This process ultimately produced testimony from 552 people: 94 witnesses who appeared before the commission, 395 witnesses deposed by commission lawyers, 61 witnesses who provided sworn affidavits, and 2 who provided statements. In assessing this entire record of testimony, and more than three thousand exhibits, the commission had the responsibility to do what federal investigative agencies do not customarily do—evaluate all the available evidence and make reasoned judgments of the conclusions that are supported by that evidence. This process is one that lawyers routinely are called upon by their clients—whether public or private—to undertake, and the commission members and lawyers had a wealth of experience in doing exactly that.

Even as the commission began to gain momentum, it was not an entirely unified team. Gerald Ford continued to chafe under Warren's style, although he was the only member who aired such complaints. Decades later, he still thought the chief justice ran a "one-man commission" and was not responsive to the views of other commission members. He characterized Warren as "pretty categorical in his views ... there was no deviation from his schedule and his scenario. He treated us as though we were on the team, but he was the captain and the quarterback." Notwithstanding his reservations, Ford made a very substantial commitment to the commission's work. Transcripts of the commission meetings do not support his criticism. Although individual members sometimes differed with the chief justice on particular issues, the transcripts show that Warren carefully sought their opinions and that the commission's decisions from beginning to end were unanimous.[39]

By the end of January, we had begun to move along an independent path. The FBI had essentially concluded its investigation and had no intention of initiating further work to supplement or amend its summary reports on Oswald and Ruby. During the commission meeting of January 27, Rankin advised the commission that the FBI's January report on Oswald "filled in some of the holes" in its first report, but left more than half of the commission's questions unanswered.[40] The hundreds of investigative requests and the tenacity of the staff in the following months uncovered important new information, developed new ways of interpreting the scientific and physical evidence, and brought us much clearer insights into how Oswald and Ruby could succeed in doing what they did.

Looking forward to February, the commission was going to hear its first witness, Marina Oswald, early in the month, with more witnesses to follow. The pending issues with the FBI had to be addressed to the extent possible, but more conflict was virtually certain. We were now ready to start dealing with the Treasury Department about presidential protection and with the CIA and the State Department about Oswald's foreign activities. As soon as Ruby's trial for the murder of Oswald, scheduled to begin in February, was concluded in Texas, our lawyers would be headed for Dallas to initiate the commission's program of taking testimony under oath from witnesses who had knowledge of the facts we needed to determine and evaluate.

CHAPTER 3

FEBRUARY 1964: THE SEARCH FOR EVIDENCE BEGINS

■

O SWALD'S WIFE MARINA WAS THE FIRST WITNESS TO TESTIFY—THE FIRST of her four appearances before the commission. Commission members and staff were never fully satisfied with her testimony, perhaps because we expected more insights than she could provide. Her appearance prompted immediate criticism of the commission's commitment to public disclosure of its work and an internal debate regarding the proper handling of commission witnesses.

■ Marina Oswald Testifies

Oswald married Marina in 1961, during his nearly three years in the Soviet Union (1959–62). She willingly left the Soviet Union to accompany her husband (with their daughter) when he decided to return to the United States. Now she occupied a place in the national spotlight like no other.

As a witness, Marina Oswald presented the commission with some difficult challenges. She spoke reasonably good English but exhibited some gaps in understanding, and already had run a gamut of intimidating interviews by federal and local officials. She had been recently widowed under horrific circumstances—after learning that her husband had killed President Kennedy and then seeing him murdered when surrounded by Dallas police.

Starting with this somewhat bewildered and frightened witness carried a substantial risk that the commission might stumble at the outset. Beginning in December, Redlich had immersed himself in preparation for her appearance. He reviewed all the available investigative reports about Lee Harvey Oswald's activities in Russia and the United States. He proposed questions that might elicit important details about his activities and motives, their life together, and their friends and associates. When he solicited suggestions from the other lawyers, several emphasized the need for more detailed questions about his emotional state to explore possible motives for his shooting of President Kennedy.

By the time Marina Oswald testified before the commission, we knew that she had lied to the Secret Service and the FBI in earlier interviews. Notably, she had denied knowledge of her husband's attempted assassination in Dallas of retired General Edwin A. Walker in April 1963 and his trip to Mexico in an effort to get to Cuba several months later. Investigative reports and exhibits provided to the commission demonstrated that these denials were false. All of us were eager to see what she would say about these incidents when she was under oath before the commission, hopefully providing a gauge whether she was believable on the many other topics the commission would explore with her.

There was a flurry of activity in the commission's office that morning. The commission was finally beginning to work in a way that the public could appreciate. Further, the commission was starting with the wife of the man who would have been the most notorious criminal of his generation if he had lived to be tried for his crime. What does she look like? What will she tell the commission? Why did she marry this loser? Many of us had these questions in mind as a few lawyers and secretaries caught a glimpse of Mrs. Oswald, her lawyer, and the commission members entering the VFW building. The impatient reporters whose grumbling and repartee could be heard through the windows on the fourth floor also had some questions.

The reporters greeted Chief Justice Warren when he arrived at the VFW building after walking over from the Supreme Court that morning. Would her testimony be made public? they wanted to know. "Yes, there will come a time," Warren told them. "But it might not be in your lifetime." He went on to explain: "I am not referring to anything especially, but there may be some things that would involve security. These would be preserved but not made public." Several reporters and commentators failed to quote the full text of Warren's comments and overlooked his reference to matters involving "security." The widely publicized shorthand for this comment became "Not in Your Lifetime."[1]

Warren's too casual comment drew immediate criticism as violating the commission's mandate "to satisfy itself that the truth is known as far as it can be discovered and to report its findings and conclusions to the American people and to the world." The *Baltimore Sun* emphasized the need for full disclosure of the facts because "there is a great deal of confusing and distressing speculation in other countries about the motives of the assassin." The chief justice's warning that "some parts of the commission's findings may not be made public during the lifetime of those of us who lived through the tragic days of November ... will feed rather than scotch speculation, for it hints of doings too dark for the public to comprehend."[2]

The immediacy and severity of this criticism drove home to all of us the intense scrutiny under which we operated. And it wasn't over yet. Two weeks later, a congressman introduced a resolution in the House of Representatives calling for full disclosure of evidence presented to the commission. A full-page "Open Letter to Chief Justice Earl Warren" in the *New York Times* by a consistent commission critic called for Warren's resignation and the creation of a new investigating group because of his apparent determination to suppress relevant information about the assassination. Several months later, Warren's "not in your lifetime" comment was identified as one of the three significant factors contributing "to the widespread impression in Europe that Mr. Kennedy was murdered by a fascist conspiracy." The same story reported that the chief justice later confided to a friend about his controversial remark: "I could have kicked myself afterward for saying that."[3]

The chief justice and Rankin scrambled to address such concerns. They issued a short statement a few days later to the effect that all results of the commission's investigation would be made public at the conclusion of its work, except those classified materials that for national security reasons could not immediately be released. As is usually the case, the accurate restatement of the commission's position never caught up with the pithier sound bite that the press and critics favored.

Although Marina Oswald's testimony had been long anticipated, the commission had not yet adopted procedures for the taking of testimony. But it never occurred to me—or other members of the staff—that Redlich would not attend the commission hearing to assist Rankin and the commission in questioning Marina Oswald. Rankin appeared to welcome and anticipate Redlich's assistance. Typically, the lawyer who prepares the questions for a witness almost always attends the session when that witness testifies and is usually the one asking the questions, for the obvious reason that he or she has the most knowledge of the facts. We had the reports of what Marina Oswald had said to others, but none of us had talked with her before she came to Washington. So it was inevitable that she might respond to questions with answers we could not always anticipate. Questioning of a witness can miss important facts or waste time on unproductive detours if the questioner has not prepared thoroughly and cannot handle the unexpected. So I and others assumed that Rankin and Warren would use Redlich's extensive preparation by letting him do most of the questioning. We were wrong.

Immediately after the session began, it became clear that the chief justice had decided that Rankin was the only person other than commission members who would question the witness. This prompted considerable consternation among our lawyers. Everyone was wondering why Redlich was not assisting in the interrogation. I raised this with Rankin at lunch and learned that he was simply deferring to the chief justice's wishes and had not proposed any different arrangement. I held my peace until after the day's testimony, when Redlich and I went to discuss the matter with Rankin.[4]

Going into the meeting, Redlich and I wanted to find out whether the chief justice had expressly told Rankin that no other staff lawyers could participate in the questioning of Marina Oswald. If he had made this decision, we had to persuade Rankin to get the chief justice to change his mind—not an easy task. I began by asking Rankin exactly why Redlich had not been allowed to help him question the witness. Surprisingly, he told us that he had not requested that Redlich assist in the interrogation at all. I told him the commission would have a seriously defective record if we did not use the expertise of the lawyers who knew the most about the facts. No matter how competent and experienced the commission members were, without the mastery of the facts they were simply not able to conduct an orderly and complete examination of the witnesses.[5]

It was our first heated exchange with Rankin—but not the last. Because Redlich's personal status was involved, I took the lead in asserting that he should have been in the hearing room. I was extremely critical of the chief justice and also of Rankin for not standing up more strongly to defend the course of action that he and the staff had agreed upon. Whenever I stopped for breath, Redlich joined in. The result was "a very devastating criticism" of Rankin, "which I am sure he did not particularly enjoy."[6]

I realized that we were challenging the judgment of one of the great appellate lawyers of his generation and a truly decent and thoughtful man. When it was his turn, Redlich peppered Rankin with questions about the day's interrogation of Marina Oswald. He reminded Rankin of the key areas in which we thought this witness had previously lied to the investigative agents. He told Rankin that no single witness could tell us as much as she could about their life in Russia, her husband's associates, and their personal relationship that might have led in some way to the assassination of the president. Redlich, although obviously disappointed with Rankin's readiness to exclude him, made his case quietly and effectively.

Lastly, I reminded Rankin that we had managed to assemble a very talented staff. They were working hard in mastering the facts. It seemed fair to suggest that unless the commission fully utilized our lawyers, we ran the risk of alienating them. I pleaded with Rankin to persuade the chief justice to allow staff lawyers to participate in the questioning of witnesses.

I learned the next morning from Redlich that he and Rankin had continued this conversation after I had left and that Rankin had agreed to let Redlich participate in the further questioning of Marina Oswald. Rankin never told me about any conversation he had with the chief justice on this subject. Rankin, as general counsel, was the only staff member who attended commission meetings and the commission members may well have assumed that this would also be the case during their hearings. They knew him; they trusted him; and expected that he was fully able to examine the witnesses—with their help, of course. I think our passion and intensity surprised Rankin. I suspect it caused him to think ahead to the dozens of witnesses likely to appear before the commission and to appreciate that he and the commission would benefit by having the responsible lawyer or lawyers participate in the hearings. It would enable him to share the burden of witness preparation and to expedite the commission's taking of testimony.[7]

My guess is that Rankin presented the question to the chief justice along these lines in a way that encouraged Warren to try this approach. Typical of his demeanor and management style, Rankin never suggested to Redlich and me that he had been offended by our vigorous advocacy that day. This was the first of a handful of instances during my commission assignment where I felt the need to challenge Rankin on matters I thought critically important.

At her first appearance before the commission, Marina Oswald admitted through her interpreter that she had previously made some misstatements to federal agents. She assured the commission that she was now ready to correct those errors. For example, she admitted that her husband had told her of his trip to Mexico. The admission that she had withheld information ended up being more interesting than the information she now volunteered. She knew only the basic facts about his Mexico trip, which the FBI had uncovered quite early in its investigation.

Marina Oswald testified for four days. It took longer than expected because of the extensive use of an interpreter. The commission's questioning led her through the story of her life and her days with Lee Harvey Oswald. She refused to speculate about his motives and provided only facts within her own knowledge. Warren declined to comment after the first day's testimony, whereas Rankin told the press that she had provided some "new things, new evidence" preceding the assassination, but what they were he didn't let on.[8]

After the second day, the chief justice was a little more forthcoming, advising the press that Mrs. Oswald had been questioned about some of the physical evidence and about her husband's attempt to kill Walker. On the last day, the commission asked her to indentify 145 exhibits, most of them Oswald's possessions. According to those at the hearing, she wept from time to time as she handled some of these possessions.[9]

We had another witness on the stand later in the month whose testimony involved Marina Oswald. After the assassination, she had hired James Martin as her business manager to deal with her extraordinary situation. By February, our lawyers had some concern that he was taking advantage of her—both financially and personally. The FBI and the Secret Service provided the commission with evidence that they were sleeping together.[10] Within the staff, we debated whether the commission needed to delve into that relationship. As he had done with Marina Oswald, Redlich had prepared for Martin's appearance. The commission had requested Martin to bring all documents relating to "any conversations and advice, instructions and other material of that kind concerning the testimony of Mrs. Marina Oswald or preparation of articles by her, or other things of that character."[11]

Warren severely restricted Redlich's interrogation of Martin. He "stated very definitely he believed that neither the character of Marina Oswald nor the business relationships" between her and Martin "were of interest to the Commission." Redlich strongly disagreed with the chief justice's decision. In a memo to Rankin the next day, he said bluntly: "We cannot ignore, however, that Marina Oswald has repeatedly lied to the Secret Service, the FBI, and this Commission on matters which are of vital concern to the people of this country and the world." He believed that the commission had an obligation to pursue all possible motives that might have prompted Oswald's assassination of the president. One of those motives might have resulted from his wife's actions. For this reason Redlich thought that Marina Oswald's character, her moral fiber, fell well within the reach of our investigation.[12]

■ Oswald's Attempt to Kill General Walker

An important aspect of Marina Oswald's testimony involved her husband's attempt to kill a well-known Dallas political figure named Edwin A. Walker. A graduate of West Point, Walker had been an Army major general, a veteran of World War II and Korea, who recently had been pressured to retire from the military for spouting anti-integration views and insinuations that various American political leaders were communists. In civilian life, his speechmaking became a big draw for right-wing audiences.

On the evening of April 10, 1963, while the general sat at a desk in his Dallas home, someone with a rifle took a shot at him. The shooter had fired from less than one hundred feet away and the bullet deflected off the window frame, but fragments still managed to wound Walker's arm. The police were unable to identify a suspect in the aftermath of that shooting until the Kennedy assassination. That's when they started wondering if Oswald had been behind the Walker attempt as well.

Marina Oswald knew about the Walker shooting—if not before, then immediately afterward. Her husband had left a note for her with instructions about what to do if he should be caught. She hid the note in a cookbook, where it remained until early December. When the FBI interviewed her, she did not tell them about his attempt on Walker because, she later said, it was unsuccessful and she didn't want to be a witness against her husband. But she admitted knowledge of the attempt to the commission.

Oswald's note wasn't his only link to the Walker shooting. Investigators had found photographs of the general's home among Oswald's possessions, and firearms identification experts told the commission that the bullet recovered at the Walker scene was the same type of ammunition used in the assassination. On the commission staff, we thought that the Walker incident provided strong circumstantial evidence that Oswald had the determination and mental capacity required to plan an assassination and was willing to kill if he thought he had sufficient reason to do so. As to what those reasons were in the case of Walker, Marina Oswald told the commission that her husband thought the general "was a very bad man, that he was a fascist, that he was the leader of a fascist organization, and when I said that even though all of that might be true, just the same he had no right to take his life, he said if someone had killed Hitler in time it would have saved many lives."[13]

At this early stage of our investigation, we were struck by certain aspects of the Walker attempt that might shed light on Oswald's culpability in President Kennedy's death. Many of the conspiracy theories about the assassination were based on the assumption that Oswald simply lacked the capacity to shoot the president without the assistance of others. As the details of the Walker attempt unfolded, we came to believe that some characteristics of Oswald's behavior relating to the Walker incident challenged this assumption.

Oswald Planned Carefully: The notebook and photographs found in Oswald's home indicated meticulous planning for Walker's assassination. Oswald had studied Dallas bus routes, which he subsequently used. He took photographs of Walker's house and possible locations for burying his rifle both before and after the attempt. And, of course, there was the note left for his wife with detailed instructions for her to follow in the event he did not return home.

Oswald Planned No Escape: Oswald faced the possibility that he might be apprehended for this attempt on Walker's life. His note advised his wife where he would be imprisoned if he was captured. He also contemplated that he might die as a result of this plan, and advised his wife regarding the money he left for her, what bills had been paid, and the assistance that friends or the Red Cross might provide her in his absence.

Oswald Left a Historical Record: In his note Oswald advised his wife to send any information in the newspapers about him to the Soviet embassy, which he said "would come quickly to your aid once they know everything." He posed for two pictures with his recently acquired rifle and pistol and copies of issues of *The Worker* and *The Militant.* Although he destroyed most of the notebook about his planning for the Walker attempt, he did not destroy the note that he left for his wife or some of the pictures that he had pasted in the notebook. He told her that he "wanted to leave a complete record so that all the details would be in it." This concern for his place in history seemed to be an important factor to consider in assessing possible motivation for the Kennedy assassination.[14]

Oswald Acted Alone: The commission and staff were well aware by this time of the widespread public perception that Oswald might have been part of a conspiracy of some kind. It was important to us, therefore, that we found no indication that Oswald had any assistance in planning for this attempt on Walker's life, in the attempt itself, or in its aftermath. His note to his wife and his conversations with her after the unsuccessful attempt never hinted of the involvement of anyone else. I am sure I was not alone in thinking: "This Walker incident is really interesting. With all the possibilities of conspiracy that have been swirling around the Kennedy assassination, Oswald seemed to have acted entirely on his own in the Walker case. Although it doesn't prove anything about the Kennedy assassination, it certainly suggests that it could have been a lone operation as well."

■ The Effort to Get Information from the Secret Service

During February, I tried to make progress on our investigation of the Secret Service. In order to prevent future assassinations, we needed to know how and why the service had failed to protect Kennedy. I knew that the Secret Service had few admirers in the law enforcement community, which tended to criticize the laxity of its training program, its pedestrian leadership, and its reluctance to modernize.

If the Secret Service was feeling defensive, one could hardly blame them. Its performance in Dallas had been vivisected by the national press; harsh (although not public) criticism from President Johnson and Mrs. Kennedy stung its leaders; and now the agency faced investigation by a commission it regarded as "political" and predisposed to look for scapegoats. The Secret Service was housed at the Treasury Department, and many commentators anticipated that the commission would consider recommending that some of its responsibilities for presidential protection be transferred to a more effective law enforcement agency. Anticipating the commission's inquiries, the Secret Service had typical Washington fears about revealing too much about its past and proposed procedures because this sensitive information might be disclosed—through leak or publication—by the commission.

James J. Rowley, chief of the Secret Service, had always managed to survive in Washington bureaucratic battles. A former FBI agent, Rowley transferred to the Secret Service in 1938, during Franklin Roosevelt's second term. He worked his way up the ladder, steadily and without controversy, until he became the director in 1961. Rowley gave the commission a report about the assassination on December 18, the day after I reported for work. I read it skeptically, looking for reasons why the Secret Service failed to discover a rifleman in a building directly overlooking the president's motorcade route through a city known for its ultraconservative political opposition to him. The report found no deficiencies in the agency's preparation for the trip or the performance of its agents in the motorcade. The defensive tone of the report couldn't help but reinforce my predisposition that the Secret Service was at fault. We did not learn until months later that several of the agents assigned to the motorcade had violated the service's regulations by drinking alcoholic beverages the night before the motorcade.

In his response to Treasury Secretary Douglas Dillon, Warren noted that the report covered only the Secret Service's advance preparations for Kennedy's visit to Dallas and the activities of its agents on that day. It said nothing about proposed improvements in the agency's policies and procedures. Warren acknowledged the service's concerns about more extensive disclosures but insisted on access to the investigative materials underlying this report, just as we had demanded of the FBI.[cxiii]

Rankin and I met with Secret Service representatives on January 7. At the meeting, Rankin asked Tom Kelley, a Secret Service inspector and the service's liaison to the commission, for all memoranda or other investigative materials the service had gathered after the assassination. Rankin also asked for a formal statement from the Secret Service specifying improvements it had made for the protection of the president in the aftermath of the assassination and any other recommendations aimed at improving its overall performance.[16]

After the meeting, Kelley called to inform me that the Secret Service had not changed any of its procedures since the assassination, except that President Johnson now rode in a closed car. Unwilling to rely on Kelley's oral representations to me, Rankin followed up with a letter asking Chief Rowley whether the Secret Service had made any changes in its procedures and for a formal statement of its recommendations regarding all aspects of presidential security.[17]

After the Secret Service provided some investigative reports, Rankin told Rowley that a staff lawyer would contact him shortly about reviewing additional reports, including those withheld as "secret." By now Sam Stern had reported for duty from his Washington law firm and begun working in the presidential protection area. Stern had considerable experience in negotiating complicated contracts between his corporate clients and foreign governments, and this commission assignment required similar skills and political sensitivities.[18]

Secretary Dillon responded in late January to Warren about Rankin's request for information about improvements in presidential protection. Dillon understood the threat the commission's investigation presented for Treasury, which had maintained control of the Secret Service since its inception in 1865. Having the Secret Service within the department gave the treasury secretary highly useful information about the president's daily schedule. A prominent Republican who ran one of Wall Street's most prestigious investment banks, Dillon had served as undersecretary of state in the Eisenhower administration. Kennedy appointed him as treasury secretary in part because of his close ties to the New York financial community.[19]

In return for his cooperation, Dillon insisted Warren agree to certain procedures to minimize the risk of disclosure of classified information by the commission. First, he proposed that information of this kind be made available only to commission personnel who had received security clearance. Second, he suggested that only commission lawyers engaged in this area of the commission's work be given access to the material. Last, he wanted no publicity given to this aspect of the commission's work and assurances that any recommendations or comments would be classified. A skilled practitioner of cabinet-level maneuvering, Dillon told Warren that he thought the commission might perform a useful service in reviewing these procedures, but nonetheless threw down a gauntlet. "However," he wrote Warren, "since the terms of the

Executive Order do not make it entirely clear how far the Commission's responsibilities extend, I should like to discuss this matter with the President and would appreciate your advice as to whether my suggestions as to the Commission's participation are acceptable." As evidence that Treasury and the Secret Service weren't being resistant to constructive change, he gave Warren a copy of his earlier memorandum instructing Rowley to draft recommendations to improve the service's protection of the president.[20]

Dillon and Warren met on February 4. The chief justice, also an adept practitioner of political maneuvering, seemed to believe that the treasury secretary would ultimately have to provide the information sought by the commission. Warren wanted to resolve this matter quickly, so Rankin asked Stern to prepare a draft letter to send to Dillon, and Redlich and I added comments from the sidelines. Stern's draft letter basically accepted the conditions proposed by Secretary Dillon.[21]

After revising it to reflect Warren's views, the commission on February 24 approved the letter to Secretary Dillon. Warren conceded in his letter that the executive order creating the commission did not specifically direct it to report on this subject. However, he advised Dillon that the commission members had all expressed the view that if any shortcomings were observed in the Secret Service's performance or procedures, they should be addressed in our report. Warren was not willing, however, to accept Dillon's proposals on the handling of materials by the commission and its staff.[22]

I thought this was a mistake, as did Stern and Redlich. We believed that the commission's response to Secretary Dillon should be firm, but accommodating enough so as to avoid a time-consuming debate between the commission and the department. We now realized that the commission members were sharply divided on the two most important issues in our dealings with Treasury: how much detailed information the commission needed to make useful recommendations on presidential protection, and what advance assurances should be given to Treasury about the confidentiality of its material given to the commission.[23]

I believed the commission needed full disclosure from the department in order to address the Secret Service's ability to protect the president. I was concerned that Treasury might try to wait us out, notwithstanding the presidential mandate in the executive order that all federal agencies should cooperate with the commission. "Slow-walking" can be an effective bureaucratic defense by an established institution like the Treasury Department in dealing with a temporary group like the commission. I feared Treasury intended to extend our negotiations, without ever formally denying our requests, until we ran out of time and had to issue our report without the information they kept from us. Stern and I did not want to be outmaneuvered by Dillon, so we kept returning to this issue in later weeks.

■ The Continuing Struggle with the FBI

Our general difficulties in extracting information from the Secret Service ran in parallel with our more focused efforts in prying information out of the FBI about its contacts with Oswald. We knew that the FBI had not alerted the Secret Service about Oswald. And we knew that Hoover would not readily give up information that supported any criticism of the FBI, no matter how important that information might be to the commission's work. At this point, we did not yet know the full extent of what the FBI knew about Oswald before the assassination, so we could not evaluate whether the FBI should have informed the Secret Service about him before November 22.

At the February 11 staff meeting, Rankin told the lawyers what he had learned about the FBI's failure to disclose information about FBI agent James Hosty found in Oswald's address book. We knew from the FBI's earlier reports and from Hoover's detailed response to Rankin on the "informant" question that the bureau had interviewed Oswald on three occasions since his return to the United States in June 1962. After the FBI learned Oswald had moved back to Texas in 1963 from New Orleans, where he'd lived for about five months, Hosty had interviewed Ruth Paine, one of Marina Oswald's friends, on November 1 and November 5, 1963, regarding Oswald's whereabouts in Dallas.

Mrs. Paine was unable to tell Hosty where Oswald was living. She told him that Marina Oswald and her two daughters, the youngest less than a month old, were living with her. Hosty left his name and telephone number with Mrs. Paine, who told Marina Oswald, which led to the inclusion of Hosty's contact information in Oswald's address book. Now, three months later, Rankin told us that the FBI had omitted this Hosty information from its report about Oswald's address book and that the commission was very concerned about this FBI failure. Like most of our staff meetings, everyone was serious and had an opinion how the commission should proceed. Some argued that the withheld information was not particularly significant and didn't require any response by us. Others thought that the deliberate withholding of relevant information (no matter how insignificant) was so important that the commission had to confront the FBI about it, although recognizing that doing so would further impair our relations with the bureau.[24]

Incensed by their blatant obstructionism, I wanted to fire off a letter right away demanding an explanation for the FBI's conduct. I was outvoted. Rankin asked me to draft a letter to Hoover, less confrontational than what I had proposed but certainly strong enough to inform the FBI of the commission's serious concern. It had to reflect our knowledge of what the FBI had done but be couched in such a way that might not damage beyond repair our working relationship with the bureau, though such a letter was probably beyond our collective creative writing skills. The letter we sent referred to the omission in the FBI report and asked: "The Commission would like to be informed of the circumstances surrounding this omission. More particularly, it would assist the Commission in appraising the significance of this matter if we knew the names of the agents, including supervisors, who prepared this portion of the report or made any decision to omit information from the report. Needless to say, we would like a full explanation."[25]

The FBI's response was a model of disingenuousness. It did not provide the "full explanation" we requested. The FBI advised the commission that the agents preparing the report to the commission based on Oswald's address book decided to confine the report to names of individuals and telephone numbers previously unknown in the investigation so that the commission staff could pursue these "leads" if they wanted to do so. Because these agents assumed that Hosty's name and other information could not possibly assist the commission in its investigation, the FBI advised us that it had decided to exclude this information from its report on Oswald's address book. We did not know at the time that Hoover had opposed the creation of the commission and that, as we got organized, he became increasingly apprehensive that the commission was dedicated to finding "gaps" in the FBI investigation of the assassination or in its handling of Oswald after his return to the United States.[26]

Although the commission staff regarded the FBI response to Rankin's letter as an insult to our intelligence, we knew there was nothing we could do. We needed the FBI agents in the field to respond to our daily investigative requests. Most of us thought our problems with the FBI lay with Hoover and his lieutenants, not with the agents on the ground. And, in fact, our lawyers and the FBI agents with whom they dealt in future months did develop a mutual respect, sometimes to everyone's surprise. For example, although FBI agents at first undoubtedly viewed Mel Eisenberg, the young New York lawyer, as an "amateur" in ballistics and other scientific areas, his quick mastery of the literature and technical issues was impressive enough to get their attention and ultimately win their respect. I believe that Redlich accurately described our collective attitude toward dealing with the FBI by saying that we came "with a professional lawyer's degree of skepticism" but without "any preconceived notion" that the FBI was always right or always wrong.[27]

Because Rankin had required that all investigative requests be reviewed by me before going to him for approval, I had more dealings than others on the staff with James Malley, the FBI inspector who was our official liaison with the bureau. There were approximately three hundred such investigative requests, most to the FBI. On occasion, Malley discussed a particular request with Rankin or me (or other lawyers) and suggested ways to rephrase or break it down into more limited requests. We almost always agreed to make these suggested changes. If the responsible lawyer and Malley could not agree, Rankin would resolve the issue. Malley described his relationship with the commission as businesslike, and I agree with that. He knew that I worked for the Justice Department and had access to high officials there. I knew that he had superiors at FBI headquarters who insisted that he keep them fully informed about the commission.

The commission's lawyers weren't hesitant about questioning the FBI's work. They understood that they had been appointed from the private sector in large measure to ensure their independence in conducting a thorough investigation. In fact, they relished proving FBI conclusions wrong. Most of our lawyers focused on finding flaws in the FBI conclusion that there were no conspiracies involving Oswald or Ruby. Many likely thought that someone (or some organization) more able and intelligent than Oswald and Ruby might have had a hand in this national tragedy and that this possibility had to be fully investigated. The team worked hard to examine every possible angle from which a conspiracy might have arisen. Conspiracies are almost always eventually revealed. No one on the staff wanted to go down in history as among those who failed to uncover the conspiracy that had taken a president's life. None of us regarded the FBI denial of conspiracies involving Oswald or Ruby as established fact.

As Rankin later said, he treated the initial FBI report about Oswald as "just an interesting document" and thought "we were probably quite offensive, especially some of the younger members of our staff who looked forward to the opportunity of finding that the FBI was wrong." Rankin never lost sight of our objective. As he remembered: "I was constantly asking for hundreds of investigations in places all over the country, and as soon as I got the reports on that and the responses, I would ask for some more, and I would ask for more complete reports on the ones that I thought were unsatisfactory." He recognized that this process created "a very difficult relationship and I don't blame them for feeling that they were being ridden pretty hard, which was true, but we never got to the place where they either apparently dared or would say they wouldn't do it. And as long as they didn't, I kept on."[28]

■ The Matter of Oswald's Legal Rights

The issue of Oswald's legal rights arose quite early in our work, when New York lawyer Mark Lane asked to represent Oswald in the commission's proceedings at the request of Oswald's mother. At its January 21 meeting, the commission rejected Lane's request. I drafted a letter for Rankin to send to Lane assuring him that every effort would be made to ascertain the facts regarding Oswald's implication in the assassination of President Kennedy as accurately and fairly as possible. As part of that effort, we invited Lane to appear as a witness, which he later did.[29]

Lane's effort to represent Oswald raised a question as to what the commission needed to do to demonstrate its desire to be fair to Oswald. The commission was functioning "neither as a court presiding over an adversary proceeding nor as a prosecutor determined to prove a case, but as a fact-finding agency committed to the ascertainment of the truth." Nonetheless, from the beginning our work focused on Oswald as the likely assassin, whether he acted alone or not. Even dead, Oswald was entitled to the consideration of evidence supporting his innocence and protection from unsupported allegations that further injured his reputation or caused harm to his wife, children, and other relatives.[30]

After rejecting Lane's offer to represent Oswald, commission members considered whether they needed to adopt additional measures to protect Oswald. In early February, they decided to ask the American Bar Association to designate one or more lawyers to serve as Oswald's defense counsel during the commission's deliberations. I was aware that both Warren and Rankin supported this proposal, but I opposed it. I worried that a large number of ABA lawyers might be required to staff a meaningful defense of Oswald. Inevitably, there would be disputes about the scope of their responsibilities, the need for time-consuming security clearances, their entitlement to subpoena power, and their access to the investigative agencies assisting the commission. I also anticipated they might retrace steps already taken by the commission (for example, the recalling of Marina Oswald as a witness) which could cause a substantial delay in the completion of the commission's work. Most important, I was convinced that the work of any ABA representatives—the establishment's lawyers—would never be accepted by Mark

Lane, Oswald's mother or brother, or the commission's critics as providing the aggressive defense of Oswald they believed necessary. I knew my views were shared by the other commission lawyers.

I stated my case in a long private memorandum to Deputy Attorney General Katzenbach about this proposed approach to the ABA. In addition to these concerns, I pointed out that designating the ABA would make the commission appear to be indecisive or untruthful with respect to its earlier expressed reason for not accepting Lane's offer to serve in this capacity. It would also give comfort to the commission's critics and the media who had been circulating Lane's contentions regarding the deficiencies in the commission's procedures. I also worried that this decision would reflect adversely on the commission members and staff by raising serious doubt as to their ability or desire to ensure that Oswald's rights and reputation were given due recognition. I did not ask Katzenbach to do anything specific, but expressed the hope that alternative methods for accomplishing the overall objective be explored. Katzenbach knew much better than I if there was any viable way to derail this train.[31]

Less than two weeks later, Warren advised the other members that he had extended the offer to the ABA's current president, Walter E. Craig, to participate in the commission's investigation and "advise the commission whether in his opinion the proceedings conformed to the basic principles of American justice." Craig had just recently been confirmed by the US Senate to serve on the US District Court in Arizona, but had not yet been sworn in. The commission issued a press release announcing Craig's appointment, stating that he could choose associates to assist him and indicating that all the materials available to the commission would be shared with him.[32]

Katzenbach called Rankin shortly after this public announcement of Craig's appointment. He told Rankin that he was "very disturbed" by this designation of Craig, among other reasons because Craig had apparently agreed with the Justice Department not to assume "any more extracurricular responsibilities which would postpone his entry on active duty on the bench." He told Rankin that he had not known that Craig personally would be representing the ABA and expressed to Rankin "a rather strong and negative view" about Craig's capabilities. Rankin assumed that I had discussed the entire matter with Katzenbach, including the identification of Craig, and was quite troubled by the whole conversation with Katzenbach.[33]

This led to an awkward confrontation between Rankin and me. I think my difficulty in dealing with Rankin's reaction to Katzenbach's call was that I hadn't known when I wrote my memo to Katzenbach that the commission would choose Craig. If I had known this then, I would have told Katzenbach and he could have had this conversation with Rankin earlier, when his reservations about Craig might have persuaded Warren and Rankin to designate someone else. Rankin assumed that I knew about Craig and had so reported to Katzenbach, which he apparently accepted as an appropriate action for me to take. I had never followed up on my memo to Katzenbach, believing that the matter was in his hands unless he indicated otherwise.

I learned later from Jack Miller that after receiving my memo, Katzenbach contacted ABA officials. According to Miller, the ABA officials confided that Warren's request was his first contact with the organization since he had resigned from the association in 1957. He had done so in response to an ABA report made public in London, where the chief justice was leading a delegation of American lawyers. Warren later described the report as a "diatribe against the Supreme Court of the United States, charging it with aiding the Communist cause in fifteen recent cases." With that history in mind, the ABA in 1964 did not feel it could very well turn the chief justice down.[34]

The commission lawyers greeted the ABA participation in the investigation with varying degrees of dismay. David Belin, the Iowa civil lawyer working on evaluating the evidence that Oswald was the assassin, was particularly upset. He and Joe Ball, the Los Angeles defense lawyer, spent thirty minutes with Rankin on February 25 discussing the proposal. Chief among their complaints—and those of the other staff lawyers—was that no one even bothered to clue them in on the proposal until it was a *fait accompli*.[35]

As explained by Rankin, the chief justice and Craig didn't discuss the mechanics of how Craig would operate. As the dust settled, this issue receded to the background. I periodically put together a large stack of materials that Rankin sent to Craig. Rather than examining the staff's investigative efforts in detail, Craig elected to undertake only a high-level review, as perhaps the chief justice and Rankin suspected he would. He attended some hearings when witnesses were testifying before the commission, as did some of his associates. Near the end of the investigation, I believe he got access in the commission office to some draft sections of the report. In retrospect, Craig provided only general oversight, which may have been useful to the commission, and he did not interfere at all in the more detailed investigative issues or judgments about the commission's report.[36]

In another matter relating to Oswald's interests, Rankin asked Stern to look into the treatment of Oswald by the Dallas police before his death.[37] He was specific about the questions he wanted Stern to answer: (1) Was undue force used in the arrest? (2) Was Oswald coerced during interrogation? (3) Was he denied access to counsel? (4) What public comments did Dallas authorities make concerning the evidence? (5) How were lineups and other identifications of Oswald handled? (6) How did it happen that Oswald was brought in front of television cameras? (7) Were Oswald's relatives provided access to him? and (8) Was he arraigned properly? These questions, of course, pale in comparison with the most elemental question bearing on Oswald's rights that Hubert and Griffin were exploring: How did the Dallas Police Department aid, or permit, Ruby to enter the basement and kill Oswald?

One of the new additions to our staff, John Ely, assisted Stern on this project. Ely had graduated from Yale Law School in 1963 and was scheduled to serve as one of the chief justice's clerks during the upcoming term of the Supreme Court. When Warren learned that Ely had some time on his hands, having completed his military service obligation, the chief justice promptly recruited him.

Three weeks later, Stern and Ely reported their conclusions and recommendations for further inquiry. Although they were able to answer a few of these questions based on the facts at hand, they recommended more detailed examination of the TV tapes and key depositions of police officials before the other issues could be resolved. Stern and Ely identified two additional issues that deserved some attention: whether there was probable cause for Oswald's arrest and the legality of the first search of the Paine residence where Marina Oswald was staying.[38]

Redlich and I endorsed these recommendations and Rankin accepted them. Both Warren and Rankin were determined to discuss these questions affecting Oswald's rights as an integral part of the commission's assignment. The commission's report addressed some of these issues. It concluded that the Dallas Police Department did not violate any of Oswald's legal rights, including his right to counsel. But the commission was very critical of the manner in which the Dallas law enforcement officials handled the interrogation sessions and the lack of control over the conditions in the police station. It emphasized the crowded and chaotic situation in the police headquarters resulting from as many as three hundred news representatives from around the world jostling to get a picture of the alleged assassin and thrusting microphones in his face as he was moved from room to room. The commission also condemned the publication by the Dallas police of virtually all of the information about the case gathered between Oswald's arrest on Friday and his murder on Sunday.[39]

■ The Lawyers Chart the Investigation to Come

Along with John Ely, we had three other additions to our staff during February. The most important was Al Goldberg, n historian from the Department of Defense. The chief justice personally undertook to find someone who could help shape the commission's eventual report and provide useful historical context. Warren found his man at the Defense Department, which, it turned out, had a virtual army of historians. Dr. Alfred Goldberg came with a PhD from Johns Hopkins University and many years of experience at the department. In his initial interview, Goldberg asked the chief justice why he wanted a historian on the commission staff. According to Goldberg, Warren said, "I don't trust all these lawyers."[40]

At his first meeting with the staff, Goldberg recommended that the lawyers might consider keeping some personal record of their work with the commission—a suggestion that resulted in my journal. He quickly focused on the documentation of the commission's efforts—the nature and organization of the files that would eventually be turned over to the National Archives. Goldberg was free to make suggestions to Rankin about our work and undertook some projects of his own with Rankin's approval. He recognized from the beginning that he was "the odd man out on the commission staff" among all these lawyers, but confessed years later that he got along quite well with most of us. In fact, he became a valuable colleague on whose judgment we relied on a wide range of issues. His outsider perspective and wry sense of humor were appreciated by all of us.[41]

Richard Mosk was another of our newly minted young associates available to work in any area where they were needed. Mosk, a recent Harvard Law School graduate, had written a polite inquiry about working for the commission, and I had drafted our routine response politely declining his offer of assistance. However, Mosk's father was, at the time, California's attorney general and a close friend of Warren's. Shortly thereafter, the chief justice mentioned to Rankin that he thought "young Mosk" possessed just the kind of credentials the commission needed, and I promptly prepared a second letter welcoming him to the staff. Mosk was completing his six months of military duty with the California National Guard and his departure for Washington was delayed for a few hours because his military superiors insisted that he complete his service with another stint of KP duty, cleaning pots and pans.[42]

Later the month, Philip Barson, an Internal Revenue Service agent from Philadelphia, reported for duty and began work immediately on the project of documenting Oswald's income and expenditures.[43] One of the possible avenues toward proving or disproving the existence of a conspiracy was whether Oswald had resources beyond his means. Some of the commission critics were already advancing allegations that Oswald's expenditures during this period exceeded his known sources of income. For this reason, we wanted a professional analysis of his income and expenditures based on the testimony and investigative materials. Barson undertook this task with the enthusiasm of a convert.

By the last week of February, the commission lawyers had completed the memoranda needed to chart the future progress of the investigation. Rankin asked Redlich and me to review these memoranda, consult with the lawyers in each area, and provide him with a frank assessment of where we stood. He and the commission wanted to know whether the lawyers had mastered the relevant information in their area, had a coherent plan for future investigation, and had identified witnesses who should be questioned by the commission or deposed by the lawyers. We needed an early assessment of potential witnesses to meet the commission's desire for more witnesses and to have our lawyers prepared to go to Dallas as soon as the Ruby trial ended.

Although the lawyers in each area had their own techniques and habits for undertaking a complicated factual investigation, each roughly followed the usual trial-lawyer process. The first step typically involved a lawyer's critical review of the material at hand. In this case the lawyers examined exhaustively the investigative reports from the different agencies and the available documentary and physical evidence. The next step was to identify the witnesses with firsthand knowledge of the critical events who needed to be questioned; the additional documents that needed to be located, produced and authenticated; and the experts who could testify on the scientific and technical issues. By far, the most tedious part of the task was the first step.

The axiom "truth is our only client" had real-world consequences in the course of the commission's investigation. First, it meant that nothing—no assertion by an investigative agency or individual—could be taken for granted. It required the development of sworn testimony on the basis of which a responsible and objective judgment could be made. Second, the judgments evaluating the evidence had to be based on a fair consideration of all the relevant testimony, recognizing that conflicts in the testimony of even well-intentioned and honest witnesses are inevitable on factual issues such as we faced.

The Ball/Belin team rigorously applied the "assume nothing" rule in their initial examination of the materials pertaining to the use of the rifle found in the depository. One example related to the conflicting descriptions of the results of the paraffin test applied to Oswald's skin to determine whether he had recently fired a weapon. Wade, the Dallas district attorney, told the press that the test "showed that he [Oswald] had recently fired a gun. It was on both hands." Dallas police chief Curry supported Wade's assessment, saying that "I understand that it was positive. . . . It only means that he fired a gun." Mark Lane's version was diametrically opposite: "The test, however, showed no gunpowder on either hands or cheek and no nitrates on Oswald's face." Therefore he concluded that there is "but one possible interpretation—that the paraffin test results were consistent with innocence."[44]

Before taking any depositions of the law enforcement officials who had administered this test, Ball and Belin consulted with Eisenberg, who had reviewed the pertinent literature regarding the paraffin test. As a result, Ball and Belin concluded that a paraffin test is wholly unreliable in determining whether a person has recently fired a weapon. As Belin later wrote, "chemicals used in the paraffin test will react positively not only with nitrates from gunpowder residues but also nitrates from any other sources and most oxidizing agents. Thus, contact with tobacco, urine, cosmetics, kitchen matches, fertilizers and many other things may result in a positive reaction to the paraffin test." In addition, the mere handling of a weapon may leave nitrates on the skin, just as the firing of the weapon might do.[45]

While a positive reaction to the test is not considered legal proof that a suspect has recently fired a weapon, the question remained whether a negative reaction on the test would be evidence that a person has not fired a weapon. We learned that the FBI had conducted tests going back to 1935 regarding the paraffin test and concluded that a negative reaction from the test did not prove that the person did not fire a weapon. To further explore the matter, the commission asked the FBI to conduct an experiment in which it used the paraffin test on an agent who fired the rifle found on the sixth floor of the depository building using the same type of ammunition as the recovered cartridge cases. The test produced negative reactions on both hands and on the cheek of the FBI agent who fired the rifle. Accordingly, the commission did not rely on the paraffin test in making its finding that Oswald was the assassin.[46]

The second point—the need to consider all the evidence—required each team to ensure that it had identified all the witness testimony, documents, physical evidence, and expert opinion that related in any way to an issue before the commission. Part of that task required the lawyers to identify conflicts in the evidence and to explain that divergence to the commission. Trial lawyers almost always work in this manner because the adversary system pits a lawyer presenting one view of the facts against another lawyer, who presents an opposing view of the facts, and the judge or jury weighs all the evidence before making its own factual findings. In the commission's investigation, our lawyers were not adversaries for one or another position on any of the facts; rather they were the first objective finders of fact. They had to consider all the evidence, evaluate competing interpretations of the evidence taking into account the credibility of the witnesses, and propose recommended findings (or conclusions) to the commission, the ultimate decision maker.

One example of the many conflicts in the evidence that Ball and Belin faced in their work related to whether the president said anything after he was hit. Secret Service Agent Roy Kellerman, sitting next to the driver, testified that President Kennedy said "My God, I am hit" after the first of two shots hit him. Secret Service Agent William Greer (the limousine driver), Connally, his wife Nellie, and Jacqueline Kennedy all testified that the president did not say a word after he was shot. Looking only at the testimony of Kellerman, a fact finder might conclude that the first bullet did not cause the throat wound, because it would have impaired Kennedy's ability to speak.[47] But weighing his testimony against the contrary testimony of four other witnesses in the president's car—plus the autopsy report and other evidence—led us to a different conclusion. All the commission lawyers made the same determined effort not only to summarize the evidence that supported our proposed findings but also to evaluate the contrary evidence.

Bill Coleman and David Slawson had the responsibility for most of the work in the foreign area. Coleman was one of the most prominent African-American lawyers of his generation, and Rankin had attached a high priority to having him on the commission staff. During his law-school years Coleman had met Fidel Castro when both had patronized jazz clubs in Harlem. Although younger than the other "senior" lawyers, Coleman had already gained recognition as a corporate counselor and effective litigator. He had made major contributions in the civil-rights arena for the preceding two decades. Coleman lived in Philadelphia at the time and commuted to Washington each Friday for his commission duties.[48]

Slawson had moved to Washington from Denver for this assignment and worked on a full-time basis. Warren had mentioned at a January commission meeting that he had just lunched with Justice Byron White, who told him Slawson was one of the best lawyers in his former law firm. Slawson had a very open manner, which the more formal Coleman seemed to appreciate. The two of them appeared to be developing a warm and respectful relationship, which resulted a few years later in Coleman recommending Slawson to serve as general counsel for a federal agency in Washington.[49]

Redlich and I discussed the memorandum from Coleman and Slawson on February 24, and later considered some unusual lines of inquiry with Slawson. We suggested a formal request to the Mexican government from our State Department seeking any information the Mexicans had relevant to our investigation, which also raised the question whether it might be better if the commission sent its own representatives to Mexico rather than depend on the State Department. We proposed exploring with State "any unofficial means of sounding out the Soviet Union as to information which they might be willing to give to the Commission"—for example, whether it applied customary procedures in permitting Marina Oswald to leave the country. We also were curious as to what action was taken by the Soviet embassy in Washington, DC, when it received a letter from Oswald a few weeks before the assassination.[50]

The Soviet Union provided the commission with all the letters it had received from the Oswalds, including the last letter written by Oswald to the Soviet embassy in Washington on November 9, 1963. It began by stating that the writer wanted "to inform you of recent events since my meetings" with Soviet officials in Mexico City. The commission learned that Oswald had spent the weekend at the Paine house working on this letter, and investigators found an earlier draft among his effects after his arrest. Comparison of the draft with the letter actually sent indicates that Oswald was trying to make his trip to Mexico sound as mysterious and important as possible. For example, whereas the draft characterized his trip to Mexico as "useless," this word did not appear in the final version. Instead, he wrote that he was unable to remain in Mexico because his Mexican visa was about to expire, which was not true.[51]

Redlich and I next turned to the memorandum produced by Bert Jenner and Jim Liebeler, which was disappointing. The Jenner/Liebeler draft lacked an overall plan setting forth their ultimate objectives and detailing how their investigative recommendations would get us there. My requirements for them were straightforward. I wanted to see a complete, well-written assessment of the known facts; a critical analysis of their investigative needs; and a proposed course of action, including a list of witnesses, which would address these needs and enable the lawyers to produce an acceptable first draft discussing the issues in their area.

The questions Liebeler and Jenner grappled with—the existence of a domestic conspiracy and Oswald's motive—were intertwined in a way that required their investigation to proceed in multiple directions. These questions were central to the commission's mission. If we could not get this part of the investigation analyzed in a thoughtful manner, we would fall far short of what the commission needed to fulfill its mandate. Redlich agreed with my assessment and my recommendation to Rankin "that these two lawyers should be given two weeks in which to fully analyze and appraise all the investigative material and that their time should not be diverted to the taking of testimony until they demonstrated complete familiarity with the basic materials."[52]

Jenner did prove to be as "indefatigable" as Warren had been told a few months earlier. Although he continued to have client commitments back in Chicago, he worked long hours when in Washington. By this point in his career, Jenner was accustomed to being in charge of any matter on which he was working, so the commission's structure was somewhat challenging for him. He brought to the investigation a trial lawyer's very practical outlook—what is the evidence on our side, what is the evidence on their side, and what is most persuasive. His assignment, however, dealing with Oswald's background, associates, and motive turned out to be more elusive than the typical antitrust case.

Liebeler was a burly, muscular man with a flaming red beard. Originally from North Dakota, he retained a prairie directness and enthusiasm that had been modulated only slightly by his years at college and law school. He worked as hard as any lawyer on the staff from his start in late January until the final days in September. As advertised, he was very combative and very smart. With Liebeler, conversation was never far from debate. Few things gave him more pleasure than decimating a colleague's reasoning or written work. Years later, when Liebeler stayed at my house for an extended period, he engaged my wife in a lively debate about what materials could or could not properly be put down the kitchen garbage disposal. One day while we were at work, he put a sign over the sink reminding her to mend her errant ways in this regard. Liebeler's challenging and argumentative approach did not mesh well with Jenner's more refined and deliberative style. I think they would agree that each did his best work when proceeding independently.

Arlen Specter and Frank Adams had the task of developing all the facts related to the assassination itself. Adams appeared on the scene late in December before any of the other senior lawyers and helped shape some of our early thinking about how the commission's lawyers should do their jobs. Although Specter liked Adams and enjoyed working with him, Adams's commitment to his law firm's work left relatively little time to help Specter. He had a major antitrust trial scheduled for mid-February, which took him away from the commission's work for long periods of time. As a result, the burden in this area fell on Specter, who took on whatever needed to be done calmly and competently. True to his collegial spirit, Specter submitted the analytical memorandum on Area 1 bearing both his and Adams's signatures.[53]

The work in this area offers a good example of the investigation's progress in February. After review of their long memo, Redlich and I suggested to Rankin that he ask Specter and Adams what specific information they expected from the witnesses identified in the memo. We expected to take detailed, sworn testimony from the most sensitive witnesses with firsthand knowledge: Mrs. Kennedy, President and Mrs. Johnson, and the Connallys. Specter and Adams were responsible also for the testimony of four key Secret Service agents who were closest to Kennedy in the motorcade, the five eye witnesses who said they saw a rifle protruding from the depository building, and the three doctors at the Parkland Hospital who treated Kennedy.

Specter responded immediately to our request. He prepared a list for the commission summarizing the topics to be developed with these witnesses, as well as those who were near the intersection of Elm and Houston Streets when the motorcade went by. Specter wanted to get depositions started in Texas as quickly as possible, but we were slowed down by various circumstances, not least of which was that Texas authorities did not want us digging around in Dallas while the Ruby trial was going on. They expected to be done by mid-March. In addition, we did not yet have the go-ahead from the commission for the extensive investigation we had planned.[54]

I had asked Charlie Shaffer to take an initial look at the work being done in Area 5, where the Hubert/Griffin team was wrestling with the factual issues about Ruby's actions and associates. After reviewing the many investigative requests proposed by Hubert and Griffin in late February, Shaffer reported to me that the matters had been resolved to everyone's satisfaction.[55]

Leon Hubert had a quiet Southern manner and was less pretentious than the other senior lawyers. Of moderate height and slim build, he was a committed chain smoker (outdoors even then) and always chased his cigarette with a Coke. He may not have exuded the self-confidence and charisma of the other senior lawyers, but he was thoughtful and thorough. Hubert worked long hours for us until early June, when his law-firm responsibilities in New Orleans and military obligations limited his availability in Washington.

Burt Griffin was a determined, hardworking young trial lawyer with a few years' experience in the US Attorney's office in Cleveland. He became an imaginative and persistent advocate for his area's investigative needs and explored relentlessly any possibility that Ruby participated in a conspiracy. Griffin had moved to Washington from Cleveland with his family, including two young sons, for the duration of the commission's work. Hubert and Griffin made a good team and early on established the challenging objective of determining as exactly as possible what Ruby had done every single day, and every single hour, in the two months or so before the assassination. If Ruby had contacts with any co-conspirators, these two were going to find them.[56]

As was our practice, Redlich and I reported to Rankin about our meetings with the lawyers and their initial memoranda. Our criticism of these basic memos was often reduced to writing. For example, my five-page memorandum to Ball and Belin raised thirty-five questions and suggestions regarding additional requests to the FBI and witnesses that should be deposed. I thought at the time that all the lawyers accepted the idea that there had to be some general oversight of their efforts and that Rankin had asked Redlich and me to help provide it. The other lawyers, both senior and junior, could always consult further with Rankin about their work and did so on many occasions. From what I observed, Rankin resolved the differences among us in a way that left everyone feeling that he had had his day in court. Some of the lawyers would have preferred that Rankin got out of his office more often and visited informally with them about their work, but that simply was not his style.[57]

After more than a month of working closely together, our lawyers—young and old—seemed to be enjoying not only the challenges of the assignment but also the collegiality that characterized our relationships. The distinction among "senior," "junior," and "associate" lawyers completely faded when debating the issues or eating a meal together. I had a wife and three young children at home in Washington who required my presence most weekdays for dinner, but I know that the lawyers from out of town often worked into the evening and frequently had dinner together. I heard that there was no shortage of gossip and jokes at these meals about "missing" senior counsel, the foibles of the commission members, and the unreasonable demands of "management" (i.e., Rankin, Redlich, and me). The strong sense of brotherhood among the commission lawyers (including even management) has persisted over the decades.

My liaison efforts to keep the Justice Department's leadership informed about the commission proceeded at my own pace. No one ever called me and demanded a report or told me to send along some memo. When I had time, I would drop by the department's main building at Ninth Street and Pennsylvania Avenue. My office at the VFW building, located near the Supreme Court, gave me a chance to walk the nine blocks or so and get some fresh air. I could almost always find Miller or Katzenbach with time to spare for me. I would report on events and issues that I thought might be useful background for them.

The results of our work in late February was a memo for the commission setting forth a tentative work schedule for the next six or seven weeks. This included the witnesses proposed for examination by the commission and by the lawyers. Before the February 24 meeting of the commission, Redlich and I asked Rankin to place before the commission the specific proposal that staff lawyers be authorized to take depositions in Dallas beginning as soon as possible after the Ruby trial ended. We gave him a rough estimate of the likely number of witnesses—thirty for the commission and seventy-five for the lawyers—which seriously underestimated the amount of sworn testimony ultimately considered by the commission. The commission readily approved this course of action by the staff.[58]

Meanwhile, the press worried about the slow pace of the commission's investigation. One story in late February reported that there were "complaints within the commission itself over the slow progress of the investigation." This Los Angeles reporter expressed concern that the commission was engaged in dealing with peripheral issues, such as "allegedly erroneous newspaper accounts of testimony which presumably have been leaked by staff members." He exhorted the commission not to let such extraneous issues divert its attention from its serious mission. That, he said, "would be tragic" because of the importance of the commission's investigation to the "preservation of the integrity of the Republic." He emphasized: "For it is the task of the Warren Commission to tell the world the truth—as far as it is discernible—about what happened that somber afternoon in Dallas last November. It is this truth, and this truth alone, which can put to rest the malicious rumors and deliberate lies about Mr. Kennedy's murder which groups within and without the United States are using for their own propaganda purposes."[59]

■ **The Genesis of the Single-Bullet Theory**

One of the most significant developments in the commission's work started to take shape in late February. Although working conscientiously on their analytical memoranda in order to meet the deadline, the commission's staff—like most lawyers—greatly preferred to confer and debate the issues. One of the important problems we faced was determining which of the bullets hit whom and when. The Zapruder film gave us a key to solving this problem. Both the FBI and the Secret Service had separately (and repeatedly) examined the film. A group of our lawyers –Ball, Belin, Eisenberg, Redlich, and Specter—did the same, often joined by FBI agent Lyndal Shaneyfelt, a photography expert who provided valuable assistance to the commission.

The first day that he reported to the commission in late January, Liebeler recalls joining "a group of staff members [who] watched the Zapruder film over and over again as well as examining individual frames. It was my first meeting with Norman Redlich, who was generally in charge of the viewing. I asked him once I had caught the drift of the meeting whether he thought more than one person had been shooting at the motorcade. His reply: 'That's what we're trying to find out.'"[60]

At this stage of the investigation, the lawyers questioned the conclusion reached by both the FBI and the Secret Service regarding the three shots believed to have been fired from the depository. Although witnesses at the scene recalled hearing between two and six shots, the largest number heard three shots, and three cartridges had been discovered on the sixth floor of the depository, so three shots became our working hypothesis.

Initially most of us thought that the first shot hit the president, the second hit Connally, and the third shot killed the president. Connally firmly believed that he had been hit by the second shot, after he heard the first shot, and that he was not hit by the same shot that first hit Kennedy. However, remnants of only two bullets were found in the presidential vehicle. Close examination of the Zapruder film gave us one way to help determine roughly when Kennedy was first hit and when Connally was hit. If the interval between the first and the second shots covered a span of less than 2.25 seconds, the time estimated to be necessary for the assassin to fire two shots, it might suggest that a second rifle was involved.

Belin worked hard in these early days to prove that a second gunman had participated in the assassination. He requested the Secret Service to ask the three physicians who attended to Connally's three wounds (back, hand, and leg) to reconstruct the position of the governor "as it must have been to receive the wounds he received." Belin received a set of drawings portraying the reconstructed position of Connally from five different viewpoints. Belin then gave these drawings to the FBI asking the bureau to compare these drawings with the Zapruder film and advise when, according to the Zapruder film, Connally could not have been hit. The FBI advised that "Governor Connally was not in the position reconstructed by his doctors at any time after frame 240." The commission's lawyers working on the problem agreed with this determination.[61]

As additional information became available, this small group analyzed, evaluated, and rejected theories. But there was one basic question that now seems very simple: Where did the bullet go after it exited the president's neck? There was no evidence on the inside of the presidential car that reflected the damage that a bullet would have caused had it followed the trajectory and had the assumed velocity of the bullet that exited the president's neck. So at some point in these collegial sessions someone, probably Specter, suggested out loud what all in the group were thinking—that the first bullet that hit the president also created Connally's wounds.

This possibility of a single bullet hitting both men, which contradicted Connally's statements (and later testimony before the commission), was also of startling simplicity. It became the much-maligned single-bullet theory. Although we were all intrigued by this new explanation, we immediately recognized its potential and controversial significance. Before this theory could be accepted by the staff and presented to the commission, it needed to be challenged and tested in a variety of ways. That, in turn, led to the reenactment of the assassination that the commission conducted three months later.

March promised to be our most momentous month yet. Not only were we looking to further testing of the single-bullet theory, but with the conclusion of the Ruby trial we anticipated depositions in Dallas at the scene of the crime. And although we didn't know it, we would soon face a showdown with yet another formidable federal entity—the Central Intelligence Agency.

CHAPTER 4

MARCH 1964: OUR INVESTIGATION EXPANDS

■

IN EARLY MARCH, WARREN WAS DEMANDING A HEAVIER SCHEDULE OF commission witnesses, and our lawyers were eager to begin depositions in Texas. On March 4, the commission heard from Mark Lane, who had avowed in countless public appearances that Oswald had been wrongly accused and that the commission could not be trusted to report the true facts. Because Lane had attracted so much attention, the commission decided to hear him in person rather than appear high-handed by ignoring him. Rankin asked Lane to bring with him all documentation relevant to the assassination of President Kennedy.[1]

Lane ignored the commission's request for documentation and repeated almost verbatim his basic lecture on the subject. Warren again denied Lane's request to represent Oswald before the commission. The commission members listened patiently as Lane asserted that Oswald had not killed the president or Officer Tippit, claiming that multiple assassins had fired five shots with the fatal ones coming from the front, and that any evidence to the contrary was the result of altered autopsy reports and distortion of witness statements. I think that Lane's failure to provide any evidentiary support for his contentions, and his refusal to acknowledge certain established facts about Oswald and his conduct, convinced the commission to schedule only witnesses with firsthand knowledge of important facts. After Lane's dramatic but empty performance, dealing with the critics in person or through correspondence became a staff job that often wound up on my desk.[2]

Lane was the last witness on the commission's schedule at that point. We on the staff were still debating which potential witnesses should appear before the commission, a question of considerable significance. The members needed to see and hear key witnesses themselves. The American justice system places a high value on hearing testimony in person. An individual's manner of speaking, tone of voice, forthrightness, and response to cross-examination provide important insights for those evaluating the evidence and determining the truth. Reading a written record of testimony provides only a distant second alternative. For us, the commission's credibility was on the line. To the extent they relied on witnesses they saw and heard in person, their decisions would carry more weight.

The chief justice wanted the commission to hear as many witnesses as possible. He wanted to concentrate initially on witnesses who saw or participated in the events on November 22. Relying on the recommendations of five of the teams (excluding presidential protection), I prepared a draft memo for Rankin proposing a group of key witnesses for the commission and another group to be deposed by our lawyers. As we revised this memo, we assumed the commission should hear witnesses on all phases of this investigation, not just a few central issues, and that this first group should reflect Warren's preferences. Rankin initially listed forty-nine commission witnesses, and offered this rationale for their selection: "[M]ost of these witnesses will supply testimony pertaining to the actual events on the day of the assassination, the medical treatment of President Kennedy and Governor Connally, the identity of the assassin, the background of Lee Harvey Oswald, and the security precautions taken by the Dallas Police Department after Oswald's arrest." Rankin left for future consideration the few "political" witnesses, such as President Johnson and Governor Connolly, because the commission had not decided whether these individuals should appear before it.[3]

As I recorded in my journal, I thought that "the adoption of this schedule is perhaps a more significant event in the internal operations of the Commission than is generally realized. It marks the commitment by the Commission to taking a considerable amount of testimony from witnesses with relevant information and to frame conclusions based on this testimony independent of the investigation conducted previously" by the FBI and other agencies. I hoped that this approach would "win for its final report a much greater degree of public support than would otherwise have been the case."[4]

Although many changes were made over the next several months to the lists of witnesses, the total number and range of witnesses demonstrated the commission's commitment to pursue an exhaustive investigation. The facts refute the contention of future critics that our inquiry was seriously defective: Appendix V to the report lists 552 witnesses whose testimony, deposition, or statement we took. Whatever flaws or deficiencies are identified in these evidentiary materials, there can be no serious doubt that the commission fully carried out its mandate to conduct a comprehensive and independent investigation.

■ A Debate about Advance Interviews of Witnesses

Before going to Dallas to take depositions, we had to await the conclusion of the Ruby trial. The Dallas district attorney indicted Jack Ruby on murder charges soon after the Oswald shooting, and a well-known defense attorney from San Francisco named Melvin Belli represented Ruby at the trial. The Texas authorities, working in the glare of worldwide publicity, did not want any slipups or unexpected events that might enable Belli to win an acquittal. Belli argued that Ruby was legally insane when he shot Oswald, but on March 14 the jury returned a verdict of murder with malice. Ruby received a death sentence.[5]

We were still hashing out policies governing the taking of testimony in early March. We were always mindful that our work was historic and would, therefore, be scrutinized for flaws by one generation after another. We traveled somewhat uncharted territory; presidential assassinations—Lincoln in 1865, Garfield in 1881, and McKinley in 1901—happened rarely and always under unique circumstances. In these instances the assassin or his accomplices were quickly apprehended and found guilty after a civilian or military trial, which provided an arena in which some of the critical facts of the assassination were made public. Without any trial for the deceased Oswald and no identified conspirators, there were few fact-finding alternatives for the task that President Johnson had assigned to the commission. Major investigations in the United States were regularly conducted by congressional committees or the Justice Department with the use of grand juries, but those federal alternatives (as well as the Texas equivalents) had been rejected here in favor of our commission. So we had few precedents for the enormous task upon which we were embarked. We on the staff shared a determination to be fair, thorough, and right. But we often differed on how to get there and discussed our differences passionately.

At two staff meetings on March 2, the staff clashed over whether commission lawyers should be allowed to interview prospective witnesses before they testified before the commission. After listening to various views, Rankin decided to appoint a committee composed of Redlich, Belin, and Liebeler to submit recommendations to him. The committee approach did not work as intended; each of its three members produced a different proposal.[6]

Belin, a trial lawyer, supported advance interviews as the best way to prepare for depositions and testimony before the commission. He did not, however, believe these interviews should be transcribed. His arguments impressed me, especially because they were strongly endorsed by his "senior" counsel,

Joe Ball. This team had perhaps the most productive partnership on the staff, despite (or perhaps because of) their different professional histories. Ball was sixty-one years old, a very successful criminal defense lawyer in Los Angeles, a teacher of criminal law and procedure at the University of South California, and a member of the US Judicial Conference Advisory Committee on Federal Rules of Criminal Procedure. Belin—a soft-spoken, formal Midwesterner who preferred bow ties—was more than twenty years younger than Ball, but quickly became fond of his more outspoken and entertaining colleague. Belin had been in private practice, primarily on the civil side, since 1954, and ran his own firm in Iowa. Together the pair had a wealth of practical experience in dealing with clients and developing a factual record.[7]

Redlich, a constitutional law professor, opposed unrecorded interviews of all witnesses by staff lawyers in advance of their testimony because of the risk that the interviewing lawyer would influence—intentionally or inadvertently—the witness's testimony to be different from what it would be without any such interview. He was concerned that "an unrecorded interview with a witness creates the inevitable danger that the witness will be conditioned to give certain testimony when he is under oath***I believe that this danger exists notwithstanding the complete good faith of the staff member and his sincere desire to obtain only the truth." Redlich proposed that interviews might take place after the witness had testified on the record.[8]

Liebeler took a middle road. He agreed with Redlich that witnesses appearing before the commission should not be preinterviewed, but contended that those deposed by staff lawyers should be. Liebeler agreed, as did Belin and Redlich, that Rankin as general counsel could authorize exceptions to any general rule.[9]

I entered this debate in part to counter Redlich's strong advocacy. This was one of the few occasions when I disagreed with him. In general, I questioned the need for any procedures regarding interviews by our lawyers. I reminded Rankin that most of our prospective witnesses had already been interviewed by at least one investigating agency and therefore the preconditioning of concern to Redlich likely had already taken place. In fact, I thought that one of the objectives of pretestimony interviews should be to provide an opportunity for a witness to reflect again on the facts, notwithstanding any prior statements, and try to present the "truth" in sworn testimony. My most serious reservation centered on the fact that the Redlich proposal reflected adversely on our lawyers and might well prevent them from doing their best work. I proposed that advance interviews be permitted with Rankin's approval so long as the responsible lawyer would make certain that any important inconsistencies between the previous statements and the sworn testimony be made part of the record.[10]

After considering these views, Rankin came to a decision: "The members of the staff are free to interview witnesses informally in the exercise of their best judgment." As he usually did, Rankin announced his decision in a memo to the staff so that everyone was informed at the same time. I would like to believe that he considered my arguments more persuasive than Redlich's, but it is far more likely that he learned that the chief justice had addressed this issue at a staff meeting while Rankin was out of town and had stated that "he had complete faith in all of the members of the staff and wanted them to be free to have unrecorded interviews with the witnesses." I never had my suspicion confirmed, but I was quite confident that the chief justice had been briefed by Joe Ball on this debate. Ball's prominence in California's legal community meant numerous encounters with the chief justice over the years when Warren had worked as a county prosecutor, state attorney general, and governor. The two had been friends for a long time and Ball could readily get Warren's ear whenever he wanted.[11]

■ The Commission Takes on a Heavier Schedule

The carefully prepared schedule for the taking of commission testimony barely survived its first week. After two days of testimony from Secret Service agents and eyewitnesses, Warren wanted changes made immediately. I needed to respond with a revised schedule promptly, but I had to deal with another urgent matter first. As mentioned earlier, I was available to listen politely to commission critics. This time, Katzenbach wanted to get Thomas Buchanan, an American correspondent for the major French newspaper *L'Express*, out of his office in a way that would not result in an adverse press article. So he sent him to me.

Buchanan had emigrated to France after he lost his Washington job as a journalist when his Communist Party membership became known. He began writing freelance articles for *L'Express* about the Kennedy assassination. He claimed that Ruby had known Oswald and loaned him money when he returned from the Soviet Union. He was among those who contended that President Johnson and his Texas oil friends were responsible for Kennedy's assassination. By March 1964, Buchanan was finishing a major book on the subject. My assignment was to listen attentively to what he said, although free to discuss his views if I wished.[12]

Buchanan spoke for about ninety minutes. All of his allegations about the assassination were being evaluated in the course of the commission's investigation, but nothing I said would have dissuaded Buchanan from his theories. His book appeared a few months later and claimed that two gunmen shot at Kennedy, one from the railroad bridge and the other from the depository. He asserted that Oswald knew about the conspiracy but did not fire any shots. Buchanan's story has significance only because his contentions, along with attacks from Mark Lane and other critics who published during the commission's work, emphasized to commission members and staff the importance of documenting our findings as thoroughly and persuasively as possible.

When I returned to the office after listening to Buchanan, Redlich "came into my office in quite a hurry and asked me to join them in the Conference Room." There I found Warren discussing the witness schedule with Joe Ball, David Belin, and Jim Liebeler. He believed that more witnesses "with significant testimony should be called before the Commission as quickly as possible." He said that the Supreme Court "was currently in recess and he wanted to complete as much of the Commission's business as possible during the next week and a half." The chief justice told us that he thought the medical witnesses "were among the most important to be heard."[13]

I told the chief justice that "we would make every effort to secure witnesses for next Friday and to change the schedule for the week of March 16 so as to meet his wishes." When Ball and Belin emphasized the difficulty of the medical testimony and the time necessary to prepare for it, Warren indicated that he was primarily interested in hearing from the autopsy doctors from the Bethesda Naval Hospital. Just when the meeting appeared to be over, McCloy joined the discussion and began asking questions about the investigation. Both he and Warren were particularly concerned about Ruby's trip (or trips) to Cuba and I told them that we would be discussing this with the CIA in a few days. According to my journal, "They were critical that more had not been done already." McCloy told us that he "was also interested in having a complete investigation of the Irving gun shop story" and I advised him that the FBI had not yet completed its investigation on this subject.[14]

McCloy's "Irving gun shop" reference concerned an allegation that, in early November 1963, Oswald had brought a rifle to the Irving Sports Shop and had a scope mounted on it. Neither the employee who found a work tag with the name "Oswald" on it nor his employer recalled that Oswald had come to the shop for any reason whatsoever. Whereas the work tag indicated that three holes were bored in the rifle, the rifle used by Oswald in the assassination had been manufactured with the scope already mounted and only two holes bored. The commission concluded that the tag was probably not authentic and that Oswald had not visited the shop.[15]

By this time, Norman Redlich and I had developed a close relationship. He knew that I had assisted Rankin in preparing the schedule of witnesses and wanted me in the meeting to respond to the chief justice's concerns and preferences. After I listened to the chief justice, I thought that his desire to get more important work done during the Supreme Court recess seemed perfectly reasonable. I knew—as did all the other lawyers at the meeting—that getting the autopsy doctors before the commission early the next week required a substantial change in our schedules. It also assumed that these witnesses would be available on these dates and could be interviewed before their commission appearances. We needed to get together to figure this out.

After the meeting with Warren and McCoy, several lawyers (Redlich, Eisenberg, Ball, Belin, Stern, Liebeler, and Ely) gathered in my office to discuss changes in the witness schedule and a new issue that had arisen during the day's hearing. Warren had apparently revealed during the hearing his "readiness to receive a clean record and not pursue in very much detail the various inconsistencies." Ball completely agreed with this approach and Specter thought that "we would have to amend our approach to correspond" with Warren's. Redlich and Eisenberg took "a strong and articulate contrary view." No conclusions were reached on this question, as we turned to scheduling Mr. and Mrs. Declan Ford later in the week and exploring the availability of the autopsy doctors for the next week.[16]

The Fords became swept up in our investigation because they were part of the Russian-speaking community in the Dallas-Fort Worth area that had become acquainted with the Oswalds. Some of this group had been born in the Soviet Union; others were Russian-language teachers; and all were interested in meeting new people who shared this interest. We hoped they might shed light on Oswald's life and his thinking that might bear on his motive for killing the president. We wanted to find every person who spent time with Oswald after he returned from the Soviet Union and learn everything that might help us shape a more complete assessment of the man. The Fords turned out to be a perfectly ordinary couple who told the commission that they had come to dislike Oswald, but sympathized with his wife because of her difficulties in coping with her new life in the United States.[17]

With respect to Warren's interest in a "clean record," I do not believe that any of our lawyers curtailed their interrogation of a witness in order to avoid any conflicts in testimony. None of us took Warren's comment as a directive that our investigation—or interrogation of witnesses—should be conducted to avoid full and truthful testimony from all our witnesses that might create inconsistencies in the record. It would have been unprofessional to pursue such an objective and impossible to achieve it; and the record we produced and made public illustrates that we did not do so. It is certainly true, however, that Warren, like a presiding trial judge, urged several of our lawyers on occasion to move on to another area of examination when he thought that a particular subject had been sufficiently explored.

On March 11, the commission questioned Buell Frazier, who worked with Oswald at the depository. Shortly before the assassination, Oswald rented a room in Dallas while his wife and two young daughters lived with Ruth Paine in Irving, about fifteen miles from the depository. Frazier would drive Oswald to Irving on Friday afternoons and back to work in Dallas on Mondays. But on Thursday, November 21, 1963, Oswald altered the routine. He asked Frazier if he could ride home with Frazier that night so he could pick up some curtain rods that he intended to put in his Dallas room. Frazier agreed. When Oswald showed up at Frazier's for his ride to work Friday morning, Frazier said Oswald carried a long paper bag. Linnie Randle, Frazier's sister who lived with him, told the commission that she also had seen Oswald with a long package that Friday morning.[18]

Some members of the staff were concerned by their testimony that "the sack carried was no longer than could fit between a cupped hand and the armpit, whereas the rifle, even when broken down, is some 35 inches, which is considerably longer than could fit in this position." Notwithstanding these observations, the commission concluded that Oswald was carrying the assassination rifle in this package rather than curtain rods. It relied on testimony to the effect that his Dallas apartment already had curtain rods; the curtain rods in the Paines' garage remained there on November 22; Oswald never discussed any need for curtain rods with Ruth Paine or his wife; and no curtain rods were discovered at the depository after the assassination. This testimony illustrated the commission's practice of seeking full and truthful testimony from its witnesses even when it resulted in inconsistencies that the commission would have to evaluate before reaching its factual conclusions.[19]

After further effort to accommodate Warren's priorities, Rankin told the commission on March 12 that he had scheduled two days for the testimony of the three autopsy doctors and two full days to take the testimony of Michael and Ruth Paine, who were among those with the most contact with Oswald and his wife while they lived in Texas. A few days later, he confirmed witnesses who would appear during the weeks of March 23 and March 30. Two weeks later, Rankin gave the commission an expanded schedule, which named the additional witnesses to be heard during the week of March 30, including experts from the FBI and outside experts to testify about their examination of the weapons and bullets.[20]

By early March, Eisenberg had mastered the scientific and technical principles sufficiently to describe the basic issues with respect to ballistics identification. The four principal questions were (1) Were there enough markings on the bullet fragments to justify a firm conclusion as to the gun from which they were fired? (2) Were the FBI Laboratory specialists certain about the origin of any of the bullets or cartridge cases? (3) How many test bullets and cartridges were fired before obtaining the test bullet and cartridge case that the FBI used for comparison purposes? (4) Was either a striagraph or a comparison camera (instruments sometimes used in ballistics identification) used in the course of the FBI's investigation? If not, why not?[21]

Eisenberg wanted to explore the ballistics identification with the FBI experts and question them about their reasons for not using comparison photographs as evidence to be presented to fact finders. He recommended that he, Belin, and Ball visit the FBI Laboratory to review the bases for the bureau's conclusions that the bullets and cartridges that had been recovered were fired from the rifle found on the sixth floor of the depository. He also told Rankin that he believed that another crime laboratory should be asked to perform a ballistics identification test on the fired bullets and cartridge cases. The results of Eisenberg's work provided an important foundation for the commission's key findings that the cartridges and bullets had been fired from the rifle owned by Oswald and found in the depository after the assassination.

Friday, March 13, was a quiet day, so I walked over to the Justice Department looking for an opportunity to discuss with Katzenbach the looming question whether the Kennedy family would allow the commission to see the autopsy pictures. Physicians often take photographs during autopsies and the doctors at the Bethesda facility had orderlies take several photos of the dead president. These photos showed his shattered head in grisly fashion, the torn throat, and other autopsy details that, if released, would tarnish the image of a charismatic president. They were quickly locked away to prevent leaks. Technically, the photos belonged to the US Government, and so the "Government" could have allowed the commission access to them. However, out of respect for the Kennedy family's privacy and desires, President Johnson decided to defer to the family whether the photos should be released. Robert Kennedy, now the head of the family, would have to make that decision. I met briefly with Katzenbach and told him that I learned that the attorney general had told Secret Service inspector Kelley that he would not permit the pictures to be examined. I suggested that the commission might need his help in persuading Robert Kennedy to revisit his reported decision on the matter.[22]

During my first three months with the commission, I had not had the occasion to visit with the attorney general. I had reported only to Katzenbach and Miller about the commission's investigation and issues I thought important for them to know about. In the middle of March, however, I was invited to a party at Robert Kennedy's house in Virginia to celebrate the recent conviction of James Hoffa for obstruction of justice. As Miller's deputy, I had worked on aspects of the Hoffa cases and was proud of the terrific lawyers in the criminal division who had worked so hard to achieve this result.

I knew most of the roughly one hundred invitees to this celebratory cocktail party and buffet supper. After dinner the lawyers who had handled the prosecution in Chattanooga were singled out for compliments and applause. On behalf of this group, Walter Sheridan, a very talented investigator who had worked for Kennedy before he became attorney general, gave Kennedy "a leather-bound book containing the jury verdict and signatures." Kennedy seemed very much a part of the evening and comfortable "in the midst of a group of men who have worked so hard toward goals which he shares." In accepting the gift,

> he spoke shortly and very sensitively of his concern that unless Hoffa had been convicted the Teamsters Union would have developed into a political and economic force whose power would have exceeded that of the federal government. In speaking of the group and thanking everybody he spoke humorously of the times when Walt would get on the phone and advise him what the next legal step should be and he always told him that he and Walt should go get themselves a couple of lawyers to advise them. During the course of his remarks the Attorney General made reference to "The President" looking down on this effort and being a part of it and it was certainly very clear to the group that he was speaking of his brother. This, plus the sight of the Attorney General by himself looking over the notebook of signatures, gave a poignant and emotional tone to the evening which it is hard to forget[23]

While I was enjoying this celebratory party, the commission's work continued unabated. In preparation for the appearance of the autopsy doctors before the commission, Specter and Ball on March 13 interviewed doctors James Humes, J. Thornton Boswell, and Pierre Finck from the Bethesda Naval Hospital. When Specter told them that they would have to testify before the commission without being able to illustrate and explain the autopsy photographs and X-rays, they offered to have some sketches made of the wounds on the president's body. On March 16, the doctors testified using three drawings made by a hospital corpsman who worked as an illustrator at the Naval Medical School. These were made without access to the X-rays or photos and were based on the verbal descriptions of the autopsy doctors. Unfortunately, as it turned out, the verbal descriptions were no substitute for access to the actual photos and X-rays. The sketches did not accurately locate the wound near the base of the back of the president's neck and were later used by critics to rebut the commission's "single-bullet theory."[23]

Dr. Humes testified that it would have been helpful if the illustrator had been able to base his work on the actual X-rays and photos. That, Humes said, would have provided the commission with a more accurate and complete understanding of the wounds. Specter, a good prosecutor, craftily used his questioning to lay a foundation for getting at the autopsy photos, which he thought were of critical importance. However, the chief justice, who thought it unlikely the Kennedys would consent to the use of these disturbing photos, asked Humes whether he would change any of his testimony if the X-rays and photos were available in the hearing room. Humes said he would not. Specter later said that if he had known that those rough sketches "would be reproduced in hundreds of books, credited with more precision than was intended, and so closely scrutinized, I would have opposed doing them. But that's twenty-twenty hindsight."[24]

■ Work Starts in Texas

Although Ruby's conviction would certainly be appealed, the end of the trial on March 14, with a finding of guilty and death sentence, removed the most important obstacle delaying the commission's investigation in Dallas. In anticipation of our work there, I contacted Harold Barefoot Sanders, the US Attorney for the Northern District of Texas, which included Dallas, to get his assistance with our Dallas depositions. Jack Miller had been in touch with Sanders since his Texas visit back in November and told me that Sanders would be the key to getting things done effectively in Dallas. A Texan through and through, Sanders's father also carried the Barefoot name, which memorialized an ancestor's achievement in traveling from Alabama to Texas without shoes. He went to the University of Texas as an undergraduate and law student, practiced with a law firm in Dallas for ten years, and then won a seat in the Texas Legislature. In 1961 Kennedy appointed Sanders to be US attorney.[26]

The depositions of about eighty witnesses began during the week of March 16. Rankin estimated that these depositions would take about four weeks. I had been working on the Dallas depositions during the previous two weeks as best I could in light of the many uncertainties. I knew that the lawyers would adjust the schedule to accommodate the facts on the ground after they arrived. Both because of the scope of our planned work in Texas and its expedited schedule, Rankin asked me to go to Dallas to explain the commission's mission in person to Dallas officials. He wrote letters to be delivered by me, his newly anointed "executive assistant," a title created for this trip only. The letter to Dallas police chief Jesse Curry, for example, described generally the scope of the proposed depositions, identified the police officers whose testimony we needed, and politely asked for further assistance in providing commission lawyers with papers or other objects from Ruby or his home which were now in the custody of the police department.[27]

Belin and I left for Dallas on Thursday, March 19, to make the courtesy calls on Dallas officials and to meet with US Attorney Sanders and local representatives of the FBI and the Secret Service. I was depending on Sanders to help us with the necessary arrangements for office space, hearing rooms, and secretaries to accommodate the needs of our lawyers.

An article in the *Dallas Times Herald* on Thursday reported that I was coming to Dallas with several lawyers from the commission to interview people about the assassination. My travel had, to this point in my life, never been newsworthy. We were the first representatives of the commission to visit Dallas since the assassination and were both curious about the city and apprehensive about our reception.[28]

Rankin wanted me to consult with Dean Storey in order to avoid, or minimize, any adverse political consequences arising from our visit. As a former dean of Southern Methodist University School of Law in Dallas, Storey knew virtually every lawyer in town, as he'd raised money from most of them. In addition to his serving previously as president of the American Bar Association, Storey had just ended a six-year term as vice chairman of the US Civil Rights Commission. Rankin valued his help.

Ours was one of the most politically sensitive investigations ever conducted by the federal government. We were well aware that local officials and residents were especially concerned about the intentions of the commission. The assassination of Kennedy and the murder of Oswald happened on their turf and resulted in the first president from Texas. Throughout the South in the early 1960s, there was intense distrust of federal authorities in general and Justice Department lawyers in particular, stemming from the school desegregation battles and civil rights protests. No one was more suspicious of federal intrusion in law-enforcement matters than Texans were.

In addition, local citizens were challenged by the widely held view that the political atmosphere in Texas, and the expressed dislike of President Kennedy by many Texans, may have influenced Oswald to assassinate the president. Just a month before President Kennedy's visit, the US ambassador to the United Nations, Adlai Stevenson, visited Dallas to celebrate UN Day. On the evening of October 24, 1963, he was "jeered, jostled, and spat upon by hostile demonstrators outside the Dallas Memorial Auditorium." In response to the local, national, and international reactions to this event, Dallas mayor Earle Cabell "called on the city to redeem itself during President Kennedy's visit." Throughout November, public officials and media had emphasized the need for Dallas citizens, regardless of their political affiliation, to treat the visiting president with dignity and courtesy.[29]

The commission's work program in Dallas now looked like this:

Belin, joined by Ball, would begin interviews on Friday, March 20, of the fourteen witnesses scheduled to appear before the commission during the next week. If this process could not be completed by Monday so that both of them could return to Washington, we agreed that one would remain in Dallas and the other would fly back and participate in the questioning of the witness (or witnesses) before the commission. They planned to return to Dallas about March 31 to take the depositions of approximately twenty-five police officials who participated in the investigation after the assassination.

Specter planned to arrive in Dallas late Thursday or Friday to take the depositions of about twenty doctors and other witnesses who were at Parkland Hospital on the day of the assassination. He hoped to complete the depositions in time to return to Washington to handle the testimony of two of these doctors before the commission. In recent weeks, Specter had assumed the full burden of the work of his team. Frank Adams was still in trial on a long-scheduled matter for his firm and could not assist Specter with these depositions.

Hubert and Griffin were going to concentrate during the week of March 23 on Dallas police officials involved with the security arrangements on the day Ruby killed Oswald. Along with Ball and Belin, they were scheduled to depose Chief Curry and Sheriff Decker the following week. During their second week in Dallas, Hubert and Griffin were going to question witnesses about Ruby's background and his activities before the assassination.

Liebeler planned to depose persons with information regarding Oswald's background. He'd be on his own. His senior colleague, Bert Jenner, was tied up in Chicago. Stern and Ely had nearly completed their report to Rankin on how the Dallas police officials had handled Oswald's civil and legal rights while holding him in custody. If any depositions were required regarding those issues—as seemed likely—Stern, too, would come to Dallas and join in deposing police officials.

On this initial Dallas trip, I spent most of my time in cabs hurrying from office to office, or in government buildings engaged in polite exchanges with local officials. I visited with Dallas mayor J. Erik Jonsson and deputy chief of police Charles Batchelor, who both assured me of complete cooperation. Joined by Ball and Belin, I visited with Roy Truly, superintendent of the Texas School Book Depository, and made arrangements to interview several depository employees.[30]

After fulfilling these obligations, I finally had a chance to meet Barefoot Sanders in person. Of medium height, with a slim and athletic build, Sanders gave the impression that he could be very efficient when he needed to be, but would rather take the time to put his feet up on the table and get to know you personally. He knew I was close to Jack Miller, which obviously sat well with him. I gave Sanders the schedule of depositions for the next two weeks, thanked him for the space and secretarial arrangements, and told him to call me personally if there were any problems regarding the commission's work or personnel.

I found Sanders to be a generous, open person very skilled in Texas politics. He had a great sense of humor and certainly spoke the local lingo with gusto. I could call him up, as I had to do many times, for things as mundane as finding a room for our lawyers or locating a court reporter to handle a deposition on short notice. He seemed to know everyone in town. He fronted for us with Texas officials and interpreted for us when we could not understand why they acted as they did.

I told Specter that the agents in charge of both the Secret Service and the FBI had offered their assistance and that he and the other lawyers should make an effort to meet with them. I also asked him (and Leon Hubert) to make certain that a press release went out each day reporting the names of the witnesses who had been deposed.

Jim Lehrer of the *Dallas Times Herald* (and later a fixture at PBS) published two stories about the commission's work in Dallas. He won me over with his description of me as "a tall, soft-spoken executive assistant in the department's criminal division." Based on our discussion, he reported that at least fifty people in Dallas would be asked to give their depositions. He described the categories of the witnesses, but not their names. I identified the lawyers who would be handling the depositions. He also reported that I had made successful courtesy visits with the deputy chief of police and the mayor.[31]

Lehrer's articles squared with what I observed during this short visit to Dallas. Everyone I spoke with in Dallas understood the need for our investigation and none expressed any concern about the commission's members or their intentions. No one in a position of authority probed to find out exactly what the commission was doing or when its report would be published. To the extent a generalization can capture the city of Dallas in March 1964, I would say that it had recovered from the trauma of November 22, if not fully. If there was any backlash, it was directed at right-wing activists. Otherwise, Dallas seemed to have resumed doing what it did best—supporting the oil industry and enjoying the benefits of economic prosperity.

Even with a full schedule of depositions, commission lawyers found the time to conduct some legwork of their own to verify the testimony of important witnesses. One of the witnesses at the depository stated in an early FBI interview that he had heard the sound of the bolt action of the rifle and the sound of the empty cartridge cases dropping on the floor above him. Belin and Ball tried to determine if that was even possible. Belin stationed himself on the fifth floor of the building with the depository worker interviewed by the FBI, and Ball was at the assassin's window a floor above with a Secret Service agent who fired a bolt-action rifle using the same type of cartridge cases found after the assassination. Belin stated: "I distinctly heard the operation of the bolt as well as the sound from the dropping of the cartridge cases. The floor seemed to act as a sounding board for the cartridge cases as they hit."[32]

When Belin went to the sixth floor to discuss their successful reenactment with the Secret Service agent, Belin was disappointed, and quite frustrated, to learn that the agent had used heavier live ammunition, not empty shells. Belin was unable to arrange for another such experiment until May 9, when he was with three members of the commission—Cooper, Dulles, and McCloy. When empty cartridges were used on this occasion, Belin reported that the sound of the cartridges hitting the floor was very similar to the first test.[33]

When I returned to the office on March 23 and was catching up on the accumulated workload, Rankin asked me to join him in meeting with Inspector Malley, the FBI liaison to the commission. Malley delivered two complaints from Hoover: (1) commission lawyers were taking depositions of depository employees at the same time the FBI was obtaining their signed statements; and (2) the FBI was reluctant to have its own experts testify on such matters as ballistics when the commission intended to hear from non-FBI experts as well. At Rankin's request, I responded to Malley's first point by stating that no depositions were being taken of depository employees at this time; some of them were being interviewed in preparation for their appearance before the commission and others would be deposed later, but only after we got their signed statements from the FBI. On the second issue, Rankin explained that the commission "is under considerable criticism for depending exclusively on the work of the FBI and that [the use of outside experts] is desirable" for both the commission and the bureau. Malley said "he would carry these views back to the Director."[34]

Over the next several days, much of my work involved facilitating the taking of testimony before the commission and the depositions in Dallas. The deposition program was going well and we received daily reports from Dallas about the progress being made there. We did receive, however, a complaint from District Attorney Wade about Burt Griffin's questioning of Sergeant Patrick Dean, a police officer.[35]

Griffin, who had been a federal prosecutor for two years, did not tolerate what he regarded as evasive or untrue testimony. He was exploring two important issues with Dean. First, Dean made a statement on television within minutes of Ruby's shooting Oswald that was interpreted as indicating that he saw Ruby enter the basement before the shooting. Two weeks later, the *Dallas Times Herald* repeated this Dean statement. Because Dean had responsibility for the security arrangements in the basement, this was an important matter. Dean later denied these reports to his department superiors, saying that he had not seen Ruby enter the basement. Second, Dean claimed for the first time in February 1964 that Ruby had said that he was contemplating shooting Oswald on November 22, 1963, two days before he actually did so. However, none of the other officials involved in the Ruby interrogation had heard any such statement. Dean's testimony on Ruby's "premeditation," based on this statement, was critical in the trial of Ruby and, in particular, was relied on to prove the malice required under Texas law to support the death penalty.

Griffin pressed hard to get at the truth on these two issues. At one point, he went off the record and had a conversation with Dean about his responses to Griffin's questions. After this discussion, Dean complained to Wade that Griffin insinuated he was not testifying truthfully. When Wade's complaint reached Rankin, he asked Griffin for a written report about the incident. Griffin wrote several memoranda to Rankin and me regarding Wade's letter, his deposition of Dean, and the basis for his concerns about Dean's truthfulness. Griffin proposed more testimony on the two areas of concern. He also provided a memorandum of his twenty-minute off-the-record interview of Dean.

In his memo, Griffin stated that during his off-the-record discussion with Dean he told the policeman he didn't believe aspects of his testimony about Ruby's entry into the basement and Ruby's statement on November 22 that he planned to kill Oswald. Griffin emphasized the importance of the commission's investigation and told Dean that "if he had a statement to make to the commission which was more truthful than the one which he made that every effort would be made to give him the kind of protection that was necessary in order to permit him to correct that statement."[36]

Griffin reported that Dean insisted that he was telling the truth and that he could not understand why Griffin felt otherwise. Griffin responded that he had read enough of the relevant file to convince him that Dean hadn't told the truth, but would not provide any fuller explanation for his concerns. Dean ended the discussion asserting that he had been truthful.

In response to Wade's specific complaints, Griffin told Rankin that he had not called Dean a liar, but conceded that he had told Dean that he believed that Dean was not telling the truth. Griffin also denied that he had told Dean that he was going to file perjury charges against him and that Dean was not entitled to a lawyer because he had waived that right. On this latter point, Griffin told Rankin that it was his customary practice to advise any witness whose deposition he was taking that the witness was entitled to counsel. He believes he may have suggested that, if Dean elected to change his testimony in the future, he might seek the advice of a lawyer so that his rights in the matter would be fully protected.[37]

Of the two Dean statements that Griffin was challenging, he recognized that the statement regarding Ruby's premeditation was, if false, the more reprehensible of the two, because the finding of premeditation in the Ruby trial was based largely on Dean's testimony. Griffin was dubious about Dean's recollection of a premeditation statement by Ruby on November 22 because Dean had never mentioned it before his February 18 report to Chief Curry. Dean had several opportunities to report Ruby's incriminating statement before he did so—in his report to Curry on November 26, during an FBI interview on December 2, in another report to Curry on December 8, in another FBI interview on December 10, and during a long television interview on November 24. In addition, Dean consistently stated that Dallas Secret Service chief Forrest Sorrels was present on November 22 when Ruby allegedly made this statement. However, Sorrels maintained and later testified before the commission that he did not recall such a statement by Ruby and that, if it was made, it was not while Sorrels was in the room.[38]

In his report to Rankin, Griffin discussed his brief conversation with Deputy Chief of Police Batchelor. Griffin told Rankin that he had emphasized in this conversation Dean's statement regarding Ruby's entrance into the basement rather than the more important statement about Ruby's intention to kill Oswald. He did not want to highlight this other statement because it might affect the recent conviction of Ruby. Even so, Griffin reported to Rankin that "Batchelor indicated by his manner of speaking that this was his primary concern."[39]

Dean's delay for about three months in reporting Ruby's alleged premeditation and the lack of corroboration by Sorrels or any other person certainly supported Griffin's concern that Dean was not telling the truth on this critical issue. I thought his conduct was appropriate under the circumstances and that no punishment of any kind was warranted. Warren entered the picture during Dean's later appearance before the commission, when he said "no member of our staff has the right to tell a witness that he is lying or that he is testifying falsely. That is not his business." Contrary to at least one published report, Rankin did not remove Griffin from the Dallas investigation and assign him to purgatory in our Washington office.[40]

Strange as it may seem, Ruby regarded Dean as one of his many friends in the Dallas Police Department. After his conviction and death sentence in part because of Dean's testimony, Ruby invited Dean to visit with him in custody and gave him a copy of the Warren Commission report with a fond inscription. Reading about the trial of Ruby left me with two firm convictions: he was very poorly represented at trial and he was mentally and emotionally impaired in a way that was not fairly considered at the time. The Texas Court of Criminal Appeals ultimately reversed Ruby's conviction because the alleged statement by Ruby testified to by Dean was inadmissible under Texas law.[41]

■ Shaping a Report to the Nation

Very early on, I focused on the structure and substance of the commission's report. I had two cardinal rules. First, every conclusion in the report would be based on facts developed or checked independently through our own efforts. Second, every fact in the report would be supported by sworn testimony, authenticated documents and physical exhibits, or verified scientific and technical work.

Al Goldberg, our historian, prepared the first draft outline of the report and circulated it on March 14. Goldberg emphasized that the report should use simple, straightforward language, and his draft outline provided a good start. Goldberg had consistently advocated a narrative approach and suggested as well that the report should include additional matters of a historical nature. We had general agreement that a narrative of the events from November 22 through November 24 should be included near the beginning of the report. Some lawyers opposed any discussion of earlier assassinations because it might suggest to the reader (or critic) that the commission had concluded that Oswald was a disturbed person, as had been the case in previous presidential assassinations in the United States. We agreed that our discussion of the key issues should be sufficiently well documented to address other publicized hypotheses regarding the assassination. However, the staff recognized the need for an appendix to the report dealing specifically with the multiple rumors and allegations circulating about our investigation.

Rankin asked the lawyers to comment on the Goldberg draft and reassured them that they would have the prime responsibility for the report's sections dealing with their areas. I had the occasion to discuss the proposed report with Rankin one evening in late March—one of several such private sessions where he and I could reflect on what we were doing and where we were going, after a day full of meetings, hearings, telephone calls, and correspondence. During these sessions, he would often tell me more about his conversations with the chief justice or other commission members. In turn, I would comment about any current issues with the staff or investigative agencies. On this occasion, I told him that I thought "we were underestimating our capabilities to produce a complete and documented report" and expressed my "strong conviction that we should publish as much material as possible" simultaneously with our report. Rankin responded favorably to these suggestions and agreed that we should discuss them at our next staff meeting.[42]

As the comments on Goldberg's draft came in over the next two weeks, Rankin asked Redlich and me to produce a revised outline incorporating the best suggestions we received. We had not turned to this task by the morning after my evening conversation with Rankin, when Rankin told us that the chief justice had asked for an outline of the report and would be arriving in the afternoon to get it. I told Rankin that we "were not prepared" to give Warren a draft outline and he said "we would have to in any event." So Redlich and I went off to produce a draft outline, worked for three or four hours, and completed a draft dated March 31, 1964, which we gave to the chief justice that afternoon with some trepidation. This experience reflected another consistent aspect of the commission's work: if the chief justice wanted a draft outline of the report—or anything else—we would move heaven and earth to get it for him.[43]

Our draft outline was circulated to the staff and discussed at a meeting a few days later. Following up on our earlier conversation, Rankin proposed that the transcripts of testimony before the commission and accompanying exhibits should be published at the same time as the commission report. After some debate, we agreed that this commitment to publish should extend also to our deposition transcripts. Rankin asked that Redlich and I prepare an assignment sheet indicating which lawyers were to be responsible for the review of particular transcripts.[44]

■ **Oswald's Foreign Activities Engage the CIA**

During March, the Coleman/Slawson team made significant headway in getting information from the Central Intelligence Agency and the State Department about Oswald's activities in Russia and Mexico. To determine whether there was a foreign conspiracy to assassinate President Kennedy, we needed to explore whether Oswald was an agent of the Soviet Union or Cuba, and whether Marina Oswald was telling the truth about the life she and her husband had in Russia.

Allen Dulles, Rankin, and I had met Richard Helms, the CIA's deputy director for plans, and two of his associates on January 14. On a personal level, I recall the obvious respect and affection that the agency officials had for Dulles, a former director. Rankin told Helms that the commission believed a request should be made to the Soviet Union soliciting information regarding Oswald's activities there. In addition, he asked for as much information as possible from CIA sources about Oswald's activities in the Soviet Union and Mexico.[45]

At the time, we knew the general outline of Oswald's nearly three years in the Soviet Union, his encounters with the US embassy, his work assignment in Minsk, and his living quarters. We had begun to get additional information about his life there from Marina Oswald's first appearance before the commission. We were trying to find out as much detail as possible about his encounters with Soviet officials, the nature of his work there, his recreational activities, and his associates. We hoped this information would contribute to our making a reasonable assessment of whether he had ever been a Soviet agent.

Helms said the CIA was preparing a report about Oswald based on the agency's files, but advised us that it would be limited in scope because of restrictions on the CIA's jurisdiction over Americans abroad. He did, however, offer help in the preparation of questions to the Soviet Union. We agreed to obtain security clearances for the commission lawyers working in this area and to provide the CIA with investigative reports obtained from other agencies. In return, the CIA would provide its completed report on Oswald to the commission as soon as possible and help in preparing questions for Marina Oswald's appearance before the commission. After this meeting, the CIA provided us with a proposed list of questions for the Soviet Union. It also provided a detailed chronology of Oswald's stay in the Soviet Union and an alphabetical list of people there who were known to or mentioned by Oswald or his wife.[46]

We knew relatively little about Oswald's activities in Mexico when we first met with the CIA. He had gone to Mexico City on September 26, 1963, by bus from Houston and came back to Texas, again by bus, on October 3. We knew he wanted a visa to enter Cuba, but whether his final destination was the Soviet Union or Cuba itself was uncertain. In late January, the CIA provided us with a report setting out what they knew about his trip to Mexico. We were especially interested in any transcript, notes, or other recording of the interview of Silvia Duran by Mexican officials. She worked at the Cuban consulate in Mexico City, and Oswald had approached her in his effort to secure a visa from the Cuban Government to transit Cuba, ostensibly on the way to Moscow. At our request, the CIA provided the commission with the translations (from the Spanish) of interviews conducted by the Mexican police of Silvia Duran and her husband.[47]

The commission had a second objective in dealing with the CIA, which was to determine how forthcoming the agency had been with other federal agencies before the assassination. Sam Stern needed to understand what the FBI, Secret Service, and CIA knew (and were doing) about Oswald before the assassination, as well as their intelligence capabilities and their policies on inter-agency sharing of information. On Stern's recommendation, Rankin in February asked the CIA for a copy of the contents of the CIA file on Oswald as of November 22, 1963, and for a report of the dissemination, if any, of those materials to other federal agencies before that date.[48]

Coleman and Slawson thought carefully about the objectives and problems in their assignment. They recognized the uncertainty regarding the veracity and motivation of any Soviet response to questions from the United States, but they still hoped to explore some of the unresolved questions about Oswald's stay in the Soviet Union. Did Oswald get preferential treatment in the Soviet Union and, if so, why? Why did the Soviets not grant him citizenship despite his strong urging and the obvious propaganda advantage resulting from such "full asylum"?[49]

In late February, Coleman and Slawson provided Rankin with an interim report on their investigation of Oswald's trip to the Soviet Union, his stay there, and his return to the United States. They discussed three major issues: (1) Oswald's application for a passport in 1959 and his trip to Russia, (2) his actions at the US embassy renouncing his American citizenship, and (3) the reissuance of his US passport and return in 1962 to the United States with his wife and daughter. Coleman and Slawson wanted more information from the State Department about its contacts with Oswald. They also wanted State to use its diplomatic channels to get information from the Soviet Union. Slawson produced a draft request to State regarding its activities involving Oswald and a proposed letter to State Secretary Rusk from Warren outlining the information needed from the Soviet Union.[50]

State responded with a draft letter to the Soviets for our review, but Slawson and I wanted more specific information about Oswald's stay in the Soviet Union. In particular, Slawson proposed seeking more information about any physical and mental examinations of Oswald and his wife, and records regarding Oswald's entry into, and exit from, the Soviet Union. I suggested we get information about Oswald's places of employment and residences in the Soviet Union and any statements from Soviet citizens who knew him. The proposed letter from the chief justice to Rusk incorporated our suggestions, and they were accepted by State. Rusk delivered the letter to the Soviet ambassador on March 11.[51]

Rankin subsequently submitted a series of questions prepared by Slawson to State, some of which sought to take advantage of the department's expertise in evaluating Oswald's life in the Soviet Union. For example, we asked State to advise us whether resident foreigners in the Soviet Union could travel (as Oswald did) from Minsk to Moscow without permission from Soviet authorities. Others related to the way that State and the Immigration and Naturalization Service handled the various permissions Oswald and Marina needed. Slawson also wanted to know how State and other federal agencies communicated with each other about Oswald.[52]

An important addition to the commission's work in this area came at the end of February, when the FBI delivered a memorandum containing information about Oswald from Yuri Ivanovich Nosenko, a recent defector from the Soviet Union. Nosenko described himself as a high official in the counterintelligence division of the KGB, the Soviet secret police. He said he had supervised the examination and treatment of Lee Harvey Oswald for the KGB when Oswald first entered Russia in 1959. He said that he also reexamined Oswald's file after the assassination to determine whether he had ever been used by the KGB as an agent. Nosenko said flatly that the KGB at no time used Oswald as an agent.[53]

The bureau said it planned to interview Nosenko further "in an attempt to determine the accuracy of his statements. He is, of course, in the custody of the Central Intelligence Agency and our interviews will be contingent on other assessments of his time." The FBI cautioned that Nosenko's "reliability has not as yet been established." Nosenko's claim of firsthand knowledge about Oswald's stay in the Soviet Union could not be used by the commission until the CIA delivered its final assessment whether Nosenko was a real defector or a double agent. Some within the CIA maintained that Nosenko was a fraud, sent by the Soviet intelligence service to confound the CIA. Others in the CIA and apparently most in the FBI thought that Nosenko was genuine. However, the commission well understood what would happen if it relied on Nosenko's statements and the CIA subsequently concluded he was a double agent. The veracity of Nosenko's information became the subject of a multi-year controversy within the CIA and between the CIA and the FBI far exceeding the life of the commission.[54]

In addition to the conspiracy possibility raised by Oswald's connections to Russia, the commission had to investigate Oswald's time in Mexico and his connections to Cuba. Coleman and Slawson wanted (1) further information regarding the activities of the American embassy in Mexico City after the assassination, (2) information regarding investigative work of the Mexican authorities regarding Oswald, (3) permission from Mexican authorities to use their investigative materials in our final report, (4) additional investigative activity by Mexican authorities, (5) further investigative activities by American government agencies abroad, and (6) meetings in Mexico City to discuss the matter with Mexican authorities and US investigative agencies.[55]

We met with CIA representatives on March 12 to discuss Nosenko and these questions about Mexico. As to Nosenko, all they would tell us was that the commission should "await further developments." With respect to Mexico, Helms, who attended along with CIA officials David Murphy and Raymond

Rocca, suggested that it might be useful for commission representatives to go to Mexico because both the CIA and FBI had agents "on the ground" there. We told the CIA officials that the commission needed to address rumors or allegations that Oswald was an agent of the CIA. Helms proposed several different ways of demonstrating that Oswald was not their agent. These included affidavits from the responsible officials, testimony of CIA officials before the commission, and permitting access by commission staff to whatever CIA files they regarded as necessary to review. We pursued all of these avenues over the following months.[56]

Moving to what I assumed would be a contentious subject, we discussed the failure of the CIA to comply fully with some of the commission's recent inquiries regarding pre-assassination documents in the CIA files on Oswald. Helms, one of the most fluent and self-confident government officials I ever met, exhibited not the slightest embarrassment at our complaint about his agency's failure to comply fully with our request. He smoothly explained that the agency had not provided materials that utilized confidential communication techniques and revealed confidential sources. I responded that the commission did not need to know these confidential aspects, but it certainly needed more than the summaries provided by the earlier CIA memorandum. After some discussion, we reached a compromise that required the CIA to provide the commission with a paraphrase of any message or other writing requested by the commission, the original version of which would reveal a confidential source or confidential communications technique, and the commission staff would be permitted to review the actual messages to ensure that the paraphrases were complete and accurate.[57]

Having met with CIA representatives on several occasions over the past two months, I was impressed with their competence and apparent willingness to cooperate with the commission. They were always polite, seemingly accommodating when we requested information, and respectful of the commission's obligation to conduct a thorough investigation of the assassination. I thought it might be "because they do not have any special axe to grind" in our investigation. As it turned out, I could not have been more wrong. The CIA had huge interests at stake in our efforts. As was revealed by congressional investigations in 1975–76, they were determined to keep extremely important information from the commission. We never knew that, among other things, the agency had been busying itself with various plots to assassinate Castro during 1960–63, including one plan scheduled to be implemented on November 22, 1963. Helms knew all about this as he looked at me across the table and promised full cooperation in providing any information that might be relevant to our work.[58]

Still, not everyone in the agency was obstructing us. None of the other CIA officials who worked with us was aware of these covert plans. Slawson developed a very close relationship with Ray Rocca, the key liaison CIA official assigned to the commission, and felt that he could communicate freely with him, make informal oral requests for assistance, and depend on his integrity in dealing with the commission.[59]

The next meeting with the CIA took place two weeks later at the agency headquarters and involved Stern, Slawson, and me. Stern went off with Rocca to review certain CIA files from which materials had been supplied to the commission. Slawson and I discussed the Mexican aspects of our investigation with Helms and Jack Whitten, who worked for Helms. Neither of them thought that "anything of importance could be developed at this time in Mexico but that representatives of the Commission should probably make the trip to satisfy themselves as to the scope of the investigation already conducted by the Federal Bureau of Investigation and the Mexican officials." They made it clear that the primary US agency responsible for the investigation in Mexico was the FBI—not the CIA.[60]

When Stern examined the files of the CIA, he found two sets of documents that had not been previously provided the commission. The first set consisted of cable reports from the CIA station in Mexico on November 22 and 23, 1963, relating to photographs of a person who had visited the Cuban and Soviet Embassies in Mexico City during October and November 1963, and reports on those cables furnished on November 23 by the CIA to the Secret Service. The second set of materials included a cable of October 10, 1963, from the CIA station in Mexico City to CIA headquarters reporting on the Oswald contact at the Soviet embassy, and an October 10 message from CIA headquarters to the Mexico City station of background information on Oswald. Although the CIA had not provided these documents to the commission, Stern reported that the CIA had provided accurate summaries of both sets of materials. It appeared that the compromise was working.[61]

■ Presidential Protection: Impasse with the Treasury Department

As of late February we had reached an impasse with the Treasury Department. The commission's last letter to Treasury advised Secretary Dillon that the commission was interested in almost everything relevant to presidential protection, future planning as well as evaluation of the performance of the Secret Service in Dallas, and would accept no limitations on the commission's use of the materials received from the department. The secretary had suggested taking the matter to the president, and there it stood. We urgently needed some resolution of the matter.

Treasury refused to make available materials relating to security precautions until it received acceptable assurances regarding the use of this material in any report by the commission. Rankin, Stern, and I had a meeting scheduled for Friday afternoon, March 6, with Treasury representatives and we got together in the morning to explore a way out of this impasse. Each of the possible approaches to the problem seemed flawed in some important respect.[62] From the staff point of view, the Secret Service appeared to be neither alert nor careful in protecting the president. Their personnel probably were not very well trained; and they didn't seem to have current technology to use. We did not believe they could obtain significant intelligence on threats to the president through their own resources or that they got much cooperation or respect from other law enforcement or intelligence agencies. But we needed facts to support any final judgments, and it seemed like we were not going to get them readily.

Our discussion with Rankin revealed a fundamental disagreement between the staff and the chief justice. We were convinced that the commission could not make any useful recommendations without detailed information about existing Secret Service procedures. For example, what were the duties of the agent riding in the front seat of the presidential vehicle? What were the procedures for checking buildings along the motorcade route? But Rankin told us that the chief justice did not think that the commission or the staff should have access to precisely this type of detailed information. We were frustrated, to say the least, and wondered whether in this instance a majority of the members would disagree with Warren. It also prompted our curiosity as to why Warren had been reluctant to accept the limitations on our access and use of Treasury Department materials as urged by that department, when he shared their concerns about confidentiality.

The meeting in the afternoon with Treasury Department representatives was almost as frustrating. We met with Robert Carswell, special assistant to Secretary Dillon, and G. d'Andelot Belin, the department's general counsel. Carswell, who had come to Treasury from a major New York law firm, was a very accomplished practitioner—careful, methodical, and protective of his client. With similar backgrounds in law practice, Carswell and Stern had established a good professional relationship over the previous several weeks. Carswell insisted on establishing procedures to limit the publication of Secret Service material in the commission's report and that these procedures had to be approved by the president. He stated that his department had no idea how to respond to the commission's last letter and thought that the issues should be resolved now. Rankin agreed that Treasury should consult with the president before making any materials available to the commission.[63]

Carswell told us that the most important single document was the report submitted by Secret Service chief Rowley to Dillon after the assassination. He indicated that this report identified certain deficiencies in the agency's practices and made recommendations for change. Rankin said he did not want Rowley's report in the commission's public records, but that it would be appropriate for Stern to read the report and make written notes for the commission's use. Carswell seemed amenable to this approach, subject to the president's approval.[64]

I briefly described this situation to Katzenbach when I visited him on Monday, March 9. He believed that "this was a needless problem which should be resolved without too great difficulty." He suggested that I might wish to discuss it with McCloy—a prescient comment as it turned out. That is exactly what happened when I returned to the commission's office that afternoon, where the chief justice was discussing the commission's schedule with several of our lawyers. McCloy soon joined the meeting.[65]

McCloy inquired about the discussions between the commission and the Treasury Department, mentioning that he had just come from a meeting with Secretary Dillon. The chief justice responded that "so far as he knew the matter was settled" and that Stern was getting information informally from Treasury. I told them both that this was not the case and reviewed briefly the Friday meeting with Treasury representatives and the impasse with respect to the commission's access to Secret Service materials. Warren expressed his views quite emphatically, stating that the commission had no need to examine any detailed information regarding the operations and procedures of the Secret Service. At that point he left the room to take a telephone call.[65]

McCloy asked for my views about the commission's responsibilities in the area of presidential protection. I made a strong statement on the subject—probably more vigorous than it would have been if Warren were in the room—and said that my views were generally shared by the staff. In particular: "I emphasized the amount of time that had already passed without any work being done in this area, the need to gain access to detailed information before any recommendations could be made, and the fact that the Commission is missing a great and unique opportunity to make a substantial contribution in the field of security precautions." I also referred to the Rowley report to the Treasury secretary, which I said (based on our discussions with Treasury) contained "detailed criticism of Secret Service operations and proposed certain recommendations for improvements in the areas of interest to the Commission."[67]

By this point, Warren had returned to the meeting and claimed that this was the first time he had ever heard of this report. He was "obviously disconcerted that it had not been submitted to the Commission." While the rest of us sat quietly, McCloy and Warren "engaged in a heated discussion." McCloy argued that the commission "should get access to all the relevant materials from Secret Service and then agree to consult with them regarding publication of these prior to the final report." Any debate on this matter, he said, "could be resolved by the President at the appropriate time." Warren responded that "this would put the President on the spot and that if he decided not to release any of this material he would be accused of covering up the investigation of the assassination." His other major concern was that "if detailed information was made known to members of the Commission and staff they would be primary suspects in the event of any leak which resulted in another assassination attempt." The meeting ended with no resolution.[68]

John McCloy and I had several intense conversations during my work with the commission. McCloy presented an interesting mix of strong personality, acute intelligence, and unusually broad experience. I never could anticipate where he might wind up on any given issue. McCloy literally came from another century; he was born in 1895 and was nearly seventy years old when he served on the commission. He fought in World War I as a second lieutenant and served as an assistant secretary of War during World War II. A Harvard-educated lawyer, McCloy became president of the World Bank, which had been created at the Bretton Woods Conference in 1944. Then he served as high commissioner for Germany and witnessed the creation of the Federal Republic of Germany, commonly known as West Germany. Following that, he served as chairman of the Chase Manhattan Bank, and at the time he joined the commission, he was chairman of the Ford Foundation. McCloy certainly did not hesitate to tangle with the chief justice. He always gave me the impression of wanting to hear all the details—warts and all—about issues of interest to him.

Presidential protection was one of those issues. When he gave me the opportunity at this meeting, I was eager to express my frustration with the situation while the chief justice was out of the room. In his "heated discussion" with Warren, McCloy embraced my main points and gave every impression that he would try within the commission to overrule the chief justice on this critical question of access to Treasury Department documents. Unfortunately, McCloy was not present at the next meeting, where Warren explained his views to Treasury representatives.

Two days later, the chief justice met with Carswell, representing Secretary Dillon, and Chief Rowley. Rankin, Stern, and I attended the meeting, which was scheduled at Warren's request so that he could personally tell Treasury representatives what he told McCloy at the last meeting. According to my journal, "It was a unique meeting in that I remained quiet from beginning to end. This proved to be a wise course of action."[69]

Warren opened with a fifteen-minute presentation in which he stated where he stood on commission's role in evaluating presidential protection. He emphasized his lack of interest in learning any details regarding Secret Service policies and procedures and his concern for putting the president on the spot. As he stated his position, Chief Rowley "could do nothing but agree enthusiastically," offering irrelevant digressions "seemingly designed to prove to the Chief Justice the wisdom of his action." For example, Rowley referred to the recent infiltration of "syndicates" into counterfeiting "and suggested that this was another reason why the Commission should not become informed regarding his operations."[70]

Carswell tried to get the meeting back on a track where it might accomplish something of value to both his client and the commission, but succeeded only in getting his boss, Secretary Dillon, and McCloy "into greater disfavor" with Warren. When it became clear that the chief justice was offended that another commission member had met with Secretary Dillon, Carswell explained that the March 9 meeting between Dillon and McCloy had been at the secretary's request. Carswell suggested that the Secret Service procedures and issues related to November 22 in Dallas "could be isolated from the procedures and issues looking to the improvement in the operations of the Secret Service." Warren seized on this distinction and the meeting ended with an agreement that Stern would work with Carswell to prepare a series of questions and answers that would give the commission the information it needed to know, but would respect Treasury's security concerns about future Secret Service policies and procedures.[71]

I was extremely discouraged by this outcome. Basically, it made the commission "a public relations adjunct to the Treasury" and made it impossible for us "to do any significant work in this field." When I discussed the meeting later with Rankin, he characteristically had a more optimistic view. We agreed (as we had to) that any progress was welcome and that the question-and-answer routine might serve to (1) supply the commission with information of value and (2) highlight the issues more sharply so that they might be discussed further. Rankin hadn't given up in this area and for this I was grateful.[72]

Stern submitted the first seventeen questions for the Secret Service on March 24. The four areas covered were (1) protective research, (2) liaison activities, (3) particular protective measures, and (4) supervision of the Secret Service. Rankin told the Secret Service: "Although some of the questions are, in form, susceptible of a single affirmative or negative response, the commission would appreciate instead a reasoned response to each question, in reasonable detail and with any substantiating materials as seem appropriate." We expected Treasury would continue to slow-walk our requests, and they did. We didn't hear much from them again until we summoned their officials to testify in late April.[73]

■ **More Troubles with the FBI**

Our relationships with the FBI were not improving. Rankin submitted five pages of questions to the FBI in late March as part of the commission's inquiry into what various law enforcement agencies knew of Oswald before the assassination. The questions emerged from the staff's review of reports from the FBI and other government agencies. Rankin noted politely that the commission "would appreciate . . . a reasoned response to each question, in reasonable detail, and with such substantiating materials as seem appropriate." We anticipated that this detailed letter might not be warmly received at the FBI and Rankin undertook to deliver it personally to Malley.[74]

I don't know how Malley reacted to the letter, but his FBI superiors were quite upset with it. The FBI frequently considered the commission's investigative requests to be oppressive and much too detailed, and one bureau official had this to say about this particular letter:

> While complimenting the Bureau for its cooperation, the President's Commission ... forwarded what purports to be 30 questions (by actual count there are 52 as some of the enumerated questions have more than one part) to which they request a reasoned response in reasonable detail and with such substantiating materials as seem appropriate. The questions are those of a cross-examining attorney and it is evident that this is a cross-examination of the FBI or a part of it in the case of the assassination of President Kennedy.

This FBI official got it exactly right. The commission staff was doing precisely what Senator Russell in December had urged—to act as a "devil's advocate" who "would take this FBI report and this CIA report and go through it and analyze every contradiction and every soft spot in it, just as if he were prosecuting them or planning to prosecute. . . ."[75]

Notwithstanding their complaint about the letter, the FBI responded promptly in a detailed two-page letter with fifteen pages of answers to the commission's questions.[76] Hoover expressed his certainty about the only conclusion the commission could reach:

> At the outset, I wish to emphasize that the facts available to the FBI concerning Lee Harvey Oswald prior to the assassination did not indicate in any way that he was, or would be, a threat to President Kennedy; nor were they such as to suggest that the FBI should inform the Secret Service of his presence in Dallas or his employment at the Texas School Book Depository.[77]

Hoover was not telling the truth. Immediately after the assassination, Hoover ordered an investigation to identify any deficiencies in the handling of the Oswald case. On December 10, he received a report from Assistant Director James Gale, which stated that there were a number of failures in the Oswald security case. The report concluded: "Oswald should have been on the Security Index; his wife should have been interviewed before the assassination, and investigation intensified—not held in abeyance—after Oswald contacted Soviet Embassy in Mexico."[78] Gale recommended that seventeen FBI employees be censured or placed on probation for "shortcomings in connection with the investigation of Oswald prior to the assassination" and that this action be taken promptly despite the possibility that the Warren Commission might learn about it during the commission's existence.[79]

Other FBI officials took the contrary position. Assistant Director Cartha DeLoach suggested that disciplinary action be deferred until the commission's findings were made public. Hoover did not agree and implemented Gale's recommendations on the same day he received the report, personally ordering that all seventeen FBI officials who had been involved in the FBI's dealings with Oswald before the assassination be disciplined. His view was that "such gross incompetency cannot be overlooked nor administrative action postponed."[80]

Assistant Director Alan Belmont suggested in an addendum to Gale's report that it was significant that all of the agents, supervisors, and officials who had considered the issue had concluded that Oswald did not meet the criteria for the Security Index. Under these circumstances Belmont proposed that, rather than discipline the seventeen individuals, the criteria should be changed, as recommended by Gale.[81] Hoover rejected this suggestion with a handwritten notation next to Belmont's addendum: "They were worse than mistaken. Certainly no one in full possession of all his faculties can claim Oswald didn't fall within this criteria." Hoover's deliberate false statement to the commission did not come to light until ten years later, after Hoover died, when a congressional committee investigated the FBI's failures in connection with the assassination of Kennedy.[82]

After a month full of proposals for more testimony and investigative requests, we were surprised to learn from an Associated Press story at the end of March that our investigation was almost over. The story ran in several papers around the country and stated, "The end is in sight so far as questioning witnesses and examining other evidence is concerned, it was reported, but writing the definitive report is expected to be a long job after the hearings close." The story referred to the commission's interest in trying to dispel the many rumors of various kinds of conspiracy, but "the case against Oswald lacks a motive explicable by the workings of an ordinary mind." It is hard to believe that the source of this story was anyone on the commission or the staff in light of our intensified activities in March and their anticipated continuation for the next several months. As was true of other such "leaked" stories about the commission in the future, we never were able to ascertain who the source was.[83]

Looking toward April, it was apparent that the commission had major unresolved issues with the FBI, Treasury, and the CIA and a full docket of commission witnesses and depositions. We decided to send a team to Mexico to look into Oswald's activities there as suggested by Helms, and I planned to be on it.

CHAPTER 5

APRIL 1964: MEXICO AND THE
CUBAN CONNECTION

■

I F THERE WAS INDEED A CONSPIRACY BEHIND JOHN F. KENNEDY'S ASSASSINA-
tion, we suspected from the outset that Oswald's eight-day trip to Mexico
from September 26 to October 3, 1963, only seven weeks before the assassination, would likely be the place we could unearth it. The CIA clearly thought
so too, which is why CIA director John McCone focused on Mexico in briefing
President Johnson on the morning of November 23, 1963. That same day,
Helms informed his deputy, Thomas Karamessines, and James J. Angleton,
chief of counterintelligence, that a desk officer in the western hemisphere division would be in charge of the CIA investigation. Helms said that this officer
had professional expertise in conducting counterintelligence investigations for
the agency. On November 24, the CIA Mexico station provided the names of
all known contacts of certain Soviet personnel in Mexico City. McCone met
again with the president that day and briefed him regarding CIA operational
plans against Cuba.[1]

On November 26, President Johnson told McCone that the FBI had responsibility for investigating the assassination and directed him to assist the bureau
with all available CIA resources. According to a report probably originating from
Rocca, who was the key CIA official working with Coleman and Slawson, the
CIA believed that the FBI may have been derelict in its handling of Oswald
before the assassination. That was one reason the CIA wanted to keep its investigative effort as independent as possible from the FBI's work. Over the next
few weeks, the CIA received information from its Mexico station about its
own investigation, actions taken by the Mexican government, and suggestions
from Ambassador Thomas Mann of additional investigative initiatives.[2]

In late December, the CIA desk officer in charge of the investigation
completed a memo summarizing the agency's investigation, which went to President Johnson. The officer did not have the benefit of the FBI report regarding
the assassination, so he did not know that in April 1963, Oswald had shot at

General Walker. At a meeting late in December, Angleton, a good friend of the CIA's station chief in Mexico, suggested that his own counterintelligence division take over the investigation, and Helms agreed. One of Angleton's analysts was designated to be the "point of record" for all matters relating to the assassination and the Warren Commission in January 1964, when the CIA began to respond to requests for information from the commission.[3]

■ Oswald's Trip to Mexico

When Helms suggested that it might be useful for us to go to Mexico City to deal directly with American representatives there and Mexican law enforcement officials, Rankin quickly agreed. Helms cautioned that the Mexican government was likely to be defensive about any potential connection with the assassination. With Rankin's approval, I joined Coleman and Slawson on this trip. We thought that having a lawyer from Robert Kennedy's Justice Department on the team would bolster our credentials with Mexican law enforcement officers, and probably wouldn't hurt in getting cooperation from the FBI in Mexico City as well.

On April 7, the day before we were scheduled to leave Washington, Coleman, Slawson, and I met with Thomas Mann, who was then the assistant secretary of state for Latin American affairs. Mann had been ambassador to Mexico at the time of the assassination and had personally directed the US investigatory effort and relations with the Mexican law enforcement authorities. In his file on the assassination, Mann had written that Oswald was "probably involved in a sinister fashion, especially by way of taking a bribe, with the Cuban Embassy in Mexico City or with some other Castro agency." When we asked him about this at our meeting, Mann acknowledged that he had no particular evidence to support these suspicions. He said, rather, that he had "the general feeling 'in his guts' that Castro was the kind of dictator who might have carried out this kind of ruthless action, either through some hope of gaining from it or simply as revenge." Mann knew about the rumors and speculations implicating Cuba, but he told us his suspicions of Castro's involvement rested only on Oswald's visits to the Cuban and Soviet embassies during his Mexico trip and Mann's own assessment of Castro's character. The CIA had been concerned about Mann spreading his unsubstantiated suspicion in the immediate aftermath of the assassination, worried that it could lead to a "flap" with the Cubans. At the time the CIA concern seemed appropriate in the absence of any hard evidence to support Mann's suspicions, but in retrospect the CIA was probably more concerned about any inquiries that would expose its recent covert efforts to get rid of Castro, including plotting his assassination—information withheld from the Warren Commission and the American public until 1976.[4]

At the very end of our meeting, Mann asked Slawson whether, "with the benefit of hindsight," we believed that his insistence on certain investigative efforts shortly after the assassination had been appropriate or whether we thought they were unduly rash. With the polish of an experienced diplomat, Slawson assured Mann that, although our investigation had shown that the allegations were in all probability fabricated, Mann's actions were fully justified based on the information known at the time.[5] As the meeting ended, Mann offered one piece of unsolicited advice—that we should conduct our business in Mexico as quietly as possible, without any newspaper publicity.[6i]

This advice came up later that day when we met with Jack Whitten of the CIA. Whitten offered to make arrangements to get us into Mexico "completely unnoticed if we desired to do so," but I thought this just wouldn't work. We could not be seen to be sneaking around, particularly with the assistance of the CIA, while conducting a formal investigation that necessarily involved meetings with high-level Mexican officials. We intended to present ourselves as representatives of the commission and hoped only, if possible, to avoid any newspaper publicity or public announcements. Whitten advised that we should deal in Mexico City with Winston Scott, the CIA station chief, who he assured us was one of the agency's top foreign operatives.[7i]

Any effort to disguise our identity as commission representatives would have collapsed immediately upon our arrival in Mexico City on the evening of April 8. When Bill Coleman had a minor issue with Mexican officials over his recent vaccination history, an Eastern Airlines representative resolved the problem by announcing with pride that Coleman was a representative of the Warren Commission. Within minutes, I was approached by an unidentified man and asked whether it was true we were coming to investigate the assassination. I declined to confirm the report. Regardless, two Mexico City newspapers announced our arrival the following morning, identifying us by name and reporting that we had come to Mexico on Warren Commission business. If it had not been for Coleman's delinquent vaccinations, we might well have blended into the busy crowd at the airport without any notice.[8]

We met the next day, April 9, with Ambassador Fulton Freeman, who had been on duty for only two days, along with Winston Scott from the CIA and Clark Anderson, chief of the FBI field office in Mexico City. Coleman explained our purposes in coming to Mexico and our desire to avoid doing anything that might disturb the good relations between Mexico and the United

States. We wanted to find out what investigations were under way so we could determine how best to fill the gaps about Oswald's activities in Mexico during his visit. Coleman said we also hoped to visit some of the Mexican officials who had conducted their investigation after the assassination. In particular, we wished to find out as much as possible about Silvia Duran, the clerk at the Cuban embassy who had dealt on several occasions with Oswald. Last, he raised the question of authenticating the evidence obtained in Mexico that would be relied upon by the commission and to do so, if possible, by the taking of depositions or inviting witnesses to testify before the commission.[9]

Freeman said we could probably interview Mexican citizens, but this would require approval by Mexican officials and assurances that all interviews would be wholly voluntary and done at the US embassy. He thought that our interest in meeting with Duran created a highly sensitive matter because of her (and her husband's) communist views and the need to avoid any appearance of US interference with a Mexican law enforcement investigation. He said that his staff would identify the Mexican officials likely to be most helpful and to assist in making appointments. Freeman also pointed out that the taking of formal depositions in a foreign country would be a very difficult matter and suggested that we discuss this matter with the consulate section at the embassy.[10]

Later in a meeting with the FBI, we reviewed the bureau's investigation about Oswald's activities in Mexico. We knew about his visits to the Cuban and Soviet Union embassies and wanted to learn as much as possible about those visits. But more immediate was our need to discuss allegations suggesting that Oswald was implicated in some kind of a conspiracy related to the assassination and decide what additional investigation in Mexico was necessary.

We focused first on a charge made by a young Nicaraguan named Gilberte Alvarado Ugarte, who was known to the CIA as a former informant of a Central American security service used to penetrate communist guerrilla groups. Alvarado told US authorities after the assassination that in mid-September 1963 he saw Oswald receive $6,500 to kill Kennedy at a meeting of three persons outside the Cuban consulate in Mexico City. He described one as "a tall, thin Negro with reddish hair, obviously dyed, who spoke rapidly in both Spanish and English" and identified another person as being Lee Harvey Oswald. He stated:

> A tall Cuban joined the group momentarily and passed some currency to the Negro. The Negro then allegedly said to Oswald in English, "I want to kill the man." Oswald replied, "You're not man enough. I can do it." The Negro

then said in Spanish, "I can't go with you, I have a lot to do." Oswald replied, "The people are waiting for me back there." The Negro then gave Oswald $6,500 in large-denomination American bills, saying, "This isn't much."

Four days after this allegation was first reported, Mexican authorities notified their American counterparts that Alvarado had admitted to fabricating the entire story, hoping it would help gain him entry into the United States. Subsequently Alvarado claimed that Mexican authorities had pressured him into retracting his original claim. But American authorities discovered serious deficiencies in Alvarado's story and, after a polygraph examination indicated that he was probably lying, Alvarado conceded that he "must be mistaken."[11]

The FBI gave us a detailed summary of their findings on Oswald's northbound travel by bus. The agents also reported that their examination of the Hotel del Comercio, where Oswald stayed in Mexico, did not reveal evidence that the hotel was a known gathering place for Cuban travelers. But the FBI did pick up some useful information from the maid at the hotel and the proprietress of the little restaurant next door where Oswald frequently ate. Both told the FBI that Oswald was always alone; that his Spanish was very poor; and that on one occasion another hotel guest sat at a table with Oswald because no other table was available.

We asked what they had learned about Pedro Gutierrez Valencia, a credit investigator for a Mexico City department store. Gutierrez had reported that he was at the Cuban embassy on September 30 or October 1, 1963, and saw a Cuban leave the embassy with an American engaged in a heated discussion in English involving "Castro, Cuba, and Kennedy." He told the bureau that the Cuban was counting American dollars and that both men departed the area in an automobile. After the assassination, Gutierrez contended that the American was Oswald. The FBI agents credited Gutierrez with being sincere and eager to cooperate with the investigation, but believed that his identification of the man as Oswald was very weak. However, they continued to try to locate the automobile that he had described.

The FBI also briefed us on Silvia Tirado de Duran, the clerk at the Cuban embassy whom we hoped to interview. The FBI had obtained a copy of her signed statement from the Mexican police. Duran was a Mexican national in the visa section of the Cuban embassy, and she remembered dealing with Oswald on his request for a visa to go to Cuba in transit to the Soviet Union. She was twenty-six, well educated, married to a forty-year-old industrial designer named Horacio Duran Navarro, and had a young child.

In support of his application for a visa, Duran recalled that Oswald showed her several documents to demonstrate his previous residence in the Soviet Union, his marriage to a Russian woman, and his commitment to Castro and the Cuban revolution. She was apparently interested enough in his situation to call the Soviet embassy to inquire what she could do to facilitate the issuance of a visa to Oswald. The Soviet authorities told her that it would take about four months to issue a visa allowing Oswald to enter the Soviet Union. When Duran relayed this information to Oswald and told him that she could not give him a Cuban visa without his first obtaining a Soviet Union visa, he got "very excited or angry," which prompted Duran to enlist the assistance of the consul, Eusebio Azque. When Oswald persisted in demanding that he should be given a visa "as a sympathizer in Cuban objectives," Azque ended the sharp argument in English by telling Oswald that "if it were up to him, he would not give him the visa."[12]

Anderson thought that our effort to interview Duran might pose problems for the Mexican authorities, but agreed that we could try. He identified the acting minister of the interior, Luis Echevarria, as the official we should see about this and other investigative matters. Anderson said that he and Scott got along well with Echevarria.[13]

Near the end of our meeting we reviewed the various allegations suggesting some form of conspiracy involving Oswald. The agents identified six relating to Mexico and Cuba, all of which had previously been considered by commission lawyers. The FBI had investigated each of the allegations and advised us that three involved misidentification, lack of corroboration, or retraction by the witness. Slawson had originally thought three might be serious, including the Gutierrez allegation, and said it now appeared that only the Gutierrez matter was important enough to warrant continued investigation. The FBI agents agreed. Anderson added that he was confident that there was no foreign conspiracy arising out of or connected with Mexico. If such a conspiracy had existed, he said, the FBI would have had some firm indication of it by now.[14]

We were pleased with how the meeting with the FBI had gone. They had answered all our questions with no hint of evasion and even volunteered helpful information we hadn't asked for. In the absence of any further leads suggesting a conspiracy, or requiring more investigation, I was inclined to accept Anderson's judgment regarding the lack of any conspiracy.

We had a similar meeting later in the day with the CIA team consisting of Winston Scott and his deputy, Alan White. Scott gave us a detailed summary of the CIA's activities in connection with Oswald beginning in September 1963, when the agency first learned that he had appeared at the Soviet and Cuban embassies. After the assassination, the CIA had ordered all its Mexican agents to concentrate on Kennedy. They had produced dossiers on Oswald and anyone in Mexico with whom he had some contact. This, of course, included Silvia Duran, her supervisor at the Cuban Embassy, and a KGB representative at the Soviet Embassy. The CIA had previously been interested in all three of them. They also put anyone who had contact with Oswald under surveillance. The CIA subsequently learned that Minister Echevarria and President Lopez Mateo immediately after the assassination had ordered the Mexican border closed for travel both ways, without having been requested to do so by the United States. Scott described the border closure as so thorough that busloads of schoolchildren were trapped on both sides.[15]

Based on Scott's account and documents he gave us, Slawson and Coleman recognized that the information we had received in Washington on Oswald's trips to the two embassies in Mexico City had important gaps. On the spot, we started to reconstruct our chronology. What the CIA had given us in Mexico City by itself justified the trip. It also served to validate the aphorism attributed to Helms to the effect that "there is no substitute for the 'case officer' being 'on the spot.'"[15]

The CIA representatives did not have anything new on the Gutierrez inquiry, which, they pointed out, rested with the FBI. They told us they hadn't seen any increases or unusual variations in cable traffic from the Soviet and Cuban embassies during Oswald's time in Mexico City. We were disturbed to learn at this meeting that the CIA in Washington had not forwarded certain material developed elsewhere to Scott, even though these materials might have reasonably related to the Mexican investigation. For example, the contents of the letter that Oswald wrote to the Soviet embassy in Washington after he returned to the United States, describing certain aspects of his Mexican trip, had never been disclosed to Scott or his staff. We showed them this letter at our meeting. The lack of coordination between CIA headquarters and the Mexico City station made it even more difficult for the officers in the field where the actual investigation was under way.[17]

We asked Scott and his deputy for their opinion regarding the possibility of a foreign conspiracy arising from Mexico. Both gave the same response as Anderson had—that if there had been a conspiracy involving people in Mexico, evidence would have surfaced by then. We asked Scott to arrange a meeting for us with Echevarria as soon as possible and asked that he and Anderson come along. Their personal relationships with the minister could be useful. Plus, their fluency in Spanish might come in handy as interpreters. The meeting was set for 11:30 the next day.[18]

Before our meeting with Echevarria on April 10, we gathered at the FBI office to review our strategy and, if possible, to see the locations known to have been visited by Oswald. I was called out of this FBI meeting by Clarence Boonstra, head of the consulate section at the US embassy. With a great sense of urgency, he told me senior officials in Washington were demanding an explanation of the publicity that had appeared in the local press about our visit. Apparently, any inquiry from Washington demanded immediate attention, so Boonstra and I collaborated in an effort to soothe his department superiors. We sent a telegram assuring State officials in Washington that their embassy officials and commission representatives were working together and had the matter well in hand.

After the FBI meeting, Rolfe Larson, an FBI agent temporarily assigned for duty in Mexico City, took Coleman, Slawson, and me on an automobile tour of the various sites that Oswald visited—the bus stations, travel agency, hotel, restaurant, and Cuban and Soviet embassies. We saw for ourselves that the two embassies were close enough together so that Oswald almost certainly walked back and forth between them when necessary. In addition, they were not easily reached by bus. The Hotel del Comercio was a reasonably neat and clean hotel conveniently located near the bus station where Oswald's journey to Mexico City ended. Upon his arrival, Oswald had probably asked where he might find a suitable hotel and been directed to this nearby neighborhood where there were a number of inexpensive hotels. We saw that both the Soviet and Cuban embassies were surrounded by high adobe walls blocking the view of their interiors. The Cuban consulate, where Oswald went to get his transit visa, was a small separate building in the Cuban complex with a front door that opened onto the street. Unlike the embassy buildings, this permitted easy observation of people entering and leaving the consulate by the CIA or other interested observers.[19]

Following this brief tour, we picked up Anderson and Scott at the embassy for the meeting with Echevarria. It lasted for about thirty minutes. By prearrangement, Coleman opened with statesmanlike remarks, including Chief Justice Warren's personal thanks. We asked for a complete report from the Mexican government on its investigation into the assassination and its other actions, such as the closing of the border. Echevarria readily agreed, indicating that an overall report had already been prepared and would be delivered on forty-eight hours' notice after receiving a formal request. To allay Echevarria's concerns, Coleman assured him that the commission would not publish anything based on the report without clearance from the Mexican government. Echevarria volunteered his opinion that no foreign conspiracy connected with Mexico was involved in the assassination of our president.[20]

When we raised the subject of interviews of Mexican citizens, Echevarria was hesitant. He told us that he did not believe that any such interviews should be at the US embassy because it would appear that the United States was conducting an official investigation on Mexican soil. This, he suggested, would be very sensitive politically for the Mexican government, with an upcoming presidential election in a few months. During the Cold War, Mexico was insistent on resisting any ideological affiliation with either the Soviet Union or the United States. Once it had satisfied itself that no persons in Mexico were involved in the assassination, the Mexican government did not wish to appear subservient to the United States.

Echevarria also suggested that the interviews be informal, perhaps at lunch or over coffee, but we needed to think that over. Given his concern, we decided to raise the issue of an interview with Silvia Duran from a different perspective. We emphasized the importance of Duran's testimony and Echevarria agreed, stating that he had relied most heavily on it in concluding that Oswald's activities at the two embassies were limited to his efforts to obtain a visa and had nothing to do with President Kennedy. However, prior to any more conversation on this subject, he excused himself to meet Queen Juliana of the Netherlands for lunch.[21]

After Echevarria left, we continued talking to his aide, Santiago Ibanez. Anderson told him that unrecorded interviews over lunch in a public place with witnesses were not what we needed. Ibanez proposed conducting the interviews at his own Interior Ministry. Although this alternative also had its problems, we left the meeting with the possibility still open (a bit at least) that we might get an opportunity to interview Duran.[22]

After we returned to the embassy, the three of us, along with Scott and Anderson, met with Boonstra and discussed at length our interest in getting access to Duran. Based on her interview with Mexican officials and corroborating information available to the CIA through wiretaps (termed "confidential sources" in the reports) we thought that her statements regarding the purpose of Oswald's visit to the Cuban embassy could be relied upon by the commission. Oswald's discussions at the Cuban embassy were completely consistent with his stated reason for the trip—to obtain a transit visa through Cuba in order to go to the Soviet Union—and did not provide any basis for concluding it was in furtherance of a conspiracy to kill President Kennedy. However, she had not been interviewed by either the FBI or the CIA. Perhaps, if willing to be interviewed, she could provide details regarding Oswald's appearance and behavior as well as any remarks he might have made in the process of seeking a visa. We considered how an "informal" session with her might be arranged and discussed briefly the possibility of trying to persuade her to visit the United States and testify before the commission.[23]

Boonstra thought it unlikely we would be given the opportunity to meet with Duran at all. He reminded us that the Mexicans were too politically sensitive to risk having her picked up a third time under arrest. Additionally, given the fact that she and her husband were both communists and he reportedly a rather bitter person in general, it was unlikely that she would agree to a voluntary appearance. Nevertheless, he said he would not object to our further attempt to arrange a meeting with her. Anderson would contact Ibanez to try to work out some arrangement regarding Duran while we were in Mexico City. We would defer any consideration of other approaches, such as requesting her to come to the United States, until Anderson had his conversation with Ibanez. Later in the day, Anderson reported that Ibanez was agreeable to our making arrangements to see Duran, subject to Echevarria's approval.[24]

We subsequently had a longer meeting with the CIA station chief and his deputy at the CIA office. This gave us an opportunity to review with them our reconstructed chronology of Oswald's activities in Mexico City based on the source materials they had given us. Scott and White thought we had it right. We then discussed in some detail how we could use the information available to the agency through confidential sources in the commission's report. This presented legitimate problems because of our different missions. The CIA needed to protect the identity of its confidential sources or risk losing those sources; we needed to identify the source of every fact we used in reaching our conclusions. We eventually decided on an approach that accommodated the CIA's concerns; the agency would prepare a report containing the information needed by the commission, but omitting any reference to the means by which the information was obtained.[25]

On Saturday morning we spent about three hours at the FBI office with Anderson and Larson. In the course of reviewing again the Gutierrez investigation, we asked the FBI to pursue several specific lines of inquiry. We wanted to know the exact time of arrival of Oswald's bus in Mexico City on September 27; we needed the hours that the Cuban and Soviet consulates were open to the public and if there was any common practice to stay open beyond these stated hours. We wanted them to generate for us an itemized list of the goods and services that Oswald probably purchased while in Mexico and during his travels. We asked them to determine the procedures customarily used by the Cuban embassy, especially as they relate to the granting of visas and the various travel permits which would be available to someone in Oswald's circumstances. Probing of this kind was essential to the overall objective of not overlooking anything that might suggest a conspiracy in operation.

Anderson again assured us that he had told us everything he knew, but that assurance had some limitations for us. As the FBI's highest-ranking official in Mexico, he proceeded under the "impression" conveyed to him by FBI headquarters that Oswald was the lone assassin. As we learned later, his investigation in Mexico was directed toward establishing Oswald's activities while in Mexico rather than looking for possible connections to a conspiracy.[26]

On the same day as our meeting with the FBI, we followed up with a brief visit to the CIA office. Scott and White gave us a report regarding the time periods covering Gutierrez's visits to the Cuban Embassy and indicated that no individuals or automobiles matched the descriptions provided by Gutierrez. The agency was continuing its surveillance of the Cuban embassy in an effort to find the car. Subsequently, Gutierrez failed to identify Oswald when shown his photograph. Like Anderson with the FBI, Scott assured us that his office had now told us everything developed in its Oswald investigation.

On Monday morning, Slawson again met with both agencies. In his meeting with Larson and another FBI agent, Slawson displayed copies of the physical evidence that he had brought to Mexico City to see if they might suggest further useful investigation by the FBI. Except for page forty-seven of Oswald's address book, none of the items seemed to offer any promising lines of further inquiry. Page forty-seven listed a number for the Cuban Airlines office in Mexico City, but further investigation uncovered no evidence that Oswald visited that office while in the city.[27]

When Slawson and I met with Anderson later in the morning, I told him that we were favorably impressed with the high quality of the FBI agents we had met in Mexico City and with their efforts on the assassination. I thought the high-quality work dated from late February and asked why agents familiar with Mexico had not been assigned earlier to the job. Anderson replied that embassy officials initially thought that the FBI would get the best results by working primarily with the Mexican authorities, who were highly motivated to discover any conspiracy that might have involved their country, and that an initial deployment of FBI specialists might have had adverse political effects.

But when the subsequent results of the Mexican investigation were simply not good enough, the FBI's own agents were assigned to the job.[28]

Confusion as to which US agency was responsible for the investigation in Mexico also limited the FBI's effectiveness. The FBI believed that the CIA and the Department of State were the only agencies with jurisdiction. Mann thought there was a Cuban conspiracy, but later it appeared that both the FBI and the CIA considered his views overblown and rejected suggestions that they seek information from their Cuban sources in the United States. They feared that such an approach would promote rumors and perhaps have serious repercussions with Cuba. In addition, although the FBI sent a supervisor from Washington to look into the allegation involving Oswald's receipt of $6,500 from a Cuban consulate employee, this specialist did not know of any "investigation in Mexico to determine if there was Cuban involvement in the assassination of President Kennedy." As soon as the source of this allegation admitted fabricating the story, this supervisor went back to Washington without any further effort to deal with a possible Cuban conspiracy.[29]

In our last meeting at the embassy, Slawson, Anderson, and I revisited the Duran problem with Boonstra. Boonstra told us that Minister Echevarria had "reacted coolly" to our suggestion about arranging an informal meeting with Duran. We discussed the possibility of a letter from the commission that would be sent to her by registered mail from the embassy in Mexico City. But after talking it through, we agreed that we couldn't be sure what Duran would do with the letter. It might be used for propaganda purposes by the communists or pro-Castro Cuban groups in Mexico if, for example, Duran claimed harassment based on her political views or the Cuban groups alleged that the United States was trying to implicate Castro's government in the assassination. With such possible risks, we agreed to let high-level officials at the State Department evaluate the possibilities.[30]

We also considered an official request by the US government through Swiss channels that the Cuban government forward its complete file on Oswald to the commission. The Cuban government had in fact acted on his application for a visa and authorized its issuance conditioned on his first obtaining a Russian visa. Both Boonstra and Anderson thought that this was a good idea, might actually be welcomed by the Cuban government, and appeared not to have any material adverse political consequences. But Boonstra thought that this idea, too, ought to be resolved in Washington.[31]

After we returned from Mexico, Slawson and I were briefing Rankin about the trip when the chief justice abruptly joined our discussion. We emphasized the positive results of the trip. First, we now had a more accurate picture of what Oswald had done in Mexico City. Second, the Mexican government was ready to provide us with a report of its investigation of any Mexican involvement in the assassination. Third, based on our conversations with the FBI and CIA agents in the field, we were better able to advise the commission about the allegations involving Oswald that had been pursued by the two agencies at our request.[32]

After listening to our report, Warren told us not to pursue any effort to bring Duran to Washington. He objected because she and her husband were communists, and the husband was already incensed over his wife's treatment by the Mexican officials. In Warren's opinion (not an unusual one in those Cold War days), Duran's communism meant she could not be a credible witness. In light of his position, we postponed further discussion of possible access to Duran.

A month or so after our Mexican trip, Slawson and I learned from the CIA's Rocca that Duran and her husband had changed their minds and were willing to come to Washington. After getting Rankin's approval to pursue the matter, we asked Chief Justice Warren whether he wanted to reconsider his earlier decision. He declined. Although Duran's appearance before the commission might have been useful, Slawson and I recognized that bringing Duran and her husband to Washington involved certain risks—including antagonizing Mexican law enforcement authorities—and we understood Warren's position. We already had a clear and documented report of her encounters with Oswald, based on the Mexican authorities' interview of Duran, corroborated by the wiretaps, and the additional information she might have provided about Oswald was unlikely to be important enough to justify assuming these risks.[33]

Even though our attempts to interview Duran ultimately failed, our pursuit had raised the possibility of obtaining from the Cuban government the documents reflecting its action on Oswald's request for a visa. Slawson and I visited the State Department to discuss a possible request to Cuba through neutral channels regarding Oswald's Mexican trip. Based on this conversation, Slawson prepared a draft letter from Warren to Rusk requesting the State Department's assistance in obtaining information and documents from the Cuban government "through appropriate channels" regarding Oswald's visit to the Cuban embassy in Mexico City. State planned to discuss with the Swiss ambassador in Havana the desirability of approaching the Cuban government to obtain this information. After approval by Rankin in late April, Slawson delivered the letter informally to the State Department. I learned later that Warren did not support this strategy, which was implemented without his approval.[34]

■ The Cuba Connection

The commission's investigation of Oswald's possible entanglement in a conspiracy involving Cuba was not limited to whatever he had done in Mexico. We had good documentation of his activities in support of the pro-Castro Fair Play for Cuba Committee in the United States and we explored these political activities to determine whether they may have involved more serious and threatening objectives beyond the distribution of handbills on the streets of New Orleans or elsewhere. Of course, we were well aware that the United States and Cuba were engaged in a political confrontation that had already led to one military encounter at the Bay of Pigs in 1961 and a near catastrophe during the thirteen-day Cuban Missile Crisis in 1962, after the Soviet Union began building a missile base on the island. The willingness of Castro's Cuba to be a proxy for the Soviets in this hemisphere increased US resolution and candor about a regime change in Cuba.

At the commission, in addition to focusing on pro-Cuba groups in the United States, we also resolved to learn more about anti-Castro Cuban groups because of the widespread sentiment among these groups that President Kennedy had failed to honor his commitment to support them. We knew that Oswald had been involved in a conflict with anti-Castro Cuban refugees.[35] In early August 1963, while living in New Orleans, Oswald volunteered his services to Carlos Bringuier, a lawyer from Cuba then active in anti-Castro projects. Oswald claimed that he had received guerrilla-type training in the Marine Corps and offered to use his expertise in training Bringuier's group. Bringuier was intrigued by Oswald's offer and was initially friendly to the young man. However, very soon after, a member of Bringuier's group observed Oswald distributing Fair Play for Cuba Committee literature. Bringuier promptly challenged Oswald on the streets of New Orleans. The altercation led to the arrest of both men. Oswald was convicted of creating a public disturbance and fined ten dollars.

Soon thereafter, in the middle of August, Bringuier sent one of his followers to Oswald's home posing as a pro-Castro Cuban interested in working for Oswald. Oswald received Bringuier's plant courteously and the two discussed Cuban politics into the evening on Oswald's porch. Marina Oswald testified that Oswald told her after the conversation that he strongly suspected his visitor was an anti-Castro agent pretending to be pro-Castro. The end result: both Bringuier and Oswald failed in their attempts to infiltrate the other's organization.[36]

Aware of their ideological differences, a local radio broadcaster arranged for a debate between Oswald and Bringuier on a daily public affairs program on August 21, 1963. According to the broadcaster, Oswald defended the Castro regime and discussed Marxism, handled himself very well, and appeared to be "a very logical, intelligent fellow." However, his advocacy was seriously weakened when his defection to the Soviet Union was revealed at the beginning of the debate, forcing him to assert that the Fair Play for Cuba Committee was "not at all Communist controlled regardless of the fact that I had the experience of living in Russia." As a result of this publicity and disclosure of his defection, Oswald believed that he was "open to almost unanswerable attack by those who opposed his views."[37]

Jim Liebeler and David Slawson pursued these leads to explore Oswald's activities in New Orleans. Liebeler worked (along with Bert Jenner) on exploring every aspect of Oswald's life in the US to determine if he was involved in a domestic conspiracy. Cuba was the intersection between these assignments. Slawson thought that the anti-Castro groups deserved particular attention. They were his "prized suspects" because they hated Castro and were very angry at Kennedy over the Bay of Pigs failure. The assassination of the president by a known communist connected in some way with Cuba would serve their purposes of getting revenge on Kennedy and possibly triggering an invasion of Cuba by the United States. In Slawson's view, "this was the only conspiracy theory that I ever heard that made sense." I agreed that we should pursue this particular conspiracy theory—no matter how implausible or complicated it might appear—because of the zealousness of the anti-Castro exiles in the United States.[38]

Because of his strong anti-Castro views and contacts with Oswald, Carlos Bringuier was an important witness. Liebeler took his deposition in New Orleans on April 8, 1964. Afterward, he prepared a four-page investigative request for the FBI, citing various leads provided by Bringuier, such as the reported appearance of Oswald at the Habana Bar in the summer of 1963 in the company of a person believed to be either Mexican or Cuban, and his apparent knowledge of the existence of an anti-Castro military training camp in New Orleans. Liebeler was also concerned about earlier FBI reports of interviews of Dean Andrews, the lawyer who represented Oswald in connection with the street disturbance involving Bringuier. In these reports Andrews stated that Oswald came to his office on several occasions accompanied by several different people, including a person of Mexican extraction, but was hesitant about identifying the Mexican. Liebeler wanted the FBI to interview Andrews again to see if his memory could be refreshed as to the identity of this man and, if possible, determine whether that man was the same person believed to have accompanied Oswald to the Habana Bar.[39]

■ Making Our Work Accessible to the Public

By mid-April, the staff had been working for about three months and Rankin sensed that the commission, the White House, and the media would soon be pressing for a projected completion date. Rankin decided to assess the remaining investigative work so that he would be better informed in any discussion of a proposed target date with the commission members.

On April 16, he asked the lawyers to focus on what remained to be done before they could start writing a draft report. Specifically, Rankin asked that each team: (1) explain the remaining areas of investigation that needed to be explored and why they were important, (2) indicate whether these areas of investigation would require further testimony or whether they could be handled through the investigative agencies, and (3) report the date on which he could reasonably expect that each team would begin writing the report in its area.[40] This memo certainly got everyone's attention, forcing the lawyers to stop what they were doing and address Rankin's specific questions.

Arlen Specter responded on that same day. He recommended that President Johnson, his wife, Lady Bird, and Jacqueline Kennedy be asked to testify before the commission. He recommended that Texas senator Ralph Yarborough, a passenger in the vice-presidential limousine in Dallas, also be asked to appear. Kenneth O'Donnell, one of the White House staffers involved in the planning of the trip, needed to be interviewed. Among the tasks remaining, Specter listed the need to "plot the position of the President's automobile at the times of the three shots to calculate, as precisely as possible, distances and angles." He also wanted Rankin to revisit the issue of commission access to the autopsy photos and X-rays, recommending that these be examined and additional depositions be taken as necessary on the medical issues.[41]

Hubert and Griffin reported that their investigation of Ruby had a long way to go. Ruby's diverse activities with colorful characters over the decades—involving one (or more) trips to Cuba, relationships with known criminals, management of a small nightclub, and friendships within the Dallas Police Department—required an expansive inquiry by the commission. Hubert and Griffin told Rankin that they were still waiting for the FBI to respond to a large number of investigative requests sent in late March. Depending on the results, they suggested that additional depositions might be required. In addition, they pointed out the need to decide whether to seek testimony from Ruby, whose murder conviction was now on appeal, and a possible deposition of his brother Earl Ruby. They needed to complete the depositions of George Senator, Ruby's roommate in Dallas, and Captain John Fritz of the Dallas Police Department. They still wanted a full investigation of names and telephone numbers found on Ruby, in his home, or in his car and to track rumors of associations between Ruby and Oswald and others. But they noted that their continuing investigative work wouldn't delay their work on the draft report.[42]

As the progress reports were submitted to Rankin, I began to have a deeper sense of the difficulty we faced in explaining to the public exactly what happened. We had pretty good evidence that there had been three shots at the motorcade, but we did not know with certainty which shots hit Kennedy and Connally. We did not even know why Oswald wanted to kill the president. By now, most of us suspected that both Oswald and Ruby acted alone, but knew that our final judgment on this issue depended on the results of our further investigation. At the end of the day, however, we would likely confront the truly daunting task of proving two negatives—no foreign conspiracy and no domestic conspiracy. That essentially meant we had to account for every contact Oswald and Ruby had in the months leading up to the shootings and decide whether any of those contacts suggested a conspiracy that needed to be fully explored. And we were being stonewalled by Treasury in our inquiry into the Secret Service's failure to protect the president.

We had established procedures for correcting errors in our transcripts and preparing them for publication. The commission had not yet decided to publish the deposition transcripts, although I strongly supported doing so. I told Rankin we should proceed to process the depositions without any decision as to their publication. I thought the question whether these materials should be published could be considered more carefully if the editing was completed than if it appeared that this process would delay the commission's report. I also thought publication of these materials would be well received by the news media and the public generally, and would help address any concern that the commission was concealing aspects of its work. When I visited briefly with Katzenbach on April 22, he told me that he was "being kept informed by Mr. McCloy as to what was going on in the Commission, and that he believed that the Commission should publish as much as possible." When I heard later from Rankin that the commission was tending in this direction, I told him that this was "progress of an important sort and that we could afford to deal with any minor problems at this point if we could proceed along these lines in publishing all this material."[43]

Another staff meeting about the report took place two days later. In retrospect, these discussions about the publication of the report as well as the accompanying supporting materials might seem thoroughly predictable. That was not the case. We lawyers were personally committed to producing a final product that could withstand the kind of critical examination that we knew it would provoke. We hoped that the commission fully shared this objective, but did not know if that was the case. Commission members would discuss such issues only at their official transcribed meetings where Rankin was the only nonmember attending. Several of the staff, both lawyers and historians, had occasional discussions with commission members about particular subjects on which they shared a special interest. Dulles, for example, often sought out Slawson to see what he was doing and thinking. I had some occasional conversations with McCloy. But I do not believe that the staff as a group had any informed understanding of what the members were contemplating by way of their report. It seemed to me that it was our job—Rankin and the entire staff—to consider these issues and present our best thinking to the commission by proposing a course of action for its consideration.

We felt strongly that it was our mission to produce a well-documented report that reflected the extent and substance of our investigation. To do this, we needed to support our factual statements with footnotes to the relevant transcripts or exhibits. But proceeding in this manner meant that we needed to commit to full publication of the supporting materials. And that in turn meant much more detailed work by everyone concerned, with an increased risk that our documentation would in some instances be less than perfect.

At a staff meeting on April 24, we debated the extent of the transcripts, documents, and exhibits that could be published with our report. I worried that any effort to publish all of the data simultaneously would only delay the report's publication. Apparently reflecting the commission's views, Rankin argued that we should not cite materials in the report that are not simultaneously published. I took issue with this, arguing that "the public did not expect this, and would be overwhelmingly satisfied by publication of the transcripts and exhibits, so long as the Commission indicated that additional material would be published" within a reasonably short period after the report was released. In an effort to eliminate (or minimize) this problem, we instructed the staff to identify any materials on which they intended to rely that were not currently in the transcripts or exhibits so that they could be published as part of the commission's records.[44]

At the commission meeting on April 30, Rankin summarized the staff's work on the report and plans to publish the materials on which it would be based. To his surprise and disappointment, the members present disagreed with this course of action because publication of the supporting materials would be too expensive. I learned of this decision when I joined a meeting late in the day with Rankin in the conference room and was told by Belin and Liebeler that there was "shocking news" awaiting me. As I recalled later:

> Mr. Rankin, in a very tired and chastened mood looked at me in such a way that I knew the Commission had reached another of their impossible decisions. Such was in fact the case. Mr. Rankin informed me that the Commission had decided not to publish the transcript simultaneously with the Final Report. Apparently the chief consideration was one of expense and there was not extensive consideration of the policy issues between members of the Commission who discussed the matter.[45]

I was of course disappointed by this seeming lack of foresight by the members.

We had worked very long hours on the transcripts so that all of our depositions would be made public at the same time as the report. Indeed, the report would recite the page numbers of various depositions where witnesses discussed the facts we were reporting. To make a decision not to publish all this work seemed perverse. In response to the news:

> I asked [Rankin] immediately how many of the Commission were present and voted on the issue. He replied that only three were present—The Chief Justice, Mr. Dulles and Mr. McCloy. I indicated to him quite briefly that this was a decision which could not be permitted to stand, and I could see that he felt very much the same way. The Commission members had indicated to Mr. Rankin that they would reverse themselves if the Congressional members of the Commission voted otherwise. Mr. Rankin planned therefore to contact Senator Russell and the other Congressional members as soon as possible on Friday morning. It was no good however to engage in any harangue on the subject although Messrs. Belin and Liebeler were certainly inclined to do so.[46]

I thought it was quite unusual to have a commission meeting that not a single elected member attended. However, the commission was doing its job during one of the most productive legislative sessions in the history of the United States—with enactment of the Civil Rights Act of 1964, a major tax cut, and antipoverty legislation. In fact, during April and May 1964, President Johnson was fully engaged in urging the Senate to approve the civil rights legislation that the House of Representatives had passed earlier in the year. Under these circumstances it is not too surprising that the congressional members were unable to attend our meeting.[47]

I saw a bit of daylight in Warren's willingness to defer to the members of Congress on the commission. If they thought the expense would not become a political issue, the other members could rely on that judgment. As I recorded: "By this time in the work of the Commission, Mr. Rankin and I enjoy some sort of brotherhood in adversity and have managed to overcome other adverse decisions of the Commission. It was hoped that we could do likewise here."[48]

Just as I had hoped, the four Congressional members of the commission reversed the tentative decision. After meeting with Senator Russell Friday morning, Rankin told me:

> Senator Russell had indicated very clearly that the entire transcript should be published as soon as possible without regard to expense. Mr. Rankin subsequently contacted all the other Congressional members who agreed with Senator Russell. When he conveyed this information to the Chief Justice, Mr. Dulles and Mr. McCloy they all agreed that the position of the Congressional members should be adopted.[49]

It seems apparent that the three non-elected commission members were overly sensitive to the financial costs involved in publication of the supporting materials and underestimated the willingness of the elected members to do what best served the overriding public interest in the commission's report. I got the sense at the time that Warren, Dulles, and McCloy were much relieved by this outcome. I know that was true of Rankin. This was the first and only time during my assignment with the commission where the costs of our investigation became an issue. Failure to publish these critical materials would have only given our future critics more ammunition to challenge the validity of our findings.

The Government Printing Office now started printing the transcripts. One might imagine that correcting the report closer to publication would be a simple matter, but in the early 1960s, the GPO was still using "hot-metal" typesetting machines, which had been invented in the 1880s. Sitting at a keyboard in front of a giant hot-metal processing machine, the operator would type in the text, the machine would cast the letters into metal, and a few seconds later the thin hot-metal slug bearing one line of type would slide down onto a metal tray. These trays were called galleys. When a section or page of text was completed, the printer would "lock up" the galley with a mechanism that held the slugs tightly in place. If corrections were needed, the printer would unlock the galley, lift out the slug that needed to be revised, go back to the keyboard and type out the corrected line, retrieve the new slug, and put it back into the galley. If the mistake required changes in more than one line, the printer would replace all the slugs until he got to a place where the type and spacing were correct. The printers at GPO who operated the Linotype machines were skilled craftsmen who could type faster than the best executive secretary. But the process was time-consuming and laborious. We accepted all of this, just as we accepted the law of gravity. Looking back, compared with today's high-tech printers, it seems like these machines preceded the steam engine.

■ Starting to Fill Gaps in the Commission's Record

Under constant pressure from Warren, the staff scrambled and improvised to produce more witnesses on an expedited schedule. The members were still determined to visit Dallas to inspect the assassination site personally, but no firm date had been arranged. This uncertainty meant that our proposed schedule of witnesses might have to be altered on short notice.

By mid-April, the only public figures scheduled to testify were Connally and his wife. They testified on April 21—a date fixed so that the chief justice could be present.[50] President Johnson had not informed the commission whether he and Lady Bird would appear before the commission. No approach had yet been made, officially, regarding Jacqueline Kennedy's testimony.

Responsibility for interviewing these high-profile individuals and others who were in the motorcade rested with Adams, our senior lawyer from New York, and Specter. Adams knew Senator Ralph W. Yarborough, who had been riding in the vice-presidential limousine two cars back from the presidential vehicle, and undertook to approach him for an affidavit about his recollections. Yarborough had told the *Washington Post* that he had smelled the gunpowder and Rankin wanted his sworn testimony. After Adams had to cancel his appointment, Specter was given the task of interviewing Yarborough, known to almost everyone as "Smiling Ralph," in his Senate office. Specter later said he had listened attentively to the senator but didn't take notes. When we finished, I returned to the commission headquarters, where I prepared an affidavit. The next day I returned to Yarborough's office to secure his signature to the affidavit. The senator read the document and erupted. I had come into his office with a tape recorder without telling him, he raged. I said, "No, Senator, I didn't, but thank you very much for the compliment."[51]

When considering the proposed testimony of three Secret Service officials, I reminded Rankin that the necessary work in the presidential protection area had not been done because of the still unresolved policy issues with Treasury, including the commission's access to the Rowley report. The commission also needed to decide whether the principal Texas law enforcement officials—Chief Curry, Sheriff Decker, and District Attorney Wade—should testify before the commission.

Meanwhile, the Hubert/Griffin team doggedly followed up investigative leads regarding Ruby, and the Jenner/Liebeler team continued to log every detail of Oswald's US-based activities. When I heard that Rankin was joining Liebeler in New York to take depositions of officers and members of the Communist party, Socialist Workers' party, and the Fair Play for Cuba Committee, I thought that this provided an unusual (and desirable) opportunity for two very different colleagues to become better acquainted. Rankin lived in New York, so participation in these depositions was convenient for him and also gave him an opportunity to contribute personally to our fact-finding mission. A very modest and soft-spoken man, Rankin was by now very familiar with Liebeler's aggressive style at our staff meetings, and I thought (with a smile) that working together on a few depositions would enable each to get to know the other a little better. Despite their differences in personal style, the two shared an ironclad determination to get this job done well.

As a general matter, the lawyers taking the depositions were getting what they wanted from the witnesses—a greater degree of certainty about tentative conclusions, elaboration in areas that had not been fully developed by the agencies, and leads that prompted further depositions and new investigative requests. A memo from Hubert evaluating the results of the depositions that he and Griffin had taken in Dallas provided a good example. They wanted evidence regarding Dallas Police Department planning for Oswald's security and the transfer from the jail, and possible complicity of any department official in his death. He and Griffin also searched for evidence about Ruby's entry into the basement on that Sunday morning. This evidence might show that

Ruby had lied on this subject and had conceived a plan to kill Oswald, which in turn would trigger further investigation as to who might have known of, or participated in, his plan.[52]

Based on the interviews of thirty-seven police officers, Hubert reported that the department's security precautions when Oswald was in custody were seriously deficient. There were no plans for his transfer until the morning of November 24; and the plans announced on that date were not coordinated and were changed at least once. However, based on the evidence, Hubert believed that it was improbable that any individual or group within the Dallas Police Department engaged in a plot with Ruby to kill Oswald. Further, he and Griffin found no evidence of a conspiracy to cover up the deficient security arrangements and to blame this failure upon any one individual within the department.[53]

As to Ruby's entrance into the basement, Hubert's view at this point was more cautious. He thought that the alternative best supported by the evidence was that Ruby entered by the Main Street ramp as he claimed, although two other entrances were available to him. However, three newsmen believed they saw Ruby around the jail earlier on the morning of November 24, and Hubert and Griffin planned to take their depositions.[54]

At the same time, the Hubert/Griffin team pursued Ruby's possible Cuban associations. They had found evidence that Ruby had a connection with Robert Ray McKeown of Houston, who had been convicted of selling arms to Fidel Castro. They learned of a visit by Ruby to Havana with Lewis J. McWillie for about ten days in September 1959. They found some conflict in the reports as to whether Ruby made two trips, or only one, to Cuba in 1959. The team also decided to investigate seven or eight different rumors linking Ruby to Cuba to determine if Ruby had associated with underworld figures interested in overthrowing Castro and if those associations were connected to his murder of Oswald.[55]

They followed up with investigative requests to the FBI two days later, including a request to the FBI to investigate thirty-eight people identified as associates of Earl Ruby, Jack's brother, based on an Internal Revenue Service analysis of his telephone calls during the course of an IRS tax investigation. In early April, Hubert and Griffin planned to take an additional thirty-two depositions, most of them in Dallas, including people believed to have information regarding Ruby's presence at the Dallas police headquarters on November 24 and others with knowledge of his personal history and relationships.[56]

Meanwhile, the Ball/Belin team planned to take the depositions of an additional twenty Dallas policemen and another eight people who might have facts bearing on Oswald's culpability as the assassin of Kennedy and the murderer of Tippit. The Jenner/Liebeler team had plans to depose seventeen people in New York with knowledge of Oswald's background. The IRS team weighed in with a status report on the chronology they were preparing and advised Rankin it would be done by May 15.[57]

By this time, the commission had decided that President and Lady Bird Johnson did not have to testify, but could submit written statements to the commission if they were willing to do so. Most of us disagreed with this decision. Redlich argued that everyone who was actually in the presidential or vice-presidential cars should testify before the commission because they might have valuable information to provide. Rankin shared this view to some extent. He told me that he intended to call Abe Fortas on this subject and tell him about the commission's decision, but at the same time express his and the staff's view that Johnson should either appear before the commission or give a detailed statement.

In the midst of this, we again had to deal with the very vocal Mark Lane. In his testimony before the commission in March, Lane said he had had a conversation with Helen Markham, a witness to the killing of Patrolman Tippit. Markham denied having any such conversation with Lane. Redlich had sent the transcripts of their testimony to Belin in Dallas and suggested that he reinterview Markham. If she persisted in her testimony, then Redlich thought that the commission should consider recalling Lane or asking him to provide further confirmation of his testimony. We also had to decide what to do about Lane's failure to produce the name of an informant who he testified had information about an alleged meeting among Jack Ruby, Officer Tippit, and Bernard Weissman, the publisher of the critical "Welcome Mr. Kennedy" advertisement in the November 22 *Dallas Morning News*. In response to a follow-up letter from the commission, Lane advised that he would identify the informant later. After nearly a month, he had failed to do so. Given the worldwide publicity of Lane's wholesale attack on the commission, we wanted to make clear that we had given him every opportunity to document his contentions and that, when given the opportunity under oath, he hadn't done so.[58]

Warren wanted a clear and unequivocal record that the key government agencies had provided all relevant information in their possession to the commission. I was not convinced then of the necessity for such written assurances, because the heads of these agencies were likely commission witnesses. Although it may have seemed excessively bureaucratic at the time, I recognize now that it reflected Warren's executive experience over the years. He wanted to have a written record that these agencies had assisted the commission to the fullest extent of their capabilities in the same way that a governor, before initiating a new program, might insist that the concerned agencies in his administration be on board.

Rankin and I moved quickly to draft and send identical letters seeking these statements. They went to Hoover at the FBI, Rowley at the Secret Service, Helms at the CIA, legal adviser Abram Chayes at the State Department, Commissioner Raymond F. Farrell at the Immigration and Naturalization Service, and Kennedy at the Justice Department. The letters were all dated April 22. After thanking each agency for its assistance to the commission, Rankin asked whether the agency had any information not previously disclosed to the commission regarding Oswald's association with any subversive or criminal organization or individuals in the United States or abroad. The commission's letter requested each agency's assurance that the commission "possesses the full extent" of the agency's 'knowledge and information' concerning such associations by Oswald."[59]

The most junior members of the staff continued to make major contributions to our work. John Ely was now at work with the Jenner/Liebeler team, assisting in the taking of depositions and producing extensively documented memos on Oswald's life. In April, he investigated Oswald's military record and suggested deposing a few soldiers who knew Oswald while he was a Marine. Richard Mosk worked on proposed federal legislation making the assault or murder of the president and other federal officials a crime. He also devoted long hours to summarizing the depositions that Jenner had taken of members of the Russian-speaking community in Texas who knew Oswald. Although Jenner's meticulous and tedious questioning of these witnesses puzzled (and amused) some of our younger lawyers, his efforts produced a wealth of material that was extensively used by later authors exploring Oswald's life and motive. By this time I also had the services of Stuart Pollak, who worked in the criminal division as a special assistant to Jack Miller. I had hired Pollak, a Harvard Law graduate, for the division after his clerkship at the Supreme Court during 1962–63.[60]

■ FBI Intelligence Capabilities and Witnesses

Sam Stern was examining the operations of the Protective Research Section of the Secret Service, which had the responsibility of collecting and reviewing information to identify possible threats to the president. Stern was exploring whether the commission might recommend improvements in this vital preventive intelligence function. We already had documented serious deficiencies in the Secret Service's performance in Dallas: it had not searched any buildings along the president's route in Dallas; it had little coordination with local law enforcement officers who believed they had been relegated to crowd control; it lacked established procedures on how to prepare for a presidential motorcade; and its agents actually had no training in how to look out for assassins. We expected there might be similar problems with the intelligence operations of the agency.

I had informal conversations with James Malley, our liaison from the FBI, on this subject and the CIA had briefed us on their techniques in handling intelligence data. Stern wanted to be fully informed on data-handling practices in order to determine whether more advanced systems were available, which might be recommended to the Secret Service. On Monday, April 27, Sam Stern and I had an extended briefing by the FBI about its own filing system, procedures for conducting name checks, and the extent to which information in its files could be made available to other agencies such as the Secret Service.[61]

The FBI officials were quite confident in describing the capabilities of the bureau's routing, classifying, and filing procedures. We learned, for example, that it conducted about ten thousand name checks every day and that the filing system is basically a name index rather than a subject index. They emphasized that the FBI had not mechanized their system because there were not yet available IBM machines that could do the job. They told us that no machine could handle the information contained in the five million index cards currently in the bureau's system that had to be queried many thousands of times a day and that, in any event, a machine would not eliminate the need for the exercise of human judgment in many cases.[62]

The last meeting with the FBI in April took place a few days later and was prompted by the scheduling of FBI agents John Fain, John Quigley, and James Hosty to testify before the commission in early May. These were the agents who had responsibility for Oswald after his return from the Soviet Union. On April 30, Rankin, Stern, and I met with Malley and Assistant Director Belmont to discuss some issues that would arise during the testimony of these witnesses. Belmont told us that Hoover had directed that the bureau was to cooperate with the commission in any way possible and that the publication of these interview reports was a decision for the commission to make. Regarding the FBI's preassassination file on Oswald, we explained that the commission had to be aware of everything that was in the bureau's files and that there was nothing in those files that contradicted the FBI's stated position about its relationship with Oswald. Belmont stated that the file was available for inspection by commission members and its staff. He did indicate that there was some information in the file that the FBI did not want to have published, such as the identity of confidential informants and some coded material, but agreed to appear as a witness before the commission in early May and to bring the entire FBI file for the members to examine during the hearing.[63]

At the commission meeting on April 30, both Dulles and McCloy said they wanted to hear more about the adequacy of the Secret Service's policies and procedures. They agreed that some members should go to Dallas before the end of their investigation. They also wanted to address the conspiracy rumors so prevalent in the European press. They were concerned that the summaries of about 300 depositions, now being prepared for them by the staff, might delay the production of their report. Warren expressed his desire to interview Ruby—whether or not he was pronounced sane at an upcoming competency hearing—if Ruby was willing to do so.[64] Warren also seemed receptive to Rankin's proposal that a doctor and a commission member examine the autopsy photographs and X-rays so as to ensure the accuracy of the testimony of the autopsy doctors who did not have those materials available when they testified, but that the materials would not be included in the public record of the commission's proceedings.[65]

I was looking forward to the testimony in early May of FBI agents Fain, Quigley, and Hosty. The testimony of Hosty was already freighted with significance because of his investigation of the Oswalds shortly before the assassination. But it promised to become even more controversial after a story broke in the *Dallas Morning News* during the last week of April that an FBI agent told Lieutenant Jack Revill of the Dallas Police Department "only moments after Oswald was brought" to the department on November 22 that: "We knew he was capable of assassinating the President but we didn't believe he would do it." According to the news story, Revill testified to this effect before the commission. Revill told the Associated Press a day later that James Hosty was the agent who made the comment and that another Dallas policeman was with Revill when the statement was made. Hoover promptly told the *Dallas Times Herald*: "That is absolutely false. The agent made no such statement and the FBI did not have such knowledge." Hosty denied ever making such a statement.[66]

These stories resulted directly from the testimony of Dallas chief of police Jesse Curry before the commission on April 22. On the morning of his appearance, Chief Curry gave Rankin a written report from Revill of a conversation that Revill had with Hosty on the afternoon of November 22, 1963, when they both arrived at police headquarters shortly after Oswald had been apprehended. Curry also provided an affidavit from Revill that he had sworn to early in April 1964, confirming the accuracy of his November 22 report. The report stated that Hosty had told Revill that the FBI "had information that this Subject [Oswald] was capable of committing the assassination of President Kennedy." Chief Curry offered no explanation as to why he hadn't provided this report to the commission earlier along with other reports relevant to his department's investigation into this matter, although he acknowledged that maintaining good relations with the FBI was very important to him. He disclosed the information contained in the report to Wade and a very few other Dallas officials, and did state at a press conference that the FBI knew that Oswald was in Dallas and had not informed the department. When Hoover demanded a retraction of this statement, Curry attempted to glide over the problem by telling the press that he did not intend to suggest that the FBI had interviewed Oswald in Dallas before the assassination.[cccv]

Rankin was shocked by this obvious leak of critical information from Curry's testimony, which he had handled personally. I recall someone—either Norman Redlich or Sam Stern—charging into my office on the morning of April 24, with a copy of the *New York Times* article in hand. The extent of the disclosure, and its release within a day of Curry's appearance, certainly suggested that it came from someone close to our operations or someone in Dallas who knew about Curry's testimony. Hoover wrote the commission a few days later denying the Revill report of his conversation with Hosty.

All of this created an additional challenge for Sam Stern, who had been working with Hosty and the two other agents scheduled to testify on May 5. Stern now had to figure out a way to get a fuller and more accurate picture of the Revill report than was contained in the press stories or the Hoover denial. May promised to be a very productive month for the commission.

CHAPTER 6

MAY 1964: CRITICAL DECISIONS

■

AFTER HIS APPREHENSION FOR KILLING TIPPIT, OSWALD WAS QUESTIONED at the Dallas Police Department. FBI agent James Hosty joined the meeting shortly after it began. Immediately on learning his name, Oswald snarled at him, "Oh, so you are Hosty. I've heard about you," and started swearing, ranting, and raving about the FBI. His abusive reaction to Hosty startled the assembled group and caused them to wonder why Oswald was directing such vehemence at Hosty and the FBI. The commission wanted to get the full story of the FBI's relationship with Oswald from Hosty when he testified on May 5.

■ The FBI Lies to the Commission

An eleven-year veteran with the FBI at the time of the assassination, Hosty had been in the Dallas office since 1953. Hosty told the commission that in March 1963 the FBI had what was called a "pending inactive case" on Marina Oswald because of her status as an immigrant from behind the Iron Curtain. He wanted to locate her for the purpose of interviewing her. At the time the bureau had closed its case involving Lee Harvey Oswald, but the FBI reopened it in late March when they discovered that Oswald was on the mailing list of the *Daily Worker*, a newspaper published in New York by the Communist Party USA since 1924. When the Oswalds moved to New Orleans in June 1963, the couple became the responsibility of the FBI office in that city. Hosty had no further connection with the Oswald investigations until October 1963, when the New Orleans office informed him that both Lee and Marina Oswald had left that city a few days earlier. Marina and her daughter departed in a station wagon with a Texas license plate driven by a Russian-speaking woman, and Oswald left a day later.[1]

Later in October, Hosty learned that Oswald had been in contact with the Soviet embassy in Mexico City and that the Oswalds were now residing in Irving, Texas. Hosty was now more interested in Oswald. He heard from a neighbor that Ruth Paine lived at the same address in Irving that he had for the Oswalds, that her husband Michael did not reside there, that a Russian-speaking woman had just given birth to a baby, and that the husband involved did not reside at this address. Hosty made some background inquiries about the Paines and confirmed that Michael worked at the Bell Helicopter Company and Ruth was a part-time Russian teacher at St. Marks School in Dallas.[2]

Hosty told the commission that he interviewed Ruth Paine for about twenty to twenty-five minutes on November 1. He described her as "cordial and friendly." She told him that Marina Oswald and her two daughters were living with her and that Lee Oswald was living in Dallas, but she did not know exactly where. She said Oswald worked at the Texas School Book Depository and they both looked up the address in her phone book. Hosty recalled that Ruth Paine was "a little bit reluctant" to give him Oswald's place of employment because she told him that Oswald "had alleged that the FBI had had him fired from every job he ever had." Hosty replied that this was not true, and that he wanted the place of employment "for the purpose of determining whether or not he was employed in a sensitive industry, and when I found out that he was working in a warehouse as a laborer, I realized this was not a sensitive industry."[3]

Ruth Paine told Hosty that she was willing to have Marina Oswald and her children live with her, but didn't want Lee Oswald residing there. He was allowed to visit, and he did so primarily on weekends. Near the end of the interview, Hosty said, Marina Oswald, who had been sleeping, entered the room and Ruth Paine identified Hosty as an FBI agent. According to Hosty,

> I could tell from her eyes and her expression that she became quite alarmed, quite upset. I had had previous experiences with people who came from Communist-controlled countries that they get excited when they see the police. They must think that we are like the Gestapo or something like that. She became quite alarmed, and, like I say, I knew that she just had a baby the week before. So I didn't want to leave her in that state, so rather than just walking out and leaving her and not saying anything to her, I told Mrs. Paine to relate to her in the Russian language that I was not there for the purpose of harming her, harassing her, and that it wasn't the job of the FBI to harm people. It was our job to protect people.

After Mrs. Paine spoke to Marina, she "seemed to calm down a little bit, and when I left she was smiling." Hosty continued in his testimony. "I left her in a relaxed mood. I didn't want to leave her alarmed and upset, a woman with a new baby." Before he left, Hosty gave Mrs. Paine his name and telephone number—the information that later found its way into Oswald's address book and generated the controversy between the commission and the FBI back in February. He was very certain that he did not leave either his address or his car license number—information that was also included in Oswald's address book.[4]

Hosty testified that he next saw Ruth Paine on November 5. She had said that she would attempt to learn where Lee Oswald was living, so Hosty dropped by to see if she had done so. She told him that Oswald had visited over the weekend, but she still hadn't managed to find out where he was living. She added that she considered Oswald "a very illogical person" and that he had mentioned over the weekend that he was a "Trotskyite communist." When asked by commission members if her reference to "Trotskyite communist" signified anything to him, Hosty responded: "Well, yes. The Socialist Workers party is the Trotskyite party in the United States, and they are supposedly the key element in the Fair Play for Cuba Committee . . ." So, Hosty testified, it "would follow" from Oswald's membership in the Fair Play for Cuba Committee that he would claim to be a Trotskyite. Hosty testified he was aware that Oswald had lied to a New Orleans–based FBI agent when he said that he had married a girl in Fort Worth. The FBI knew that he had married a Russian woman while he was in the Soviet Union.[5]

Hosty took no further action on the Oswald case before the assassination. He explained that he had between twenty-five and forty cases to handle at any one time, and he had satisfied his primary concern—that Oswald was not employed in a sensitive industry. So he told the commission that he felt he could afford to wait until the New Orleans office forwarded the relevant case files to him. "It was then my plan to interview Marina Oswald in detail concerning both herself and her husband's background." Only after that interview, Hosty said, would he make a decision what further steps, if any, would be needed.[6]

The commission members then moved to the crux of the matter: Did the FBI's information on Oswald at that time require alerting the Secret Service about him because of President Kennedy's impending trip to Dallas on November 22? When asked what his reaction was to learning that Oswald was the alleged assassin, Hosty replied: "Shock, complete surprise." He said: "I had no reason prior to this time to believe that he was capable or potentially an assassin of the President of the United States."[7]

Hosty then described his encounter with Lieutenant Revill when they both arrived at police headquarters in the early afternoon of November 22. Hosty testified he told Revill "that Lee Harvey Oswald had been arrested about an hour ago, that he was an employee of the Texas School Book Depository, and that he was the man who had defected to Russia and had returned to the United States in 1962." Hosty was then shown the letter dated April 27, from Hoover to the commission, enclosing the *Dallas Morning News* story of April 24 and Hosty's own affidavit. Hosty said he prepared the affidavit to "refute the story that appeared in the *Dallas Morning News* on April 24, 1964, to set the record straight as to what actually did take place in my conversation with Lieutenant Revill." Hosty testified:

> I want to state for the record at this time that I unequivocally deny ever having made the statement to Lieutenant Revill or to anyone else that, 'We knew Lee Harvey Oswald was capable of assassinating the President of the United States, we didn't dream he would do it.' I also want to state at this time that I made no statement to Lieutenant Revill or to any other individual at any time that I or anyone else in the FBI knew that Lee Harvey Oswald was capable of assassinating the President of the United States or possessed any potential for violence. Prior to the assassination of the President of the United States, I had no information indicating violence on the part of Lee Harvey Oswald.[8]

Hosty testified that he attended Oswald's interrogation at the department and that Oswald became very hostile when Hosty entered the room. According to Hosty, "He reacted to the fact that we were FBI, and he made the remark to me, 'Oh, so you are Hosty. I've heard about you.' He then started to cuss at us, and so forth, and I tried to talk to him to calm him down. The more I talked to him the worse he got, so I just stopped talking to him, just sat back in the corner and pretty soon he stopped ranting and raving." But, Hosty said, Oswald wasn't done ragging on the FBI. "He said, 'I am going to fix you FBI,' and he made some derogatory remarks about the Director and about FBI agents in general. ... He was highly excited. He was very surly, I think would be about the best way to describe him, very surly; and he was curt in his answers to us, snarled at us." When asked by McCloy whether Oswald had complained about Hosty abusing his wife, Hosty replied: "He made the statement, 'If you want to talk to me don't bother my wife. Come and see me.' He didn't say that I had abused his wife in any manner, and I hadn't. He did criticize me for talking to her. He said, 'Come talk to me if you want to talk to me.'"[9]

McCloy and Cooper pressed Hosty as to why he had not considered Oswald a candidate for referral to the Secret Service. They emphasized what

was known at the time by the FBI: Oswald was a defector; he had an association with the Fair Play for Cuba Committee; he had engaged in a demonstration
in New Orleans; he had lied to the FBI about his wife and the place of their
marriage; he had contacted the Soviet embassy in Mexico City; and he had
proclaimed himself to be a Trotskyite communist. Hosty firmly stated that
under the existing criteria Oswald had not qualified as a person who was capable of violence and had not given any indication that he "planned to take
some action against the safety" of the president.[cccxv]

Because Hosty's account of his conversation with Revill differed so dra-
matically from Revill's, the commission summoned Revill to testify on May
13. Revill told the commission that he had been a lieutenant in the Dallas police
force since 1958 and on November 22, 1963, was in charge of the criminal intelligence section. He had known Hosty since 1959, when Revill took charge
of the intelligence section. He said that on November 22 he and Hosty had arrived at the same time in the basement of the municipal building where the
Dallas police had their headquarters. He recalled:

> And Mr. Hosty ran over to me and he says, "Jack"—now as I recall these
> words—"a Communist killed President Kennedy." I said "What?" He said "Lee
> Oswald killed President Kennedy." I said "Who is Lee Oswald?" He said: "He
> is in our Communist file. We knew he was here in Dallas." At that time Hosty
> and I started walking off, and Brian [another Dallas policeman], as well as I
> recall, sort of stayed back, and as we got onto the elevator or just prior to getting
> on the elevator Mr. Hosty related that they had information that this man was
> capable of this, and at this I blew up at him, and I said, "Jim"—

Lee Rankin interrupted Revill to ask: "What did he say in regard to his
being capable?" Revill replied that Hosty said that

> "We had information that this man was capable"—
> "Of what?" Rankin asked.
> "Of committing the assassination."

When asked whether these were Hosty's exact words, Revill told the
commission he wanted to

> give him the benefit of the doubt; I might have misunderstood him. But I
> don't believe I did, because the part about him being in Dallas, and the fact

that he was a suspected Communist, I understand by the rules of the Attorney General they cannot tell us this, but the information about him being capable, I felt that we had taken a part in the security measures for Mr. Kennedy, and if such, if such information was available to another law enforcement agency, I felt they should have made it known to all of us, and I asked Hosty where he was going at that time.

Hosty told Revill that he was going up to the department's homicide and robbery bureau "to tell Captain Fritz the same thing." There's no evidence that Hosty repeated what Revill attributed to him to Fritz or anyone in the Dallas Police Department.[11]

Revill told the commission that he was sorry to give this testimony, saying that he and Hosty were friends "and this has hurt me that I have involved Hosty into this thing, because he is a good agent, he is one of the agents there that we can work with; that has been most cooperative in the past, and I worked with him just like he is one of us." Revill said that he immediately reported the details of his conversation with Hosty to Captain Gannaway, who instructed him to write a report about the conversation, which Gannaway told him he would give to Chief Curry. Revill said he prepared the report within an hour of this conversation.[12]

Revill had a copy with him when he testified. He stated that the original went to Curry, who later asked Revill to swear that the report was true and correct and he did so in April. Revill said he didn't know why his report had not previously been given to the commission, but acknowledged that he had hoped that the information would not get out for fear it would impair the existing good relations between the department and the FBI.[13]

Revill denied giving the report to the press. "This would have been the last thing I would have done," he said, adding that he didn't know who had. He noted that one of the stories about the report had quoted "the last paragraph of the report verbatim," from which he concluded that at least one reporter had an actual copy. But Revill did repudiate the part of the published stories claiming that Hosty had also told him that the FBI did not believe that Oswald would actually assassinate the president.[14]

Despite the conflicting statements of Hosty and Revill, the commission did not undertake any investigation in an effort to make an informed judgment which of these two witnesses to believe. The commission did ask Chief Curry to explain why a copy of Revill's report of his conversation with Hosty, which Revill had directed be placed in the official department file on Oswald, had not been provided to the commission before Curry's appearance to testify on April 22. Curry never provided a satisfactory explanation. The commission appears to have concluded that, having heard from the two participants in the conversation and determined that no one else heard the conversation, further inquiries were likely useless. In its report the commission summarized the testimony of both Hosty and Revill regarding the conversation, but expressed no view as to who was the more credible. This seemed reasonable at the time.[15]

Using Hosty's testimony and our review of the FBI files on Oswald, the commission was creating the record on which it would determine whether the FBI should have notified the Secret Service of Oswald's whereabouts in Dallas before the president's trip. In later testimony, Hoover supported Hosty's conclusion that "There was nothing up to the time of the assassination that gave any indication that this man was a dangerous character who might do harm to the President or to the Vice-President." On the other hand, the commission now was aware of the breadth of the information about Oswald possessed by the FBI's Dallas and New Orleans field offices, as had been stressed by the members in their questioning of Hosty. It turned out, however, that the FBI knew much more than it ever told the commission.[16]

As discussed previously, in December 1963 Hoover had ordered disciplinary actions against seventeen FBI agents for their failure to identify Oswald as a security risk who should have been reported to the Secret Service. Hosty was one of those disciplined for his failure to conduct further investigation of the Oswalds based on information in FBI files supplemented by what he learned from Ruth Paine in early November 1963. Disclosure of Hoover's own assessment of his bureau's performance to the commission would have enabled it to probe more critically the FBI's handling of the Oswalds before the assassination. The commission did not necessarily have to agree with Hoover whether the criteria then in effect required notification of the Secret Service, but his inexcusable dishonesty denied the commission the opportunity to reach its own conclusion based on all the relevant information.

Congressional inquiries after Hoover's death in 1972 revealed further evidence of the FBI's failure to be truthful with the commission. The Church Committee in 1976 examined the handling by the FBI of the Oswald security case. Sworn testimony from FBI agents and others demonstrated that the FBI failed to give the commission the administrative cover page of Special Agent John Fain's report on July 10, 1962, of his interview with Oswald after his return to the United States, which discussed Oswald's refusal to be polygraphed. The FBI also did not tell us that it learned on October 22 of Oswald's activities in Mexico

City and his contact at the Soviet embassy there with Vice Consul Valeriy Kostikov. The FBI's Soviet experts believed that Kostikov was an agent in the KGB department that carried out assassination and sabotage. Hosty, who was aware of this information, remained content to wait until the complete files arrived from New Orleans before he did anything further regarding Oswald.[17]

An even more significant revelation was the FBI's destruction of a critical preassassination document resulting from Hosty's interviews of Ruth Paine on November 1 and 5. An unidentified source informed the FBI in 1975 that Oswald had delivered a note to Hosty in November 1963 referring to these interviews. The Church Committee investigated and confirmed that Oswald visited the FBI field office in Dallas in November and left a note for Hosty. The note was no longer available because Hosty destroyed it right after the assassination.

The Church Committee developed conflicting evidence on two key issues: whether the note was threatening in nature and at whose instruction it was destroyed. On the first point, the FBI receptionist who received the note in an unsealed envelope from Oswald told the committee that it read as follows:

Let this be a warning. I will blow up the FBI and the Dallas Police Department if you don't stop bothering my wife. Signed—Lee Harvey Oswald.

Hosty testified before the committee that the note's wording was:

If you have anything you want to learn about me, come talk to me directly. If you don't cease bothering my wife, I will take appropriate action and report this to proper authorities.

Given what we knew about Oswald's character and the lack of self-interest on the part of the receptionist, it seems very likely that her recollection of the note's content is closer to the truth than Hosty's. Although efforts were made to impeach the credibility of the receptionist in subsequent proceedings, there seems to be no doubt that the note was definitely threatening.[18]

The note rested in Hosty's workbox until the day of the assassination, when his supervisor and Gordon Shanklin, the head of the FBI's Dallas field office, asked him about it. Hosty testified that he prepared a memorandum at Shanklin's request about the note and his recent interview of Marina Oswald at the Paine residence. He gave the memorandum to Shanklin on the evening of November 22. Before the Church Committee, Hosty testified that after Oswald's murder Shanklin told him to destroy both the note and the memo, and he did so. Shanklin, however, testified that he had no knowledge of the note until July 1975. The officials at FBI headquarters denied that they had any knowledge of the note or its destruction.[19]

If Hoover or other FBI officials in Washington had known about the destroyed note at the time of the Warren Commission's investigation, two conclusions seem likely. First, Hoover would have more severely disciplined Hosty and his superiors in the Dallas office and, second, the FBI would not have advised the commission of the note's existence. If the commission had been given all of the relevant information about the FBI's investigation of Oswald in 1964, including the Oswald note to Hosty, it could have conducted a more thorough investigation of the FBI's performance in handling the Oswald case, including detailed examination of the FBI receptionist and many of the agents who were disciplined by Hoover. The result would certainly have produced a more detailed and critical assessment of the FBI's failure to report Oswald to the Secret Service before the assassination. If Hosty had responded to the note (and the most recent information in his file about Oswald's activities) by interviewing Oswald before November 22, it is unlikely that Oswald would have assassinated President Kennedy.

Knowledge of the Hosty note might also have persuaded the commission to conclude that Revill, rather than Hosty, was telling the truth about their conversation on the afternoon of November 22. As Hosty approached Revill in the basement of the municipal building, he knew about the note that Oswald had left with his office some ten days earlier threatening violence if Hosty did not stop bothering his wife. Hosty told the commission that he was shocked and surprised when he heard that Oswald was the likely assassin. He probably was experiencing other feelings as well when he approached his friend Jack Revill in the basement—panic, fear, shame, and guilt all come to mind. In the midst of the chaos surrounding the assassination and his own complicated and intense emotional state, Hosty most likely blurted out the truth about his knowledge of Oswald to Revill without intending to do so and without realizing the full consequences of what he was saying. The American legal system assigns a high level of credibility to such "spontaneous declarations"—defined as "an excited utterance that is made without time for fabrication"—because of the special circumstances and human instincts that give rise to them.[20]

Burt Griffin has identified another important way in which knowledge of this note would have assisted the commission. He suggests that the commission's knowledge of this incident certainly would have supported the proposition that, at least about ten days before November 22, Oswald was unlikely to have been contemplating the assassination of the president. As Griffin has written: "A rational, calculating person considering an assassination would not want to subject himself to heightened scrutiny from the FBI by contacting the agency and leaving a caustic note for the individual assigned to watch him." This conclusion seems persuasive whether the individual was contemplating an attack on the president by himself or as part of a conspiracy.[21]

In 1975 the Department of Justice conducted an investigation of the destruction of the note. After interviewing the FBI officials with some knowledge of the incident, the criminal division concluded that Shanklin had committed perjury when he denied knowing about the note before 1975. Although the department considered prosecuting Shanklin, it decided not to proceed more than a decade after the event. In 2003, the new FBI building in Dallas was named the J. Gordon Shanklin Building.

■ Continued Work on the Report

While the FBI story was unfolding in early May, I was involved in the usual mix of duties—including a short visit with Katzenbach on May 4. I told him about my interview at his request of Buchanan, the Paris-based journalist who had just published his book. I also asked him whether he wanted someone else in the department to examine the commission's principal documents. I thought he might believe the department would be required to endorse the commission's report when it came out because of my presence on the staff. After "a moment's reflection," Katzenbach said that he did not want to see the report before its publication and that my position at the commission "would not prejudice the Department or the Attorney General so far as their response to the report was concerned."[22]

I can't imagine what prompted me to ask this question. His response was consistent with his view of the department's relationship with the commission from its inception—namely, that the department would not interfere in any way with the commission's investigation or conclusions. His comment that my commission role would not inhibit the department's (or the attorney general's) freedom to criticize the commission's report was neither comforting nor surprising. We all knew that the quality and public reception of the commission's report would mark our professional reputations for decades to come.

Al Goldberg, our historian, continued work on the report outline that had been approved by the commission at its April 30 meeting. Warren and Rankin wanted the report to have an appropriate historical context and it was Goldberg's responsibility to provide it. Goldberg thought that historical material of particular interest would include the role of the president, previous assassinations, and presidential protection over the years. He also wanted to have a narrative of the events leading to the president's visit to Dallas—the decision to make the trip, the president's arrival, advance publicity, and the planned visits to other Texas cities. He pointed out that the outline did not include any discussion of the conduct of the press and TV in the Dallas police headquarters from November 22 to 24. He thought that the relationship between the police and the press and the effect of the press on security arrangements were of considerable historical significance and should be assessed in the report.[23]

One of the most challenging issues raised by Goldberg was how to address the public reaction worldwide to the president's assassination. As Goldberg correctly observed, "It was this public reaction—disturbed, confused, suspicious, uncertain of the truth—that apparently helped President Johnson decide to appoint this Commission." He recommended that the report include a section "with particular reference to the suspicions, allegations, rumors, and theories that came into existence immediately after the event and have persisted until now." He thought that: "These public fears and rumors should be dispelled positively by considering and disposing of them rather than negatively by ignoring them. They are a part of the historical context of the event just as the century of myth-making since Lincoln's assassination is a part of that event. Failure of the Commission to destroy these myths while they are still in their infancy may permit them to persist as long as have the Lincoln myths."[24]

After Rankin and I discussed Goldberg's suggestions, Rankin asked him to start drafting sections dealing with the role of the president, previous assassinations, and presidential protection, using the materials prepared by Richard Mosk and the Secret Service on these subjects. We also asked him to draft a section discussing the role played by the press and TV in the Dallas police station, and to analyze newspaper reports and other media coverage of the assassination. Goldberg accepted the assignment in good humor, saying that he had "learned his lesson" and "would never write another memorandum."[25]

Rankin and I discussed whether the commission report should address right-wing extremism in the United States as a possible contributing factor to the assassination. I do not remember whether Rankin or I raised this subject, although I do recall discussing the general subject with him on more than one occasion. I had opposed any testimony from an official of the Birch Society, which continued to claim that the Soviet Union was responsible for the assassination. In addition to the fact that the Birch Society did not have any knowledge of facts relating to the assassination, I thought that calling as witnesses representatives of any right-wing group would be viewed as an effort by the commission to assign responsibility for the assassination, at least in part, to an atmosphere of extremism in Dallas. I considered this to be a particularly troublesome question and believed that the commission in its report "should not wander into this swamp unless it was absolutely essential."

I believe that these reservations were generally shared by other members of the staff, and also within the commission. Rankin recognized this problem and told Goldberg that he would like this to be handled without in any way suggesting that the climate in Dallas was more inclined toward extremist movements than any other metropolitan area of the United States. I did not think any of us knew enough about extreme political activity in any US city to make a judgment about Dallas. We certainly were aware of General Walker's right-wing activities, including his involvement in the attack on Adlai Stevenson in October 1963, and how much Oswald hated Walker. What we did not find was any personal involvement by Oswald with specific people and organizations in Dallas pursuing extremist goals, which might have motivated him to kill the president.[cccxxix]

In early May, Rankin was exhorting the lawyers to draft sections of the report in their areas. He had personally set a goal of May 20 for a draft of the entire report. I told him in mid-May that this was impossible and "that it was very unlikely that he would have a workable draft of the entire report for several weeks." By the end of May, we had only a few draft sections for the commission's review—a foreword, description of the events of November 22, and a brief history of presidential protection. We didn't yet have anything on Oswald or Ruby, and I remained pessimistic that we would see anything soon, based on recent meetings with Liebeler and Griffin. The senior lawyers working on these projects had less and less time to spend in Washington, and the junior lawyers were generating a flow of investigative requests to the FBI or other agencies seeking facts needed before shaping their conclusions.[28]

■ A Right-Wing Attack on the Staff's Integrity

By May, another issue that had been simmering below the surface for three months came abruptly into the open. The commission had asked the FBI in January to determine if its staff could receive security clearances, and the FBI probably dug a bit more assiduously into our backgrounds than they ordinarily did for temporary government employees.

Some time later, a few congressmen and others began raising questions about Norman Redlich's associations, including his membership in the Emergency Civil Liberties Council, which had criticized the work of the House Committee on Un-American Activities. Created in 1938, this congressional committee was charged with investigating alleged disloyalty and subversive activities on the part of private citizens, public employees, and organizations suspected of having communist ties. Although this committee (and its Senate counterpart) had labeled the Emergency Civil Liberties Council to be a "Communist-front" organization, the Justice Department had not included it on its list of such organizations. Beyond that organizational connection, Redlich had co-authored an article with someone who allegedly had "far-left" views. Critics seized on these facts to argue that Redlich never should have been hired by the commission.[29]

Rankin was worried about what the FBI was likely to report after finishing its full field investigation. Redlich was Rankin's friend, but more important, over these first four months Redlich had become an integral part of our operation. His commitment to high standards, his analytical skills, and excellent judgment were of enormous help to everyone. Rankin persuaded the commission members to withhold judgment until the FBI investigation was completed.

Rankin raised this subject with me on at least two occasions early in the commission's work. I told him that these associations had nothing to do with Redlich's character or his ability to contribute substantially to our work. But it seems in retrospect that Rankin was not as interested in my views on the subject, which were undoubtedly similar to his, as he was in determining whether any of my superiors at the Justice Department had expressed concerns about Redlich. I had not discussed the criticisms against Redlich with anyone at the department, and I had no intention of doing so. I was confident that Katzenbach and Miller would regard this as a matter for the commission to resolve—with the expectation that Warren was most unlikely to be swayed by the allegations against Redlich.[30]

The commission met on May 19 to consider the results of the FBI's investigation of its staff. The first issue wasn't about Redlich, but about Joe Ball. The FBI reported that Ball had been a member of the National Lawyers Guild many years earlier and had signed a petition criticizing the House Committee on Un-American Activities. The House Committee achieved considerable notoriety and influence in the late 1940s and early 1950s, but had declined significantly by the late 1950s when it was widely criticized for its unsupportable accusations of disloyalty. In 1959, the committee was denounced by former President Truman as the "most un-American thing in the country today."[31] Warren, who had known Ball for years, defended him, and without debate the commission approved his retention on the staff.

Now it was Redlich's turn. Rankin began the discussion by describing how he had met him as a result of teaching an evening course at the NYU Law School, where Redlich was on the faculty. He knew of Redlich's academic standing and his credentials from the Yale Law School, but said he had not known of his membership in the Emergency Civil Liberties Council when he hired him. He reported that the NYU faculty had written a letter testifying to Redlich's loyalty, competence, and integrity.[32]

Each of the first five commission members to speak (Russell, Boggs, Ford, Cooper, and Dulles) expressed serious reservations about Redlich's past associations and activities. They all praised Redlich's work on the staff and didn't doubt his loyalty to the United States. But each said Redlich should never have been hired because of his "extreme" views and the likelihood that his presence would taint the commission's report. Notwithstanding the decline in the House Committee's reputation, it was still active in the early 1960s and certainly (surprisingly to me) influenced the views of these commission members.[33]

Warren wasn't having it. Speaking last, which was his practice at meetings of the Supreme Court, he admonished his fellow members that we do not judge people by their views. He reminded them that lots of people had opposed the House Committee. He also said that he thought that Redlich and his family had already suffered because of the unanswered attacks on his loyalty. "I think that should we decide that if there is any question of his loyalty," Warren intoned, "that the least we could do would be to give him a trial, where he can defend himself, and where he can show that he is a good American citizen and is not disloyal. That is the American way of doing things."[34]

There were only two courses of action he told his commission colleagues: either accept Redlich as a loyal member of the staff or give him a hearing to answer the charge of disloyalty. He rejected out of hand the suggestion of letting him resign and depart along with a few other staff members who were returning to their law firms. "The idea of just dropping him now and letting him go off quietly would serve no purpose except to make a great many people despise us for not being willing to face an issue," Warren concluded.[35]

McCloy, who arrived at the meeting during Warren's remarks, threw his support to Redlich, although he couched his position as a matter of expediency rather than principle. The commission, he said, "would be better advised to carry on with him than to ask him to step down." Cooper observed that cutting Redlich loose now wouldn't spare the commission criticism in any case.

Redlich had been on the staff for five months and had already seen all the classified materials in the commission's possession. Rankin weighed in to agree with Warren's point that the staff would "feel deeply offended ... that one with whom they have worked so closely and so fraternally in this important work going on six months should be so unjustly accused."[36]

When the vote was finally taken, the commission unanimously agreed to approve Redlich's continued employment. There was some discussion off and on the record about what kind of statement the commission, or individual members, might make about this resolution of the matter. Both Ford and Boggs were under considerable pressure by some of their colleagues in the House of Representatives to take a tough stand regarding Redlich. Ford admitted as much three decades later, when he told then Senator Specter that his reservations about Redlich were prompted by three or four members of his Republican caucus— "extreme right-wing Republicans . . . who used to give me a hard time on the floor of the House" for employing "left wing people" on the commission.[37]

Rankin never discussed the commission's deliberations with me. Knowing him as well as I did at this time, I have no doubt that he and Warren had agreed in advance on a strategy (a mix of principle, expediency, and potential staff revolt) that was so successful in persuading the other members to do the right thing.

■ **The Dallas Reenactment Project Supports the Single-Bullet Theory**

One of the commission's critical decisions came in May, when, after lengthy discussion, it approved a reenactment of the assassination on-site in Dallas. This project, completed on May 24, was independent of anything the FBI, CIA, or Secret Service had done. Our lawyers designed, developed, and supervised every detail. The project was invaluable in supporting key commission conclusions.

The reenactment project arose initially from February discussions, when an informal group of our lawyers—Ball, Belin, Eisenberg, Redlich, and Specter—were studying the Zapruder film of the assassination. Both the FBI and the Secret Service concluded that there were three shots, all fired from the depository, and that the first shot hit the president, the second hit Connally, and the third killed Kennedy. Our lawyers thought those conclusions might be wrong, and were considering the possibility that the first bullet that hit the president also caused Connally's wounds. But this alternative hypothesis needed to be tested.

In March and early April, most of our lawyers were handling depositions in Dallas, New York, and New Orleans. By late April, we were ready to focus again on the course of the bullets and the cause of the injuries suffered by Kennedy and Connally. We all recognized that the commission members were likely to find the single-bullet theory "implausible" at best. Three decades later, Liebeler characterized the staff's challenge in these terms:

> Plausibility has no innate qualities. It depends on what alternative hypotheses are available. The question must always be: "Plausible as compared to what?" Explanations dubious at first look better if all other possibilities are even more unlikely. The staff opted for the single bullet theory because all the alternatives were more implausible. They opted for it, in other words, because they believed it best explained what actually happened.[38]

Redlich, Specter, and Belin had been considering how to reconstruct the path of the bullets fired from the depository. I had not been involved in this planning, but I fully supported the project. Now, five months into the investigation, I was troubled that we had still not come to a definite conclusion regarding the trajectory and points of impact of the bullets that was supported by the available medical, ballistics, and photographic evidence. To the extent possible, certainty on these issues was essential to our report's conclusions about the number and identity of the assassin(s).

On the afternoon of April 29, 1964, we met with FBI and Secret Service representatives to discuss work in Dallas to ascertain with greater precision the range of probabilities about the location and time of the three shots fired by the assassin. Rankin and I were joined by Belin, Redlich, Eisenberg, and Specter. Before the meeting, both the FBI and Secret Service had advised Warren and Rankin of "their reluctance to go down to Dallas with any sort of further reenactment of the assassination." Although the lawyers sponsoring this project were convinced that it was essential, Rankin was not fully persuaded.[39]

Before the meeting, Redlich presented Rankin with a strong statement of why the reenactment was necessary. "Our report presumably will state that the President was hit by the first bullet, Governor Connally by the second, and the President by the third and fatal bullet," Redlich wrote. He went on to say:

> The report will also conclude that the bullets were fired by one person located in the sixth floor southeast corner window of the TSBD building. As our investigation now stands, however, we have not shown that these

events could possibly have occurred in the manner suggested above. All we have is a reasonable hypothesis which appears to be supported by the medical evidence but which has not been checked out against the physical facts at the scene of the assassination.

Redlich explained the need to evaluate the medical testimony, Connally's testimony, and the Zapruder film against the facts on the ground. He pointed out some significant gaps, and possible inconsistencies, in the commission's record. Redlich said that he had always assumed that the report would indicate the approximate location of the vehicle at the time of each shot, but now he advised Rankin that such a conclusion cannot be reached "without establishing that we are describing an occurrence which is physically possible." He emphasized:

Our failure to do this will, in my opinion, place this Report in jeopardy since it is a certainty that others will examine the Zapruder films and raise the same questions which have been raised by our examination of the films. If we do not attempt to answer them with observable facts, others may answer them with facts which challenge our most basic assumptions, or with fanciful theories based on our unwillingness to test our assumptions by the investigatory methods available to us.

Redlich ended his memo with this cautionary reminder:

I should add that the facts which we now have in our possession, submitted to us in separate reports from the FBI and Secret Service, are totally incorrect and, if left uncorrected, will present a completely misleading picture. It may well be that this project should be undertaken by the FBI and Secret Service with our assistance instead of being done as a staff project. The important thing is that the project be undertaken expeditiously.

Redlich had delivered to Rankin one of the most important questions he had to address during his service as general counsel of the Warren Commission.[40]

The April 29 meeting lasted for more than two hours. Each time Rankin emphasized the inability of the commission to make "precise judgments" regarding the location and timing of the shots, FBI Inspector Malley "confirmed this and generally expressed skepticism about the entire project." At the end of the meeting Malley stated that the FBI "was opposed to such further investigation" but that if the commission were to request it, the bureau would consider doing the work. Rankin ended the meeting with a decision that the staff should draft such a letter to the FBI requesting the work to be done on the project, which Rankin would then present to Warren for his approval.[41]

Although his lawyers were passionately in favor of the reenactment project, Rankin had to consider why it might not be a good idea. I believed he was concerned by the opposition of the FBI and the Secret Service, the difficulty of explaining the need for the project to certain commission members, the possible critical reaction in Dallas, and the expense and delay involved in such an undertaking. It may also have been the case that he was simply looking for the best opportunity to get the chief justice to focus on the question. During the next week, we continued to urge Rankin to get Warren's approval for the reenactment. After the commission heard testimony on May 6, Rankin advised the staff that he had obtained Warren's approval. The chief justice instructed that Rankin was to personally supervise the project.[42]

After the necessary arrangements were made by the FBI and Secret Service, Rankin decided that he, Redlich, and Specter would oversee the reenactment project on May 24. I had great confidence in the commission lawyers who advocated and developed this project. To the critics who later complained that the commission's overall investigation was constrained by its excessive dependence on the FBI, the commission's defenders have many persuasive responses. But the Dallas reenactment provides a singular and dramatic response; it emerged solely from the commission staff and was strongly opposed by the FBI and the Secret Service until the commission made clear that the project was necessary. FBI officials were well aware by this time that the bureau's initial reports regarding the assassination were in error on some significant issues, and the proposed reenactment had the potential to expose those errors in graphic detail.

Rankin wrote the FBI asking for its assessment on three aspects of the reenactment: (1) probable time range within which the first two shots occurred, (2) the timing of the third shot and the location of the car at that time, and (3) plotting trajectories from the railroad overpass.[43]

The first line of inquiry started with the estimate that Connally was shot sometime between frames 230 and 240 of the Zapruder film. This determination was based on his testimony, the medical testimony regarding the nature of his wounds, and the opinions of those lawyers who had most carefully examined the film. Both Connally and his wife believed that he was hit by the second shot. Acknowledging that it was impossible to determine "the exact point at which the first two shots were fired," Rankin wanted "to determine whether it was possible for a person located in the sixth floor southeast corner window of the TSBD building to fire two shots at the Presidential car, the second of which occurred no later than frame 240." The staff lawyers had planned the reenactment in great detail, involving the placement of the vehicle, and the taking of photographs (including some from the Zapruder camera, which was now in the commission's possession) from the road to fix the vehicle's location on the Zapruder film and from the assassination window. Their goal was to demonstrate when the assassin had a clear view of the vehicle and when his view was obscured by the large oak tree in full foliage that stood between the depository and Elm Street. They also wanted to determine whether a gunman could fire Oswald's rifle twice in 2.25 seconds.

The second and third lines of inquiry were not as complicated. The timing of the third shot was fixed at particular frames of the Zapruder and two other available films. The goal was to identify the location of the president's vehicle at that moment. To do that, the investigators planned to place a vehicle at the approximate location corresponding to these films, and to take photographs from the three places where the moviemakers were when they filmed the assassination so as to establish the accuracy of the location of the vehicle when the third shot was fired. Finally, the investigators planned to explore whether a second assassin could have fired bullets from either end of the overpass that could have reached the rear seat of the presidential vehicle without hitting the windshield. This inquiry required accurate and precise determination of the location of the car at the moment of each shot. At Rankin's request, the Secret Service had furnished us with photographs, surveys, and measurements, which we had used in our examination of the films. We sent these along to the FBI for use in the reenactment.[44]

On May 24, everyone involved in the reenactment was assembled in Dallas. Because the presidential limousine was not available, the Secret Service follow-up car, similar in design, was used. Two FBI agents with approximately the same physical characteristics as Kennedy and Connally assumed the positions in the car that their real-life counterparts had on November 22. Each had a mark on his back where a bullet had hit Kennedy or Connally. On the sixth floor of the depository building, the conditions present on November 22 were replicated as exactly as possible. The assassination rifle used by Oswald—we had use of the actual one—had a camera mounted on it that recorded the view as seen by the shooter. The three cameras that had photographed portions of the motorcade were available so that their locations on November 22 could be determined more precisely.

FBI special agent Robert Frazier sat at the window of the depository with Oswald's rifle pointed out the window. At a signal, the substitute limousine with its two simulated victims set out on the precise route taken six months earlier by the original, down Houston Street and left on Elm Street, at the same speed the driver had maintained for Kennedy's motorcade. Frazier drew a bead on the X mark on the back of the stand-in for President Kennedy. As the car moved along, Frazier, looking down the telescopic sight on the rifle, could see the two men "both in direct alignment" with "the Governor . . . immediately behind the President in the field of view."

That alignment proved the plausibility of the single-bullet theory, which sent ripples of excitement from Dealey Plaza back to Washington, where we received their calls. Everyone understood immediately the impact of the reenactment. The bullet that passed through the president then either struck the automobile or someone else in the car. But there was no damage in the car that could have resulted from a bullet exiting Kennedy at its known velocity. If the bullet with that velocity had hit the car it would have penetrated any other metal or upholstery surface of the automobile. But nothing like that was found.[47]

Where that bullet had gone was into Connally. And it wasn't simply the alignment of the two victims that strongly suggested it. The angle of the bullet's trajectory was also consistent with the bullet exiting Kennedy's neck and striking Connally's back.[48]

Although the reenactment had produced convincing evidence, the commission recognized that the "alignment of the points of entry was only indicative and not conclusive that one bullet hit both men." Additional experiments conducted by the Army Wound Ballistics Branch gave us more evidence that the same bullet passed through both Kennedy and Connally. These experiments replicated Connally's wounds and supported the proposition that those wounds would have been different (and more serious) if the bullet had not already hit and exited the president. Based on the medical evidence of the wounds of the two men and the wound ballistic tests, the experts from the Army Wound Ballistics Branch testified that it was probable that the same bullet struck both.[49]

The reenactment also enabled us to approximate the point at which the president was struck by that bullet—as reflected in part by his reaction recorded on the Zapruder film.

Neither the reenactment nor other evidence before the commission enabled it to conclude whether it was the first or the second shot that hit both men.[50]

The sense of accomplishment after the reenactment project buoyed our staff greatly. We had all been through five months of chasing down detail after detail, questioning witness after witness, and writing memo after memo. We now had some solid results that supported much of what we were drawing out of the sworn testimony.

Not surprisingly, the appearance of a presidential-looking vehicle and numerous law enforcement officials in Dealey Plaza did not go unnoticed. The following week KRLD-TV in Dallas reported on the conclusions from the reenactment based on the proverbial "highly placed source close to the Warren Commission." Published in newspapers across the country, the report stated that the reenactment had demonstrated that the previous thinking about the three shots was incorrect and that the commission now believed that the first shot hit both the president and Connally, the second shot fatally wounded the president, and the third shot missed completely. The story also reported that unidentified medical testimony to be discussed in the commission's report "will show that chances for the President's recovery from the first wound would have been excellent" if the shot had struck Kennedy a fraction of an inch lower. The suggestion in the KRLD-TV report that the commission's report would be released "in a few weeks" came as news to all of us.[51]

■ Presidential Protection Still a Problem

Two key witnesses from the Secret Service testified in late April: Robert Bouck, the agent in charge of the Protective Research Section, and Winston Lawson, the agent who did the advance planning for the president's trip to Dallas. These two witnesses were the best equipped to describe in detail how the Secret Service performed critical functions on the president's trip, and the commission members actively questioned them. They were accompanied by the Treasury Department's deputy general counsel, Fred Smith, who intervened occasionally to ensure that these agents did not answer questions (or volunteer information) about proposed changes in the service's policies and practices.

Bouck explained that the Protective Research Section had many functions other than the assessment of information regarding people who might threaten the president or vice president. When Bouck testified that he had only five agents processing threat information and a total of twelve agents in his section, McCloy was quick to express doubt that he had enough people to do the job. Bouck said that in the two years before the assassination the service had investigated 1,372 potential threats (another 7,337 did not meet the service's criteria). Bouck said that the Secret Service's criterion for determining whether anyone was a potential danger to the president "is broad in general. It consists of desiring any information that would indicate any degree of harm or potential harm to the President, either at the present time or in the future." He added that the Secret Service had not developed any more specific guidance about applying this broad criterion and did not know how the FBI or other federal agencies decided what information to provide his agency.[52]

The commission members questioned whether Oswald should have been referred to the Secret Service based on the derogatory information about him possessed by several federal agencies. Although Bouck was not ready to indict the FBI for its failure to tell his agency about Oswald, he stressed—in addition to the general criterion—the importance of access to the president, or an unusual vantage point (as in the depository building), which would have warranted precautionary action by the Secret Service.[53]

Bouck was followed by Winston Lawson, the agent responsible for advance work on Kennedy's trip. Lawson had joined the Secret Service in 1959, in the Syracuse office. He testified that the Protective Research Section had informed him that there were no individuals in its files who required his attention. He explained that the agent in charge of the local Secret Service office played a major role in assisting the advance agent, especially in consulting local law enforcement officials about their involvement in an upcoming visit by the president. It was Lawson's responsibility to choose the motorcade route and, after consulting local and federal officials, he chose the most expeditious way to the Trade Mart, where Kennedy was to speak at a luncheon. The motorcade route initially proposed by Lawson and Sorrels on November 14 was approved without change by local police officials and published in the November 19 newspapers. Lawson also described his discussions with the local police about their role, which he defined as principally to control the traffic and prevent spectators from interfering with the motorcade.[54]

Commission members were keen to hear exactly what advance precautions had been taken regarding possible threats along the motorcade route. Lawson told the commission that his agency had been aware of the demonstration against Ambassador Stevenson a few weeks before the president's visit. He obtained photographs from the Dallas police department of some of the demonstrators, which were to be used by Secret Service agents and local police officers in screening persons who would attend the Trade Mart luncheon.[55]

In response to Ford's question, Lawson said local police had the responsibility to check the windows and the crowd, but that the Secret Service agents in the motorcade also had that duty. He said he had discussed this with the Dallas Police Department before the motorcade but, in response to another question from Ford, said he had not followed up to see if these instructions were put in writing for the officers accompanying the motorcade.[56]

When McCloy questioned whether the Secret Service agents in the motorcade could be relied upon to observe carefully all the windows in the buildings passed by the motorcade, Lawson conceded the difficulty of the assignment. "[A]gents," he said, "are supposed to watch as they go along." Lawson also said that no arrangements had been made to inspect buildings along the route and that no list of specific responsibilities for the local police had been provided by the Secret Service. On this last point, Ford's comment suggested a future commission recommendation:

> But I would think for every Presidential visit there would be certain mandatory things that would have to be done, areas of responsibility of federal officials, areas of responsibility for local officials. . . .
>
> Such a memorandum or checklist I should think would be helpful in defining the areas of responsibility, being certain that there is no misunderstanding as to whose responsibility it is for A, B, C, or D operations.

Lawson had little choice but to say, "I agree."[57]

The serious deficiencies confirmed by this testimony had a decided impact on the commission members. They were even more insistent that their report had to recommend improvements in presidential protection because of the obvious failures in Dallas. It also whetted their desire to get their hands on the still-withheld Rowley report, which they understood contained recommendations from Rowley to Secretary Dillon of changes in Secret Service policies and practices resulting from the assassination. At their April 30 meeting, the commission members decided to go further into the presidential protection area than had been previously contemplated by the chief justice. They decided to request the Rowley study and other studies under way, with the understanding that these materials would be made available only to Rankin—not to the commission members themselves or other staff. In his letter to Dillon implementing these commission decisions, Rankin also assured him that the commission would not publish any information furnished by Treasury without that department's approval.[58]

Stern had already obtained considerable information about the supervision of the Secret Service within Treasury, preventive intelligence, Treasury's liaison with other intelligence and law enforcement agencies, Secret Service procedures and resources, manpower assistance from other agencies, and improved protective measures. He believed that Treasury had receded from its original position that nothing should be published by the commission regarding presidential protection. Based on his conversations with Carswell, Stern told us that the Rowley report and other studies might be available to the commission, although it was unclear whether Treasury would still insist that presidential approval was required. During the past few months, Stern had been doing what he always did very well—to look for some reasonable basis on which the parties to a dispute could find middle ground.[59]

Unfortunately, Secretary Dillon took a different course. Shortly after receiving Rankin's most recent letter, Dillon advised us that President Johnson had instructed him not to supply the requested material to the commission until the president had discussed the matter with the commission. I never heard who in the White House might have participated in this decision by the president or whether the president (or someone on his behalf) consulted with the chief justice or Rankin regarding the commission's purpose in seeking to review such materials. In light of Warren's strongly held view that the president should not be involved in any aspect of the commission's deliberations, I concluded at the time that Dillon's success in securing the president's endorsement of Treasury's position effectively barred any further commission inquiries into Treasury's plans for improving the Secret Service.[60]

In light of these developments, Rankin put the issue back before the commission on May 14. He reviewed the staff's efforts to negotiate a solution with Treasury, and acknowledged that the executive order establishing the commission did not specifically instruct it to review arrangements for presidential protection. He argued, however, that there were good reasons for supporting a broader construction of the executive order. The commission's analysis of presidential protection arrangements might lead to constructive suggestions that could help avoid another assassination. The commission, he observed, had the political clout to get those improvements implemented. Noting the serious lapses the commission had already discovered, he concluded that he did "not believe the Commission could conscientiously remain silent."[61]

If the additional material requested (including the Rowley report) was provided, and Rowley testified, Rankin believed that the commission would be equipped to make significant recommendations. Even if the commission did not propose recommendations, Rankin emphasized that the commission could perform an important public service by identifying questions about the Secret Service and recommending that some other institution undertake an authoritative examination of its policies and practices. The commission deferred any further debate on this subject until after they heard from Chief Rowley.[62]

■ **Integrating the Work of Commission and Staff**

The commission members worked harder in May. As the staff prepared drafts reflecting their investigative work, Warren and Rankin wanted the members to assess the drafts promptly and comment on the report's ultimate content, tone, and recommendations. The flow of paperwork from the staff to the commission was primarily my responsibility. Commission members in May were getting relatively noncontroversial sections of the report, such as the proposed foreword and memoranda reflecting the staff's research and analysis on issues that might be discussed in the report. So long as the drafts were readable and useful, I did not spend any time editing them. Rankin's objectives, which I fully shared, were to maintain pressure on the staff to produce drafts based on their current investigative results and to make certain that the commission had as much to read as we could generate.

Rankin had decided early in April that the commission needed to be informed of the evidence being developed by the staff in their depositions, so that the members could suggest further lines of inquiry and be better equipped to evaluate draft sections of the report. Several lawyers complained about Rankin's directive to prepare summaries of their depositions. They thought that the summaries were unnecessary because the commission would have access to the full transcripts and supporting exhibits when they reviewed draft sections of the report. Redlich and I shared these views. But Rankin was adamant on this point. As a result, I spent two days in early May assembling the summaries of deposition testimony prepared by our lawyers and incorporating them into a memo for the commission members. Rankin also asked me to revise the introductory chapter of the report dealing with the formation and operation of the commission and incorporate some of the material contained in a draft section of the report apparently written by the chief justice, although Rankin "did not want this known."[63]

The memorandum summarizing the depositions went to the commission on May 12. Rankin told the members that this "is just a brief statement regarding each witness" and offered to provide the full testimony of any witness if any member wanted that. The fifty-two page memorandum listed the 288 witnesses deposed by the staff through May 7. Every one of these depositions required long hours of preparation—reading documents, consulting the testimony of other witnesses, assessing expert opinions and physical evidence—so that the questions put to the witness would seek to elicit everything the witness knew pertinent to our investigation. The summaries of the testimony were succinct, but provided the commission members with what we hoped was a useful overview of the investigation to date.[64]

Rankin also gave the members a list of tape recordings of various radio and television programs that the commission had acquired. We provided a tape recorder in the commission hearing room for use by the members and staff. Sam Stern had alerted Rankin in late March about the need to organize a commission effort to obtain and examine the tapes of television and radio programs broadcast in the days following the assassination. He reported that the Secret Service at his request had made the necessary inquiries in Dallas and had provided a list of the materials available in Dallas and the cost of reproducing them. Stern also advised Rankin that the Library of Congress had formally requested all tapes from the networks soon after the assassination and that the Kennedy Library had a parallel effort under way.[65]

Later in the month, our historian emphasized the importance of these tapes to the commission's investigation. Al Goldberg pointed out that these materials represent an important primary source for what happened during November 22, 23, and 24. He urged that these sources should be exploited to the fullest extent possible and, based on his own viewing, suggested a few examples where the tapes might be used in verifying certain allegations involving Ruby's activities at the police station or elsewhere. Looking to the future, he warned that "these sources will undoubtedly be used in the preparation of future books and TV-documentation, and if they reveal new or substantiating information that we also could have found, it would be most embarrassing for the Commission."[66]

Some of the most important witnesses were still to come. The directors of the FBI and the CIA were scheduled to appear on May 14. Jacqueline Kennedy and Robert Kennedy were still on the list of possible witnesses, as well as Chief Rowley of the Secret Service and experts from the FBI who could discuss the results of the Dallas reenactment. We were still considering the Russian defector Nosenko and Jack Ruby as possible witnesses, although we knew that both raised special problems. I did not believe that the commission wanted to hear testimony from Nosenko, based on the CIA's current disinclination to vouch for his credibility. As for Ruby, we did not know if his lawyers would allow him to testify.

At this point, we had about forty witnesses remaining to be deposed by staff lawyers. Six of the forty witnesses were already scheduled—four in Dallas to be deposed by Joe Ball and two in Chicago to be taken by David Belin.[67] The remaining thirty-six potential witnesses were on the list because of some connection to Oswald's background and activities before November 22, his trip to Mexico, or to Ruby's background and activities during the period November 22–24. We also wanted Abraham Zapruder to testify about his filming of the presidential motorcade on November 22.[68]

Before the commission decided whether or not to ask Jacqueline Kennedy to testify, we wanted to get a clearer sense of what her potential testimony might offer. An unexpected opportunity to pursue this question arose when Rankin and I were asked by the attorney general's secretary to meet with William Manchester, the author retained by the Kennedy family to write the "authorized" book of the assassination.

In 1962, Manchester had written an admiring book about John Kennedy entitled *Portrait of a President*. He had interviewed the president on several occasions in writing that book and enjoyed the experience. Both men were ex-servicemen, with families in Massachusetts, and had World War II experiences in the Pacific. Manchester later wrote that the president "was brighter than I was, braver, better-read, handsomer, wittier, and more incisive. The only thing I could do better was write."[69]

Manchester and I had lunch together before his afternoon appointment with Rankin. He impressed me as a quiet, competent, and thorough writer. We discussed at great length the scope of his responsibilities and the extent to which they overlapped the work of the commission. He emphasized that his interest went far beyond the events in Dallas and that he had just begun work on that particular phase of his assignment. He told me that he had met with high officials in Washington about the assassination and the following few days when the control of government transferred from President Kennedy to President Johnson. "Without divulging any details he indicated that the feelings of many people ran very high regarding some other people and as a result he did not feel free to publish ever some of the information which he now had recorded." One of these interviewees was Jacqueline Kennedy, who, during the course of his lengthy interviews, "made a variety of very frank accounts about people in the course of her recollection." Substantively, he said, "she really had very little to contribute." He told me that he could not publish his work until five years from the date of the assassination unless Mrs. Kennedy and she alone allowed him to publish at an earlier date.[70]

In the later discussion with Rankin, it became clear that both Rankin and Manchester had concerns about his relationship with the commission that had to be clarified. Manchester, for example, had the impression from a conversation with the chief justice that he might be asked to review the work of the commission to determine whether it satisfied the Kennedy family. Rankin and I assured him that this would not be appropriate. Rankin, on the other hand, was concerned that Manchester might seek access to all our investigative materials before our report was published. Manchester told us that he was not seeking immediate access to our materials and was content to wait until we had completed our assignment.[71]

Although I spoke to Manchester on a few occasions after this initial meeting, he pursued his research independently of the commission. His book *The Death of a President* was published in April 1967 "after more than a year of bitter, relentless, headline-making controversy over the manuscript [which] nearly destroyed its author and pitted him against two of the most popular and charismatic people in the nation: the slain president's beautiful grieving widow, Jacqueline Kennedy, and his brother Robert F. Kennedy." Manchester refused to make all the deletions in his book desired by Mrs. Kennedy, whose ten hours of recorded interviews with him were full of intimate details and commentary that she did not wish to share with the public. The litigation was eventually settled with compromises by both sides and an agreement that her full interviews would not be disclosed until 2067—one hundred years after the book's publication.[72]

■ The Investigation Continues

One of my primary goals in May was to start wrapping up the investigative work and highlighting what remained. Meanwhile, the three IRS agents completed their assignments with painstaking care. Edward A. Conroy and John J. O'Brien finished the task of reviewing all the investigative reports received by the commission and preparing a chronology of the activities of Oswald, Ruby, and other principal figures in the investigation. Philip Barson completed an extensive memorandum reporting on Oswald's income and expenditures from his return to the United States on June 13, 1962, until the day of the assassination.

During May, Slawson followed up on several aspects of Oswald's trip to Mexico. At his request, Rankin asked the State Department to obtain affidavits or sworn testimony from Mr. and Mrs. John B. McFarland of Liverpool, England, before an official of the US Consular Service. In an earlier interview, the McFarlands said they had traveled to Mexico in September 1963 and that a man later identified as Oswald got on their bus at Houston in the early morning of September 26. Oswald told them that he was the secretary of the Fair Play for Cuba Committee in New Orleans and that he was traveling to Mexico City so that he could go from there to Cuba to meet Castro. In his letter Rankin suggested several questions that might be asked of the McFarlands, including the nature of Oswald's clothing, the number of suitcases he was carrying, and names or places in Mexico that Oswald might have mentioned.[73]

The commission had not yet received the official report of the Mexican government on its investigation of Oswald's activities in Mexico City, so Rankin sent a follow-up letter to legal adviser Abram Chayes at the State Department. Echevarria had assured us that he could deliver the report to us within forty-eight hours after the request was made, but here we were four weeks later, and still no report. Rankin asked State to ascertain the status of the request and, if possible, to quickly obtain the promised report from the Mexicans.[74]

The speed with which Oswald obtained his passport from State in June 1963 warranted further investigation by the FBI. The record showed that Oswald had applied on June 24 for a passport at the New Orleans Passport Office and it was issued one day later. State reported that the authority to issue passports, at least from the New Orleans office, was routinely granted by Washington approximately twenty-four hours after the application was filed. Slawson prepared a letter for the FBI asking that an investigation be undertaken to test the accuracy of this information, including the review by the bureau of a random sampling of passport applications from the New Orleans office between the dates of June 17 and July 1, 1963, to determine how long it took for the necessary authorization to reach the New Orleans office.[75]

Coleman and Slawson also examined the State Department's report that the initials "NO" found on Oswald's passport application were routinely placed on all applications from the New Orleans office. Rather than request the FBI to conduct this inquiry, Slawson decided to visit the State Department. On May 20, without advance warning, Slawson showed up at the passport office accompanied by Richard Frank, a State Department lawyer assisting the commission. Slawson looked at the telegrams that had arrived from the New Orleans office dproximately fifty to sixty telegrams examined had the letters "NO" written on them in red pencil, which appeared approximately two-thirds of the way down the page on the right-hand side, the same place the letters appeared on the message referring to Oswald.[76]

By the end of May, nothing further had been done to obtain information from the Cuban government about its response to Oswald's visit to its Mexico

City embassy. Although I do not recall what prompted this delay, it may be that Coleman, Slawson, and I might have dropped the ball and not informed Rankin that our strategy involved a possible letter from Warren to the Swiss government asking for its assistance in making a request on our behalf to the Cubans. We were waiting for advice from State whether this approach was acceptable.[77]

Slawson later recalled that Warren didn't want to make such a request of the Cuban government because "he did not want to rely upon any information from a government which was itself one of the principal suspects." Slawson disagreed:

> The CIA and I nevertheless came to the conclusion that any information that we could get we ought to get. We would worry about trying to authenticate it after we got it. As I told you, I simply disobeyed orders and went ahead and made the request through the State Department—it had to come from Dean Rusk, I remember we got his signature—to the Swiss Government and we got the information. Then of course I had to tell the Chief Justice that we got it and I pretended that I had misunderstood his previous statement. I think that is the only time I disobeyed orders.

When the information did arrive from Cuba, Slawson discussed the issue of authentication with Ray Rocca of the CIA. Rocca asked Slawson whether he wanted the CIA to authenticate the Cuban documents through a "top-secret" method that involved some risks. Slawson authorized the CIA to proceed and Rocca subsequently advised him that the Cuban documents dealing with Oswald's request for a visa were what they purported to be.[78]

On May 14, I reviewed a memo from the Hubert/Griffin team regarding additional investigation in the Ruby area. I disagreed with many of their suggestions, which resulted in a very spirited discussion with Griffin in the morning and Hubert in the afternoon. I didn't lack respect for Hubert or Griffin. I admired them both for their tenacity in pursuing the investigation relating to Ruby. They were determined to examine every contact Ruby made before the Oswald murder to see if we could detect any signs of conspiracy. They were in complete command of the facts in their area, gave no ground in debate, and almost always succeeded in getting what they wanted. But Griffin and Hubert didn't believe they had adequate help in achieving our shared goal of a complete and thoughtful investigation. It was my job to solve the problem.[79]

When I read their memo, I was initially troubled by three aspects. First,

I had hoped that by now we would be near the end of the Ruby investigation. Back in February and March, Charlie Shaffer (my Justice Department colleague) and I had reviewed certain investigative requests made by the Hubert/Griffin team and had advised Rankin that they seemed excessively broad in scope. I did not recall, however, to what extent (if any) these earlier requests had been modified before being sent to the FBI. I would have appreciated some warning from them in April that they would be seeking Rankin's approval of further investigation. When I raised this concern, Hubert and Griffin stated that their earlier memoranda had outlined the scope of the necessary investigation and that their new memo simply reaffirmed their early judgment.[80]

My second problem was their definition of the assignment. They wanted to answer three questions: Why did Ruby kill Oswald? Was Ruby associated with the assassin of President Kennedy? Did Ruby have any confederates in the murder of Oswald? But in their memo, Hubert and Griffin said that "although the evidence gathered so far does not clearly show a conspiratorial link between Ruby and Oswald, or between Ruby and others, *the evidence also does not clearly exclude the possibilities* [emphasis added] that (a) Ruby was indirectly linked through others to Oswald; (b) Ruby killed Oswald, because of fear; or (c) Ruby killed Oswald at the suggestion of others."

I had no objections to the questions posed, but their view that the evidence in the commission's possession had to "clearly exclude" any and all possibilities struck me then and now as unreasonable and unachievable. I said so. Ironically, the next time I saw something like this "clearly exclude" standard was in the final report of the House Select Committee in 1979, which used the equally unacceptable phrase "evidence does not preclude," in its misguided denunciation of our work.

Either because they agreed with me on the merits, or to placate me, Hubert and Griffin produced a second version of the May 14 memo, in which the offending sentence was modified to read that "evidence should be secured, if possible, to affirmatively exclude [the same three possibilities]." Either version of the investigative goal, of course, would support an aggressive investigation of leads bearing on these questions. But the second formulation suggested that, at some point, the investigation of these (or similar) questions would permit reasoned judgments as to whether such conspiratorial relationships existed even if they had not been "clearly excluded." The question of "what is enough" is raised regularly in the practice of law, and it was becoming of paramount importance to the commission as our staff moved from the investigative stage to drafting the report.[81]

My third problem was their vigorous complaint that Rankin had focused staff resources on investigating Oswald while neglecting the Ruby area. They said, "Depositions have been taken from less than one-seventh of the persons who are known to have talked to or seen Ruby on November 22 and 23. Had such an omission occurred in connection with the Oswald investigation, we believe the Commission would consider the work of the staff inadequate both by investigative and historical standards." This paragraph was deleted from the second version of their May 14 memo.[82]

Once we had discussed these issues, however, we needed to move forward. Hubert and Griffin wanted further investigation on seven subjects that illustrate just how complicated it is to try to prove another negative—Ruby was not part of a conspiracy in killing Oswald:

1. Although the FBI had thoroughly investigated Ruby's nightclub operations, it did not appear to have explored in detail his other business or social activities.

2. Ruby was a person who looked for moneymaking activities and his promotion of a device known as a "twist board" had not been investigated fully to see if it was a front for an illegal enterprise.[82]

3. Ruby had long been close to people pursuing illegal activities and a reasonable possibility existed that he maintained a close interest in Cuban affairs to the extent necessary to participate in gun sales or smuggling.

4. Bits of evidence linking Ruby to others who may have been interested in Cuban affairs had not been pursued.

5. Although Ruby did not witness the motorcade, he may have had a prior interest in the president's visit as suggested by the two newspapers dated November 20, 1963, found in his automobile.

6. Neither Oswald's Cuban interests in Dallas nor Ruby's Cuban activities had been explored adequately, in particular possible links through Earlene Roberts, manager of the rooming house where Oswald lived.

7. Background checks had not been made on possible co-conspirators with whom Ruby made, or attempted to make, contacts on November 22 and 23.[84]

Hubert and Griffin said, "In short, we believe that the possibility exists, based on evidence already available, that Ruby was involved in illegal dealings with Cuban elements who might have had contact with Oswald. The existence of such dealings can only be surmised since the present investigation has not focused on that area."[85]

Hubert and Griffin worried about other deficiencies in the Ruby investigation. They did not think they had a sufficient understanding of who Jack Ruby was and what motivated him. They thought that substantial periods in Ruby's daily routine from September 26 to November 22 had not been accounted for; and they estimated that forty-six people who saw Ruby from November 22 to November 24 had not been questioned by commission lawyers, although there were FBI reports of interviews with them. People who had been interviewed because of known associations with Ruby generally had not been investigated themselves so that their truthfulness could be evaluated. Much of our knowledge of Ruby had come from his friends, but no investigations had been undertaken to corroborate their information.[86]

Hubert and Griffin persuaded me that these matters needed to be investigated. I suggested that the broader requests not directly related to these aspects of the investigation be deferred, and they agreed. As a result of these discussions, over a ten-day period, Rankin sent to the FBI numerous specific requests for investigation addressed to the areas of concern identified by Hubert and Griffin. It ranged from such minutiae as an effort to determine why the November 20 newspaper of one J. E. Bradshaw was found in Ruby's car on November 24 to a more extensive review of long-distance telephone calls of a list of persons who may have had contact with Ruby during recent months based on information found in Ruby's possession or disclosed in previous FBI reports. It is to the credit of Hubert and Griffin's thoroughness and tenacity that once we had the results from the FBI in response to these (and later) requests, we were able to shape our conclusions about Ruby with more precision and a higher level of confidence.[87]

At Rankin's request, Hubert took the depositions of seven witnesses in Dallas on May 28 and May 29. He also took three depositions in Washington during early June of two brothers of Jack Ruby (Hyman Rubenstein and Earl Ruby) and Nancy Perrin, who had been employed by Ruby for a few months in 1961 and whose previous husband, Robert Perrin, had had some kind of altercation with Ruby. This was a very substantial load of new work for Hubert in light of his commitment to return to his law firm by June 8.[88]

Both Rankin and I hoped that these investigative efforts would produce valuable information. There was no question that both Hubert and Griffin had worked very hard and had produced good results. I now recognized that we had earlier underestimated the need of the Ruby team to cover more ground than any of the other five areas of the commission's investigation. But of equal importance, we wanted Hubert and Griffin to be satisfied that Rankin supported the investigative effort that they thought was necessary. The commission depended on Rankin, and he depended on the rest of us to be fully committed to the commission's work so that our report would have the unanimous support of the staff. The events of June would test that desired unity more than we could have expected.

CHAPTER 7

JUNE 1964: CRUCIAL WITNESSES

■

O N MONDAY, JUNE 1, THE *NEW YORK TIMES* CARRIED A FRONT PAGE STORY
on our investigation, the conclusions reached, and a projected publication date of our report by the end of June. Relying on a "Commission spokesman," the article reported that the commission would conclude that
there was no credible evidence of any conspiracy. The reporter—Anthony
Lewis—described the commission as "aware and concerned about the foreign
skepticism" and considers "that its job is to dispel uncertainty and suspicions
about the assassination as far as possible."[1]

Lewis reported that the commission would conclude that three shots
were fired—the first wounded Kennedy but probably not fatally, the second
fatal shot followed, and a third bullet, "fired either before or after these two,
went wild." According to the unidentified "spokesman," the commission's report "would completely explode the theories published by such persons as Mr.
Buchanan" and anticipated that "not even the authors of the theories would
stand by them." In short, the "spokesman" said, "We'll knock them out of those
positions." I could not believe that anyone on the commission or its staff could
have broadcast such an improbable assessment of our likely impact on the conspiracy theorists.

The commission could hardly ignore this article. When they discussed
it on June 4, they wondered if there was a "Commission spokesman" and, if
so, who it was. After unanimously denying that each was the "spokesman,"
they authorized the release of a short public statement: "The Commission is
nearing the conclusion of the taking of testimony and is giving thought to the
content and form of its report. The Commission has reached no final conclusions and has not discussed final conclusions as a Commission."[2]

The *Chicago Tribune* seized upon the *Times* report as further evidence
of an effort by the Johnson administration "to dictate the conclusions of the
Warren commission on the Kennedy assassination."[3] The *Tribune* reported that
the commission members were disturbed by the numerous alleged reports of

their conclusions that Oswald acted alone and there was no foreign involvement in the assassination. The article stated that "The White House and state department, for diplomatic reasons, reportedly are adamant" that the commission reach these conclusions and that newspapers "frequently chosen by the Johnson administration for the hoisting of trial balloons began carrying such stories ... before the Warren commission could even set up shop." It observed that "a rash" of such stories appeared this week "in newspapers from coast to coast" and that the commission "met in special session" and issued its release about not having reached any conclusions. Newspaper speculation aside, June did prove to be the month in which the commission started making the key decisions that would be presented in its report.

■ Jacqueline Kennedy Testifies

The commission members had not yet decided how to secure the testimony of Mrs. John F. Kennedy about the events on November 22. Everyone recognized the sensitivity of the matter, not wanting to intrude unnecessarily into the details of the assassination that would be deeply emotional to the still-grieving widow. Rankin asked me to raise this issue with her brother-in-law and my boss, Robert Kennedy. The commission also wished to know whether he would testify or file a statement asserting that the Justice Department had no evidence showing a domestic or foreign conspiracy. As the commission's liaison with the Justice Department, discussing these sensitive questions with the attorney general was my responsibility.

Before I met with the attorney general, I consulted with Ed Guthman on May 28 and with Nick Katzenbach on June 3. Guthman was the department's public information officer and a close friend of Robert Kennedy. Guthman agreed that Mrs. Kennedy should be questioned and said that he would take it up with the attorney general. We also considered the question of Robert Kennedy's appearing before the commission or, alternatively, submitting a statement informing the commission that the department had no evidence of any domestic or foreign conspiracy. Guthman thought that such a statement might reduce the need for Kennedy to make a public statement after the commission issued its report. He promised to discuss these matters with the attorney general and get back to me the next week.[4]

After the meeting with Guthman, I prepared a draft statement for Robert Kennedy's consideration. I proposed that he say that he was familiar with the executive order creating the commission and had received reports from the FBI and others about the commission's work, but did not have any detailed information about its investigation. I thought he should also say that all of the information that had come to his attention relating to the assassination had been sent to the FBI or to the commission for appropriate investigation. On the critical element of conspiracy, my draft statement suggested that Kennedy state that, although he was aware of allegations of a domestic or foreign conspiracy involved in the assassination, he knew of no credible evidence to support these allegations.[5]

I also prepared a memo for him about a proposed interview of Jacqueline Kennedy. I explained that the commission wanted to hear from all of those in the presidential vehicle, and she might have particular recollections about the events that could clarify some of the unresolved questions. "The area of the greatest importance to the Commission concerns the few seconds during which the shots were fired," I wrote. "The Commission would like to have Mrs. Kennedy's recollections regarding the reactions and statements made by the occupants of the Presidential car during this period of time. Answers to questions such as those attached to this memorandum may supply detail which will be helpful to the Commission."[6]

If this memo seems insensitive and unseemly under the circumstances, the attached questions were even more so. But they had to be proposed. While everyone on the commission staff was concerned for Mrs. Kennedy, we needed whatever she knew if we were to complete a thorough investigation of her husband's murder. There was no getting around it. If we did not get her testimony at some point before publishing our report, the commission would get lambasted and the integrity of the report would be questioned.

Specter had prepared a list of over one hundred questions for Mrs. Kennedy, probably with input from Belin, Redlich, and others. It was thorough and specific—perhaps too much so for this witness at this time. His outline of proposed questions was divided into seven sections: events of November 22 preceding the assassination; general questions about President Kennedy; the shooting; immediate post-shooting events; activities at Parkland Hospital; the return trip to Washington; and other general information.[7]

The list of questions attached to my letter to the attorney general was much shorter, only forty questions in total. I consulted with Rankin about reducing the number of questions for Mrs. Kennedy and he agreed that Specter's list was simply too long and detailed.

My proposed questions addressed the circumstances before, during, and immediately after the president was shot. They began with the conversations in the presidential vehicle shortly before the shots, and then her recollections as to where she was looking at the time of the individual shots, the interval between the shots, the president's reaction to each shot, what he said if anything, the reactions and words spoken by each of the six occupants in the vehicle including herself (the others being the two Secret Service agents, Governor and Mrs. Connally, and President Kennedy). Additional questions sought her recollection as to what was going on outside the vehicle, the vehicle speed at the time of the shots, her observation of bullet fragments in the car, comments by Secret Service Agent Clinton J. Hill, who was in the car immediately behind the presidential limousine and when the shots were fired jumped onto the back of the car to shield Mrs. Kennedy, what happened when she crawled onto the trunk of the vehicle, the condition of the president on the way to the hospital, her observations of his wounds, what was said en route to the hospital, and what happened after the vehicle arrived at the hospital.

We were only going to get one opportunity to talk to Mrs. Kennedy, so our questions had to get to the point. Still, I thought that this streamlined approach was more likely to be accepted by Robert Kennedy. Rankin was the only person at the commission whom I kept informed of my dealings with the attorney general.

I took the proposed statement for the attorney general and my memo regarding Mrs. Kennedy's testimony to my next meeting at the Justice Department, this time with Guthman and Katzenbach. After reviewing the proposed questions for Mrs. Kennedy, Katzenbach said that they were still too detailed. When discussing the attorney general's own participation, he suggested another alternative—an exchange of letters between Robert Kennedy and Warren. He thought that a letter from the attorney general could meet the commission's needs and thereby justify the commission's decision not to call him as a witness. They both agreed that the statement I had prepared was "a sterile and unsatisfactory device"—which it was.[8]

Accompanied by Katzenbach, I met with Robert Kennedy on June 4 for about thirty-five minutes. In my three years with the Justice Department I had been in the attorney general's office on a few dozen occasions. Several of these were substantive meetings when Jack Miller took me along to participate in discussing particular investigations, pending lawsuits, or congressional inquiries. As I gained confidence, I felt increasingly comfortable in answering Kennedy's questions and offering my views. This meeting with him, however, was a wholly different matter. The room seemed larger; he seemed smaller; and the intensely personal nature of our discussion was palpable.

Notwithstanding the circumstances, the attorney general "was quite cordial and easy to speak to about these problems. He asked me what we wanted to ask Mrs. Kennedy about, reviewed the questions and found some of them a little less significant than others and indicated that he would make the necessary arrangements." He then asked my advice about how the interview should be handled and I suggested that the chief justice and Rankin should be present, along with a court reporter. He said that he was "perfectly willing for the Chief Justice and a reporter to be present as well as himself, but that he wished to reserve judgment until he met Mr. Rankin and saw how Mrs. Kennedy responded."[9]

The next subject was Kennedy's participation in the work of the commission. As Katzenbach had suggested, I had prepared two letters for the attorney general's review. The first was a draft letter from Warren asking whether Robert Kennedy was aware of any information relating to the assassination that had not been sent to the commission, particularly information regarding an alleged conspiracy. The draft letter also asked Kennedy if he had any suggestions to make about the commission's investigation.[10]

The second letter was a proposed response to Warren's letter. This draft acknowledged Robert Kennedy's awareness of the extensive investigation conducted by the FBI and the allegations of a possible conspiracy. The draft proposed that he say: "Based on reports I have received from the Director of the Federal Bureau of Investigation and other persons familiar with the investigation, I know of no credible evidence to support these allegations." The letter concluded with his statement that he had no suggestions for the commission and was willing to appear as a witness if the members so requested.[11]

The attorney general told us that he was "willing to do anything necessary for the country and thought that he making a statement about the nonexistence of a conspiracy would be desirable." Although he did not say so, I got the clear impression that he would prefer not being a witness before the commission and hoped that the exchange of letters would be an acceptable alternative. He commented that the draft letter prepared for his signature was inaccurate in that he had never received any reports from the FBI regarding the assassination. He said that his only sources of information about the assassination were Warren, Katzenbach, and me. Based on these reports, he was "perfectly willing to make a broad and definite statement regarding his confidence in the commission and the adequacy of the investigation." The meeting ended with the understanding that the exchange of letters was the preferred course of action and I was asked to prepare them for signature.[12]

Unlike President Johnson and Jacqueline Kennedy, Robert Kennedy was not in Dealey Plaza on November 22, 1963, and was unable to provide information about the shooting. In contrast with the directors of the FBI, CIA, and Secret Service, his Justice Department (except for the FBI) was not engaged in any investigative work on the assassination, because that responsibility went to the commission. The only reasons for his appearance before the commission would be to tell the members that the Justice Department had provided all relevant information to the commission, he had no knowledge of any possible conspiracy, and he had confidence in the commission. The commission concluded that the proposed exchange of letters between Warren and Kennedy would satisfy its desire for these assurances.

I was pleased to hear Robert Kennedy express confidence in the commission's work. We certainly hoped that he would publicly approve our final conclusions. But—as he said on so many occasions—nothing was going to bring his brother back to life. He had very little interest in the scope of the commission's investigation (except any possible Teamsters aspect). Because the FBI reports on the investigation to the Justice Department were routinely addressed to the attorney general, I was initially surprised that Kennedy had decided that all such reports should go directly to Katzenbach and Miller. But I recognized soon after November 22 that Kennedy did not wish to be personally involved in the government's response to the assassination, leaving that role to Katzenbach.

During the meeting, Kennedy asked me about the commission's work. I told him that I thought the commission was doing a good job. When he asked whether we were going to be critical of the Secret Service, I replied that I thought we would be. When he asked the same question about the FBI, I told him that I expected the commission would be "critical to a much lesser extent." I volunteered that the commission "was not meeting the difficult issue," specifically whether the responsibility should be transferred from the Secret Service to the FBI. The attorney general commented that he did not believe that the Secret Service was "very capable" although both he and Mrs. Kennedy had "reservations" about the FBI as well. Katzenbach weighed in to express his view that the FBI was better suited to handle this responsibility. At the end of the meeting, the attorney general told me to "tell the Commission to consider this issue."[13]

On June 11, the letter from Warren to Robert Kennedy was mailed. The next day, I sent a copy of the letter to Katzenbach, as well as a copy of the proposed response from the attorney general that I had prepared. I advised Katzenbach that Warren believed that the proposed response by Robert Kennedy would eliminate any need for him to testify before the commission.[14]

One day after our meeting, the attorney general arranged for Mrs. Kennedy to testify before the commission. The questioning took place in her Washington apartment, with only Warren, Rankin, Robert Kennedy, and a court reporter present. Rankin conducted the brief interrogation, which lasted only nine or ten minutes.[15]

Specter was waiting at the commission office late that afternoon to see Rankin about Specter's proposed trip with Warren to Dallas on Sunday. When Rankin told him that he had just been at Mrs. Kennedy's apartment taking her testimony, Specter recalled, "He braced for my response. I didn't say anything. I didn't have to. Rankin knew I was livid."[16]

Belin and Specter were extremely critical of Rankin's interview of Mrs. Kennedy. Rankin did not advise Specter (or anyone of the staff to my knowledge) about Warren's decision not to call her before the full commission. Specter had assumed that he would take the lead in questioning her, using his list of more than one hundred questions. He later reviewed the transcript of the "abbreviated, nine-minute session" and concluded that the interview "omitted most of the lines of questioning I had proposed. It was almost worthless."[17]

Rankin asked twenty-six questions during the interview.[18] He started with Mrs. Kennedy's recollections of the motorcade as it approached the Texas School Book Depository. She remembered Mrs. Connally's comment about the friendly welcome that the people of Dallas were giving the president. When asked what she recalled about the shooting of her husband, she testified:

> You know, there is always noise in a motorcade and there are always motorcycles besides us, a lot of them backfiring. So I was looking to the left. I guess there was a noise, but it didn't seem like any different noise really because there is so much noise, motorcycles and things. But then suddenly Governor Connally was yelling, "Oh, no, no, no."[19]

Rankin asked "Did he turn toward you?" Mrs. Kennedy replied:

> No: I was looking this way, to the left, and I heard these terrible noises. You know. And my husband never made any sound. So I turned to the right. And all I remember is seeing my husband, he had this sort of quizzical look on his face, and his hand was up, it must have been his left hand. And just as I turned and looked at him, I could see a piece of his skull and I remember it was flesh colored. I remember thinking he just looked as if he had a slight headache. And I just remember seeing that. No blood or anything. And then

he sort of did this [indicating], put his hand to his forehead and fell in my lap. And then I remember falling on him and saying, 'Oh, no, no, no.' I mean, 'Oh, my God, they have shot my husband.' And 'I love you, Jack,' I remember that I was shouting. And just being down in the car with his head in my lap. And it seemed an eternity.[20]

Mrs. Kennedy testified that she did not recall climbing onto the trunk of the car. Nor did she remember Special Agent Hill of the Secret Service coming to help. She did recall someone yelling, "Get to the hospital." When Rankin asked her whether there were one or more shots, she testified:

Well, there must have been two because the one that made me turn around was Governor Connally yelling. And it used to confuse me because first I remembered there were three and I used to think that my husband didn't make any sound when he was shot. And Governor Connally screamed. And then I read the other day that it was the same shot that hit them both. But I used to think if only I had been looking to the right I would have seen the first shot hit him, then I could have pulled him down, and then the second shot would not have hit him. But I heard Governor Connally yelling and that made me turn around, and as I turned to the right my husband was doing this [indicating with hand at neck]. He was receiving a bullet. And those are the only two I remember. And I read there was a third shot. But I don't know. Just those two.[21]

She testified also about the drive to the hospital, but could not recall any conversations that took place in the presidential vehicle. When Rankin asked her whether she could think of anything more about these events, Warren interrupted and said, "No, I think not. I think that is the story and that is what we came for. We thank you very much, Mrs. Kennedy."[22]

To his credit, Rankin was not deterred from asking her whether she recalled anything that the president's bodyguard, Roy Kellerman, who was in the front seat of the president's car, said to her after the vehicle turned the corner and proceeded down Elm Street. She said she could not recall any such conversation. In response to Rankin's very last question, she assured him and Warren that she had told them everything she remembered about the entire event.[23]

Specter's description of this testimony as being "worthless" was harsh, but it is true that any reasonably competent lawyer could have taken this testimony and proceeded, detail after detail, to question her further about her recollections, which if done thoroughly would have taken more than an hour. Whether more detailed, and persistent, questioning would have produced additional information is a matter of speculation. I am confident that Specter would have admitted that his outline included many questions on general subjects that need not have been put to Mrs. Kennedy. And I am equally sure that he would have conceded that in light of Mrs. Kennedy's answers many of his proposed questions would not have been appropriate. However, Specter had prepared for the interrogation as thoroughly and competently as he did all of his commission assignments. Years later, he made this final important point: "Extensive questioning of Jacqueline Kennedy would probably not have produced any revelations. But we will never know. I continue to believe that far more questions should have been put to the former first lady."[24]

It was clear to me that more vigorous questioning of Mrs. Kennedy wasn't going to happen. We had to tread a thin line. Robert Kennedy had made it clear that he wanted to keep the questioning as brief as possible in order to protect his sister-in-law from the more horrific recollections that she alluded to in her brief session with Warren and Rankin. I knew also that Warren, whose courtliness and concern for women would seem archaic today, was eager to limit the questioning of Mrs. Kennedy. Given these obstacles, I was prepared to accept what we were able to obtain from her testimony and tried to persuade my colleagues that further complaints on the subject would not be productive. Upon reflection after several decades, I believe that the commission got from Mrs. Kennedy all she had to give on issues important to our investigation.

On the other hand, I believed that no such justifications could explain the commission's decision that same week to do without direct testimony from President and Mrs. Johnson. Again, most of the commission lawyers were critical of this decision. They thought that the testimony of all the riders in the vice president's car (as well as the presidential car) should be obtained, not only because they might have some recollections that were significant to the investigation but also so that the commission's investigation could be seen for what we wanted it to be—namely, thorough in all respects without any special treatment for grieving widows or the current incumbent in the White House.

To this day, I think the public would have taken President Johnson's willingness to testify as evidence of his commitment to the commission and might have helped defuse the more salacious rumors about conspiracies involving him or his Texas oil industry supporters. The commission was pursuing these allegations along with all others that came to its attention. But I also don't believe that either the president or Mrs. Johnson would have said anything that would have caused us to conduct additional investigation or alter our report.

I met with Katzenbach on June 17 to follow up on Mrs. Kennedy's testimony and the attorney general's response to Warren's letter. I told him: "I would prefer that the letter not be answered immediately." By way of explanation, I mentioned that "I expected there would be a considerable difference of views between the Chief Justice and the staff regarding the quality of the report." If this situation developed, I told Katzenbach, "I intended to fight for a report I considered satisfactory, and indicated that a delay in sending this letter would bolster my position." Katzenbach said that he would hold the letter while the attorney general was in Europe from June 23 to June 30.[25]

I had no reason at the time to believe that Warren (or the other members of the commission) might try to limit the investigation or shape its conclusions in a way that would be unacceptable to me or other members of the staff. I may have been thinking of our difficulties with the Treasury Department on presidential protection issues. But I was obviously anticipating the worst, and being able to employ the persuasive force of the Justice Department and Robert Kennedy, if necessary, was a precautionary step that seemed appropriate at the time. As it developed, the attorney general did not answer the letter for about seven weeks.

■ The Autopsy Photographs and X-rays

Securing testimony from Mrs. Kennedy had been difficult, but getting our hands on the autopsy photographs and X-rays proved even more so. Although the public might accept our delicate handling of Mrs. Kennedy, we doubted they would be as sympathetic to our failure to get the hard evidence that the autopsy materials represented. The Kennedy family had deep, long-term, emotional interests at stake but, for us, it was much more difficult to take a pass on this issue. We all believed we could not back down.

Most of the staff was convinced that the commission's failure to consider these materials carefully in its report would be used to attack our competence and integrity. Specter had taken the testimony of the three autopsy doctors three months earlier, at a time when neither he nor the doctors had access to the autopsy X-rays and photographs. He and others were satisfied that the testimony of the doctors did accurately reflect the trajectory of the bullets and the nature of the wounds suffered by both Kennedy and Connally. However, the corpsman's sketch introduced during this testimony was inaccurate as to the location of the wounds and to that extent inconsistent with that testimony.

President Kennedy and Chief Justice Warren, whose names would be forever intertwined, are here shown with their wives at a White House reception honoring the judiciary on November 20, 1963, the evening before the president departed for Texas.
(National Archives)

(left) The President and the First Lady are welcomed in Dallas on November 22 after flying from Fort Worth, where they had spent the night after a busy schedule in San Antonio and Houston the previous day.   *(JFK Presidential Library)*

(below) The close relationship between the president and the attorney general made my service in the Justice Department under Robert Kennedy a very special professional experience.

(Library of Congress)

As shown here, President Kennedy, Mrs. Kennedy, Texas Governor Connally, and Mrs. Connally were very pleased with the warm reception they got from the Dallas crowd as their limousine moved slowly down Main Street. The motorcade turned into Dealey Plaza just moments later. *(Library of Congress)*

HOMICIDE REPORT

POLICE DEPARTMENT

CITY OF DALLA

Last Name of Person Killed	First Name	Middle Name	Race	Sex	Age	Residence of Person Killed	Offense Serial No.
KENNEDY, John F (PRESIDENT OF U. S.)			W	m	47	Washington, D. C. (White House)	F-8599

Reported By — Title or Relationship

Offense as Reported (Crime)	After Investigation Changed to
MURDER	

Place of Occurrence — Street and Number or Intersection	Division	Platoon	Beat	Officers Making Report	I.D. No.	Name
Elm St. (approx. 150' W of Houston)	H&R)	2	101	CN Dhority 476 HH Blessing 698		

Day of Week	Date of Occurrence	Time of Day	Date Reported	Time Reported	Report Received By	Received—Time—Typed
Fri	11/22/63	12:30PM	11/23/63	5:10PM	Mayo	5:10PM

DESCRIPTION OF DEAD PERSON

Age	Height	Weight	Eyes	Hair	Beard	Complexion	Identifying Marks, Scars, Etc.	Clothing

Coroner Notified	Name of Coroner Attending—Time of Arrival		Name of Prosecutor Attending—Time of Arrival
Joe B. Brown		A.M. / P.M.	

Pronounced Dead by Physician — Address — Person With Whom Accused Lived or Associated

Dr. Kemp Clark, 1PM, Parkland Hospital

DETAILS OF OFFENSE (Give Circumstances of Occurrence of Offense and its Investigation) Use Both Sides of This Sheet.

The expired was riding in motorcade with wife and Governor John Connally, and his wife. Witness heard gun shot and saw the expired slump forward. More shots were heard and the expired fell in his wife's lap. Governor Connally was also shot at this time. Car in which they were riding was escorted to Parkland Hospital by Dallas Police Officers.

Witness Taken Into Custody	Address	Witness Taken Into Custody	Address
All witnesses affidavits are in Homicide Office.			

The official homicide report prepared by the Dallas Police Department records the murder of President Kennedy on November 22, 1963 and the testimony of witnesses at the scene. *(Library of Congress)*

(left) If he had lived, Oswald, shown here escorted by police officials, would have been tried under Texas law for the murder of President Kennedy because there was no US law at the time making assassination of the president a federal crime.

(Library of Congress)

(below) As shown here in London, the news of President Kennedy's assassination spread immediately around the world and raised concerns about the motives of the alleged assassin and whether some conspiracy was involved. *(Library of Congress)*

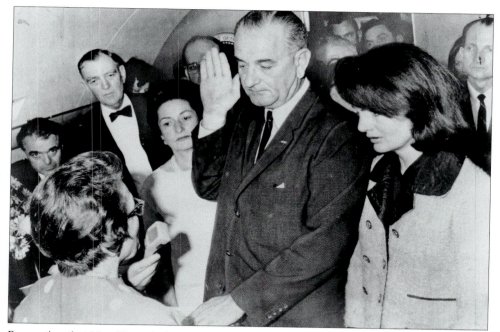

Requesting that Mrs. Kennedy be at his side on the presidential plane to reassure the nation of the passage of power, Lyndon B. Johnson was sworn in as the 36th President of the United States by Federal District Court Judge Sarah T. Hughes. *(Library of Congress)*

Journalists and bystanders swarmed Dallas police headquarters during Oswald's incarceration, and public statements at press conference like the one shown prompted worries in Washington whether Oswald could get a fair trial in Dallas. *(Library of Congress)*

(above) On the morning of Sunday, November 24, Jack Ruby went to Western Union to send a money order to an employee, walked one block to police headquarters, entered the basement down an auto ramp, and fatally shot Oswald before millions watching on television. *(Library of Congress)*

(left) Jack Ruby, shown here being taken into custody for shooting Oswald, maintained from the moment of his arrest that he had acted alone. In a polygraph test conducted by the FBI, Ruby testified to that effect without any indication of lying.

(Bill Winfrey Collection / The Sixth Floor Museum at Dealey Plaza)

On November 29, 1963, President Johnson appointed a commission chaired by Chief Justice Warren to investigate the assassination. From left to right, this picture shows Representative Gerald R. Ford, Representative Hale Boggs, Senator Richard B. Russell, Chief Justice Earl Warren, Senator John Sherman Cooper, John J. McCloy, Allen W. Dulles, and General Counsel J. Lee Rankin.

(Courtesy of the author's personal collection)

(left) The first witness who appeared before the Warren Commission was Lee Harvey Oswald's wife, Marina, shown here with counsel approaching the commission's offices on February 3, 1964.

(©Bettmann/CORBIS)

(right) Marina Oswald testified that she took this picture of her husband holding a rifle, a pistol, and issues of two newspapers later identified as the *Worker* and the *Militant* at his request before he attempted to kill General Walker in April 1963.

Lyndal L. Shaneyfelt Collection / The Sixth Floor Museum at Dealey Plaza)

(above) This rifle was purchased by Oswald and found on the sixth floor of the depository. Ballistics experts determined that it fired the bullets that hit Kennedy and Connally. *(National Archives)*

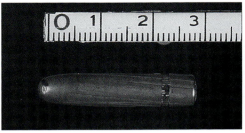

(right) Rigorous testing and forensic analysis concluded that this nearly intact bullet caused the Kennedy's back and neck wounds and subsequently caused Connally's wounds. *(National Archives)*

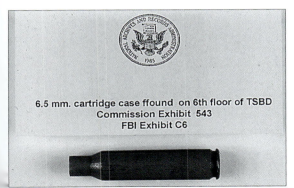

6.5 mm. cartridge case ffound on 6th floor of TSBD
Commission Exhibit 543
FBI Exhibit C6

(left) This is one of the three cartridges found on the sixth floor of the depository, which led the commission to conclude that three shots had probably been fired by Oswald and that one of those shots had missed the limousine and its occupants. *(National Archives)*

(right) Oswald purchased this revolver using an alias. Experts testified before the commission that he used this weapon to kill Patrolman Tippit when the officer got out of his police car to question Oswald.

(National Archives)

These boxes were piled high in the corner of the sixth floor of the depository so that Oswald would not be seen when he was at the window aiming his rifle at the presidential limousine.

(Library of Congress)

(above) The commission tried to learn as much as possible about Oswald's life in the Soviet Union where he and Marina Oswald lived in Minsk, as pictured here.

(National Archives)

(left) Jack Ruby failed to get his trial removed from Dallas and was convicted on March 14, 1964, for murder with malice and received a death sentence. Ruby died of cancer before his conviction was reversed by the appeals court in 1967.

(Library of Congress)

(above) Assistant counsel David Belin (at left) and I visited the depository in Dallas in March 1964 where we arranged to take the sworn statements of several employees.

(©Bettmann/CORBIS)

(left) J. Edgar Hoover, director of the FBI at the time, testified before the commission on May 14, 1964, that the FBI had no obligation to identify Oswald to the Secret Service before the assassination, even though in December 1963 he punished seventeen officials and agents in his organization for their failure to do so.

(Library of Congress)

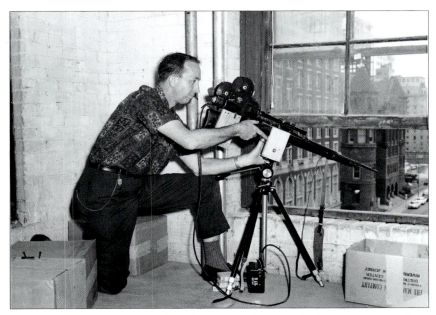

Using the actual assassination rifle with an attached camera, the FBI agent pictured here was able to determine that Kennedy and Connally were aligned in the vehicle so that a bullet exiting Kennedy's throat would necessarily hit Connally.

(Lyndal L. Shaneyfelt Collection/The Sixth Floor Museum at Dealey Plaza)

he Secret Service provided this limousine for use in the reenactment on May 24, 1964. Two stand-s for President Kennedy and Governor Connally were used in the analysis.

(Malcolm E. Barker Collection / The Sixth Floor Museum at Dealey Plaza)

(left) Assistant Counsel Norman Redlich played a critical role in assisting Rankin to supervise the commission staff and was instrumental in persuading Rankin that a reenactment of the assassination was necessary to ensure the accuracy of the commission's conclusions. *(Barton Silverman/The New York Times)*

(right) This is how I spent much of my time at the commission, at my desk dealing with assorted documents and talking on the phone. *(Courtesy of the author's personal collection)*

(above) Assistant counsel Arlen Specter—later a long-serving senator from Pennsylvania—accompanie␣ Warren to Dallas on June 7, 1964, to take Jack Ruby's testimony and used the occasion to discuss th␣ evidence supporting the single bullet hypothesis while the two men stood at the assassin's window ␣ the depository. *(Arlen Specter Center for Public Policy at Philadelphia University␣*

All members of the commission visited Dallas to inspect sites related to the assassination; here Senator Cooper, Senator Russell, and Representative Boggs (left to right) are seen leaving the depository.

(©Bettmann/CORBIS)

This picture shows Allen Dulles (far left) and John McCloy (fourth from the left) looking up at the depository along with David Belin (at McCloy's left side) and local law enforcement officials.

(Bill Winfrey Collection / The Sixth Floor Museum at Dealey Plaza)

THE ATTORNEY GENERAL
WASHINGTON

September 2, 1964

Dear Howard:

On my last day as Attorney General, I want to thank you for your excellent service to this Department during my tenure.

When we look back four years and see how much was needed to be done, and now how much has been accomplished, you can take great satisfaction in having made an important contribution to the country in a time of maximum need. President Kennedy would have wished to thank you for that--and for your loyalty.

I am proud to have served with you--and I am grateful for your friendship.

With kind regards,

Sincerely,

Bob

Robert F. Kennedy

Mr. Howard P. Willens
Executive Assistant
Criminal Division
Department of Justice
Washington, D. C.

(right) When he resigned as attorney general in order to run for the US Senate, on September 4, 1964, Robert Kennedy sent me this nice letter.

(Courtesy of the author's personal collection)

(above) On September 24, 1964, Chief Justice Warren, the members of the commission, and Le Rankin presented the report to President Johnson and it was released to the public three days later.

(Cecil Stoughton / LBJ Library

Specter and other lawyers pressed Rankin hard on this issue, emphasizing the need for these materials in order to make more definitive judgments regarding key issues in the investigation. Specter believed that Secret Service inspector Thomas Kelley, who had reportedly talked to the attorney general about this matter, might not have fully appreciated why these materials were necessary and that the commission should present its own reasons to Robert Kennedy. At the commission meeting of April 30, Rankin obtained Warren's approval to try and obtain access to the X-rays and photos.[26]

Specter thought that the autopsy records were "indispensable" in determining with certainty the origin of the shots and identifying any major variations between the autopsy images and the artist's drawings used by the doctors in their testimony. He was convinced that James Humes, one of the autopsy doctors, could use the photographs and X-rays to pinpoint the exact location of the entrance wound on the president's upper back, the exact location of the entrance wound on the back of the president's head, and the exact area of his skull that was hit by the second bullet. In addition, Specter proposed that the specifics of Kennedy's wounds be examined closely in the photographs and X-rays to determine whether they were characteristic of entrance wounds under the criteria used by the autopsy doctors and by the Dallas doctors who examined the president after he was shot. Specter proposed that Humes, after examining these materials, indicate whether he needed to make any changes in his earlier testimony. Unknown to Specter, the question of the commission's access to these materials was still unresolved when I met with Katzenbach on June 17.[27]

I understood at this time that the attorney general had agreed to let Warren and Rankin see the autopsy materials. I urged Katzenbach to get Kennedy's approval for Specter rather than Rankin to examine them. I told him that it was very important to have the most knowledgeable lawyer on the staff assume this responsibility and that Specter was known to the attorney general as the prosecutor who had successfully won the Roy Cohn Teamster case in Philadelphia.[28]

Katzenbach raised the question a few days later with Kennedy, who decided that Warren could view these materials on behalf of the commission, but that no one else could be present and the X-rays and photographs would remain in the possession of the custodian who brought them. Kennedy was understandably wary of any opportunity to copy them.

Warren promptly arranged to have the materials brought to his chambers at the Supreme Court. He looked at them reluctantly and only briefly. He reported back to Rankin, and presumably the other commission members, that the photographs were so gruesome that he did not believe that they should be included among the commission's records. Due to Warren's extreme distaste for these materials and his previous public commitment to publishing everything relied on by the commission, Rankin concluded that there was no possibility of Specter being permitted to view these materials to confirm the accuracy of Humes's earlier testimony.

With the exception of Rankin, the commission's lawyers considered this decision by Warren to be a serious mistake. I agreed. Without the autopsy photos, we had to deal only with a medical corpsman's sketch made several months later based on a doctor's memory of his examination of the patient. The sketch opened the door to all kinds of speculation about the wounds, and therefore the shots that caused the wounds, that could have been avoided easily if we had the X-rays and photos. We were right in the conclusions we drew from the corpsman's sketches and the testimony of the doctors, but we could have supported our conclusions better if we had the documentary evidence as well as the medical testimony.

As it happened, our fears were realized and critics eagerly embraced the corpsman's inaccurate sketch to question the commission's conclusions about the nature of the wounds and the single-bullet analysis. David Belin later characterized it as "a disastrous decision" which "gave rise to wild speculation and rumor." Belin attributed the decision to the Kennedy family, and especially Robert Kennedy, claiming that they "did not want these pictures and X-rays to become a matter of public display." Belin believed passionately that the family's "desire for privacy was outweighed by the need for public knowledge on what actually happened in Dallas on Nov. 22." He worried that such deference to the Kennedy family was indicative of "a dangerous trend toward preferred treatment for high governmental officials."[29]

Specter shared Belin's assessment. He also attributed the decision to the Kennedy family and their worries that "those ghastly images might reach the public." Specter believed this concern could have been met by including "an analysis of the autopsy materials in the commission report without including the images as a commission exhibit. That approach should have satisfied the Kennedy family." Specter did not learn that Warren had examined the autopsy materials until long after the commission report was filed. He recalled that he and Belin had dinner together "after the commission nixed the photos and X-rays" and discussed resigning from the commission staff. But neither of them seriously considered doing that.[30]

It is clear that the Kennedy family's objections to releasing the images found a sympathetic ear in Warren. As Redlich later recalled:

My impression, and I cannot be more precise than that, my impression was that the Kennedy family was concerned about the publicity, about a public display of the President's skull in those pictures. The Chief Justice was very sensitive to that. He felt that that family had undergone just tremendous trauma, and he was very sensitive to that, perhaps by retrospect overly sensitive. But he was very sensitive to it. Now, I don't believe that it would be fair to the Kennedys, at least on the basis of anything I know of, to conclude that it was because of their directly saying to the Chief Justice that we want it this way, that it was done this way. I have no information of that kind.[31]

I do not have any information of that kind either. Based on my conversations with Robert Kennedy, I believe that he might have been persuaded to let the autopsy materials be used for the forensic purposes described by Specter so long as they did not become part of the commission's records. Because Warren responded so negatively to any commission use of the materials—with no apparent challenge from other members—Rankin and the staff never had the opportunity to develop such a proposal and present it to Robert Kennedy, with the strong endorsement that I believe Katzenbach and Miller would have provided.

Rankin, however, later defended Warren's position on this question:

We thought we had good evidence from the doctors who were involved at the hospital in Dallas and also at the autopsy, and we did not want the President's memory to be presented in that manner, and we had already promised the American people that the investigation, that everything that we obtained, except for such matters as involved national security, would be made available to them, so we would have had to publish it, if we used it ourselves.[32]

I did not find this explanation acceptable—and still don't. It invited further questioning by the critics as to what else the commission may have excluded from its records to avoid embarrassing individuals or agencies. Once the commission had decided to suppress *anything* from its published records, including documents withheld in the name of national security, the withholding of the X-rays and photographs could have been explained in a way that I believe would have been accepted by the vast majority of the American public. Whatever criticism the commission might have received for such withholding would have been trivial compared with the criticism it did receive (and deserve) for not letting these materials be used by the testifying doctors to make certain that their testimony was accurate.

■ On Other Investigative Fronts

Meanwhile, our investigative work in other areas was moving along well. On June 4, the commission heard the testimony of three FBI agents and Inspector Kelley of the Secret Service about the results of the Dallas reenactment project. The agents were now able to provide detailed information regarding the location, timing, and approximate distances of the shots from the depository.

On June 8, District Attorney Henry Wade testified concerning his role in the investigation of the assassination, statements made by him to the press, and conversations with Secret Service agent Forrest Sorrels and police officer Patrick Dean about what Jack Ruby said on November 22. Rankin led the interrogation of Wade, with both Redlich and Goldberg available to assist him.[33]

Wade, a onetime FBI agent, had been the Dallas district attorney since 1951. He described how he first heard about the assassination, consulted with US Attorney Barefoot Sanders to confirm that this was a local rather than federal matter, and went to the hospital to visit with Governor Connally, who was a friend of his. He then went to the Dallas police headquarters, whose officers had the responsibility for investigating both the assassination and the murder of Patrolman Tippit, arriving there at about seven in the evening. Immediately upon his arrival, Chief Curry showed him the report by Lieutenant Revill regarding the statement by FBI agent Hosty earlier in the day. When Wade asked Curry what he was going to do about the Revill report, Curry responded that he didn't know.[34]

Wade described in colorful detail the "mob scene" at police headquarters on the evening of November 22. He recalled seeing Ruby amidst the crowd of an estimated three hundred news reporters and bystanders in the hallways. He told the commission he was focused on ensuring that Oswald be advised of his right to counsel and resolving the confusion over what kind of charge to file under Texas law for his killing of President Kennedy. He was not personally involved in any questioning of Oswald. He denied answering any of the many questions from the press about fingerprints and other evidence, although he did say that he referred to the statement by Oswald's wife that her husband had a gun—a statement that Wade said would be inadmissible under Texas law. He also said that Ruby, whom he didn't know at the time, was in the group of reporters and bystanders when Wade made a reference to Oswald's reported connection with the "Free Cuba Movement" and Ruby yelled out to say, "No, it is the Fair Play for Cuba Committee."[35]

Wade told the commission that Ruby's appearance at the department on Friday night caused him to believe that Ruby had decided then to kill Oswald. He said that he had not heard of Dean's testimony on this subject until the day before he put Dean on the stand in the Ruby trial a few months later, because he had been busy picking a jury. Wade told the commission of the many rumors and allegations about the assassination that passed through his office, but emphasized that his responsibilities were limited to preparing for the Ruby trial and he sent all information or allegations about Oswald to the FBI or some other agency.[36]

Wade's testimony was followed by that of Officer Dean, who had requested the opportunity to appear after his deposition had been taken in Dallas. In response to Rankin's questions, Dean said that his deposition testimony was truthful in every regard and that he had nothing to add to it. He testified that he was shocked and offended by Griffin's suggestion that he was not telling the truth regarding Ruby's entry into the basement on November 24, and his statement about Ruby wanting to kill Oswald two days earlier. Rankin asked Dean why he had not reported Ruby's statement on November 22 until his report on February 18, before the Ruby trial. Dean's only response was that his earlier report within the department related only to the basement security issue and not the interview of Ruby at which he and Sorrels were present.[37]

When Dean complained about Griffin accusing him of perjury, Warren said: "I have never talked to Mr. Griffin about this. I didn't know that you had this altercation with him, but I want to say this: That so far as the jurisdiction of this Commission is concerned and its procedures, no member of our staff has a right to tell any witness that he is lying or that he is testifying falsely. That is not his business. It is the business of this Commission to appraise the testimony of all the witnesses." I don't recall that Rankin ever told the staff of Warren's statement to Dean, whose appearance before the commission marked the end of the Griffin/Dean controversy.[38]

■ The State Department Defends Itself

From September 4, 1959, when he applied for his first passport, until shortly before the assassination, Oswald had numerous dealings with the Department of State, the American embassy in Moscow, and the Immigration and Naturalization Service (INS) within the Justice Department. To respond to Oswald's various requests, the State Department and INS had to decide many legal and administrative questions under the applicable US laws. Within hours of the identification of Oswald as the alleged assassin, speculations arose about the legality and propriety of the decisions made by State—a favorite target of the press—that permitted a defector to return to the United States, to be reissued a passport, and to travel to Mexico for the stated purpose of returning to the Soviet Union.

Bill Coleman and David Slawson wanted to know if Oswald's dealings with federal agencies were lawful and handled in the normal course of business. On June 9 and 10, the commission heard from the two consular officers who had dealt with Oswald in Moscow, officials in Washington responsible for the passport decision, the State Department's legal adviser, Abram Chayes, and Secretary of State Dean Rusk. Most of the commission members participated actively in these hearings—in part reflecting the widespread public suspicion that some of these State decisions *must* have been flawed in some critical way.

The first consular witness was Richard Snyder, who was second secretary and consul in the American embassy in Moscow from 1959 through mid-1961. He testified about Oswald's appearance at the embassy on Saturday, October 31, 1959, when he declared his desire to renounce his US citizenship. Snyder recalled that Oswald told him that he had applied for Soviet citizenship because, he said, "I am a Marxist." In his report, Snyder described Oswald as "arrogant and aggressive" and had volunteered that "he had offered to the Soviet authorities any information which he had acquired as an enlisted radar operator in the Marines." Consistent with State Department policy, Snyder proposed to delay completing the renunciation procedure "until the action of the Soviet authorities on his request for Soviet citizenship is known or the Department advises." Snyder retained Oswald's passport after Oswald left his office.[39]

Snyder told the commission that Oswald subsequently complained about the embassy's failure to proceed with the renunciation and Snyder advised him in writing of the need to follow regulations. Over the next several months, the State Department received inquiries about Oswald's whereabouts, some resulting from his mother's complaints. State actually considered a request to the Soviet government for assistance in locating Oswald. As of early 1960, Snyder and the State Department still considered Oswald an American citizen because he had not completed the appropriate forms implementing his proposed renunciation.[40]

Snyder next heard from Oswald in February 1961, when a letter arrived from him at the embassy requesting the return of his passport and expressing his desire to return to the United States. From Minsk he wrote that he was unable to come to Moscow to complete in person the requisite forms but, in fact, he showed up a few months later. According to Snyder, this was now an important matter; Oswald's mother had enlisted the assistance of Texas representative (and later Speaker of the House) Jim Wright from Fort Worth to help get her son back home. The State Department's central concern was whether Oswald had "expatriated himself" by committing any one of the acts amounting to expatriation, such as swearing allegiance to a foreign country or serving in its armed forces. State concluded that Oswald had not committed any of these acts and was therefore still a United States citizen and entitled to his passport.[41]

Commission members examined Snyder closely about his initial decision to delay Oswald's request to renounce his citizenship, as reflected in this exchange with Ford:

> REPRESENTATIVE FORD: In retrospect, assuming the tragic events that did transpire last year didn't take place, and this circumstance was presented to you again in the Embassy in Moscow, would you handle the case any differently?
>
> MR. SNYDER: No, I don't think so, Mr. Ford. You mean in terms of would I have taken his renunciation? No, I think not.
>
> REPRESENTATIVE FORD: In other words, you would have put him off, or stalled him off, in this first interview, make him come back again?
>
> MR. SNYDER: Yes; I would have.

Snyder explained that he was influenced by the fact that Oswald was young—barely twenty when he first showed up at the embassy—and he thought it was important to give Oswald some time outside the office, for even a few hours, to consider the significance of what he was seeking to do.[42]

The next State witness was John McVickar, who served as consul in the American embassy in Moscow along with Snyder from 1959 to mid-1961. McVickar shared an office with Snyder at the embassy and generally confirmed Snyder's testimony about the substance of his conversation with Oswald, in which McVickar did not participate, and Snyder's description of Oswald's appearance and attitude. The commission members and Bill Coleman questioned McVickar about his recollection that Oswald appeared to have had some knowledgeable assistance in seeking renunciation of his US citizenship. McVickar said his assessment of Oswald's competence was based in part on Oswald's going to Helsinki to obtain a tourist visa to enter the Soviet Union. Oswald's choice of Helsinki, McVickar said, was a shrewd one because it was an unusual place for an individual tourist to seek a visa. McVickar testified that "[i]t is a well enough known fact among people who are working in the Soviet Union and undoubtedly people who are associated with Soviet matters" that Helsinki would be a good place to go to get a visa into Russia, but that "it was not a commonly known fact among the ordinary run of people in the United States."[43]

McVickar had occasion to meet with Marina Oswald as well, in July of 1961, a few days after her husband had returned to the embassy to regain his passport in order to return to the United States. As part of this initial security interview, Marina Oswald told McVickar that she was not a member of the Communist youth organization but was in her factory union. McVickar accepted her answer and initiated the process for the State Department to consider granting her a visa to enter the United States with her husband.[44]

Shortly before he left Moscow in September, McVickar submitted a petition to the department to classify her status as eligible for an immigrant visa and enclosed Lee Oswald's sworn statement of July 11, 1961. The State Department would not generally process such applications for visas to enter the United States until the applicant had obtained permission to leave the Soviet Union. However, McVickar recommended approving Marina Oswald's petition and a waiver of the sanctions otherwise applicable under the law— and described this action as "a routine request which would have been made in any similar case using almost exactly that type of language." He told the commission that her membership in the trade union for medical workers would be considered involuntary and therefore not a potential bar to her admission. McVickar emphasized that it "was my responsibility to make these recommendations, and I did so of my own free will as the officer-in-charge of this particular aspect of the case."[45]

Bernice Waterman had the responsibility in State's Passport Office to consider Oswald's request for reissuance of his passport in 1961. She testified that the passport could be returned only after the embassy had thoroughly questioned Oswald about his residence in the Soviet Union and his possible commitment of acts of expatriation. In August 1961, she concurred in the embassy's conclusion that he had not expatriated himself. Ford challenged this statement and quoted again from Oswald's initial written declaration of his desire to renounce his American citizenship. Waterman insisted that such a statement alone was not sufficient and Oswald was required to complete the necessary forms in order to achieve this termination of his citizenship, and he never did so.[46]

Frances Knight, the head of the Passport Office, addressed some of the same issues and confirmed the decisions reached. In addition, she addressed the issuance of a new passport to Oswald in June 1963 when he was living in New Orleans. There simply was no legal basis for declining to give Oswald his passport, she informed the commission. She emphasized that "there was no request in the file from any Government agency or any area of the Government for a lookout card on Oswald ... at the time that his 1963 passport was issued."[47]

Abram Chayes, legal adviser to the State Department, testified further about State's decisions about Oswald. He had not heard of Oswald before November 22, 1963, and was asked by Under Secretary of State George Ball immediately after the assassination to review State's files on Oswald. In discussing his opinion that Oswald had not officially renounced his citizenship in 1959, Chayes referred to several court decisions imposing a heavy burden on the State Department in proving the expatriation of an American citizen. Later in his testimony, Chayes agreed with Ford that if Oswald had returned to the consular office on a workday and persisted in his desire to renounce his citizenship—and filled out the requisite forms—that the consular officers would have been obligated to approve the renunciation. Regarding the issuance of a passport to Oswald in 1963, Chayes reminded the commission that State was not entitled "to withhold a passport on grounds related to political association and beliefs" and, accordingly, the Passport Office had acted properly in issuing a new passport to Oswald in 1963.[48]

Ford vigorously questioned Chayes about the decision to let Oswald return to the United States and then to issue a new passport to him in 1963, despite all the information in the file including his willingness to provide information to the Soviet Union acquired during his service in the Marines. Chayes defended State's decision and, at one point, emphasized again the restrictions imposed by the US Supreme Court on State's discretion to deny passports to persons with anti-American views by referring to the fact that "[w]e have got Malcolm X traveling across Africa making one speech after the other about how terrible our policies on the race question are." He also pointed out that the FBI had interviewed Oswald after his return to the United States and that neither that agency nor any other investigative agency asked that a lookout card be placed in State's file regarding any future issuance of a passport.[49]

Secretary of State Dean Rusk testified before the commission on the afternoon of June 10. He and several other US officials had been on their way to Japan at the time of the assassination, but turned back to return home after getting the news. During the flight back, Rusk said, he reflected on "the dozens and dozens of implications and ramifications of this event as it affects our foreign relations all over the world" and asked himself "could some foreign government somehow be involved in such an episode."[50]

> So far as the Soviet Union was concerned, Rusk testified:
> I have not seen or heard of any scrap of evidence indicating that the Soviet Union had any desire to eliminate President Kennedy nor in any way participated in any such event. Now standing back and trying to look at that question objectively despite the ideological differences between our two great systems, I can't see how it could be to the interest of the Soviet Union to make any such effort.... I do think that the Soviet Union, again objectively considered, has an interest in the correctness of state relations. This would be particularly true among the great powers, with which the major interests of the Soviet Union are directly engaged.

Soviet Premier Nikita Khruschev and Kennedy, Rusk said, shared "a certain mutual respect" and realized that they "necessarily bear somewhat special responsibility for the general peace of the world." In his opinion, "it would be an act of rashness and madness for Soviet leaders to undertake such an action as an active policy. Because everything would have been put in jeopardy or at stake in connection with such an act."[51]

Rusk acknowledged that Cuba presented a more difficult question because the United States had so few contacts with the Castro government. However, he expressed the same basic conclusion—that he had seen no evidence pointing in the direction of Cuba's involvement in the assassination. He went on to say that "it would be of even greater madness for Castro or his government to be involved in any such enterprise than almost for anyone else, because literally the issue of war and peace would mean the issue of the existence of his regime and perhaps of his country might have been involved in that question."[52]

The commission questioned Rusk about a report in the *Washington Post* on November 24, 1963, that the State Department had "no evidence indicating involvement of any foreign power in the assassination." Rusk defended the statement as reflecting the situation at the time and said that "the implications of suggesting evidence in the absence of evidence would have been enormous." He elaborated on this point by emphasizing that State could not afford "to leave the impression that we had evidence that we could not describe or discuss, when in fact we didn't have the evidence on a matter of such overriding importance could have created a very dangerous situation." When Ford suggested that a response of "no comment" might have been just as effective, Rusk responded that the press would certainly have taken such a response to confirm that there was in fact evidence that could not be disclosed.[53]

■ Marina Oswald Testifies Again

After hearing from these State Department officials, the commission on June 11 had a second opportunity to question Marina Oswald. The principal reason for calling her back was to explore her recollection that her husband had threatened to kill former vice president Richard Nixon, a fact not mentioned in her earlier testimony. She apologized for this omission and told the commission she had not intended "to deceive you the first time."[54]

She testified that Oswald's remark about Nixon came after his General Walker attempt on April 10, but before he left for New Orleans on April 24. After Oswald returned from getting the morning newspaper, she said, he put a suit on and took his pistol. When she asked where he was going, he answered: "Nixon is coming. I want to go and have a look." She expressed concern about the "look" he was intending to have with his pistol, went into the bathroom in tears, and reminded him of his promise after the Walker incident never to do anything like that again. When he came into the bathroom, she tried to keep him from leaving. She had not seen or heard anything about Nixon coming to Dallas.[55]

When pressed, she became uncertain where they lived at the time and whether she did struggle to keep him in the bathroom, but "there is no doubt he got dressed and had a gun." She did not remember her husband previously expressing any hostility toward Nixon, but said he told her the next day that Nixon had not come to Dallas after all.[56]

Mrs. Oswald testified she and her husband argued about this incident and that he became angry at her. She told him that she was pregnant and reminded him repeatedly of his previous promise not to repeat the Walker attack. He took the pistol out of his belt and put it back in his room. When asked how he reacted to her interfering with him, she said:

At first he was extremely angry, and he said, "You are always getting in my way." But then rather quickly he gave in, which was rather unusual for him. At the time I didn't give this any thought, but now I think it was just rather a kind of nasty joke he was playing with me. Sometimes Lee was—he had a sadistic—my husband had a sadistic streak in him and he got pleasure out of harming people, and out of harming me, not physically but emotionally and mentally.

Under questioning by Cooper, she recalled that her husband told her that "I am going to go out and find out if there will be an appropriate opportunity and if there is I will use the pistol." She testified that he did not seem angry at the time: "He looked more preoccupied and had sort of a concentrated look." She said that the whole incident took about twenty minutes.[27]

The commission members found her testimony on the Nixon event inconclusive and unsatisfactory. Dulles questioned her about her reactions to this incident in light of the assurances she had gotten from her husband earlier. She admitted the Walker attack had made a strong impression on her, but as for her reaction to the Nixon threat she said: "I don't know. I was pregnant at the time. I had a lot of other things to worry about. I was getting pretty well tired of all of these escapades of his." When asked whether her husband had made any other threats at other persons, including President Kennedy, she said that he had not.[58]

After informing her that Vice President Johnson had come to Dallas around April 23, the commission questioned whether it might have been Johnson that her husband wanted to take a "look" at. She was still certain that it was Nixon, rather than Johnson, that her husband was interested in. She said: "Yes, no. I am getting a little confused with so many questions. I was absolutely convinced it was Nixon and now after all these questions I wonder if I am right in my mind." She added: "I never heard about Johnson. I never heard about Johnson. I never knew anything about Johnson. I just don't think it was Johnson. I didn't know his name."[59]

The commission pursued several other subjects that had developed in the investigation. She was asked about signing a card using the alias "A. J. Hidell" that he had previously used. She testified that Oswald asked her to sign the name so he could plausibly claim more than one person was involved in the Fair Play for Cuba Committee chapter. He threatened to beat her if she did not sign the card. Although she initially said she signed only one such membership card, she later indicated it might have been two or three cards.[60]

The commission also wanted to learn more about the couple's life in Minsk. When asked how Lee spent his leisure time, she replied that "he was a great lover of classical music and used to go to concerts a lot, and theaters, and movies, symphony concerts, and we used to go out on the lakes around Minsk." She said Lee did not read very much because reading books in Russian was difficult for him. He did belong to a Russian hunting club, she testified, "in order to be able to acquire a rifle because only apparently members of such hunting clubs have the right in the Soviet Union to own a rifle." She recalled only one time that he went out with friends to shoot game, but was unsuccessful. She said her husband was friendly with many Cuban students who, he told her, were not impressed with the Soviet Union and worried that life in Castro's Cuba might become too much like the Soviet Union.[61]

When asked about any marital difficulties in Minsk, she answered that their only difficulty arose when, contrary to Lee's wishes, she told her uncle and aunt that she and Lee were going to leave for the United States. They had some additional arguments after arriving in the United States, one prompted by her telling their Dallas landlady that she was from Russia. Her husband had told the landlady she was from Czechoslovakia and "he became very angry with me for telling her I was from Russia, and said that I talked too much." She testified that her husband would get angry with her because of her association with Russian-speaking friends. She said that "he was jealous of me and didn't want me to see them." She said that he hit her on occasion.[62]

■ Jack Ruby Testifies

Jack Ruby had been on everyone's list of witnesses since the investigation began. After he was convicted in mid-March, we debated whether we should even discuss his murder of Oswald in our report. Hubert and Griffin recommended at one point that the commission report not discuss Ruby's murder of Oswald, worried that any commission assessment of Ruby's responsibility for Oswald's death might prejudice either his appeal or the prosecutor's effort to sustain the jury's verdict. Hubert and Griffin questioned whether it was proper for a prestigious commission to comment extensively about a person whose case was on appeal and likely headed for the US Supreme Court. They recommended that the commission state in its report that "conclusions relative to any aspect of Ruby or his activities are considered improper because of his pending appeal and that a report will be made later."[63]

I urged them to address the remaining issues about Ruby as thoroughly as possible. I told them that the staff could not make the decision about publication of the Ruby material at this time, and we should proceed as though Ruby would definitely be included in the report. Rankin agreed with me that we should reserve decision on this problem until we had a draft in front of us.[64]

The commission had not decided whether to question Ruby, but the possibility of a polygraph examination had been raised. Hubert and Griffin opposed it, believing that it was not an accepted method of arriving at truth. In fact, the commission had rejected an earlier proposal to use a polygraph test with Marina Oswald because the results of such an examination were not admissible in court.[65]

David Belin, taking depositions in Dallas during March and April, had heard of a possible polygraph examination of Ruby. During the summer of 1963, Belin had met Hillel E. Silverman, the rabbi of a Dallas synagogue that Ruby attended. After the murder of Oswald, Silverman visited Ruby regularly in the Dallas County Jail. Belin met with Silverman, who was convinced that Ruby had not been involved in any conspiracy. Belin proposed a strategy for Silverman to discuss with Ruby—Ruby would ask to be given a polygraph examination even though it was probable that his attorneys would advise him against it. After considering the matter carefully, Silverman later advised Belin that Ruby had agreed to request a polygraph test. Belin did not disclose his role in this matter until many years later.[66]

By the commission's April 30 meeting, Warren had decided he wanted to interview Ruby if he was willing. Ruby had been insisting that he wanted to take a polygraph examination in order to prove that he hadn't been involved in any conspiracy. In early May, Rankin asked Ruby's counsel if they would agree to his testifying. We were aware that a motion had been filed seeking a hearing on Ruby's mental competency. Some commission members thought that Ruby's appearance should be postponed until all post-trial motions were resolved. Rankin asked Ruby's lawyer, Joe H. Tonahill, what he wanted to do.[67]

Ruby's lawyers told Rankin that Ruby's mental condition prevented them from consulting with him and for that reason they were obliged to decline any waiver of the attorney-client privilege. Ruby's lawyers had presented a defense of insanity at trial, and his appellate lawyers were unwilling to undercut this defense by having Ruby be found by the commission to be competent to testify for its purposes. Hubert thought the commission would be criticized for obtaining testimony protected by the privilege where the client involved could not make the waiver decision himself. Hubert advised Rankin that he and Griffin also believed that Ruby's mental condition precluded any appearance before the commission.[68]

Warren was not deterred. If Ruby wanted to testify, the chief justice wanted to hear that testimony. We scheduled Ruby to give his testimony on Sunday, June 7, at the sheriff's office in Dallas. Warren planned to preside at this session, accompanied by Ford and Specter from the staff. Warren also wanted a complete tour of the various locations that figured in the investigation. Rankin proposed an agenda that would have taken an entire week, but Warren said that he only had that Sunday, because he had oral arguments in the Supreme Court the next day.

Rankin wanted Specter to educate Warren on the critical elements of the single-bullet theory. Although Warren had heard considerable testimony supporting this theory, Rankin sensed some reservations among the commission members and thought that this trip provided a unique opportunity for Warren to better understand the issue. On the morning of June 7, after flying together to Dallas, Specter and Warren stood together by the sixth floor window at the southeast corner of the depository, where the assassination scene had been recreated with the requisite number of cartons arranged to shape Oswald's "nest."

According to Specter, Warren "assumed a silent and thoughtful pose at the window" as Specter detailed the evidence that supported Oswald's identity as the assassin. He summarized the medical evidence regarding the wounds suffered by Kennedy and Connally, the ballistics results and the speed of the bullets, the trajectory of the shots at the moving vehicle, the reactions of the two victims as shown on the Zapruder film, and the alignment of the two men in the vehicle at the critical time, as confirmed by the reenactment two weeks earlier. Specter told Warren that it

> all boiled down to one key fact. When the bullet exited the President's neck, the limousine was in such a position that the bullet had to strike the car's interior or someone in it. Our exhaustive examination of the limousine had shown that no bullet had struck the car's interior. Then there was Connally, sitting right in the line of fire, directly in front of Kennedy, about to collapse from gunshot wounds. Could the President's neck wound and all of the governor's wounds have been caused by a single bullet?

Specter told Warren that the physical evidence, ballistics experts' analyses, wound tests, and clothing examination all supported the conclusion that the nearly whole bullet found on Connally's stretcher struck both men.[69]

Specter identified for Warren two of the major criticisms of the single-bullet theory: (1) the condition of the apparently whole bullet demonstrated that it could not have caused all the wounds; and (2) the holes in the president's clothing were inconsistent with the projected path of the single bullet at issue. Specter summarized briefly the evidence that countered these possibilities and the staff's conviction after the reenactment project that the single-bullet theory was the only logical and supportable explanation of what actually happened. When Specter completed his explanation, Warren "remained silent. After a moment he turned on his heel and stepped away, still saying nothing."[70]

In the afternoon, Warren was accompanied by too many federal and local officials—each asserting his obligation to be personally involved—to fit into

Sheriff Decker's small kitchen, where Ruby was to be questioned. The only person that Warren thought he could exclude was Specter, who happily went off to watch a baseball game on television. An hour later, a Secret Service agent rushed in and asked Specter to return to the kitchen because Ruby was insisting that there be one Jewish person in the room. Specter did as he was told and joined the crowd in the kitchen. But he steadfastly refused to acknowledge Ruby's silent mouthing of an inquiry to get him to confirm that he was Jewish.[71]

When the session began, Ruby asked for a "lie detector test" as orchestrated by Belin and Rabbi Silverman. Warren refused to answer Ruby's question about Warren's confidence in such a test, saying, "I can't tell you just how much confidence I have in it, because it depends so much on who is taking it, and so forth. But I will say this to you, that if you and your counsel want any kind of a test, I will arrange it for you. I would be glad to do that, if you want it."[72]

Ruby started his testimony by reiterating that he never engaged in any conspiracy with anyone, and had acted entirely on his own on November 24. He said that he always had a gun in his bag of money, and shot Oswald on the spur of the moment in order to save Mrs. Kennedy the ordeal of a trial.[72]

On the flight back to Washington, Warren told Specter that he regretted agreeing to a polygraph examination for Ruby, presumably because he thought it was inappropriate for him to be appearing to endorse a controversial interrogation technique. Specter, who did not customarily instruct chief justices, told Warren that we had no choice now but to go forward and honor his commitment.[74]

Ruby's testimony before the commission and a possible polygraph examination did not affect Griffin's assessment of his investigative mission. For Griffin, many details still required follow-up. Both Rankin and Redlich participated with me in the discussion about the need for further investigation in the Ruby area. I wanted to be certain they understood the extent of the investigative effort to date, the strongly expressed conviction of Hubert and Griffin that much additional effort was needed, and that the investigation involving Ruby's background, associations, and actions over the weekend of November 22 to 24 required more time and effort than we had anticipated earlier. I confess that, as a matter of bureaucratic self-interest, I did not want to be the sole decision maker on what *needed* to done in the Ruby area as contrasted with what *might* be done.

Griffin now had the assistance of Murray Laulicht, a recent graduate from the Columbia University School of Law who was recommended to me by a Justice Department friend. Rankin hired him with the initial thought that Laulicht would serve as his law clerk. But, in light of Hubert and Griffin's complaints about a lack of manpower, we decided to assign Laulicht to work exclusively with them. His work was excellent. He brought fresh eyes to problems that Hubert and Griffin had been working on for months. Griffin particularly welcomed his arrival because Hubert would have limited future availability for our work.[75]

Hubert told Rankin that he could not remain with the commission "on a permanent-duty status" after June 3, though he was prepared to return to Washington on weekends or to go to Dallas if necessary. In a handwritten note to the commission staff on June 5, Hubert advised all of us of his need to return to New Orleans and said: "I cannot leave however without saying to all of you that I have never been associated with a group of people as able and dedicated as this group." Later in June, Rankin took advantage of Hubert's offer, and asked him to obtain the testimony of twenty-two additional witnesses in Dallas.[76]

I asked Griffin on June 1 to give me every investigative request he believed was necessary to complete his investigation. He and Hubert agreed to do so with the qualification that additional requests might be required due to future developments in Ruby's criminal case. Their investigative requests to the FBI—more than 30 in number—began arriving on June 1 and kept flowing through the full month. Some were very small—like Griffin's desire to follow up on the deposition of Hyman Rubenstein (Ruby's brother) about an allegation that Ruby years ago had attempted to hit a person with a chair who made a derogatory remark about President Franklin D. Roosevelt. Some were more involved—such as a request for a review of the arrest records and summaries of FBI reports about any alleged criminal or subversive activities of ten acquaintances of Ruby and an exploration of a 1959 FBI report describing Ruby as a "known Dallas criminal."[77]

In their entirety, these requests reflected a prodigious effort by Griffin to supervise an investigative effort that met his professional standards and to be prepared to draft portions of the commission's report with a high level of confidence in the facts. No lawyer on the staff worked more diligently or thoughtfully than Griffin.

■ The Commission Starts Making Decisions

By mid-June, most of the teams, except the Ruby lawyers, had finished their investigative work and were drafting portions of the report. During this process, questions inevitably emerged that stimulated requests to the FBI, the Secret Service, the Department of State, the National Security Agency, and the CIA.[78]

Rankin, Redlich, and I agreed on our shared role in editing the report. In a discussion with Rankin on June 8, I told him that "I thought my function during the next several weeks in the course of preparing the report would probably be to make his life unpleasant." I recommended that nothing should go to the commission unless he, Redlich, and I agreed that it met our standards. I was confident he would not be offended by the suggestion and would recognize that, together with Redlich, we were already operating in this manner. I also recommended that no one person should have final responsibility for any section of the report, but that each section should be reviewed (and edited) by several persons to ensure consistency of style and quality of the final product. [79]

When Redlich joined the meeting, we took several steps to implement these objectives. He agreed to review and edit the draft foreword which I had prepared, and he agreed that his draft summary of conclusions should not go to the commission until the members had reviewed all the chapters in the report. We decided that the report's discussion of the source of the shots that hit the president should be a separate chapter rather than included—as it currently was—as part of Specter's draft narrative of the events of November 22 and the Ball/Belin chapter dealing with Oswald as the assassin. I reshaped this material, including the first draft of a separate chapter discussing the shots, starting with the material presently in the Ball/Belin and Specter drafts. I did not realize at the time how contentious this decision would become. [80]

We now had established a routine of sending draft sections of the report—in no particular order—to commission members for their review after clearance by Rankin. On June 12, Redlich sent Dulles five separate drafts: the foreword, drafted by me; a section dealing with the basic facts of the assassination, drafted by Specter; a draft dealing with presidential protection, written by Stern; a section dealing with Oswald's life from birth through his military service, written by Ely; and a memo on foreign conspiracies from Coleman and Slawson. [81]

Three days later, I sent two draft chapters of the report to Warren with a brief explanation of how we proposed to present the material in the report. The first was a draft chapter entitled "The Trip to Dallas." I explained that this draft "incorporates material from earlier drafts prepared by Mr. Specter and Mr. Stern which you have seen. The effort here has been to minimize duplication and to bring together in one chapter all the material dealing with the selection of the motorcade route, the composition of the motorcade, the reaction of the Secret Service personnel to the assassination, and the subsequent events at Parkland Memorial Hospital." [82]

The second was a draft chapter entitled "The Shots from the Texas School Book Depository." I explained that this draft

> was prepared to bring together all the evidence which might be relied upon by the Commission for the conclusion that the shots were fired from the sixth floor of the Depository. The chapter includes, for the most part, material prepared by Specter, supplemented by the discussion of eyewitness testimony and ballistics evidence which was prepared initially by Ball and Belin. If this organization of the material is approved, it is planned that this chapter and the chapter dealing with the trip to Dallas will be revised by the responsible attorneys and footnoted appropriately.

I also included a draft prepared by Ely dealing with Oswald's pre-Russian period. I advised the chief justice that it was being reviewed by Jenner and Liebeler.[83] Unfortunately, I made the mistake of not forwarding to each commission member everything sent to Warren. The chief justice forcefully brought this lapse in our administrative process to our attention a few weeks later.

At this point, our available manpower was shrinking. Both Belin and Specter found it increasingly difficult to work on a full-time basis in Washington in light of their responsibilities in Des Moines and Philadelphia. We had lost Ely in mid-June because of a military commitment, but we still had the full-time assistance of Richard Mosk, who had been with us since February; Stuart Pollak, who had been at the commission since April; and Murray Laulicht, who had joined us for the summer.

On June 16, Rankin, Redlich, and I examined each of the six areas of our work. In the first area, we discussed my reorganization of the Specter draft. We agreed that the reorganization worked, but that the draft needed polishing and appropriate footnoting. We decided to ask Specter to undertake this task. I called him and asked him to come to Washington to consult with Rankin on the subject. Specter seemed to understand the need for an overall perspective of the report into which his work, and that of other lawyers, had to be integrated.[84]

We had a much more difficult problem with the work of Joe Ball and David Belin dealing with Oswald as the assassin. A week earlier, Joe Ball expressed his strong disagreement with the edits proposed by Redlich in the draft that he and Belin had prepared. In a meeting attended by the three of us and Ball, "Redlich tried very hard to be diplomatic and minimize the extent of his differences with Mr. Ball in handling the material. Mr. Ball really didn't seem to recognize the extent of the differences and maintained that his handling of the facts was every bit as competent as Mr. Redlich's." Rankin tried his best to mediate, but was unsuccessful. The end result was that Ball and Belin were free to prepare another draft using whatever suggestions from Redlich or me were acceptable to them. I did not think this was going to end well—and it did not.[85]

When Rankin, Redlich, and I met on June 16, this situation remained unresolved. Three major issues about the Ball/Belin draft generated this very intense discussion. First, Ball and Belin disagreed with the tentative decision to have a separate chapter, using material from their draft chapter, about the shots from the depository. Second, their draft contained a lengthy discussion of procedural issues—such as documenting in detail the chain of custody for each major piece of evidence—that seemed unnecessary. Third, the Ball/Belin team disagreed with our view—which was supported by most of the other lawyers—that we needed to present our evidence in a way that both supported our conclusions and addressed major questions raised by the commission's critics. Redlich prepared an alternative outline of the chapter, which I thought was a substantial improvement over the Ball/Belin draft.[86]

We then turned to Area 3, where Bert Jenner and Jim Liebeler were reviewing Ely's memo on Oswald's pre-Russia life. Jenner had been concentrating on various aspects of Oswald's life after he returned to the United States. In this connection, he had taken depositions and prepared long affidavits for witnesses who knew Lee and Marina Oswald during their residency in Texas. Jenner had been given a "Dutch Uncle" talk by the chief justice and promised to have his report submitted within a few days. I had received an outline from Mosk covering Oswald's life following his return to the United States, which would be used by Jenner in writing this portion of Oswald's history. We continued to worry about when, and how, we would see these various reports dealing with Oswald put together in some coherent form.[87]

In Area 4, dealing with Oswald's foreign activities, the Mexican government's report regarding its investigation of Oswald's activities in Mexico had finally arrived. The report of the Cuban government, obtained through the assistance of the Swiss government, was received later in the month. David Slawson was carrying the major burden in this area in a competent and well-organized manner. Because Bill Coleman had not been able to devote sufficient time to the commission, I had arranged for both Mosk and Pollak to assist Slawson on his various projects.[88]

An important development in this area was the FBI response to Slawson's request for detailed information on the Fair Play for Cuba Committee and certain well-known anti-Castro groups. I had previously discussed with Malley our interest in getting background information on three anti-Castro groups identified in the letter: DRE, JURE, and the 30th of November movement. We asked for information on (1) the origin and growth of the organizations; (2) their activities, both at present and over the past few years, including the interrelationships, if any, among these organizations; (3) names, places of residence, areas of operation, and activities of the organizations' leaders, both at present and over the last few years; (4) locations of the headquarters and other important or special places of activities, if any; (5) sources and methods for obtaining financing and other material support, if known; and (6) known or suspected underworld contacts, if any. We wanted the information on a national level, but also the same information regarding the organizations with contacts in Dallas, New Orleans, Chicago, Miami, Detroit, Pittsburgh, Puerto 89[cdlxxi]

The FBI responded in June with fifteen reports on leaders of these groups and forty-six memoranda from the bureau's field offices on the organizations. We learned years later from a congressional investigation that this cursory response did not reflect any supervision by the FBI official responsible for submitting it to the commission. Nor did it reflect any input from the FBI's own experts on Cuban exile organizations or from its established network of informants in key areas such as Miami. The FBI reports on the Alpha 66 group, which had attacked a Soviet vessel near Cuba in 1963, failed to advise the commission that this group continued to plan paramilitary operations against Cuba. In particular, the FBI knew that the leaders of the Alpha 66 group in September 1963 had been negotiating with those involved in a New Orleans anti-Castro training camp for the use of aircraft with which to conduct raids against Cuba.[90]

The FBI told us that the CIA and the Department of the Army might have pertinent information concerning these organizations. It did not tell us that both the CIA and the Army actually had an "operational interest," which meant "that those agencies might be using the groups or individuals for intelligence collection or in covert operations." There was no indication that the FBI contacted these two agencies itself as part of its investigation of a possible conspiracy in which Oswald was involved. Nor was there any indication that either the CIA or the Army independently contacted their sources in these groups to determine what they might be able to contribute to the commission's investigation.[91]

The FBI's inadequate response regarding Cuban groups was not accidental. Hoover had assigned the FBI's investigation of the assassination to its general investigative division, which dealt primarily with the physical aspects of the case (e.g., the weapons, the bullets, the scientific evidence), Oswald's apprehension, and his subsequent murder by Ruby. Hoover maintained effective bureaucratic walls around the principal parts of his organization so that only he and a few trusted lieutenants had an overview of the bureau's entire capabilities or its relations with other government entities. The head of the general investigative division and his personnel working on the assassination were unaware of CIA efforts to kill Castro, Castro's threat to retaliate, and any consideration of possible Cuban involvement in the assassination.[92]

When Rankin, Redlich, and I evaluated Area 5 dealing with Ruby on June 16, we faced the same concerns that we had discussed over the last few weeks—the need for more investigative requests and the difficulty in writing a draft of Ruby's background without the results of previous requests. Our new associate, Murray Laulicht, and Griffin collaborated in producing a forty-page draft that discussed primarily the Dallas Police Department's plans for transfer of Oswald on November 24 and the question of Ruby's entry into the basement. Griffin estimated that he needed two more weeks to turn out a finished draft. This was longer than we had hoped, but none of the three of us had any productive suggestions for expediting the preparation of this important section of our report.[93]

The last area we discussed was Sam Stern's work on presidential protection. Chief Rowley was scheduled to testify in a few days and Stern would incorporate this new material into his draft section on recommendations for improving presidential protection. We were still unsure whether the commission would have a chance to review the Rowley report before completing our work. Remembering my last conversation with Robert Kennedy, I told Rankin and Redlich that the commission "had to deal with the question of transferring responsibilities" from the Secret Service to the FBI. "Neither of them seemed particularly enthused about discussing this."[94]

After our review of the six areas, we considered a few additional matters. The most important was the issuance of a subpoena to Bernard Weissman for the next week. Weissman was one of the sponsors of an ad published in the Dallas morning newspaper on November 22, 1963, critical of Kennedy. Although there was no evidence that Oswald had seen this black-bordered advertisement, with several questions challenging the policies of the Kennedy administration, the commission wished to investigate the individuals behind the ad and ascertain whether they ever had any association with Oswald.[95]

■ Secret Service Chief Rowley Testifies

Chief James Rowley of the Secret Service testified on June 18. Although the commission had heard from key agency officials, it was eager to hear Rowley before making recommendations. It was uncertain whether Rowley would be permitted to testify about changes in policies and practices recommended in his report, still being withheld by Treasury. Rowley was accompanied by Robert Carswell, Secretary Dillon's special assistant who had been intimately engaged in the negotiations with the commission about the scope of its investigation. Rankin proposed that, if Rowley believed that any questions invited disclosure of confidential information, he could request that such questions and answers be conducted off the record. Warren agreed.[96]

The commission asked Rowley about the conduct of nine agents in Dallas the night before the motorcade. We had learned that these off-duty agents went to the Fort Worth Press Club and, between midnight and two A.M., drank beer or mixed drinks. After leaving the Press Club, seven of the agents went to an all-night coffeehouse that did not serve alcoholic beverages. Several of the agents stayed there until shortly before three A.M. All of them had duty assignments beginning no later than eight A.M. that day. Rowley confirmed that their drinking of any alcoholic beverage while on duty was a violation of the service's regulations. But Rowley insisted that this violation did not affect the agents' performance the next day in protecting the president, even though some of the agents involved had critical responsibilities in guarding the presidential vehicle.[97]

When asked whether the agents involved had been reprimanded, Rowley, after some equivocating, admitted they had not. "I felt that these men, by their conduct, had no bearing on the assassination of the President in Dallas," he said. "[T]o institute formal punishment or disciplinary action would inevitably lead the public to conclude that they were responsible for the assassination of President Kennedy. I did not think in the light of history that they should be stigmatized with something like that, or their families or children. And, for that reason, I took the position that I did."[98]

Warren's disapproval was clear. "Chief, it seems to me that on an assignment of that kind, to be alert at all times is one of the necessities of the situation," Warren told Rowley. "And I just wonder if you believe that men who did what these men did, being out until early morning hours, doing a little— even a small amount of drinking—would be as alert the next day as men should be when they are charged with the tremendous responsibility of protecting the President." Rowley tried to stand his ground. "Well, we checked on that, Mr.

Chief Justice, and the agent in charge reported that they were in good physical condition. I don't condone these late hours; no. This is not a rule. This case is an exception.... I don't condone this at all. But these men are young. They are of such age that I think that they responded in this instance adequately and sufficiently as anyone could under the circumstances."[98]

Despite further questioning about this incident and the publicity it engendered, Rowley insisted that no official reprimand or disciplinary action was appropriate. He found no shortcoming whatsoever in the performance of the agents accompanying Kennedy that fatal day and never could explain why several witnesses—but no Secret Service agents—saw a man with a rifle shooting from the sixth floor of the depository. Scanning the windows along the motorcade route was unquestionably one of the major duties of the agents in the motorcade. Rowley's refusal to acknowledge the failure of his agents to perform this task effectively on November 22, coupled with his refusal to discipline agents who violated regulations, provided a sharp contrast with Hoover's severe disciplinary actions for the failure of his agents to pursue the Oswald investigation more aggressively before November 22.

When the commission asked about the advance planning for the trip, Rowley stated that he had read Lawson's report on the subject and was satisfied that Lawson had done a satisfactory job. He said that the report "follows the standard procedure that we have exercised over the years, and in many of the trips we had taken with the President. He covered everything with the police and all that we have normally covered on such visits." He told the commission he thought that advance notice of a motorcade route should be as short as possible, but that presidents often preferred an earlier notice for political purposes.[100]

He was also familiar with Bouck's report and testimony regarding the Protective Research Service, but told the commission for the first time that the Secret Service had conducted "a complete reexamination of" the operations of this intelligence operation. Specifically, Rowley testified that his agency had enlisted the services of the Rand Corporation, Research Analysis Corporation, and the President's Science Advisory Committee to assist the agency in revising its criteria and analyzing the reports received from other agencies.[101]

Rowley said the Secret Service had added three new factors to the criteria for determining who represented a threat to harm or embarrass the president: "the interest of the individual or the organization, capabilities of the individual or the organization, and the activities of the individual or organization. The interests of the individual or organization is the prime factor to be considered in the criteria, but must be coupled with the capability and activity of the individual or organization in any determination for referral to the Secret Service." Rowley said this new standard had become effective three weeks earlier and that his agency would be soliciting comments and suggestions from those agencies which customarily filed reports with the Secret Service about potential threats.[102]

Under questioning, Rowley confirmed that the buildings along motorcade routes outside Washington are not examined in advance of the motorcade. When he suggested that some change in this practice may have been made, or was under consideration, the commission went off the record so that he could testify candidly about this issue. Rowley submitted statements of several agents reporting that Kennedy did not want them to ride on the rear step of the presidential limo, and thought agents in the follow-up car were better situated to respond in an emergency than an agent on the presidential vehicle's rear step. He emphasized that the president does not control the agents protecting him.[103]

After an extended discussion of the budgetary needs of the Secret Service and its recent funding by Congress, Ford brought up a matter that Lawson had raised in his testimony. Ford told Rowley of his impression that "there was no clear delineation" of responsibilities among the various law enforcement agencies during a presidential visit and asked whether "a more precise checklist, a clear understanding, would be wholesome and better." Rowley said his agency had now revised its policies to address that issue. In its manual of presidential protection, he reported, there was now "a more precise procedure for the relationships of the Secret Service on the one hand and local law enforcement agencies on the other." While commission members were skeptical of Rowley's refusal to censure his agents for drinking on duty, they did appreciate his indication that the Secret Service was taking steps to improve its procedure.[104]

■ A Staff Failure Angers the Chief Justice

As we tried to do every week, Redlich and I sent on June 19 several draft sections of the report to Warren and Ford, who had requested that drafts be sent to him on a regular basis.[105] The next day, McCloy came to the office to pick up some materials and we spent some forty-five minutes together while copies were being made of various drafts. I reviewed with him the status of our drafting efforts and some major pending issues:

Specifically I mentioned such problems as dealing with the transfer of the Secret Service responsibilities to the Federal Bureau of Investigation and the need for the Commission to at least consider this issue. I mentioned the trouble areas as being areas 3 [Oswald background] and 5 [Ruby]. I outlined to him the reorganization that had been made in Chapter 2 [on the assassination] and Chapter 3 [shots from the depository] and also the disagreement regarding the handling of the material in the projected Chapter 4 [Oswald as assassin]. He did not express himself on many of these issues. He was interested in knowing why Marina Oswald had not been cross-examined more rigorously, why former Mayor [of Dallas] and Mrs. Cabell had not been deposed, etc. I told him about some of the recent testimony of Marina Oswald, the need to conduct more investigation on the Irving Sport Shop matter, the subpoena of Bernard Weissman, and the taking of the Fifth [Amendment] by [Robert] Surry[106] during the prior week.[107]

McCloy's most telling comment was about Marina Oswald's testimony. He had not been present at her second appearance, but had apparently heard some negative comments from other members (or staff lawyers) to the effect that she had not been questioned vigorously enough. Presumably these complaints were aimed at Rankin, because the members at the hearing did participate substantially in her questioning, although they were often frustrated by her responses. I was impressed by McCloy's willingness to look at the details of the commission's work and his understanding of the staff's role. I was a little taken aback though by his outspoken criticism of Rankin and Warren for not being sufficiently aggressive with the witnesses and not moving more rapidly to prepare the report.[108]

McCloy sent in detailed comments on the draft Chapter 2 (facts of the assassination) and Chapter 3 (shots from the depository) a few days later. McCloy was most concerned with Chapter 3 because he believed that our discussion of the shots was "the most important chapter in the Report and it should be the most convincing considering the evidence we have." His comments were aimed at improving the clarity and force of the chapter's analysis of the evidence.[109]

Before he left for New York on June 23, Rankin discussed with Warren the possibility of a commission meeting to consider draft sections of the report. Warren wanted to have this meeting as soon as possible. He told Rankin that he wanted the commission to "decide the basic questions involved in the writing of the report and then have the staff prepare a draft of the report based on these decisions." Apparently some of the commission members were concerned that "certain matters were discussed in the drafts although the basic decisions had not been made by the Commission." Warren wanted to emphasize that the commission—not the staff—was responsible for the conclusions in its report. When Rankin told the chief justice that he would not be in town on Wednesday, Warren said that he would talk with Redlich and me "to assist us in preparing the questions" for the commission to decide. Rankin suggested over the phone that Jenner be present at our meeting with the chief justice because of their personal relationship and Rankin's desire to have "someone of senior status" present to support us.[110]

On Wednesday morning, the three of us met with the chief justice for about ninety minutes. Before the meeting, Redlich and I tried to figure out how to respond to Warren's comments to Rankin. The staff had the responsibility to develop the facts through investigative requests and testimony and then present findings (or conclusions), supported by the evidence, to the commission, identifying along the way the questions that required more investigation or analysis. This is the traditional way in which law-firm associates and junior partners prepare a draft memo or brief for a senior partner to review, revise, or discard as the senior wishes. The commission members wanted the staff lawyers to undertake the investigative and drafting tasks, but wanted to make certain that the ultimate conclusions reflected their judgments. Redlich and I respected these concerns and welcomed their initiative in identifying the questions to be addressed. We knew, of course, that the staff necessarily would be making *proposed* findings based on the evidence for the commission to consider and—like the senior partner—revise or discard. Although we discussed some of the questions that we thought the commission would want to decide, we decided not to present this list to the chief justice, but rather see what he had prepared and wanted to discuss with us. Rankin had told us that we were free to try to persuade the chief justice not to have a commission meeting on Thursday but to schedule it for a later day.[111]

At the beginning of our meeting Warren read forty or so questions that he had prepared earlier that day. The questions pertained principally to the facts of the assassination, and the identification of the assassin, and were quite detailed and appropriate. His recital of the questions took only three or four minutes. When he asked us what we thought of his approach, we were enthusiastic about his questions as a method for organizing the commission's discussions. "We did suggest to him, however, that in some instance the Commission might feel that they needed some discussion of the evidence before they could resolve the questions," but the chief justice "thought this might be true on only a few of the questions." Warren had written his questions on a yellow pad, a staple of lawyer work. He handed over his list to me. His questions went to the heart of the matters we had investigated, his first five being: At what hour was the President assassinated? How many shots were fired? How many times was he wounded? What was the course of the bullets through his body? Were both shots lethal?[112]

During the meeting, it became apparent that Warren assumed that each commission member had received all of the draft memos and sections of the report that he had. When we told him that was not so, he became "extremely mad." He said that he had "instructed Mr. Rankin to see that every Commissioner received everything that he had received." Redlich and I were stunned. We looked at each other with dismay and then, very hesitantly, told him that we had not received any such instructions. At this point the chief justice realized that a commission meeting the next day to address his questions was not feasible if all the commissioners did not have the necessary materials. When he was called out of the room to take a call, I checked with Rankin's secretary and learned that she had not been instructed to schedule a commission meeting for the next day. When Warren returned, Redlich told him that no meeting had been scheduled. "I thought he was going to have a heart attack but then he became very quiet and disheartened. It was clear that he felt that he had been deceived and that everyone was making it difficult for him to complete this job on time. It was either here or a little later that the Chief Justice said 'Well, Gentlemen, we are here for the duration.'" We took this to mean that our failure to distribute the drafts to the members as he had hoped caused him to fear that "the work was going to stretch on for months."[113]

Redlich and I were shaken by Warren's reaction—and watched as this commanding and self-confident giant of a man so quickly became depressed by events beyond his control. We both had enormous respect for him and admired the time and energy he committed to the commission. His proposed questions for the commission were right on point, but he clearly had lost any interest in discussing them with us. Our practice in distributing drafts to members was not the result of any policy decision Rankin made; it developed gradually as some members expressed more interest than others in getting whatever materials the staff had produced. I should have seen this problem developing earlier and taken steps to correct it. Warren's concern that this failure would cause the commission's work "to stretch on for months" seemed a bit extreme under the circumstances, and likely reflected both his fatigue and his eagerness to finish a job he had not wanted.

We tried very hard to "soothe" the chief justice and "persuade him that all was not lost." Redlich suggested that we have the meeting on Monday and we promised that we would distribute the available material to all commission members by the end of the week. We described how much material could be distributed, but he "did not seem particularly persuaded that this was any kind of accomplishment."[114]

Although by this point we all wanted to bring the meeting to a speedy conclusion, two other matters required attention. On the subject of Oswald's motive, Warren said that the commission "should not try to determine his motive with any precision. He did allow, however that we could spell out alternative motives." Our colleague Jenner, who had been very quiet during the entire meeting, "said how relieved he was" that the chief justice felt this way because he "had filled his wastepaper basket with his writings dealing with motive because of his inability to fix on any certain motive." There certainly was no lack of possible motives underlying Oswald's assassination of the president. I knew that most of the staff tended to favor one motive over others, even if they didn't agree what that dominant motive was. But the range of our views, likely to be matched by the views of commission members, would have presented a formidable challenge if we felt compelled to agree on a single dominant motive, or even a ranking of possible motives. So I too was glad to hear Warren express himself on this subject.[115]

Looking forward to the commission's consideration of the questions to be decided, we suggested that members of the staff might participate. Without hesitation, the chief justice responded "that we should find something else for the beatnik to do"—referring to Jim Liebeler's luxurious red beard. After a moment of awkward silence, I said that Liebeler "was doing a good job" for the commission and Redlich countered that "we all have different ways of expressing ourselves." The chief justice said that he did not mean Liebeler was not doing a good job, but that "his beard might antagonize some of the conservative members of the Commission." Taken aback by Warren's unexpected bias, we just let the matter drop.[116]

Warren's characterization of Jim Liebeler as a beatnik was, on the one hand, humorous because Liebeler, perhaps the most conservative lawyer on the staff, warranted the "beatnik" label less than anyone else. On the other hand, it was profoundly unfair because he brought enormous energy and intellectual force to his work and deserved our respect. Warren's disappointment about our administrative failures probably produced the frustration that prompted this comment. When we reported this conversation to Liebeler, he took it in good humor, but thought it was serious enough to justify shaving his beard shortly thereafter. This was, after all, the 1960s.

Although I had concerns about some of Warren's decisions, they had to be considered in light of the extraordinary commitment he brought to this assignment. He probably spent more time on the commission's work than the other six members combined and, at the same time, attended to his duties at the Supreme Court. I believed also that, when the facts developed by the investigation were put before him, he would listen carefully to Rankin and consider what conclusions were justified.

After the meeting, Redlich and I quickly called Rankin. He was very concerned by Warren's reactions at the meeting, but assumed full responsibility for our failure to distribute the materials as Warren had wanted. We immediately took steps to distribute materials to members who had not received them earlier. I advised each member that we would be sending additional drafts on Friday for their review before the meeting now scheduled for the following Monday.[117]

Redlich and I had each undertaken substantial writing responsibilities, which occupied me, at least, for the remainder of the week. We agreed that I would continue work on the narrative for Redlich to edit, while he would continue rewriting the Ball-Belin piece. The next few days were extremely hectic and tiring as we made an effort to edit and duplicate additional material for distribution. On Friday afternoon, Warren came to talk with Rankin, and I delivered the new drafts to him. Afterward Rankin told Redlich and me that the chief justice "was not particularly impressed."[118]

I was not surprised at his initial reaction to these various drafts. They were isolated sections of what would ultimately, we hoped, be a coherent presentation of all the relevant facts. Some were more polished than others. I was certain that Warren wanted to see more work product than we had available. His comments may have also reflected his disappointment that the commission was seemingly unable to finish its work as rapidly as he had hoped.

Despite Warren's misgivings, we now had on the table the set of questions to be decided by the commission. We also had delivered preliminary drafts of five out of eight chapters, which I thought was a considerable accomplishment. The absent chapters—Chapter 3 (dealing with the shots from the depository), Chapter 5 (dealing primarily with Ruby issues), and Chapter 7 (dealing with Oswald's motive)—either required more investigation or necessitated integrating the work of different lawyers. To assist the commission in considering the questions put to them by Warren and to begin to shape materials for appendices to the report, we also delivered a draft portion of Oswald's biography dealing with his boyhood and Marine career; a draft explaining the legal bases on which the State Department and INS made their decisions concerning the Oswalds; and a draft entitled "Press and Police in Dallas" (with a note from Rankin asking whether the commission wished to address this subject in its report).

At the following Monday's staff meeting, we discussed several necessary but relatively minor aspects of the report. This involved questions about the analysis of Oswald's finances, the inclusion of our chronology in the report, and the possibility of a subject index to the report and the other published material. The most important question—not discussed but on everyone's mind— was whether any staff lawyers would be invited to consult with the commission later that day when it begin its consideration of the seventy-two questions that Redlich and I had prepared using Warren's list as a starting point. By the end of our meeting, it was clear we were going to be excluded.[119]

This was the first staff meeting since Marina Oswald had returned to testify before the commission and stimulated some very frank comments. Jenner and Coleman (among others) complained that she had not been vigorously examined by the chief justice and Rankin. Redlich took on the task of defending Rankin, challenging the critics to identify any specific instance where they thought that more aggressive interrogation would have produced new information. In any event, he emphasized that it was evident that her testimony would not be given any significant credibility.[120]

I do not recall any discussion with Rankin after this meeting about the criticism of his handling of Marina Oswald. He and Redlich were the only two staff lawyers in the room when she testified. After reading her testimony, I think the criticism was directed particularly at the commission's inability at the time to get a straight statement from Marina Oswald about her recollection of her husband's desire to take a shot at Vice President Nixon.

The staff remained available throughout the afternoon of June 29 as the commission members considered the seventy-two questions before them. As it became apparent that no lawyers other than Rankin would be asked to discuss draft report sections with the commission, their discontent grew. Like most of my colleagues, I believed that the commission failed on this occasion and others to take full advantage of the expertise that individual members of the staff had acquired over several months. The commissioners, on the other hand, may have felt well-enough informed to decide the basic questions before them without any need for additional facts that

Rankin himself could not provide. They understandably relied on Rankin to advise whether their discussion of an issue required information that he was not personally able to provide, in which event another lawyer might have been summoned to join the discussion.

In retrospect, Warren conducted the affairs of the commission just as he did with his fellow justices (with no law clerks present) in deciding cases before the Supreme Court. He expected each commission member to be fully prepared to discuss the issues, to listen to the views of his colleagues, and then to exercise his best judgment in reaching the conclusions that President Johnson had asked each of them personally to make. This may have been an unrealistic expectation for two reasons. First, Supreme Court justices devote their full-time efforts to consider the cases before them, whereas commission members had other, in some instances demanding, obligations requiring time and attention. Second, Supreme Court justices have law clerks to help them analyze the issues raised by the cases and to conduct additional research for them, whereas commission members for the most part lacked this kind of skilled and dedicated assistance. Notwithstanding these differences, I believe that Warren, by this stage of the commission's work, had a good sense of the other members and their ability and commitment to prepare a report under his leadership that would respond to President Johnson's mandate.

When the commission ended its meeting at about 6:45, a group of us marched into Rankin's office to find out what had happened. Rankin told us that the members had done a considerable amount of reading and that "the meeting had gone well." He said that they had resolved the first fifty-one questions unanimously, reserving decision on a few matters. The commission had agreed with the staff on all of these questions. This provided considerable relief to Redlich and me as all of our drafting and editing work had been based on our assumptions how the members would decide these questions.[121]

Although the staff's collective ego was still bruised by the commission's lack of interest in its views, most of the lawyers were pleased with the outcome. There was one exception. Ball still forcefully protested the way things were being handled. He was critical of the way he had been treated as consultant and critical of Rankin and those of us who were involved in the editing process. Although I knew he was upset by our rewriting his chapter, I never understood exactly what prompted Ball's sharply worded criticism of the process.[122]

Ball, more than twenty-five years older than I was, had attained great professional success as a criminal defense lawyer, where success depends to a much larger extent (than on the civil side) on the personality, technical courtroom skills, and persuasive advocacy of the lawyer in charge of the defense. He was a charming and influential colleague, and I regret that he felt so mistreated by Rankin and those of us assisting him. We were all striving to produce a well-organized and coherent report that would assess the evidence fairly and, in the process, dispose of allegations that had been given wide circulation. Because he was a close friend of the chief justice, I thought it was especially important that Ball not become so disenchanted as to not endorse the commission's report.

One unexpected decision emerged from the commission meeting of June 29. That day, the commission learned that the contents of Oswald's diary had been published in the *Dallas Morning News*. Oswald called the diary of his mundane life in the Soviet Union a "Historic Diary," reflecting his conviction that "he personally played a historically important role." The commission was concerned by this disclosure not only because it had entrusted the confidentiality of such documents to the Dallas officials who had them, but also because evidence being disclosed piecemeal could be misleading. In addition, the commission had assured Marina Oswald's counsel during her appearance on June 11 that the commission would make every effort to preserve her legal rights to the documents and other materials that she made available to the commission.[123]

The commission unanimously voted to request the FBI to investigate this matter. The *Dallas Morning News* accepted the FBI investigation as an accolade, stating, "The American people have a right to know, particularly any facet of an assassination of a president of the United States. The American press, large and small, has an obligation to tell them." As with most such investigations, the leaker was never identified, but Warren became even more adamant about security before we published our report.[124]

Rankin made two other disclosures of importance to the press after this meeting. Rankin announced that the commission's report would not be completed until after the Republican National Convention, scheduled to start on July 13, and the commission was not prepared to announce a target date for its public release. Rankin also said that the commission did not discuss the first published comments by Attorney General Kennedy about the assassination of his brother during a recent visit to Poland. On that occasion, Kennedy was quoted as saying that there was no question that Oswald did it alone and by himself. He expressed the additional view that ideology "did not motivate his act. It was the single act of an individual protesting against society."[125]

I was as surprised as the commission members that Robert Kennedy had chosen that occasion to express such a definitive opinion on the issues under investigation by the commission and wondered who, if anyone, had recommended that he make such a statement at this time. I never asked and was never told. But our focus was elsewhere. We had a report to write.

CHAPTER 8

JULY–AUGUST 1964: A TALE
OF TRAGIC TRUTH

■

B Y EARLY JULY, THE COMMISSION HAD ANSWERED MOST OF THE SEVENTY-two questions before it, and the staff was revising draft chapters based on those decisions. During July and August, both commission members and staff evaluated innumerable drafts of each chapter. The testimony of additional witnesses and investigation of critical factual issues expanded the commission's record. Changing publication dates complicated our lives, but when the commission in August requested additional time to complete its report, the White House readily agreed. By the end of August, we were confident that the report would be ready for submission to President Johnson on schedule.

Mark Lane, the New York lawyer who by this point was making quite a good living lecturing around the world on Oswald's innocence, appeared before the commission for the second time on July 2. We were faced with an unexpected hitch when Lane was stopped by immigration authorities on his return from a European lecture tour and asked whether he had ever traveled to Cuba. Lane was outraged to learn that his name was on a "stop" list. At Rankin's request, I learned from the FBI and INS that the request had been made by an unidentified federal agency. Based on this information, I assured Rankin that the commission had nothing to do with Lane's stop at the border.[1]

Although we knew he would relish this opportunity to again trumpet his views, the commission had asked Lane to appear because he had still not produced documents he repeatedly claimed to have. Rankin asked Lane to bring all records in his possession pertaining to the assassination of Kennedy, the killing of Tippit, and the killing of Oswald, including a recording of conversations between Lane and Helen Markham, the eyewitness to the shooting of Officer Tippit. Once again, however, Lane produced no records. During the session Warren suggested that the commission had every reason to doubt his truthfulness—a statement that was widely publicized.[2]

Lane had previously testified under oath that Helen Markham had told him that the gunman was "short, a little on the heavy side and his hair was somewhat bushy." This description did not fit Oswald. In March, Joe Ball questioned Markham in a hearing before the commission. Markham denied describing the gunman in this manner to Lane or anybody else. She testified that the gunman "wasn't too heavy" and that his hair "wasn't so bushy. It was, say, windblown or something." Markham said she had never met Lane and did not know who he was. When presented with two photographs of Lane to refresh her recollection, she said, "I have never seen this man in my life."[3]

When questioned by the commission, Lane denied that he had recorded any interview with Markham or knew of anyone doing so. Lane later reconsidered and wrote Rankin for assurances that neither he nor anyone else would be prosecuted under state laws prohibiting the recording of conversations without consent, if he provided the tape recording of his conversation with Markham. With Warren's approval, Rankin provided Lane with the requested assurances of immunity if he produced the recording.[4]

The FBI transcribed the tape subsequently produced by Lane. It turned out that he had never met with Markham, but had recorded a telephone conversation with her. A transcription of this conversation was published by the commission and illustrated Lane's persistent efforts to put words into Markham's mouth and her refusal to allow him to do so. As David Belin later appraised the conversation: "Try as he could, Mark Lane, legally trained, sought in vain to lead a relatively uneducated person into saying that the man she saw kill Officer Tippit was short, stocky, with bushy hair."[5]

■ Changing Publication Dates

By the beginning of July, we still lacked even a tentative publication date for the commission's report. After our memorable discussion with Warren in late June, the commission acknowledged that its assignment would require more time than the members had anticipated. Our lawyers and historians were determined to proceed carefully and thoughtfully, well aware that each statement in the report would be scrutinized for decades. It is certainly true—as observed by many future commentators—that the staff worked under pressure. The pressure, however, came not from the White House (or the Justice Department) but from the demanding nature of this unique assignment and the standards of care, judgment, and professionalism that the staff brought to the task.

The media and other commentators constantly pressed the commission about the projected publication date, particularly given the upcoming political conventions. One well-known writer asked Rankin to make the report available to the press before its public release, so that the initial coverage could be better informed; he suggested it not be released during the Republican Convention in San Francisco when the press would focused on that event. When Robert Kennedy asked me on July 7 about the timing of the report's release, I told him we hoped it would be done before the Democratic Convention in August.[6]

Later in the month, two target dates for publication emerged from White House meetings. After one session with McGeorge Bundy on July 14, Rankin advised me the report would be published on Monday, August 10. Although Rankin knew this was completely unrealistic, he was unable to influence the decision. At that time, Bundy held the position of assistant to the president for national security affairs and chaired the National Security Council, comprising the secretaries of Defense, State, and Treasury and the attorney general.[7]

By this time, commission crises had become routine. Rankin would take from his desk drawer "a yellow pad of paper and start listing things that remained to be done;" Redlich and I would decide which jobs we should undertake and which could be assigned to others on the staff. In light of the new—and im-possible—deadline, we agreed that Redlich and I should not do any original writing but concentrate instead on editing. We decided that Goldberg should undertake drafting of the appendix dealing with rumors and allegations, and that Belin and Specter would be asked to take on new writing assignments. We undertook to recruit additional people from the Government Printing Office for technical editing and two Justice Department lawyers for source checking.[8]

Reports of discussion about the publication date found their way into the newspapers. A *Los Angeles Times* article on July 23, under the headline "Kennedy Death Report Split Told," reported that Warren "is pressing vigor-ously for publishing findings early next month"—a view reportedly shared by commission members Dulles and Ford. The article reported President Johnson was urging the report be released before the Democratic Convention in late August. However, the article detailed the contrary views of Senator Cooper, very likely the primary source for the story. Described as "[t]he quiet-mannered but firmly decisive veteran of General Patton's famed Third Army," Cooper was quoted as asking "Why the rush?" and stating that he knew of no deadline the commission had to meet. The article indicated that Senator Russell shared Cooper's view on the timing issue, but had attended only a few commission meetings—in part because he was the "leader of the Southern bloc during the historic ten-week Senate battle over the new civil rights law."[9]

During the next week, Redlich and I made every effort to complete our own projects and to check with our colleagues about their writing assignments.

The period was "one of considerable pressure, aggravation and fatigue" during which I worked on several chapters, some of which had substantial problems. Redlich and I needed to raise the publication-date issue again with Rankin. On Monday, July 20, when Rankin returned from New York, Redlich and I confronted him. I opened the conversation and suggested that "the only problem was when Norman and I should tell him that it was hopeless and impossible to meet the deadline." We reported that the writing and rewriting was taking much longer than was anticipated.[10]

The next day, Rankin had another meeting at the White House with Bundy and representatives from State, the United States Information Agency, and the Government Printing Office. A new publication date was fixed— September 14, the first Monday after Labor Day. According to Rankin, these factors influenced the decision: "(1) The difficulties encountered by the Commission in putting the report in final and accurate form; (2) the problems of printing, particularly in light of White House requests that at least half of the available copies be bound in hard covers and the possibility of repagination of a substantial number of pages; and (3) the problems with getting the most favorable press distribution and reception until after the Democratic Convention and Labor Day." Rankin was quite clear: the decision was not based on any political considerations. The White House "requested only that the report be as good as it possibly can be."[11]

At least one commission member was unhappy with this new target date. When I was at the Justice Department the next day advising Katzenbach of the changed date, McCloy joined us. When I told him of the new date, he was "not particularly pleased and made a comment to the effect that we had not been very well organized over here. I suggested to him that a lot of people had worked very hard and he shouldn't have a mistaken idea about the amount of work that had been done." I doubt that my defense of the staff persuaded McCloy.[12]

In early August, the commission faced a proposed date of September 1 for submitting the report to President Johnson, which would give him two weeks for review before making it public on September 14, as agreed earlier. Under this arrangement, everything had to go to GPO by August 20. While the staff had been struggling with these deadlines for some time, in mid-August the commission members had to face reality. On August 14, the commission discussed this timetable. Senator Russell "made a strong presentation to the effect that he could not spend sufficient time on the materials to see that they got to the President in page proof form by September 1." He referred to his various responsibilities during the past eight months, particularly his work on the appropriations bills, and said "this was why he urged the President not to appoint a Senator, or, in fact, the Chief Justice, to the Commission." Based on Senator Russell's presentation, the commission decided to request two additional weeks for its report.[13]

Rankin discussed this extension a few days later with the White House staff, placing the responsibility for the delay on Senator Russell and the other congressional members of the commission. Bundy had no problem with an extension of two weeks. He did indicate his special interest in the chapter dealing with presidential protection, emphasizing the need for the president to be fully informed so that he could respond satisfactorily to whatever recommendations the commission made on this subject. Rankin told me after this discussion with Bundy that the commission had already decided not to give the White House any galley proofs or other advance knowledge of the report's recommendations, thereby demonstrating that the commission's recommendations reflected its own judgment without any influence from the White House.[14]

Although the White House had occasionally expressed its interest in early publication of the commission's report, no one there ever insisted that the report be produced by a certain date. As reflected in Rankin's discussions with Bundy, the White House deferred to the commission's judgment about a feasible publication date. In short, the commission produced the report on its own schedule, after determining that the investigative work was completed satisfactorily and that the members had sufficient time to review and finalize the report.

■ Organizing Our Presentation of the Facts

We had been revising our outline of the report since our historian, Al Goldberg, produced the first version in mid-March. By early July, we needed to establish our final structure for the chapters and decide how to present the evidence in each chapter. Some of the proposed chapters fell neatly into the outline used for our investigation, but some did not. As was inevitable, the drafting of the individual chapters did not proceed at the same pace. Some chapters were easier to write; some required more investigation; others required more collaboration within the staff; and some received extra commission attention.

At meetings on June 29 and July 2, the commission considered the seventy-two questions that Warren wanted discussed. The members evaluated each question in light of the testimony they had heard or read and the draft sections of the report prepared by the staff. Of course, the commission reserved final judgment on its conclusions until it saw the proposed final version of the entire report, which was still some distance down the road. However, after these meetings we had our marching orders and it became the staff's job to present the evidence on which the commission's tentative conclusions were based in the most persuasive way that we could fashion.

Persuasion depends on clear organization and good writing. The commission members knew that their report would be long and complicated. Many of the facts that supported one conclusion were interwoven with facts supporting another conclusion. For example, some of the evidence supporting the commission's finding regarding the source of the shots that hit Kennedy and Connally was also pertinent to the identification of Oswald as the assassin. Any long document confronts problems of duplication, contradiction, and error. We had to find a way to minimize all three.

From early July, when the commission settled tentatively on its main factual determinations, through the end of August, the chapters in the report gradually took shape. Although we had been working for six months, a great deal of work remained. We needed to decide which facts should be in the main report and which in appendices. Warren requested that the staff submit draft chapters in sequential order for consideration by the members, who had complained of the difficulty in determining where a chapter would be placed in the report. Although this request prompted some grumbling among the staff, including me, Rankin insisted we alter our writing schedules to accommodate this request. A description of each chapter individually assists in understanding each chapter's evolution and the substantive issues that need further development.[15]

CHAPTER 1: SUMMARY AND CONCLUSIONS

This chapter had three sections: a narrative of the events in Dallas, the commission's conclusions, and its recommendations. Several of us had worked on the narrative of events, which had to reflect both the substance and the language that was used in later chapters of the report. It was my responsibility, along with Redlich, to revise this section and provide it to Rankin for his approval before it went to the commission. In early July, Redlich and I prepared a draft set of conclusions and recommendations for the chief justice, who wanted to review it before he left the country a few days later. We managed to meet his schedule and his resulting comments reflected a careful reading of the draft. About half of his suggestions related to the section on presidential protection, dealing with the performance of the investigative agencies and the preliminary decision of the commission not to address the question of removing this responsibility from the Secret Service.[16]

At its meeting on August 11, the commission considered a new draft of Chapter 1 but decided to postpone any decision on this chapter until the remainder of the full report had been considered. Although there was by now little debate about the narrative section of the chapter, the substance and wording of the commission's conclusions required careful consideration of the evidence dealing with the key issues—the shots from the depository, the evidence identifying Oswald as the assassin, the evidence about Ruby, and the evidence regarding possible conspiracies. The draft chapters dealing with these issues had not yet been approved.[17]

CHAPTER 2: THE ASSASSINATION

This chapter had been tentatively entitled "The Trip to Dallas," but was renamed over the summer. Here we discussed the planning and advance preparations for the trip; publicity in Dallas before the visit; the president's visits to San Antonio, Houston, and Fort Worth before going to Dallas; the arrival at Love Field near Dallas; the organization of the motorcade; the drive through Dallas; the assassination; the events at Parkland Memorial Hospital; the swearing-in of the new president, the return to Washington, DC; and the autopsy. Specter's first draft was supplemented by material from other areas, reorganized, and substantially edited by Belin and me. The chapter's description of the Secret Service functions and reactions at the assassination scene came from Stern's work on presidential protection.[18]

The commission concluded that the first nine questions on its list were addressed satisfactorily in a June draft of this chapter. These were:

(1) What was the purpose of the trip?

(2) Who participated in the planning of the trip?

(3) When was it decided to visit Dallas?

(4) What was the purpose of the motorcade?

(5) Who planned the motorcade route?

(6) Why was this route chosen?

(7) Why did the motorcade turn from Main Street and pass the intersection of Elm and Houston?

(8) When was the route announced to the public?

(9) What time was the president assassinated?

The commission discussed an additional seven questions addressed in this chapter:

(10) How fast was the car going?

(11) Did the car slow down after the first shot?

(12) What treatment was given President Kennedy at Parkland?

(13) What wounds were observed by the doctors?

(14) What treatment was given Governor Connally?

(15) When and where did President Johnson take the oath of office?

(16) What wounds were observed at the autopsy?

The notes from the commission meeting on July 2 reflect its conclusions that the car was going "between 11 and 12 miles per hour" and that the treatment of questions 11 through 16 in the proposed draft was satisfactory.

After receiving the commission's conclusions, we prepared another draft. Goldberg, who was familiar with the facts about the Dallas trip, suggested a new organization for the chapter and provided editing suggestions. Both Stern and Specter participated in rewriting sections of the chapter and providing the needed footnotes. I finished working on a new draft on July 21, and it was distributed to the commission that day.

At its August 11 meeting, the commission approved a revised draft with only minor suggestions and authorized its printing. After implementing the commission's suggestions and clarifying its discussion of a few points, I delivered the chapter to GPO on August 20.[19]

CHAPTER 3: THE SHOTS FROM THE TEXAS SCHOOL BOOK DEPOSITORY

When we decided tentatively in early June to have a separate chapter consider the shots from the depository, I prepared an initial draft. I used material from the reenactment project prepared by Specter, supplemented by the discussion of eyewitness testimony and ballistics evidence written by Ball and Belin. My draft was circulated to the commission and staff in mid-June.

Questions 17 through 27 on the commission's list related to the shots fired at the president. The commission's answers to the questions and assessment of the draft chapter were brief and straightforward:

(17) How many shots were fired? "A preponderance of the evidence indicates that there were 3 shots fired."

(18) How many times was the President wounded? "Twice."

(19) What was the course of the bullets through his body? "Treatment [of this subject in the proposed draft] satisfactory."

(20) Were both shots lethal? "First shot not necessarily lethal; second shot unquestionably lethal."

(21) How many times was the Governor wounded? "One."

(22) What was the course of the bullets through his body? "Treatment . . . satisfactory."

(23) Where did the shots come from? "It was agreed that all of the shots came from the Texas School Book Depository Bldg. and the treatment in the proposed draft is satisfactory."

(24) Did they all come from one place? "Treatment . . . satisfactory."

(25) Is there any evidence that the shots came from the Triple Overpass or any other place in front of the car? "Overwhelming weight of the evidence is that the shots did not come from the Triple Overpass (commission indicated that in referring to the three railroad crossings at that point on Elm Street, reference should be uniformly by the name 'Triple Overpass')."[20]

(26) What damage was done to the windshield of the Presidential car? "Treatment in draft satisfactory, but make certain that there is a comment that there was no penetration of the windshield and also that there was no roughness that could be felt on either side of the windshield."

(27) From what kind of gun were the shots fired? "Treatment satisfactory."

The commission's conclusion that the treatment of a subject was "satisfactory" meant only that it accurately reflected the commission's answer to the relevant question. It did not amount to an endorsement of either the organization of the chapter or the staff's presentation of the evidence bearing on the question. The commission members always made suggestions, both large and small, for the staff to consider in preparing the next draft. That was especially the case with this chapter, where McCloy and other members made several suggestions. I am not sure that even Rankin knew what to expect from the chief justice's decision to proceed in this manner, but after these meetings we all concluded that the process successfully engaged the members individually in deciding the key questions, while enabling the staff to exercise its judgment in organizing the chapter and presenting the evidence on each issue.

The commission's review of a draft chapter frequently highlighted the need for further investigation on specific factual issues. In this instance, we asked the FBI to address a specific question about the Zapruder film as to the time that elapsed between frame 313 and the moment when Secret Service agent Hill first reached the back of the presidential limousine. We also asked the bureau to obtain the original tapes of the radio transmissions from Channel 1 and Channel 2 of the Dallas Police Department radio station for specified hours on November 22 and November 24, 1963, and provide new transcripts based on these tapes.

Rankin also authorized Specter to take five additional depositions in Dallas on July 16, including two witnesses who might have information regarding what we called the "missing bullet." The commission had decided that "a preponderance of the evidence" indicated that three shots had been fired. However, we could account for only two of those bullets—one nearly whole bullet found on the hospital stretcher that had carried Connally and the other included the two larger bullet fragments recovered from the vehicle. We could not find the third one, and no one ever has.[21]

Based on the comments received and the results of further investigation, I put together another draft that now included discussion of the expert examination of rifle, cartridge cases, and bullet fragments; the bullet wounds; the trajectories of the two bullets; the number of shots; the shot that missed; and the time span of the shots. After reviewing the draft, Mosk recommended that he and Arthur Marmor, our second historian on loan from the State Department, sit down with the authors of the earlier drafts so that the text and footnotes could be edited to reflect the authors' intentions more accurately. In the course of undertaking this chore, Marmor advised Redlich that important information provided by a deputy sheriff had not been used in the chapter. This prompted an immediate request from Redlich to Liebeler, who was then in Texas, to take the deposition of this deputy sheriff and others.[22]

After further revision the commission considered Chapter 3 again on August 14. I rewrote the section dealing with the missed shot to reflect the testimony of James Tague and James Altgens. Altgens, a photographer for the Associated Press, took a widely circulated photograph that showed President Kennedy reacting to the first of the two shots that hit him. Altgens testified that he took the picture "almost simultaneously" with hearing a shot that he was confident was the first one fired. Tague, who was located at a position near the Triple Underpass, was hit on the cheek by an object during the shooting and shortly thereafter a deputy sheriff located a mark on the south curb of Main Street where it appeared that a bullet fragment had hit the cement. I was concerned that the current draft did not sufficiently reflect the Altgens and Tague testimony and other gaps in our knowledge.[23]

Chapter 3 was approved by the commission later in the month and, by the end of August, the chapter was ready for printing. The commission reached two conclusions in this chapter that have been challenged by critics—the number of shots fired and the probability that the bullet that pierced Kennedy's throat also caused Connally's wounds. The commission did not reach a conclusion on the second issue—the single-bullet theory—until its final meeting on September 18.

In considering the number of shots fired at the president's limousine, we began with the proposition that the physical and other evidence compelled the conclusion that at least two shots were fired. In particular, the commission report referred to the nearly whole bullet discovered at Parkland Hospital and the two larger fragments found in the presidential automobile. All three were identified as coming from the assassination rifle, and "came from at least two separate bullets and possibly from three." The report acknowledged that witnesses at the scene had varying opinions regarding the number of shots—ranging from two to six—but concluded that "the consensus among the witnesses at the scene was that three shots were fired."[24]

The commission found "the most convincing evidence relating to the number of shots was provided by the presence on the sixth floor of three spent cartridges," which were fired by the same rifle that fired the bullets causing the wounds. The commission recognized the possibility "that the assassin carried an empty shell in the rifle and fired only two shots" and that the "eyewitness testimony may be subconsciously colored by the extensive publicity given the conclusion that three shots were fired." Nevertheless, the evidence, in particular the three spent cartridges, led the commission to conclude that three shots were fired. This conclusion of three shots, coupled with the physical evidence, indicated that one of the three shots missed the automobile and its occupants. Chapter 3 discussed which of the three shots might have missed, but did not offer any conclusion on this question.[25]

Absolutely no factual evidence of additional shots has come to light since 1964. No witness has come forward who saw a person with a rifle on the overpass, or the grassy knoll, or anywhere near the assassination site. No rifle was found around the assassination site except the rifle on the sixth floor of the depository building. No bullet, other than the two that killed Kennedy and wounded Connally, hit the vehicle. The relatively minor damage to the inside of its windshield was readily attributable to fragments from one of the two bullets that hit its occupants. This lack of factual evidence to refute our findings after nearly fifty years adds further credence to the commission's conclusion.[26]

CHAPTER 4: THE ASSASSIN

This chapter produced unanticipated drama in July. Ball and Belin concentrated their investigative efforts in the area initially called "Oswald as the Assassin," which mostly ended up in Chapter 4. Ball was back in California by this time and Belin was in Iowa, resuming their law practices. After we decided to move the discussion of the shots from the depository to a separate

Chapter 3, Redlich prepared a new draft of Chapter 4. Eisenberg helped out with various scientific issues, Specter polished up the discussion of Oswald's rifle, and we included some of Ely's earlier work on Oswald's experience in the Marines and his post-arrest treatment by the Dallas police. Redlich's first draft of the revised chapter was circulated to the commission and staff late in June with a comment that it was incomplete.

The commission considered fourteen questions (28–41) addressed in this chapter and made these decisions based on Redlich's new draft:

(28) Who owned the gun? "Lee Harvey Oswald."

(29) Was Oswald at the window from which the shots were fired? "Treatment satisfactory except that it was suggested that in describing the cartons piled up near the window as a rest for the gun, there be a reference to the Rolling readers and their light weight."[27]

(30) How did the weapon get into the building on November 22? "Treatment satisfactory."

(31) Who fired the gun? "Treatment satisfactory."

(32) How did Oswald leave the building? "Treatment satisfactory except the report should be explicit that he presumably left by the front entrance and that he had a Coke in his hand when he was seen by Mrs. Reed in the office."

(33) What time was the building closed off by the police? "Treatment satisfactory."

(34) Did Oswald kill Officer Tippit? "Yes."

(35) What was Tippit's record as a policeman? "Treatment satisfactory."

(36) Was Tippit normally performing his duties? "Treatment satisfactory."

(37) Was Oswald's pistol the murder weapon? "Yes."

(38) Are Oswald's actions between the time of the assassination and the murder of Tippit consistent with his having committed both crimes? "Treatment satisfactory."

(39) Did Oswald shoot at General Walker in April of 1963? "The answer should include statement that the overwhelming evidence established that Oswald shot at General Walker in April of 1963. The Commission also commented upon the fact that there should be a reference to the pictures of the Walker house that were found and the special book that Oswald had made up about the Walker affair which he later burned."

(40) Did Oswald threaten to kill Nixon in April of 1963? "The Commission directed that in answering this question it be shown that in the original

hearing Mrs. Marina Oswald was asked whether Oswald shot at any other person in high public office and that she answered 'No.' Furthermore, that the Commission questions whether the incident did in fact occur."

(41) Did Oswald practice with his rifle during October and November of 1963? "This question should be answered by the statement that there is some evidence by reputable people that Oswald practiced with his rifle during October and November 1963 but this is a matter of their recollection without their having known Oswald, and the other circumstances tend to negate any such conclusions. There was some discussion at this point about the Irving Gun Shop incident and whether investigation had been sufficient to conclude that there was no other gun. The Commissioners commented that all the surrounding circumstances that they knew of caused them to question whether the testimony about the Irving Gun Shop incident should be believed, but they desired to have any additional, reasonable investigation made that might help to determine the matter."

After the commission's review of the chapter, we expanded the material supporting the conclusion that Oswald was the assassin. The chapter now addressed the ownership and possession of the assassination weapon, the rifle in the building, Oswald at the window, the killing of Patrolman Tippit, statements of Oswald during detention, Oswald's prior assassination attempts, and Oswald's skill with a rifle. In most of these areas, Redlich set forth the evidence and summarized the basis for the commission's conclusion on each issue. Several members of the staff reviewed this draft to ensure we discussed the issues thoroughly and accurately.

Redlich's revision prompted David Belin to renew his (and Joe Ball's) opposition to a separate chapter dealing with the shots from the depository, rather than include this evidence to support the conclusion that Oswald was the assassin. In an impassioned letter to Rankin, he complained that he and Ball were not consulted about this proposed change. He told Rankin that the failure to consult with Ball "frankly shocks me; from my work with Ball I can honestly say that I have never met a lawyer who has better insight on the practical effectiveness of presentation of argument combined with an ability to understand and judge the heart of the testimony of witnesses."[28]

Belin recognized, however, the lack of prior consultation was not the issue. "Rather, the sole question is what is the most effective way of presenting our findings." Belin argued that "[t]he evidence on the source of the shots is among the strongest evidence there is to show that Oswald was the assassin" and therefore it should be included in the chapter dealing with Oswald as the assassin. He suggested that devoting an entire chapter to the shots was an "example of gilding the lily" and expressed concern that "the overproof in this type of a separate chapter serves as a contrast to point up the weaknesses of other aspects of other evidence showing Oswald was the assassin."[29]

Belin was not one, then or later, to soften his arguments for diplomacy's sake. "My frank opinion," he wrote Rankin, "is that this report is far too much influenced by the short-range concern with Buchanan and Lane, et al. Writers of this ilk all center their attack on a claimed shot from the overpass. There can be absolutely no doubt about the source of the shots, and it does not take 68 typewritten pages to prove it. All Buchanan and Lane have succeeded in doing is to steer the Commission on the false course of meeting the short-range argument while undercutting the entire function of what should be the historical findings of fact that will serve for the next 100 years or more."[30]

Belin's argument highlighted an important difference of opinion within the staff. He and Ball had developed sufficient evidence that would likely have persuaded a jury to convict Oswald of the assassination. If Oswald had lived to be prosecuted in court, his defense counsel (putting aside any question of Oswald's mental competence) would have tried to raise reasonable doubt about the prosecution's case—through challenges to the physical evidence and cross-examination of the prosecution witnesses. In the absence of any credible evidence regarding another shooter, another weapon, another cartridge, or another bullet, an effective defense would be difficult. Because there was no such evidence, Ball and Belin reasonably concluded that there was no need for the commission report to do more than present the existing evidence—physical evidence, eyewitness testimony, and expert testimony—that proved Oswald was the assassin. They objected to the commission undertaking a rebuttal of possible alternative explanations of the crime.

Others on the staff, including me, had concluded that the Ball-Belin approach would not be sufficient to achieve the commission's objectives. Instead, we thought it was necessary to anticipate criticism directed at the commission's work. And to do that, we had to do just what Ball and Belin wanted us to avoid: marshal the evidence to rebut allegations or contentions that had been made or might be anticipated. That doesn't mean we disagreed with Belin that there "can be no doubt about the source of the shots," but we wanted to disprove to the fullest extent possible the suggestions that there were shots from the overpass, from the grassy knoll, or any source other than the depository.

Our effort to document critical facts in Chapter 4 prompted new investigative requests in July and August. While exploring a possible escape route for Oswald, we asked the Secret Service to provide additional information on city bus routes in Dallas and Greyhound bus routes southbound out of Dallas.[30] We also asked the FBI in July to follow up on an alleged report that there was no palm print on the rifle and to obtain slides or originals of a picture taken by a photographer showing Oswald being removed from the movie theater by police officers.

In August, staff lawyers continued doggedly pursuing details on Oswald's activities. New requests asked the agencies to confirm, clarify, or supplement earlier reports. Other requests sought appropriate documentation that could be used in the report. Still others pursued newly developed information. In a few instances, the requested investigation led to further testimony before the commission or by deposition.[32]

In late July, Redlich circulated another draft of Chapter 4 incorporating the suggestions of the commission and members of the staff. Several of us responded in early August with further comments on the new draft. There were forty-one suggestions in my memo, generally focusing on improving the clarity and persuasiveness of the presentation of the evidence demonstrating that Oswald was the shooter.[33]

I was concerned about how we used the testimony of Howard Brennan, an eyewitness standing on Elm Street directly opposite and facing the depository as the motorcade went by. Brennan testified that he had seen a slender man, about five feet ten inches tall, in his early thirties, take deliberate aim from the sixth-floor corner window and fire a rifle in the direction of the president's car. We had relied on Brennan's testimony in Chapter 3 to support the conclusion that the shots came from the depository, and I thought he was an accurate observer whose testimony should be relied upon in Chapter 4, even though he declined to make a positive identification of Oswald when he first saw him in the police lineup.[34]

Goldberg's review of this draft chapter included general comments and fifty-one specific observations or questions. He wanted to put the discussion of Oswald's movements after leaving the depository ahead of the section dealing with Tippit's murder, which was implemented in subsequent drafts. He pointed out the need for more precision and clarity in the discussion of the critical evidence identifying Oswald as the assassin of Kennedy and the killer of Tippit—for example, the palm print on the rifle, the various descriptions of the suspect before the Tippit shooting, Oswald's taking the rifle to the depository, the exact time of the Tippit shooting, and the eyewitness testimony regarding this event. These, too, were passed on to Redlich.[35]

We were under pressure to get a revised version of Chapter 4 back to the commission for its review. Redlich still had the editing responsibilities for the chapter and had to consider all the comments he had received about the last draft. In addition, the FBI was responding promptly to our requests and this new information had to be reflected in the next draft, which went to the commission on August 20.

After the commission met on August 21, I was surprised to learn that a few members had already returned the latest draft of Chapter 4, which had gone to them the day before. According to Rankin, one of the commissioners had said that the chapter "was all factual and that therefore there was not much controversy in it." To the contrary, most of the staff anticipated that this chapter would be of the greatest interest to the critics such as Mark Lane and the broader audience in the United States and Europe waiting to see exactly what we had to say about Oswald's involvement in the assassination. Despite all the later controversy about the commission's report, the commission members and staff believed then and now that the evidence identifying Oswald as the assassin was overwhelming and convincing.[36]

CHAPTER 5: DETENTION AND DEATH OF OSWALD

The most dramatic—and potentially significant—development about Ruby in July was his polygraph examination. Rankin wanted the FBI to handle the examination, but Hoover resisted. He was reluctant to advertise that the FBI made use of this investigative tool. Rankin assured the director that the commission was not endorsing polygraph examinations, but emphasized Ruby had requested it. Rankin agreed with Hoover that the polygraph technique was not sufficiently precise to permit absolute judgment of guilt or innocence. Rankin stressed that the commission would avoid any interference with the pending proceedings in Ruby's criminal trial. Hoover relented.[37]

The examination took place on July 18. It was delayed a few days to resolve a dispute whether anyone from the sheriff's office could be present. Sheriff Decker told Specter he had been criticized because no one from his office had been present when Ruby testified before Warren and Ford. The sheriff insisted that Allan Sweatt, his chief criminal deputy and a polygraph operator, retain custody of Ruby during the examination. Unless Specter agreed, the sheriff said that Specter would need a court order to examine Ruby. Specter retreated, but still objected to Sweatt because he was a polygraph operator who might seek to interpret the polygraph results. The sheriff became "vitriolic" in opposing Specter's position but, after District Attorney Wade intervened, Specter and Decker agreed that Chief Jailer Holman, rather than Sweatt, would be present during the examination.[38]

After Ruby entered the room at about 2:00 P.M., Specter advised him that the commission was responding to his request for a polygraph examination and asked whether he still wanted it. Ruby stated that he did. Specter advised him of his rights, as did Ruby's counsel, Clayton Fowler, who also reiterated his view that Ruby should not take the test. Ruby's other counsel, Joe Tonahill, had previously told Specter that "he was personally glad that we had come to administer the polygraph and that Jack Ruby very much wanted to take the examination." The examination lasted until approximately 9:30 in the evening with several breaks to enable Ruby to rest, including one break lasting an hour and forty minutes. Specter later reported: "Mr. Ruby was very cooperative and, as the record will show, suggested a number of questions that he wanted to be asked in addition to the ones which we had planned. We accommodated him and asked all those questions." Bell Herndon, the expert FBI agent conducting the investigation, asked fifty-five questions.[39]

The proceedings concluded with testimony from William Beavers, a psychiatrist who had previously evaluated Ruby's mental state. When questioned by Specter, Beavers said Ruby was "in touch with reality and understood the questions asked and was responsive in almost all instances, except for questions which related to whether Mr. Ruby's family had been harmed as a result of Mr. Ruby's shooting Oswald and another question as to whether Mr. Fowler was in danger because of his representation of Mr. Ruby." Although Ruby before testifying had expressed concern that his family and attorney were in danger, he refused to answer these questions during the examination. Beavers testified about those questions: "Ruby's delusional state took hold so that his response there, in effect could not be counted against him." He went on to say that the examination did not damage Ruby's mental state and that the test was "fairly administered with adequate rest periods for Ruby."[40]

When questioned by Tonahill, Beavers testified that Ruby was psychotic—a conclusion that Specter thought differed from the answers the doctor had previously given him. Specter thought that Beavers and Tonahill were "trying to ride two horses: If the results of the polygraph examination were helpful to Ruby, then they would like to contend that he understood the questions and knew the nature of his replies. If the examination should be unfavorable, they wanted to have room to fall back on the fact that Mr. Ruby is psychotic so that the test could have no validity." A few days later, newspapers in Dallas and Washington published stories that included questions and answers from Ruby's polygraph examination.[41]

FBI examiner Herndon "concluded that the absence of any physiological response on the relevant questions indicated that there was no deception." According to Herndon, the examination showed that Ruby was telling the truth when he denied ever knowing Oswald before November 22, 1963, when he denied assisting Oswald in the assassination, when he denied shooting Oswald because of any foreign influence, when he said that he shot Oswald in order to spare Mrs. Kennedy the ordeal of a trial, and when he said that everything he told the commission in his earlier testimony was the truth.[42]

The commission members knew that such examinations were not infallible measures of a person's truthfulness. In addition, Hoover advised the commission not to rely on the examination. He stated: "In view of the serious question raised as to Ruby's mental condition, no significance should be placed on the polygraph examination and it should be considered nonconclusive as the charts cannot be relied upon."[43]

Specter, who had participated in both interrogations of Ruby, believed "that the most reliable assessment came from Herndon before he consulted any of his superiors. Herndon, a top polygrapher, not only had Ruby's readings but also could see Ruby's reactions—his frowns, smiles, gestures—as Ruby fielded the questions." Specter believed that Herndon was correct in accepting the polygraph's validity, and he was surprised when Hoover overruled him.[44]

In his 1973 book, Belin raised an intriguing hypothetical about the Ruby polygraph. "[T]he Warren Commission could very well afford to say that they did not rely on the lie detector test where the results of the test showed that Ruby was telling the truth on these important matters," he wrote. "*But suppose that the polygraph examination had showed that Ruby lied on any one of these matters. Do you think that the Warren Commission could have summarily dismissed the results of the test?*" Belin emphatically answered his own question: "Of course not." He knew "there was always a tremendous risk in giving that test"—the risk that a polygraph examination would indicate that Ruby had lied even though he was not involved in any conspiracy. Regardless of the risk, Belin was determined "to leave no stone unturned in an effort to arrive at the truth" and believed that "the story behind the polygraph examination of Jack Ruby is further evidence of the fact that we lawyers performed our work with a 'total dedication to the determination of the truth.'"[45]

The Hubert/Griffin investigation provided much of the substance of

Chapter 5, which discusses Ruby's entrance into basement of police headquarters and murder of Oswald. Some of the Hubert/Griffin material belonged in Chapter 6, dealing with the possibility of a domestic conspiracy, and the detailed biography should be in an appendix, as was Oswald's.

The commission considered seven questions (57–63) on its list relating to Ruby's killing of Oswald. These were the questions and the commission's conclusions:

(57) Were the security precautions adopted by the Dallas Police adequate? "No."

(58) How did Ruby get into the basement? "Treatment satisfactory."

(59) Did he have help from inside the Police Department? "The answer should be that there is no evidence of that."

(60) Did he have any other domestic or foreign conspirators? "Same as 59."

(61) Did Ruby know Officer Tippit? "Same (but here there was a further comment about the mind reader on TV who claimed to have seen Oswald in Ruby's Carousel [Club] and the fact that this should be checked out.)"

(62) Was there any connection between Ruby and Oswald? "There was no evidence of that."

(63) What was Ruby's probable motive? "Commission does not wish to answer this question as to the probable motive of Ruby."

The Hubert/Griffin team continued to seek information on Ruby's background, associations, and recent contacts that might produce leads indicating that his murder of Oswald was part of a conspiracy. In June, they made thirty-four requests for more investigative work, principally to the FBI. In July, they sent an additional thirty-one requests.[46]

The Ruby team took more depositions during July to explore Ruby's alleged presence at Parkland Hospital on November 22; his presence at the Dallas Police Department on November 22; his activities late Saturday night, November 23; more about his childhood and parents; and more about his telephone calls during the November 22–24 weekend. Hubert went to Dallas and took depositions of twenty witnesses. He took two more in Washington, DC, and then he and Griffin deposed an additional twenty witnesses in Chicago and Dallas. Rankin authorized Specter to take four additional depositions in early August at Griffin's request—two in Las Vegas and two in Los Angeles. We had FBI interviews of most of these witnesses, but needed to get their sworn testimony to resolve questions relating to Ruby's activities during the November 22–24 period and to explore his background more fully. None of these depositions produced any indication that Ruby knew Oswald or that he was part of a conspiracy to kill Oswald.[47]

Meanwhile, our historian, Al Goldberg, was working on another angle in the Ruby investigation. He recognized that the tapes and films generated by the media and, in some instances, by private parties were an important historical resource that should be accumulated and preserved. Goldberg wrote to the leading TV stations and networks, radio stations, magazine publishers, and newspapers to obtain their photos and other materials for the commission's review. He contacted both NBC and CBS to arrange for the commission's inspection of the footage resulting from their coverage of the events in Dallas during November 22 to November 24, 1963. Goldberg arranged that all these important materials be stored and preserved by the Army Photographic Agency of the Department of Defense.[48]

On July 11, Goldberg arranged for the Ruby team to see videotapes from three Dallas television stations before their trip to Dallas. They found significant information recorded by the media concerning Ruby's presence on the third floor of police headquarters on the evening of November 22, his departure from the assembly room in the headquarters basement about an hour and a half later, and his presence in the basement on Sunday morning five or ten seconds before his shooting of Oswald. In addition, studying these materials enabled them to make more precise judgments of the timing of critical events, such as the departure of the car driven out of the Main Street entrance by police officer Rio Pierce, the arrival of the armored truck at headquarters to transport Oswald, and the interviews given by police officials and others. Some of the interviews of police officers contained information that had not been mentioned by them either to the FBI or in their depositions by our lawyers. Based on this review, Griffin prepared a three-page letter to the FBI requesting its investigation of various questions arising from the tapes and films.[49]

Griffin continued to work on Chapter 5 throughout July. Other staff members, including Goldberg, Stern, Pollak, and Ely, produced sections of the chapter. By early August, Chapter 5 began to take shape this way: treatment of Oswald in custody (a chronology of what happened, interrogation sessions, Oswald's legal rights); activity of newsmen (on the third floor); Oswald's exposure to the press during his custody at police headquarters; the activity related to the proposed transfer; possible assistance to Jack Ruby in entering the basement; adequacy of security precautions; news coverage and police policy; and responsibility of news media. I do not recall any serious concerns about the organization and substance of this chapter in August.

CHAPTER 6: POSSIBLE CONSPIRACY

By July we had made substantial progress on the section dealing with the possibility of a foreign conspiracy, based largely on the work done by Coleman and Slawson. In June they had sent Dulles at his request a memo dealing with the possibility of a foreign conspiracy and delivered to the commission two other drafts—one dealing with Oswald's life in Russia and the other on the Oswalds' interactions with the State Department and the INS.

Back in February, the FBI had provided a short memo summarizing its interview of Soviet defector Nosenko. He claimed that he would have known if Oswald was a Soviet agent, yet had seen no evidence of such a relationship. Therefore, Nosenko concluded that the Soviets were not using Oswald in such a capacity. Based on the CIA's uncertainty whether he was a true defector, the commission decided not to rely on Nosenko's statement. The issue arose again in late June because we gave the commission a draft section of the report dealing with Oswald's life in the Soviet Union that had several references to Nosenko.[50]

Ford, who had paid close attention to this line of the investigation, was concerned by these references and strongly opposed any reliance on Nosenko. He was skeptical about using the information even if Nosenko was a true defector, which was far from certain; no one knew for sure if he was a defector or a Soviet Union plant. Warren recalled that CIA Director McCone had told the commission "off the record" that the agency could not vouch for Nosenko's credibility, to which the Warren had responded that he was "allergic to defectors." All three members present (Warren, Ford, and Dulles) agreed that Nosenko's information should not be relied upon. Dulles reported that he had talked to his former CIA colleagues over the weekend and learned that they still couldn't determine whether Nosenko was a real defector.[51]

Rankin thought that the commission should indicate for the historical record what information it had received from Nosenko, but had elected not to use because of the CIA's inability (or reluctance) to verify his credibility. Rankin was also concerned that this information had come to the commission from the FBI rather than the CIA. He reported that CIA deputy director Helms had just called him and was concerned that the commission had seen any report on Nosenko because of the risk of disclosure to the public. Rankin told Helms that it might be useful for the CIA director to write a letter to the commission expressing the agency's view that this source of information should not be relied upon.[52]

Warren, Ford, and Dulles remained concerned, however, about having important information in the commission's possession but being unable to even comment on it because of the defector's uncertain status. They asked Rankin to have the staff review information about Oswald from all sources other than Nosenko to determine to what degree the Nosenko report added to this information. If Nosenko added nothing new, their decision would be easy.[53]

At its meetings on June 29 and July 2, the commission answered nine questions (42–50) dealing with the possibility of Oswald being involved in a conspiracy:

(42) Did Oswald have any accomplices at the scene of the assassination? "This should be answered by stating that all of the evidence the Commission has, indicates that Oswald was alone at the scene of the assassination."

(43) Did Oswald have any accomplices in shooting Tippit? "Same as in 42."

(44) Is there evidence that anyone helped Oswald from assassination to arrest? "The commission thought that the testimony of the one witness that someone looking like Oswald was taken away from in front of the Depository Bldg. in a station wagon should be referred to with the additional statement that the evidence shows conclusively that Oswald was on the bus (and the other places that he was during the purported time of the station wagon incident) and therefore the Commission concludes that the witness must be mistaken."

(45) Was any private conveyance used during that period? "Treatment in proposed draft satisfactory, except for matters referred to in answer to 44."

(46) Is there evidence of any domestic left wing conspiracy? "The answer should be that there is no present evidence available to the Commission, etc."

(47) Is there evidence of any domestic right wing conspiracy? "Answer same as 46."

(48) Is there evidence of any foreign conspiracy? "The Commission reserved its answer on this question and said that this would be answered later."

(49) Is there anything in Oswald's relationships with the Soviet Union which suggests that Oswald was an agent? "Answer reserved. Same as in 48."

(50) What do the investigative agencies conclude on the subject? "Treatment in proposed draft satisfactory. Commissioners all agreed that the agencies uniformly said that Oswald was a 'loner.'"

After the commission discussed the Nosenko issue and answered these questions, we revised the foreign conspiracy section of the chapter and prepared it for another review by the commission.[54]

Chapter 6 raised perhaps the commission's most difficult challenge—was there any credible evidence of a conspiracy involving either Oswald or Ruby? We all knew the difficulties inherent in trying to prove a negative proposition—in this case that there was no conspiracy. We were now completing an extensive investigation of the background and associations of both Oswald and Ruby. The only logical approach to address this question in Chapter 6 was to present the facts developed by the investigation in a way that would persuade readers that our investigation was sufficiently thorough that the conclusion finding no credible evidence of any conspiracy was a fair and reasonable one.

We decided to report our findings in Chapter 6 by discussing a few broad areas of investigation where evidence of a conspiracy might have been found. We began with an analysis of the specific circumstances surrounding the assassination event itself: the selection of motorcade route, Oswald's presence in the depository building, his bringing the rifle into the building, potential accomplices at the scene of the assassination, and his escape from the building. Next, we needed to explore Oswald's personal contacts in search of relationships that might suggest a conspiracy. This discussion would explore his residence in the Soviet Union, associations in the Dallas–Fort Worth community, political activities upon return to the United States, contacts with the Cuban and Soviet embassies in Mexico City and the Soviet embassy in Washington, DC, Oswald's contacts with the US government, and his finances. Last, we needed to discuss any possible conspiracy involving Jack Ruby, which led to an examination of Ruby's activities from November 21 to November 24, 1963; whether Ruby and Oswald were acquainted; and Ruby's background and associations. This chapter required close coordination among five different teams: Ball and Belin, together with Specter (the assassination); Jenner and Liebeler (Oswald's background and domestic associations); Coleman and Slawson (Oswald's foreign activities and associations); Hubert and Griffin (Ruby's background and associations); and IRS agent Philip Barson (Oswald's finances).

The open-ended nature of our investigation of a potential conspiracy—requiring a far-reaching investigation of the possible associations of Oswald and Ruby and exploration of allegations and hypotheses—raised the fundamental question: When could the commission responsibly decide that sufficient investigation had been done to support a conclusion there was no credible evidence of a conspiracy? We knew that not only President Johnson but also the entire world were looking to the commission for a definitive finding on this subject.

Hubert and Griffin may have been satisfied with the evidence developed on Ruby's entry into the basement and his shooting Oswald, but Griffin now worried about whether he had sufficient evidence to judge whether Ruby was involved in a conspiracy of some kind. He continued to investigate Ruby's background, associations, and activity in the weeks before the assassination. These are a few of his Ruby-related requests to the FBI during August:

- Letter asking for further investigation of Mark Lane's allegation that on November 14, 1963, there was a two-hour meeting at the Carousel Club among Bernard Weissman [drafter and signer of November 22 newspaper advertisement], officer Tippit, and Jack Ruby.
- Letter requesting interview of a witness who may have received a letter from a former secretary to Ralph Paul [Ruby acquaintance] about a conversation between Paul and Ruby on November 23, 1963.
- Letter requesting location and interview of a Dallas garage attendant who may have witnessed an hour-long conversation on November 23 that Ruby had with two witnesses deposed by commission staff.
- Letter requesting that a witness previously interviewed by the bureau be shown pictures of various persons who he might have seen at the Carousel Club and resembled Oswald.

We all recognized that Ruby was a shadowy figure, with a range of business and personal associations that demanded full investigation by the commission. To accomplish this, Griffin and Hubert had made more than one hundred investigative requests to the FBI and deposed dozens of witnesses in the search for one shred of incriminating evidence. We found none. Near the end of the commission's work, Griffin reported: "I have personally examined all reports of the Federal Bureau of Investigation for the Dallas and Fort Worth areas pertaining to subversive activities during 1963 and have found no reports identifiable with Jack Ruby or any of his known associates."[55]

The commission's investigation pursued a "ground up" approach that focused on the background, associations, and activities of Oswald and Ruby to unearth clues of possible conspiracies. You need evidence—not speculation—before concluding that a conspiracy existed. One can speculate about the "possibility" of a conspiracy directed by one of the many groups that had reason to dislike the president's (or his brother's) policies or programs. If such a conspiracy existed, however, it eventually had to manifest itself in some manner through contacts with Oswald or Ruby relating to their actions in November 1963. If, for example, the national syndicate of organized crime had decided to assassinate President Kennedy and had elected to use Oswald as their chosen assassin, there would be evidence somewhere that someone on behalf of the national syndicate enlisted Oswald for this purpose and likely (but not necessarily) assisted Oswald in some aspect of the assassination.

I spent time on Chapter 6 in early August, working with Slawson and Griffin. Because Griffin had been left alone working on all the remaining issues in the Ruby area, I asked Pollak to assist him. I was aware that the investigation of the Ruby area had proved more extensive than anticipated, and that Griffin could use some help. We managed to produce a complete draft chapter for consideration by the commission at its August 14 meeting, when we decided to seek an extension of time from the White House.[56]

The adequacy of the commission's investigation of a possible conspiracy was the subject of much debate among our lawyers. Several, including Liebeler and Griffin, thought that we had not adequately investigated the possibility of a conspiracy and referred specifically to unresolved issues raised by the "Sylvia Odio story." Others thought that the commission needed to have a section in its report dealing with Marina Oswald's credibility.[57]

The Sylvia Odio story involved an allegation made by Sylvia Odio, a fervent anti-Castro expatriate who was a member of the Cuban Revolutionary Junta (JURE) and whose parents were political prisoners of the Castro regime. She testified that in late September 1963 three men came to her apartment in Dallas in the evening and asked her to help them prepare a letter soliciting funds for JURE activities. She said that two of the men appeared to be Cuban (or perhaps Mexican) and that the third man, an American, was introduced to her as "Leon Oswald" and described as someone interested in the Cuban cause. After the assassination, Sylvia Odio was certain that this man was Lee Harvey Oswald, and her sister, who was with her at the time of the meeting, also believed this to be the case. She testified that the other two men did not give her their full names, but one of them called her the next day to tell her that it was his idea to introduce the American into the underground "because he is great, he is kind of nuts," had been in the Marines, was a good shot, and believed that some Cubans should have assassinated President Kennedy after the Bay of Pigs.[58]

Although she initially stated that the meeting took place on either September 26 or September 27, we considered the possibility that the date was

September 25, because we knew that Oswald crossed the border into Mexico on September 26. This allegation was of particular importance to Slawson and Liebeler, who took her deposition in Dallas on July 22, 1964. When the transcript of that deposition became available, we sent a detailed four-page letter to the FBI requesting an investigation of all aspects of the matter. This included examining the possibility that Oswald may have left New Orleans on September 24 rather than September 25, the identification of other persons who might have met with Odio and been introduced as "Leon Oswald," and alternative means of transportation, if any, that Oswald would have had available to make his trip to Mexico if he had been in the meeting with Odio.[59]

Although the investigation was not finished when the commission issued its report, the commission concluded that "the evidence was persuasive that Oswald was not in Dallas on September 25" when Sylvia Odio said that she met with him. The commission acknowledged that no evidence had been developed that showed exactly how Oswald left New Orleans—by air, bus, or private car—and then (after a meeting with Odio) traveled from Dallas to Houston in time to take the bus that left Houston for Laredo at 2:35 A.M. on September 26. The commission had circumstantial evidence that Oswald took this bus from Houston, which was consistent with the Mexican immigration records showing the time he entered the country. The possibility that Oswald, whose pro-Castro sentiments were well known in New Orleans, would be able to persuade two fervent anti-Castro supporters to drive him from New Orleans to Dallas for a meeting with another such supporter, and then to Houston after the meeting with Odio, seems most unlikely, but not impossible. I think the commission was justified in reaching its conclusion based on the evidence before it, among other reasons because Liebeler, after taking her deposition, told me that he thought Odio was a credible witness but was wrong in her recollection of this alleged meeting with "Leon Oswald."[60]

Griffin agreed with the proposed conclusion about Ruby in Chapter 6 "that our investigation into the question of whether or not there was any conceivable tie-in between Ruby and the assassination is adequate to conclude that there was no tie-in" and that "there is insufficient evidence to conclude that any particular person assisted Ruby" in the shooting of Oswald. After discussion with him, Rankin, and Redlich, we agreed that Griffin would be responsible for further work on this section of the chapter.[61]

The commission lawyers differed on the appropriate treatment of Marina Oswald. Griffin thought that "Marina Oswald's possible function as a Soviet agent deserves particular attention, and her conduct deserves treatment in a single subsection." Pollak advised Redlich that not including a subsection on Marina Oswald's possible involvement in the conspiracy chapter "is an exceptionally obvious and glaring gap in the chapter as it now stands." Slawson, in response to an invitation by Rankin, wrote a memo recommending that Marina Oswald be called back to testify before the commission on the subject of Oswald's job at the Minsk Radio Factory, his activities in Moscow in 1959, Marina's exit interview with Soviet authorities in 1961, and the similar interview that she and her husband had in 1962. Three commission members—Russell, Cooper, and Boggs—were accompanied by Rankin and went to Dallas in early September to explore these, and other, issues with Marina Oswald.[62]

In the end, the commission's report did not include a separate subsection discussing Marina Oswald, her credibility, and her possible role as a Soviet-sponsored conspirator with her husband. There were two reasons for this. First, the commission found that "Marina Oswald's lack of English training and her complete ignorance of the United States and its customs would scarcely recommend her to the Soviet authorities as one member of an 'agent team' to be sent to the United States on a difficult and dangerous foreign enterprise." Second, I believe that the commission, after hearing her on three occasions and becoming more familiar with the facts of the investigation, concluded (after some initial misgivings) that she was a credible witness who did not know of, and certainly did not participate in, her husband's plans to assassinate Kennedy. I believe the commission was right on both points.[63]

Although we debated how much information was needed in our report and where to include it, there was agreement among the staff that the commission was correct to conclude that there was no evidence implicating either the Soviet Union or Cuba in a conspiracy to assassinate the president. Coleman and Slawson had done all that was feasible in exploring Oswald's activities in Mexico with the assistance of the FBI and CIA officials there. As for Oswald's conversations with Duran at the Cuban Consulate, the commission stated that it "has been advised by the CIA and FBI that secret and reliable sources corroborate the statements of Senora Duran in all material respects, and that the Cuban Government had no relationship with Lee Harvey Oswald other than that described by Senora Duran."[64]

Secretary of State Rusk testified that after the assassination "there was very considerable concern in Cuba as to whether they would be held responsible and what the effect of that might be on their own position and their own safety." Slawson told me recently that some of the confidential sources on which Rusk may have based this assessment were still undisclosed as of

December 2011. In the Warren Commission files at the National Archives there is a folder of materials from the CIA. Under a cover sheet identifying certain transcripts of the intercepted calls from the Russian and Cuban embassies in Mexico City, the folder contains the transcripts that the commission had seen and relied upon. Next in the folder there is a cover sheet entitled "Transcript of telephone calls between two high officials of the Cuban Government." Under the cover sheet, there is no transcript. Whether these telephone calls related to Cuba's reaction to the assassination or some other matter remains unknown in the absence of the transcript. Whatever agency concluded that these transcripts remain classified should have been more careful and removed the cover sheet from the folder as well.[65]

In an article written on the thirtieth anniversary of the assassination, in 1993, two of the most experienced and well-connected reporters with the *Washington Post*—Walter Pincus and George Lardner Jr.—wrote that no high-level United States officials believed that the Soviet Union was behind the assassination because it "simply had too much to lose from the repercussions of such an act, and were as mindful of the delicate balance of superpower relations as the Americans."[66] They went on to say: "Top-secret intercepts by U.S. and allied eavesdropping agencies reassured them. Communications between Moscow and the Soviet Embassy in Washington and between Moscow and Havana showed surprise and alarm over what had taken place, according to Warren Commission lawyers who were given access to the records."[67] I doubt that Coleman and Slawson (or any other commission lawyers) were given access to such intercepts if they existed but, if they did see them, such information would not have been shared with anyone else on the staff except Rankin. I am confident that they would not have given this information to any reporters.

As the end of August approached, Norman Redlich and I were disappointed with the status of Chapter 6 and the inherent problems in supporting our conclusion that there was no conspiracy. We unwisely vented our frustrations in a meeting with Jim Liebeler, suggesting that he was partially responsible for our lack of progress in dealing with possible domestic conspiracies. He got upset and wrote a memo challenging our statements. He gave us a little history lesson regarding the allocation of work between him and Jenner, reminding us that as of two months ago Jenner was to be responsible for the handling of any domestic conspiracy, whereas Jim was going to concentrate on Oswald's motive. Liebeler said: "I am more than willing, if able, to accept my full share of responsibility for the work of this staff. I cannot, however, leave myself in the position implied by the above-described oral statements made by both of

you which I hope you both will admit, upon reflection, are false and unfair."
He was right. We were wrong. Both of us apologized on the spot.[68]

CHAPTER 7: OSWALD'S BACKGROUND AND POSSIBLE MOTIVES

By July, the Jenner/Liebeler team had completed most of its investigation, including a large number of depositions in Texas, New Orleans, New York, and elsewhere. The commission discussed Liebeler's memo "Possible Personal Motive" at meetings in late June and early July and addressed six questions:

(51) Was Oswald's act the act of a psychotic individual?

(52) Was Oswald motivated in part by his adherence to Castro's regime?

(53) Was Oswald motivated in part by his adherence to Marxism or communism? If so, how?

(54) If Oswald was not politically motivated and if his act was not psychotic, what are the factors which may have contributed to his act?

(55) Is it possible that any specific events in his life shortly prior to November 22 may have contributed to his acts, e.g. his relationship with Marina, the rebuff in Mexico City, etc.?

(56) What was Oswald's possible motive in shooting at General Walker and does this shed light on his motive to commit the assassination?

After reviewing Liebeler's memo and these questions, the commission found the Liebeler draft well written but shied away from assigning any particular motive to Oswald or getting involved in psychiatric theories or terminology. Instead, they wanted these six questions to be answered by presenting all the essentials of Oswald's life that might have contributed to his motivation to kill Kennedy. They thought their report might suggest various motives that may have influenced Oswald, but not attempt to identify any of greater importance.

The commission members did question one aspect of Liebeler's draft: they thought it was soft on Oswald, too sympathetic. They thought it didn't adequately reflect the strength of his character, which they considered "steely" as demonstrated by some of his actions. They also were struck by Marina Oswald's observation that her husband's unhappiness in the various countries in which he lived—Russia, United States, and even Cuba if he could reach it—suggested that he would be happy "only on the moon, perhaps."[69]

We began reworking the chapter in light of the commission's comments. Meanwhile, we asked the FBI in July to run down some additional details regarding Oswald's political activities and associations. We asked for further investigation of a report identifying a witness who saw a young man in New Orleans in or about June 1963 distributing Fair Play for Cuba Committee leaflets to a crowd waiting to board a US aircraft carrier and in checking the deposition testimony of a witness who claimed that he saw Oswald in the Habana Bar in New Orleans on or about August 9, 1963. Following up on all such possibilities was essential to our consideration whether Oswald could possibly have been involved in a conspiracy to kill President Kennedy.

We also decided to seek the assistance of experts in examining Oswald's motives and on July 9 met with Dr. Dale C. Cameron, superintendent, St. Elizabeths Hospital, Washington, DC; Dr. David A. Rothstein of the Medical Center for Federal Prisoners; and Dr. Howard P. Rome from the Mayo Clinic. In advance, we provided the psychiatrists with a detailed memo summarizing key facts from Oswald's life, together with the depositions of his mother, brother, and experts who had examined him earlier in his life, a set of his known writings, including some letters, and a copy of his "Historic Diary."[70]

The consultants declined to advance any firm opinions about Oswald's personality and motives based on these materials. One or two commented on the desirability of more information about his military service and his stay in Russia. Nonetheless, their discussion identified some of the factors which were included in the final paragraph of Chapter 7: Oswald's overriding hostility to his environment, his inability to establish meaningful relationships with other people, his perpetual discontent with the world around him, his expressions of hatred for American society and his actions in protest against it, his doomed search for a perfect society, and his desire for recognition as a "great man." These professional insights gave most of us additional confidence in our assessment that this tragic event was a random act of violence by a lone assassin.[71]

Chapter 7 was divided into these sections: the early years, New York City, return to New Orleans and joining the Marine Corps, interest in Marxism, defection to the Soviet Union, return to the United States, personal relations, employment, attack on General Walker, political activities, interest in Cuba, possible influence of anti-Kennedy sentiment in Dallas, and his relationship with his wife. Most of the investigative work was done by the Jenner/Liebeler team, with some overlap with the Coleman/Slawson foreign affairs team. The extensive investigation of Oswald's entire life was necessary to enable the commission to address two distinct questions: (1) Was there credible evidence in Oswald's background and associations indicating his assassination of

Kennedy was part of a conspiracy? (2) In the absence of such a conspiracy, what motivated Oswald to assassinate the president?

After the commission's discussion of the issue, Liebeler continued to investigate aspects of Oswald's life and associations trying to discern his motivation for shooting Kennedy in the absence of any conspiracy. The public wanted to know "why" in 1964 and still does to this day.[72]

Rankin, Redlich, and I met with Liebeler on August 20 to discuss our differences about how to assess the importance of Oswald's Marxist views in the chapter on motive. Liebeler's current draft stressed Oswald's Marxist views and, by this stage of our investigation, he believed that there was a conspiracy among the staff to downplay the fact that Oswald was a Marxist. On the other hand, Rankin seemed principally concerned about what "the Far Right would do with any such discussion in our report rather than by what the facts actually show." This debate continued into September, until Chapter 7 was finally sent to the printer.[73]

CHAPTER 8: THE PROTECTION OF THE PRESIDENT

The commission had two major decisions to address in this area: (1) Should the FBI have informed the Secret Service of the information in its possession before November 22, 1963? and (2) Should any of the functions of the Secret Service be transferred to the Justice Department? The commission heard from FBI director Hoover in May and had received draft sections of this chapter before its meetings in late June and early July.

When Hoover appeared before the commission, he strongly defended his bureau's handling of Oswald before the assassination. Referring to the three interviews of Oswald by FBI agents, Hoover told the commission that the bureau's motive was to find out whether he had been recruited by the Soviet Union intelligence services. He stated: "We found no indication at all that Oswald was a man addicted to violence. The first indication of an act of violence came after he, Oswald, had been killed, and Mrs. Oswald told us about the attempt on General Walker's life by Oswald. No one had known a thing about that." Under the criteria then in force at the FBI, Hoover told the commission that the FBI had no obligation to provide Oswald's name to the Secret Service.[74]

Hoover advised the commission that he changed the FBI criteria in December 1963 following the assassination to provide that "all defectors automatically go on the list to be furnished to the Secret Service. There are thirty-six defectors that we know of in this country who have been under investigation. Some of those men may have changed their views sincerely. Some of them may not have. But as a matter of general precaution, as a result of the Oswald situation, we are seeing that all go to the Secret Service." With respect to the original criteria, "which we felt were sound and sufficient and which we felt no one, not even the most extreme civil rights proponent could take exception to, we limited the furnishing of names to [the Secret Service] to persons potentially dangerous to the physical well being of the President. We included emotionally unstable people who had threatened the President or Vice President."[75]

What Hoover did not tell the commission was that in December 1963 he had disciplined seventeen FBI agents and officials for their mishandling of the Oswald case and their failure to refer his name to the Secret Service. As discussed earlier, these actions came to light during the Church Committee investigation in 1976. Directly contrary to his commission testimony in 1964, Hoover had concluded a few months earlier that Oswald did_fall within the criteria in place at the time and proclaimed, "Certainly no one in full possession of all his faculties can claim Oswald didn't fall within this [sic] criteria."[76]

Notwithstanding Hoover's vigorous (and dishonest) defense of the FBI's actions regarding Oswald, the commission concluded that the FBI should have done more with the information in its possession about Oswald. The commission report stated:

> Although the FBI, in the normal exercise of its responsibility, had secured considerable information about Lee Harvey Oswald, it had no official responsibility, under the Secret Service criteria existing at the time of the President's trip to Dallas, to refer to the Secret Service the information it had about Oswald. The Commission has concluded, however, that the FBI took an unduly restrictive view of its role in preventive intelligence work prior to the assassination. A more carefully coordinated treatment of the Oswald case by the FBI might well have resulted in bringing Oswald's activities to the attention of the Secret Service.[77]

If Hoover had disclosed his disciplinary actions in 1963 to the commission as he should have, the commission could have explored in more detail exactly what the disciplined agents and officials had done, and not done, in the course of the Oswald investigation. It might have led to the commission learning about the Oswald note to Hosty, which was unknown to Hoover and had been destroyed after Ruby's killing of Oswald. Knowing about the disciplinary actions would have certainly resulted in more complete and stronger commission findings about the FBI's performance before the assassination.

The members considered six questions relating to presidential protection (64–69), but the notes prepared by Rankin reflected their responses at this point to only the first two. The commission's report reflected its decisions on the remaining questions as summarized here:

(64) Were the advance preparations for the Dallas trip adequate? "The answer is 'No, they were not. They were much too casual.'"

(65) Should the Secret Service have known about Lee Harvey Oswald? "The answer here is that under the criteria of the Secret Service they could not be expected to know about Lee Harvey Oswald although the Commissioners thought the criteria should have been such that they would have been informed about him."

(66) What did other agencies know about Oswald?

The commission reviewed in its report the information about Oswald possessed by the FBI and the CIA and concluded that the agencies failed to share this information with the Secret Service.

(67) What criteria were applied by the Secret Service prior to November 22 in defining persons who present a threat to the President?

The commission heard testimony regarding the criteria in effect on November 22 as well as the revisions adopted by the Secret Service during the commission's investigation.

(68) Did the Secret Service adequately fulfill its protective responsibility during the trip? (a) in San Antonio, Houston and Fort Worth? (b) in Dallas?

The commission report addressed the service's performance only in Dallas and specified several serious shortcomings in its advance planning and performance of the agents during the motorcade.

(69) What recommendations does the commission wish to make in this area on such matters as federal legislation, a Board of Overseers, intelligence criteria, use of the presidential car, etc.?

The commission did make recommendations on all these subjects in its report.

The last three of the seventy-two questions (70–72) considered by the commission were labeled "Miscellaneous Questions" and the commission's conclusions as of early July can be readily inferred:

(70) Was Lee Harvey Oswald an agent or informant of any federal agency?

The commission concluded that there was no evidence of any such relationship.

(71) Were the decisions made by the State Department with respect to Lee and Marina Oswald appropriate in light of existing law and practice?

The commission concluded that the State Department had acted properly and legally in its dealings with the Oswalds.

(72) Did the Dallas law enforcement authorities adequately meet their responsibilities during the period of November 22–24, 1963?

The commission's answer was no, and its report details the many shortcomings by Dallas law enforcement personnel in its handling of Oswald.

After revising the draft chapter in accord with the commission's comments, we submitted another draft to the members. McCloy responded promptly with detailed comments regarding the staff's discussion of the protective measures taken in advance of the trip and the information available to the FBI about Oswald that was not communicated to the Secret Service. McCloy wanted the report's comments about the Secret Service and the FBI to be both more specific and more critical.[78]

At its July 2 meeting, the commission discussed the broader issue whether any presidential protection responsibilities should be shifted from Treasury to the Justice Department. I learned from Rankin that Dulles and Ford were the only two members supporting a transfer of some protective duties to the Justice Department, but that Warren believed the commission should disavow its competence to address this question.[79]

Although this question was considered at later meetings, the two proponents of transfer gained no additional support. After the July 2 meeting, Dulles wrote a memo to Rankin explaining why he thought more radical measures were required than his commission colleagues. Dulles believed that one of the most important functions involved in the protection of the president was to provide "high-level guidance" defining "the general nature of the dangers in the world of today in both the domestic and foreign areas which affect Presidential security." He concluded that this and the other important functions "can only be fulfilled through high-level direction from an office or a body having great prestige" and proposed that these duties be assumed by the National Security Council. He suggested that the NSC allocate to the Secret Service "all of the physical measures for the protection of the President" but that the "task of pinpointing the suspects as potential assassins would be assigned to the FBI." Under this approach, Dulles anticipated that the FBI "would then take over full responsibility for the human detection analysis in consultation and collaboration with local police authorities in any areas the President might visit in the USA, with the CIA performing somewhat parallel duties, in consultation with local security and protective agencies, in any friendly foreign countries the President may visit."[80]

On July 13, Stern sent me sections of the chapter dealing with the evaluation of protective measures followed in Dallas, and I worked with him on these and other portions of Chapter 8 during the remainder of the month. When we were finished, this chapter had sections on the nature of the protective assignment, evaluation of presidential protection at the time of the assassination of Kennedy (intelligence functions relating to presidential protection at the time of the Dallas trip, liaison with other government agencies, other protective measures and aspects of Secret Service performance), and recommendations (making assassination a federal crime, creating a committee of cabinet officers to oversee the presidential protection function, responsibilities for presidential protection, general supervision of the Secret Service, preventive intelligence, liaison with local law enforcement agencies, inspection of buildings, Secret Service personnel and facilities, and manpower and technical assistance from other agencies).

At a commission meeting in August, Dulles campaigned for more than an hour to persuade the other members to adopt his proposal or some similar approach that might improve the quality of presidential protection. He was not successful. Although the Dulles proposal seems attractive in retrospect, the commission's failure to recommend a transfer of presidential protection duties was understandable. As earlier pointed out by Secretary Dillon, the executive order creating the commission did not expressly direct it to consider this issue. Of more importance was the concern that careful examination of this transfer question would have involved issues unrelated to the assassination—including statutory, budgetary, and organizational questions affecting the departments involved. Of course, the commission was well aware of the strong opposition of the Treasury Department and J. Edgar Hoover to any transfer of responsibilities to the FBI. With these considerations in mind, the commission decided that the matter was best left to the executive branch and the Congress.[81]

In August, I asked Lloyd Weinreb, our newest "associate," to review the draft and propose any editing changes. Weinreb was a classmate of Stuart Pollak at Harvard Law School, had just completed his Supreme Court clerkship, and was planning to join the criminal division at the Justice Department as a special assistant to Jack Miller. Weinreb provided a new, much improved draft to me on August 12. I made only a few changes, the most important being an effort to clarify the section dealing with the relocation of the Secret Service's responsibilities. This draft was delivered to the commission on August 19. After the draft was delivered to the commission, but before its meeting, Redlich and I were summoned to meet with Warren at his office.[82]

It was by far the most pleasant meeting with the chief justice that I had during my commission assignment. He was very cordial and began the meeting by stating that he was pleased with the current draft of Chapter 8. He offered a few suggestions for improving the draft and then turned to the two major questions that had likely prompted the meeting.[83]

First, he suggested that the proposal making assassination a federal crime should not explicitly provide for the death penalty. He told us that he "did not have strong views one way or the other on capital punishment" but did not wish to involve the commission in this controversial subject. He suggested that it might be sufficient for the commission to describe the need for, and the scope of, the proposed legislation and not address the issue of punishment. Redlich and I agreed that this could easily be done, either by referring to other federal statutes that could serve as models for this one or by leaving the question of punishment open for congressional decision. The commission's final report makes no reference to the punishment that might result from violation of the proposed federal law.[84]

Second, Warren thought the last paragraph of Chapter 8, which was the last paragraph of the report, was "too much of an admonition" to future presidents to be more conscious of security risks. He suggested that it "should be addressed more to the people of the United States than to the President." I told the chief justice that an earlier draft had referred to President Kennedy by name and expressed "the hope of the Commission that its work might minimize the dangers of another assassination" and that these sentiments seemed appropriate for the last paragraph in the report. Warren seemed amenable to revisions along these lines. With this encouragement, we redrafted the last paragraph to capture these suggestions.[85]

The commission discussed Chapter 8 on two consecutive days that week, with further consideration of the question of shifting the responsibility for presidential protection. After their deliberations on August 20, Rankin reported that the members "were pleased with the chapter although they were very methodically reviewing it page by page." They finished with their review of the chapter the next day and McCloy undertook to draft some language that might bridge the gap between the members on the issue of transferring some duties to the Justice Department.[86]

The Appendices

By mid-July, the commission had generally approved what material would be in the report itself and what would be relegated to appendices. We had tentatively designated about three hundred pages for the appendices, including a biography of Oswald, an analysis of his finances, an evaluation of the contacts between the Oswalds and the State Department, a biography of Ruby, a review of forensic tests (such as ballistics), a refutation of known rumors and theories, and a history of presidential protection. We had also decided to include in the appendices selected documents relevant to the investigation (such as the autopsy reports), and the documents relevant to the composition and operation of the commission. I wanted to get the appendices finalized because these materials, like the transcripts, could go to the printer well ahead of the report itself. The commission's report ultimately included eighteen appendices, the last one listing the endnotes for the entire report.[87]

Appendix XII, "Speculations and Rumors," was perhaps the most difficult appendix to write. Both the commission and staff had recognized from the beginning of the investigation that an appendix would be an appropriate place to address the most significant of the rumors and speculations, which were constantly increasing in number and intensity. But, as reflected in the debate about Chapter 4, we also wanted to rebut some of these allegations in the body of our report. Although I originally had an interest in drafting this appendix, we decided that Goldberg was the better candidate for this assignment.

Goldberg made substantial progress during July. On July 21 he reported that he had collected between 125 and 150 allegations that should be addressed. He advised Rankin that answers to most of these could be found in the draft report and in other appendices. However, he identified for Rankin eleven allegations that were not presently considered in the report; so, we needed to decide whether, and where, each might be addressed. Acting on Goldberg's suggestion that a few allegations needed further investigation, Rankin sent a letter to the FBI asking for its assistance on four allegations from Goldberg's list: (1) it has been FBI policy for twenty years to report to employers those of their employees who are communists or suspected communists; (2) Patrolman Tippit violated a procedure covering radio cars when he failed to notify headquarters that he was stopping to question a suspect; (3) prior to the assassination Dallas police searched other buildings in the area of the Texas School Book Depository but not the depository building itself; and (4) precautions taken by the Dallas police on November 22 before the assassination included surveillance of many people, among them some who did no more than speak in favor of school integration. The FBI told the commission that none of these allegations had any factual support.[88]

Goldberg circulated a draft of the proposed rumors and speculation appendix to the staff on July 24. He proposed that the answers to the allegations be footnoted by references to the report, other appendices, and, if necessary, the transcripts and other commission documents. He asked for comments on recommended additions or deletions, the accuracy of the answers, and whether answers to some allegations should be incorporated into the report. Goldberg received numerous, and detailed, comments from the staff. With these and other comments in hand, Goldberg was able to produce another version of the appendix for the commission in August.[89]

■ Our Fact-Checker Corps

As a matter of policy, we required that each fact in our report come from sworn testimony, or from a document that we had verified for accuracy, or from scientific or technical testing for which we had verified results. As was customary, our lawyers used footnotes to identify the source for each fact. It was necessary, however, to have someone other than the drafters confirm the accuracy of the footnoting—a process called "cite-checking."

In July and early August, we began to assemble a truly outstanding group of young lawyers to be our independent fact-checkers, whom we counted on to bring independent eyes and demanding standards to check the accuracy of our work. Drafted by Warren, they were, for the most part, recent law-school graduates who were incoming (or departing) law clerks for the Supreme Court justices. One of these was Stephen G. Breyer, a clerk for Justice Goldberg, who a few decades later returned to the Supreme Court as one of its justices.

As they arrived for work at our offices, we explained the materials they would be reviewing. By now we had more than 10,000 pages of transcripts, piles of test reports, a great many photographs and other exhibits, and a growing number of draft chapters that ultimately would amount to 469 pages with another 410 pages of appendices. Every fact in these materials would have to be checked to see if it was correctly supported by its footnote. Literally thousands of hours were spent on this task.

Murray Laulicht, also pressed into duty as a fact-checker, recalled an example of the importance of this process. He noted a comment in Chapter 4 that nine fingerprints on cartons surrounding Oswald's "nest" on the sixth floor had not been "identified." Other members of the staff, including Griffin and Liebeler, had also focused on this problem. They questioned whether the author meant "unidentifiable"—meaning that they had been examined but no conclusion could be reached as to their origin. Pursuing the matter, they learned that this was not the case—that in fact these prints had not been fully investigated. So we requested that these prints be compared with the prints of the local police officials or FBI agents or clerks who handled these boxes. The results showed that all nine sets of fingerprints belonged to state or federal officials and the text was accordingly modified to eliminate what otherwise would have been an unresolved issue. Dozens of such questions were raised on a daily basis during the nearly two-month period that this cite-checking took place.[90]

■ Publication of the Commission's Underlying Investigative Materials

The commission had decided early on that it wanted to make all of its non-classified documents public. Warren had announced this policy shortly after his impromptu comments before Marina Oswald's testimony in February, and it was repeated frequently in later statements by commission representatives. We had already decided to publish all of the transcripts of witness testimony and evidentiary statements, all evidentiary materials cited in the report, and our most important underlying investigatory materials.

During August, we consulted with the National Archives about the handling of the remaining materials. These were primarily correspondence, inter-office memos, drafts, TV films, radio recordings, newspapers and magazine articles, less important investigative reports, and miscellaneous materials that had been sent to us or collected along the way. I learned that under current National Archives policies the commission's investigatory and other materials would not be made public—regardless of the commission's desires. I reported this policy to Rankin and he raised it with the commission. I learned two days later that the commission had considered the matter.[91]

According to Rankin, the commission members thought "that it would be desirable if all the material of the Commission were not available to the public for a year or two after the report comes out." Although some time delay was inevitable because of the required organization and screening of these materials, it appeared that their "principal interest here is making sure that sufficient time elapses before any real critics can get access to material other than those which the Commission desires to publish simultaneous with its report." Rankin told me that the chief justice intended to talk with the National Archivist about its future handling of the commission's documents that are not published simultaneously with, or shortly after, its report.[92]

I do not know whether Warren ever discussed this issue with the National Archivist. Even if he had expressed his (and the commission's) view that all of the commission's documents (except those with a national security classification) be made public after the necessary organization and screening of the materials, it is unlikely that the National Archives would have departed from its customary procedures. President Johnson took steps in early 1965 at the chief justice's urging to ensure that most of the commission's records would be made public after normal processing by the National Archives.[93]

The commission's desire to defer access by "any real critics" to its unpublished materials for a limited time should be evaluated in light of its decision to publish promptly the commission's most important evidentiary materials. This supplementary material ultimately filled twenty-six substantial volumes and was available to the public two months after the commission report was released by the president. I think it was a perfectly natural instinct for the commission members to hope that the evaluation of their work would initially be based on the contents of their report and the supporting materials in the twenty-six volumes. However, I know the members recognized that "real critics" would find reasons to challenge the commission's conclusions regardless of the amount of supporting material eventually published.

■ Alleged Pressure from Outside

The repeated claim by critics that the White House, a federal agency, or unspecified powerful forces influenced the extent of the commission's investigation or the content of its report is simply false. I am certain that no one attempted to persuade the commission members to alter the substance of their report to meet any allegedly overriding national interests. If there had been an effort to compromise the independence of the commission in this manner, I would have known about it. The commission members, although certainly not flawless in their attendance or decision making, were men of integrity and strength, and not lacking in a sense of self-importance. They would not have deferred to any such influences.

The commission's lawyers who came from the private sector were instinctively more inclined to distrust—rather than trust—the federal government. They would not have acquiesced in an indefensible commission investigation and report and would have gone public with their disagreement if that became necessary. As the only assistant counsel who was on a government payroll, I served as a representative of the Justice Department and Robert Kennedy with only a single mission—to assist the commission in conducting a far-reaching and intensive investigation of the facts and in writing a report that would accurately reflect that investigation. We were none of us perfect, but it would have been difficult to deceive us individually, and impossible to do so as a group.

The commission members were steadfast in their defense of their schedule and independence. Gerald Ford testified later that the commission set "its own schedule for completion of its work" and pointed out that when the commission concluded that a July 1964 deadline was unrealistic, it extended the deadline as necessary. He understood why Katzenbach or others in the federal government might have wanted an early statement from the commission on its investigation as soon as possible. But Ford stated firmly that President Johnson, his associates in the White House, the Justice Department, or other federal agencies did not hurry the commission to conclude its work. Ford also denied that there were any political pressures influencing the substance of the commission's work. Cooper agreed with Ford's statement that the commission was not pressured by anyone.[94]

McCloy stated that the commission "came to a judgment in due course" although there were some "questions of style in regard to the preparation of the report" that required time to address. The earlier deadlines for June were abandoned, and the deadlines in July, August, and September were extended. The commission decided when it was ready to complete its work and no one pressured it to finish before then.[95]

The staff had the same perspective. Rankin acknowledged that there were time pressures because the country was anxious for answers to whether there had been any conspiracy. But he made it clear to the commission staff "that our only client was the truth" and he thought that "we never departed from that standard, any of the Commission or myself or the staff." Rankin said that some commission members thought it would be better if our report came out before the November election, principally to avoid any suspicion that President Johnson for political reasons wanted to delay the report. But there were no pressures exerted from the White House or elsewhere on us to meet that, or any, deadline if it meant not completing the investigation or writing the report as we believed necessary. Redlich added that if any member of the staff had approached Rankin or Warren and said that the staff needed more time to complete the investigation, the additional time would have been provided. I agree with that assessment.[96]

Rankin rejected the suggestion that pressures were exerted on the commission "not to find a foreign conspiracy" and stated that the commission undertook an aggressive effort to discover whether any kind of conspiracy existed regarding the assassination of President Kennedy. Specter in his later testimony rejected any theory that the commission's objectives included the allaying of public fears, the prevention of an international crisis, or the facilitation of a smooth transition in national leadership. No member of the commission or staff ever charged that we had been pressured in any way to limit the scope of our investigation or the substance of our report.[97]

Of course, we felt personally the incredible sense of national dismay and anxiety caused by the assassination of President Kennedy, followed by the assassin's murder by Ruby. President Johnson's decision to appoint a distinguished presidential commission—rather than rely on the normal processes of the Justice Department or the uncertain course of a congressional investigation—challenged the commission and its staff to address this national emergency in a professional manner so that the critical questions surrounding the assassination could be addressed in a timely and effective manner. I believe we met that challenge.

By the end of August, I was confident that we could finish our work on schedule in September. The commission was still deliberating on two major conclusions—the single-bullet theory and the phrasing of its conspiracy findings—and four of the eight chapters needed substantial editing, but the finish line was near.

CHAPTER 9

SEPTEMBER 1964: THE LAST DEBATE

■

THE RELEASE DATE OF THE REPORT WAS SET FOR SUNDAY EVENING, SEPtember 27. The White House agreed to give us three extra days to accommodate printing. We received galley proofs of most of the chapters in early September and I distributed them by hand to commission members and staff in Washington. Even this late in the process, I knew that we still had a lot of work to do.

By this time, the 1964 election campaign was in full swing. In office for less than a year, President Johnson wanted the personal endorsement that an overwhelming electoral victory would provide. Reports circulated that Robert Kennedy tried to force his way on the ticket as the vice-presidential candidate, leading to a Johnson announcement that no cabinet members would be considered for that slot. Shortly after Senator Hubert Humphrey was selected as the vice-presidential choice, Kennedy resigned as attorney general to run for the US Senate in New York. Meanwhile, Republican challenger Barry Goldwater, from Arizona, had alienated moderate Republicans shortly before the party's convention by voting against the Civil Rights Act of 1964, a signature piece of President Johnson's legislative program in the aftermath of the assassination. Johnson led in the polls by very large margins during the entire campaign.

None of these political developments affected our work at the commission. Kennedy's decision to run for the Senate certainly came as a surprise and produced a new wave of Kennedy publicity. Katzenbach formally became the acting attorney general, and remained the official most informed about the commission's efforts to complete its assignment. Most of us were too busy to do more than glance at the daily headlines and exchange casual comments about the political campaign. The White House announcement of a late-September publication date for the report managed to quiet, at least temporarily, those critics charging that President Johnson wanted to delay the report until after the election. I welcomed the fact that the media were preoccupied with matters other than our work.

■ The Final Debate on the Single-Bullet Theory

The commission had not yet approved the final wording of its conclusion on the path of the first bullet that hit Kennedy. Governor Connally had been adamant in testifying, based on his memory of the gunfire he heard, that he was not hit by the same bullet that struck the president. He was a man of considerable self-confidence and was obviously not persuaded by the expert testimony that his wounds would have been different and more serious if he had been struck by a pristine bullet. The commission members held him in high regard, and Senator Russell and others were reluctant to sign off on this question if it conflicted with Connally's testimony. They were also concerned that Connally would criticize their report if it rejected his testimony, which might in turn adversely affect the report's acceptance by the public. I had hoped that Warren and Rankin would be able to avoid any dissent among the members to the conclusion compelled by the facts—that a single bullet wounded both men.

Out of deference to Connally and in pursuit of unanimity, the commission produced a compromise statement on the single-bullet question. At its last meeting on September 18, the commission decided to adopt this conclusion:

> Although it is not necessary to any essential findings of the Commission to determine just which shot hit Governor Connally, there is very persuasive evidence from the experts to indicate that the same bullet which pierced the President's throat also caused Governor Connally's wounds. However, Governor Connally's testimony and certain other factors have given rise to some difference of opinion as to this probability but there is no question in the mind of any member of the Commission that all the shots which caused the President's and Governor Connally's wounds were fired from the sixth floor window of the Texas School Book Depository.[1]

By coincidence, President Johnson called Senator Russell on the evening of September 18 to discuss some disturbing events in the Gulf of Tonkin off the coast of Vietnam. Russell had returned to Georgia after the last commission meeting. Russell told the president that he "was just worn out, fighting over that damn report." He said that "they were trying to prove that the same bullet that hit Kennedy first was the one that hit Connally . . . went through him and through his hand, [and] his bone, into his leg and everything else. . . ." He told the president that it didn't "make much difference" which bullet hit the governor, but "Well, I don't believe it. . . . And so I couldn't sign it. And I said that

Governor Connally testified directly to the contrary, and I'm not gonna approve of that." Russell said to Johnson that "I tried my best to get in a dissent, but they'd come 'round and trade me out of it by giving me a little old thread of it." President Johnson asked whether the report was unanimous, and Russell replied that it was.[2]

This result should come as no surprise to those familiar with the ways of Washington. I knew that Warren thought that a unanimous report was very important. But Russell—and the commission members who deferred to him— were indisputably mistaken. There were no "certain other factors" in addition to Connally's testimony and it did, in fact, make a difference which bullet hit Connally.

The problems with the commission's equivocation are obvious. If the members were certain that all three shots came from the depository's sixth floor but also rejected the single-bullet theory, it left critical questions unanswered. If the first bullet to hit the president did not also cause Connally's wounds, and we knew an additional bullet that hit Kennedy did not hit Connally, then there must have been a further bullet (either second or third) that did hit Connally. Considering his wounds and the trajectory of the bullet that hit him, the bullet necessarily came from behind. However, the assumption of a separate bullet hitting Connally raised a different question not considered by the members: Could Oswald have fired such a second shot within the assumed time interval between Kennedy showing a reaction to being hit and the point at which Connally could not have suffered the wounds he did incur? In wrestling with this question, the commission would have to acknowledge there was no evidence that any bullet fragments in the car came from a rifle other than the one fired by Oswald.

Furthermore, the possibility of such a separate shot would leave us with the question that stimulated the staff's inquiry in the first place: Where did the bullet go after exiting the president's neck on a downward trajectory? It also invited further debate about whether Connally's wounds were caused by the bullet found on his stretcher or a pristine third bullet, raising the question where that bullet—also on a downward trajectory—came to rest. As discussed earlier, the commission's investigation revealed no evidence that a third bullet hit the vehicle, anyone in the vehicle, or anywhere else in the vicinity.

I was disappointed and angry—as most of us were—by this clumsy effort at compromise that endangered the credibility of the whole report. Rankin made an effort to explain it to Redlich and me, but we could not accept the excuses that he offered on behalf of the commission. It was incredible to us then—and to me some fifty years later—that the members would reject persuasive scientific and other evidence in order to avoid suggesting that a single prestigious witness may have been incorrect in assessing, from memories of a traumatic event, which bullet hit him.

In retrospect, Warren (and to a lesser extent Rankin) failed to exercise the leadership necessary to avoid this outcome. They—or perhaps Dulles or McCloy—should have ascertained long before September 18 that Russell was going to insist on not contradicting Connally. If they had done that, we could have urged our most knowledgeable lawyers to again present the evidence supporting the single-bullet conclusion and the problems inherent in any compromise like the one they adopted. It is unlikely that these discussions would have dissuaded Russell. But a powerful staff explanation to the commission might have persuaded Warren and other commission members that the single-bullet conclusion was the only supportable interpretation of all the evidence and the implications of not saying so might have led to a more defensible compromise.

■ Resolving Some Oswald Facts

Although the commission's deliberations about the single-bullet conclusion focused on our proposed conclusions in Chapter 3, they also related to our findings about Oswald as the assassin in Chapter 4. In September we pursued some allegations about Oswald's activities before the assassination, including his appearance at a rifle range or a car dealership, but developed no new evidence of importance. When we learned from Marina Oswald that she still had some items in her possession related to her husband's trip to Mexico, we quickly requested the FBI to get the items and add them to the commission's inventory of all the property possessed by Lee and Marina Oswald as of November 22, 1963. We wanted to be assured that no such property remained in the possession of Marina Oswald or anyone associated with the Oswalds.[3]

Liebeler got the galley proofs of Chapter 4 on September 4 and submitted detailed comments two days later. Although Liebeler was aware of the controversy about this chapter and the decision to treat the shots from the depository in another chapter, I do not believe that he had reviewed earlier drafts of Chapter 4. Liebeler had a passion for detail, a keen eye for lack of clarity, and a deep love of identifying potential improvements in the work of his colleagues, especially Redlich and me. With Chapter 4 already in galley proofs, it was a very difficult time to deal with the range and detail of his suggestions. But Liebeler's concerns—ten pages' worth—were important. They did not challenge the conclusions reached about the assassin, but instead the evaluation of the evidence and the clarity of the writing.[4]

This was the first of several memos about galley proofs that Liebeler wrote in September. His memos have been widely circulated by commission critics as evidence of the report's deficiencies and Liebeler's disagreement with its conclusions. When questioned about these memos in 1978 by a congressional committee, Liebeler unequivocally supported the commission's conclusions and expressed confidence that his memos were taken seriously by those at the commission responsible for putting the report in final form.[5]

I did not realize at the time that this was the first of four such memos that Liebeler would be delivering to me and Rankin, who expected me to manage this project and bring it to a successful conclusion on time. The accumulated pressures and emotions after eight months did not promote reasoned and calm deliberation. I was not pleased with Liebeler's last-minute decision to be the staff gadfly who would bring me detailed criticisms of chapters that had already been approved by Rankin and the commission. I am quite sure that I expressed my frustration.

But even at this eleventh hour, I knew it was essential to carefully consider all of Liebeler's suggestions. I made changes responding to about fifty of his eighty comments. About fifteen of his eighty suggestions required no changes, either because they were not substantive or had already been addressed. The remaining fifteen involved questions of judgment on which reasonable observers might disagree, and I decided to stick with what had been written.

Some of his changes could be readily accomplished because they involved substituting just one or two lines. Others were more difficult to accommodate in a way that did not disturb the already "set in metal" galley. Sometimes we were able to modify the language in a less disruptive way that still met his concerns. But some of Liebeler's concerns did not require any changes because they simply reflected his views on nonsubstantive aspects of the chapter, such as the use of headings, length of particular sections, or small changes in language not affecting the analysis or conclusions in the chapter. In any group project like this one, there are as many possible variations in structure and language as there are participants. There comes a time—and this certainly was the case in September 1964—when individuals have to subordinate their personal preferences and support a final product that incorporates the judgments and styles of many other contributors.

About fifteen of Liebeler's eighty comments included substantive aspects of the chapter where Liebeler would have preferred a more extensive, or modified, discussion of the evidence. He raised questions, for example, with respect to the photograph of Oswald with a rifle and whether the commission could reasonably conclude that the rifle in the picture was the assassination weapon, even though the FBI expert testified he could not make a positive identification of the rifle. He questioned aspects of the "curtain rod story" with respect to Oswald's transport of the rifle to the depository, urged more discussion of Oswald's capability with the rifle, and thought the commission should acknowledge that luck may have played a role in enabling Oswald to hit the president with two shots in what might have been a short period of time. I did not make these proposed changes because I believed that commission members and other staff members, if presented with these suggestions in plenty of time, might have reasonably decided not to change the chapter's language.

I was impressed with Liebeler's request for a more nuanced statement of the facts, and I would have supported some further editing if I had gotten the suggestions before we had galley proofs in hand for final approval. But they would only have added nuance, not substance, and by this time I limited changes to those that significantly clarified the commission's conclusions.

■ More Work on Assessing Potential Conspiracies

In September, the commission examined two more witnesses on conspiracy questions. The first was Revilo Oliver, a University of Illinois faculty member who had "recently leveled accusations against a member of the President's cabinet" in connection with the assassination in a conservative magazine. The commission decided that Professor Oliver's fulminations justified taking his testimony in order to dispel any false rumors he was spreading. Bert Jenner arranged for his deposition in Washington.[6]

At the beginning of the deposition, Jenner summarized Oliver's article. It contended that the "assassination was a part of a Communist plot engineered with the help of the Central Intelligence Agency; that Lee Harvey Oswald was a Communist agent trained in sabotage, terrorism, and guerilla warfare, including accurate shooting from ambush, in a school for international criminals near Minsk, Russia, [and that] under order from Secretary of Defense Robert S. McNamara, the U.S. Army began to rehearse for President Kennedy's funeral more than a week before the funeral actually took place"—in short, before the assassination. The exhibits produced by Oliver at the deposition—and relied upon for most of his conspiracy allegations—were principally news articles. Oliver was unable to offer any new information or analysis that challenged the facts upon which the commission was relying.[7]

The second witness was Marina Oswald, called to testify before the commission for a third time. Commission members Russell, Cooper, and Boggs, accompanied by Rankin, traveled to Dallas on September 6 to interview her. The session lasted from 3:20 in the afternoon until 8:00 P.M. Robert Storey, who was acting as special counsel to the Texas attorney general, and two interpreters were present to assist. Rankin had requests from our lawyers (including Liebeler and Slawson) for subjects they wished to have covered, and Rankin did his best to do so.[8]

Russell, serving as chairman at the session, began by asking Marina Oswald about her husband's reason for coming to the Soviet Union. She recalled that he had told her "that the Soviet Union is the outstanding Communist country and he wanted to see it with his own eyes." However, he later told her that he had declined citizenship in the Soviet Union "because he said that in case he did not like the way they do things in the Soviet Union, it would be easier for him to leave the country than if he did become a citizen." After their marriage, she said he did complain about many aspects of his life in the Soviet Union. He did not like his job or his living quarters. He felt he was not paid enough and that the prices of goods were too high. He resented the restrictions on his travel within the country and the need to report every three months to the government.[9]

On the subject of his association with Cuban friends, she testified that he and Erick, a medical-student friend, had some Cuban friends, but she did not know any of them. She confirmed that her husband was interested in Cuba and Cuban matters, but had no details to provide about the nature, or extent, of that interest. When asked whether he had Cuban friends in New Orleans or Texas when they returned to the United States, she responded: "No. I don't think he had."[10]

She told the commission about the couple's experience with Colonel Aksenov in trying to exit the Soviet Union. Although her husband was not permitted to see the colonel, she met with him on a later occasion. She testified that her uncle worked for the Soviet government, although not in the same area as Aksenov, but did not discuss the matter of exit visas with Aksenov or any other government official. She told the commission her uncle "would have been afraid to talk about it. When my uncle knew that Lee and I were planning to go back to the United States, my uncle was afraid for his own job and his own welfare." She said she had heard of another Russian woman married to an American who had difficulty leaving the country and that "to the very last moment we did not believe that they would let us out of the Soviet Union."

She testified that she was not questioned about her reasons for leaving the country, other than the fact that her husband wanted to return to the United States, and filled out the requisite questionnaire stating she was leaving for permanent residency in the United States. She said she found this lack of questioning "surprising."[11]

About her husband's trip to Mexico, she testified that she did not know definitely when he left New Orleans, but believed that she and Ruth Paine left for Texas one day before he went to Mexico. Oswald told her that he intended to visit the Soviet and Cuban embassies in Mexico. She said he was very anxious to get to Cuba. After the trip, he complained that both embassies were bureaucracies and that he did not get any good results from the visits.[12]

Russell asked her whether Lee was a "good" or "bad" husband and whether she had been truthful in her earlier commission appearances. She asserted that all her previous testimony about him was true and that he was a "good" husband when he helped with the children and the housework, but a "bad" husband when he beat her. Although she had previously testified about only one such beating, she now told the commission that he beat her on several occasions. She thought his suggestion that she return to the Soviet Union was made before the attempt on Walker's life, and she was unsure what his motivation was, because it was obvious that she would have taken the children back with her. On the one hand, she took his expressions of love in their domestic life as evidence that he did love her and the children, but "the fact that he made attempts on the lives of other people showed to me that he did not treasure his family life and his children, also the fact that he beat me and wanted to send me to the Soviet Union." Her basic assessment of her husband: "Frankly, I am lost as to what to think about him."[13]

Marina explained how she found the ticket stub for her husband's trip from Mexico to Dallas and why the FBI had missed some of his possessions at the Paine residence. She testified that she took a small suitcase with her after the assassination when she went to stay at a hotel, and she included in that suitcase some of her old magazines and books in English for the children and the stub was found in one of them.[14]

Cooper asked her about her feelings after the Walker attempt and whether she thought, or feared, that he would use the rifle on a future occasion against a high government official. She responded that she "was afraid that he did have temptation to kill someone else." She reaffirmed her earlier testimony that her husband never expressed hostility to President Kennedy. She volunteered for the first time that she believed that her husband was shooting at Connally rather than Kennedy, because the governor had approved Oswald's dishonorable discharge from the Marine Corps Reserve. But she went on to say that he never expressed "displeasure or hatred" for the governor. She stated that she had no doubt that her husband killed Kennedy. She did not know whether her husband knew that Connally would be in the motorcade on November 22. We later added a paragraph to Chapter 7 of the report about the unreliability of this testimony and why it was unlikely that Oswald had the governor as his target.[15]

Near the end of her testimony, Rankin returned to some of the subjects raised by the staff. He probed further about her knowledge of her husband's activities in New Orleans after she and Ruth Paine had left. She said that he spent the first night in the house where they had lived and then he stayed one or two nights with his Aunt Lillian. She could not identify anyone in the photograph of her husband handing out leaflets for his pro-Cuba committee. She also knew nothing of any meeting that her husband might have had in Dallas with Sylvia Odio. In New Orleans, her husband spent most of his evenings at home; he never discussed meeting Cubans or others at bars in the city; and she said she was surprised that he would have been in bars because he never showed any signs of drinking.[16]

Our recent investigative requests dealing with Chapter 6 had not produced any information requiring revision of our proposed findings. On September 1, Rankin distributed to the commission a section of Chapter 6 discussing whether Oswald had any accomplices in the planning and the execution of the assassination. This section also considered Oswald's defection and residence in the Soviet Union. By September 4, I had a complete draft of the chapter, which I hand delivered to Liebeler, Slawson, Griffin, and Laulicht, who were still in our Washington office, and mailed copies to Jenner and Coleman. Everyone responded quickly as we had few loose ends or outstanding questions at this point.[17]

The revised Chapter 6 was approved by the commission on September 8. Galley proofs of the chapter appeared a few days later. When Liebeler looked at the proofs, he focused quickly on the fact that none of his proposed language had been included. Liebeler sent me three separate sets of comments on the galley proofs—on September 14, 15, and 16—just days before our entire report had to be finished. During these last weeks, Rankin was preoccupied with the members as they discussed the conclusions and supporting evidence. He expected comments on the galley proofs from the members and staff and his instructions to Redlich and me were clear—regardless of timing or substance, they needed to be evaluated carefully.

In his first memo on September 14, Liebeler commented on three sub-sections dealing with Oswald's background, including whether he had been an agent for the United States government and an analysis of his finances. Again, most of his estimated fifty comments were directed at the substance of the discussion, usually with specific editing proposals, but sometimes he simply raised questions to be checked before the galley proofs were returned to the printer. On a few occasions he referred to suggestions written on the galley proofs but not summarized in the memo, so without his copies of the proofs, I cannot determine whether his recommended changes were made.[18]

I made changes in the final text that were responsive to twenty-two of his comments. In thirteen cases I concluded that no action was required—usually because he raised a question regarding the evidentiary support for a proposition, which could be checked without making any change in the text, or because he simply made a comment for my information. In ten instances, changes were not made in the text as Liebeler suggested, including specific proposals related to the commission's investigation of the Sylvia Odio testimony and its detailed summary of Oswald's finances. In both instances, I thought Liebeler's comments were reasonable, but I also believed that the commission could legitimately conclude that the text was accurate and supported by the evidence.[19]

As discussed earlier, the commission had concluded that there was "persuasive evidence" that Oswald had not been the "Leon Oswald" that Sylvia Odia believed she met in Dallas in late September 1963. Liebeler now was questioning the commission's judgment that the evidence was "persuasive." Unless one believes that "persuasive" evidence must meet the test of "beyond a reasonable doubt" applicable in criminal prosecutions, I think the commission was justified in reaching this conclusion based on the evidence before it.

Likewise, Liebeler's comments about the treatment of Oswald's finances illustrate a reasonable difference in judgment. The main issue here was the amount of detail on this subject in the commission's report. The study of Oswald's finances from his return to the United States on June 13, 1962, until November 22, 1963, concluded that he had income of $3,665.89 and disbursements of $3,501.79, leaving a balance of $164.10. This estimated balance was within $19 of the $183.87 in Oswald's possession at the time of his arrest. Liebeler thought the discussion was "too long and detailed" and ran the risk of it being "too apparently precise to be readily believable." But one could also conclude that this was one of those instances where detailed information was necessary to make the main point under examination; namely, that if Oswald were a part of a conspiracy or an agent of any government, either his income or expenditures would likely show more financial resources than this very careful analysis revealed. In fact, Liebeler made this exact point in his 1978 testimony before a congressional committee.[20]

Liebeler's next set of comments regarding the chapter's galley proofs came on September 15 and covered the portion of Chapter 6 entitled "Circumstances Surrounding the Assassination," and the subsections about Oswald's residence in the Soviet Union and his associations in the Dallas-Fort Worth Russian-speaking community.[21]

Of the sixty-three suggestions in this memorandum, about thirty-three resulted in revisions in the galley proofs. For example, Liebeler recommended eliminating all references to Oswald's wife by her first name only, correcting the spelling of a Russian official, and eliminating long clauses separated by semicolons. I did that. Many were more substantive: editing of the chapter's introduction to describe more accurately the nature of the commission's investigation, correcting factual errors regarding the evidence described, and shortening the description of Oswald's and his wife's relations with the Russian-speaking community in Dallas and Fort Worth. I made these changes too.[22]

But many of Liebeler's suggestions didn't work or were unnecessary at this stage. In some cases, his comments suggested only that a particular fact or citation be checked to confirm its accuracy, which I did. In other instances, he simply expressed a view about the need for a particular discussion in the chapter or a stylistic change. Much more difficult were his recommendations that several portions of the chapter be substantially reduced in length. These sections of the report had principally been written and reviewed by lawyers who did not share Liebeler's emphasis on brevity. Because his suggestions did not involve any criticism of the conclusions reached, I concluded that they should not be implemented at this late stage in the printing of the report. In no case, though, did I reject a suggested change that was necessary to clarify or support the report's findings.[23]

I am sure there came a time in this process when I insisted that Liebeler expedite, and hopefully end, this flow of critical comments. Liebeler's third and last memorandum about Chapter 6 considered the discussion of Oswald's political activities upon his return to the United States. It contained twenty numbered paragraphs, some of which advanced more than a single suggestion. Of these comments, about ten of them resulted in changes in the text of the chapter. On several occasions he suggested that a footnote was required, but in some of these instances I disagreed. My disinclination to add new footnotes was definitely influenced by the fact that this would require renumbering of all the subsequent footnotes. The commission's assertion that Oswald acted "purportedly" on behalf of the Fair Play for Cuba Committee seemed like a fair characterization, given the range of his unauthorized activities in the name of the committee, despite Liebeler's reservation about the use of the word.[24]

Liebeler's comments were more numerous than those of his colleagues, but no one should make the mistake of interpreting Liebeler's memos as reflecting his disagreement with the conclusions of the commission. The lawyers on the commission staff were trained to challenge each other's ideas and assessment of the evidence that had been developed in our investigation. Liebeler's memos exemplify how this process worked within the staff and improved the quality of the report.

My association with Jim Liebeler on the commission staff led to a close personal relationship over the decades before his death in 2002. We did have some intense discussions about the commission's work in 1964, as we did in later years on other topics. He and his wife stayed at my home for weeks, occasionally months, at a time when they were consulting, or considering employment, with federal agencies during the 1980s.

I know from my many personal discussions with Liebeler over the years that he firmly supported our work. In addition to his testimony before a congressional committee in 1978, he reaffirmed it in his 1996 manuscript comparing the conclusions of the commission with those of the same congressional committee eighteen years later. He often said that the questions raised in his memos were to be expected in a project of this complexity and importance. He acknowledged the differences of judgment within the staff about how best to present the commission's conclusions. But he became one of the most eloquent and effective defenders of the commission's work, which had benefited greatly from his persistent, specific, and substantive contributions.

■ The Commission's Conclusions on Possible Conspiracies

In the final text, the commission "concluded that there is no credible evidence that Lee Harvey Oswald was part of a conspiracy to assassinate President Kennedy." It made the same finding about Ruby. The commission emphasized that these findings were based on the evidence developed by the commission's own investigation. According to Ford, the members wanted to be clear that they were not saying, "there was no conspiracy," but were saying that "there was no evidence of a conspiracy." None of us on the staff objected to this phrasing of the commission's conspiracy conclusions. It seemed reasonable under the circumstances.[25]

To make this point even more emphatically, the commission pointed out: "Because of the difficulty of proving negatives to a certainty, the possibility of others being involved with either Oswald or Ruby cannot be established categorically, but if there is any such evidence it has been beyond the reach of all the investigative agencies and resources of the United States and has not come to the attention of this Commission." In support of its conclusion that the available evidence did not reveal a conspiracy, the commission listed those officials of the United States government who endorsed this conclusion, including the secretaries of State, Defense, and Treasury; the attorney general; the director of the FBI; the director of the CIA; and the chief of the Secret Service.[26]

On August 4, Robert Kennedy signed the letter to Warren that I had left with Katzenbach several weeks earlier. He said that he had received "periodic reports about the work of the Commission from you, Deputy Attorney General Katzenbach and Mr. Willens of the Department of Justice, who has worked with the Commission for the past several months." He concluded: "In response to your specific inquiry, I would like to state definitely that I know of no credible evidence to support the allegations that the assassination of President Kennedy was caused by a domestic or foreign conspiracy."[27]

When he appeared before the commission, Hoover had testified about a possible conspiracy:

I know of no substantial evidence of any type that would support any contention of that character. I have read all of the requests that have come to the Bureau from this Commission, and I have read and signed all the replies that have come to the Commission. In addition, I have read many of the reports that our agents have made and I have been unable to find any scintilla of evidence showing any foreign conspiracy or any domestic conspiracy that culminated in the assassination of President Kennedy.

Hoover assured the commission that "so far as the FBI is concerned, the case will be continued in an open classification for all time. That is, any information coming to us or any report coming to us from any source will be thoroughly investigated, so that we will be able to either prove or disprove the allegation."[28]

Hoover did not refer to organized crime in his testimony before the commission, and no one asked him specifically about the topic. What Hoover chose not to divulge was that the FBI was engaged in an illegal electronic surveillance program directed at organized crime. Because of my position at the criminal division, I was personally aware of the program, but had no knowledge regarding its scope or results.

When the transcripts of this surveillance were reviewed by an independent expert in the field fourteen years later, they revealed no evidence that the national organized crime syndicate was involved in the assassination of Kennedy. Under those circumstances, Hoover could justify his failure to discuss organized crime during his commission testimony. If there had been information implicating organized crime, I believe that Hoover would have provided it to the commission under terms similar to what Treasury negotiated regarding the Rowley report. If he elected not to, I believe that other officials in the FBI who had close relationships with Robert Kennedy, Jack Miller, or other Justice Department officials would have revealed it in confidence to one of them.[29]

Years later, Rankin was pressed on whether he would have requested information obtained through the FBI's electronic surveillance program if he had known of its existence. He responded:

> Well. I don't know. That is highly speculative. I will tell you my problem with that would be that I would have on the Commission the Chief Justice of the United States [and] all of these other Government officials who would be involved in using material that was in my opinion highly illegal, violation of people's constitutional rights and whether I should put them in that kind of position knowingly would be a serious question. I don't think that their duties as Commissioners would require that they step up and violate the Constitution. I have not ever thought that a man in public office had a duty or a right to violate the law in order to carry out his official position.[30]

When the committee lawyer suggested that these materials might have helped in the investigation, Rankin tersely replied: "Yes; I think that is just like saying it would have been a good thing not to have Castro around and, therefore, you should proceed to assassinate him regardless of what laws you are breaking."[31]

■ Closing Off Possibilities Regarding Oswald's Motives

We had the galley proofs of Chapter 7 before we got the comments of the three outside psychiatrists consulted in July about Oswald's personality and possible motives. We asked them to review the current draft of Chapter 7 and each responded in early September.

Dr. Cameron from St. Elizabeths Hospital in Washington complimented

Liebeler for "what appears to me to be a very unemotional, straightforward presentation of factual material about Lee Harvey Oswald." He agreed with the "decision to draw no ultimate conclusions about Oswald's motivations to be the best possible course." He suggested some language changes relating to Oswald's feelings for his children, the possible existence of a conspiracy, and clarification of Oswald's transfer from active to inactive duty followed by his discharge under undesirable conditions. These changes were made.[32]

The comments from Dr. Rothstein of the Medical Center for Federal Prisoners produced two changes to the galley proofs of Chapter 7. The commission decided to include in its report the findings of a New York Youth House psychologist based on Oswald's drawings and additional language from Oswald's letters to his brother after his defection to the Soviet Union in 1959.[33]

When Oswald was thirteen years old and examined by Youth House professionals in New York City, a psychologist interpreted a human figure drawing test as follows:

> The Human Figure Drawings are empty, poor characterizations of persons approximately the same age as the subject. They reflect a considerable amount of impoverishment in the social and emotional areas. He appears to be a somewhat insecure youngster exhibiting much inclination for warm and satisfying relationships to others. There is some indication that he may relate to men more easily than to women in view of the more mature conceptualization. He appears slightly withdrawn and in view of the lack of detail within the drawings this may assume a more significant characteristic. He exhibits some difficulty in relationship to the maternal figure suggesting more anxiety in this area than in any other.[34]

In a letter of November 26, 1959, Oswald tried to explain to his brother Robert his defection to the Soviet Union and his desire to see the US government overthrown. Oswald complained about various aspects of American life and then stated:

> So you speak of advantages. Do you think that is why I am here? For personal, material advantages? Happiness is not based on oneself, it does not consist of a small home, of taking and getting. Happiness is taking part in the struggle, where there is no borderline between one's own personal world and the world in general. I never believed I would find more material advantage at this stage of development in the Soviet Union than I might of [sic] had in the U.S.[35]

The letter from Dr. Rome from the Mayo Clinic contained a twelve-page analysis of Oswald's reading disability. He suggested that Oswald's misspelling of names, apparently on a phonetic basis, was caused by a reading-spelling disability. The report added a new paragraph referring to this disability.[36]

■ Final Debate on Presidential Protection

At their last meeting on September 18, the commission unanimously agreed not to recommend transfer of any of the responsibilities of the Secret Service to the Federal Bureau of Investigation.

Treasury Secretary Dillon's testimony on September 8 was influential in persuading all the members to reach this result—even Dulles and Ford, who had previously argued for some reallocation of responsibilities. Dillon told the commission that, among other changes he was instituting, his department had established an interagency committee to develop more effective criteria for reporting information to the Secret Service and he had requested funds for five additional agents for the Protective Research Section to serve as liaison with law enforcement and intelligence agencies. A day later, Warren wrote Dillon seeking financial information for fiscal years 1960 through 1965, including the Secret Service budget request to the Treasury Department; the Treasury Department budget request for the Secret Service as submitted to the Bureau of the Budget; the presidential budget for the Secret Service as submitted to the Congress; and the Secret Service budget approved by the Congress. The secretary's prompt response contained all the requested information.[37]

Chapter 8 was revised to incorporate this information. The commission endorsed the increased use by the Secret Service of agents from other federal law enforcement agencies, which Dillon had successfully tried recently. It also urged the Bureau of the Budget to promptly review the budgetary requests of the Secret Service and to authorize a request for the necessary supplemental appropriations as soon as it could be justified.[38]

■ The Commission Concludes Its Work

During nearly ten months, the commission members had met in executive session more than twenty times; heard the testimony of ninety-four witnesses at more than fifty hearings; considered dozens of drafts reviewing the evidence; debated seventy-two specific questions central to their conclusions; and approved 469 pages of text for their report to the president.

The commission members understood their assignment. Several members, especially Russell and Boggs, failed to attend most of the hearings at which the commission heard witnesses.[39] To most of us on the staff, the failure to attend more hearings was indefensible. However, each commission member received a copy of the testimony of every witness who appeared before the commission and most of them had staffers who assisted them. President Johnson did not select the commission members because he expected them to have an admirable attendance record. He wanted them to use their experience and best judgment in reaching, and supporting, the conclusions resulting from the largest criminal investigation in the nation's history.

The process by which the commission put together its report provided one of the most convincing, although rarely explained, bases for the accuracy of its facts and the undeniable support for its conclusions. After four months of basic investigation by staff, the commission approved a proposed outline of the report at its April 30 meeting. From then through mid-September, the members received a steady flow of memos, reports, and drafts. The members consistently focused on how their conclusions on the seventy-two questions would be expressed and how the evidence to support them would be most effectively explained. Throughout the commission's work, Warren and Rankin talked at least two or three times each week about the investigation, schedule of witnesses, interagency problems, and much more. As should be evident, there was no "rush to judgment" here. The commission supervised Rankin's handling of the investigation on a regular basis and considered every part of the report carefully during the three months from mid-June to mid-September.

On September 21, 1964, Rankin distributed his last memorandum to the staff regarding the final steps before publication of the commission's report. For each chapter and appendix he identified the person (or persons) responsible for any final changes "which are essential" to the text and appendices. Our first order of business was to revise the galleys containing all our footnotes and return them to the printer. We needed to include all the footnotes in the volume of the report that we submitted to the president. We were trying to get all of the changes in the text of our report to the printer by the close of business on Tuesday, September 22. Although this may seem like we were asking all the commission members and staff to read the entire report overnight, the only sections that needed scrutiny were those we had changed in the final day or so. At this point, we could make only those changes that were absolutely essential to ensure the accuracy of our work. Mercifully, these were very few in number.[40]

I wrote my last memo to Rankin on September 21 dealing with administrative matters that had to be addressed after submission of our report. We had discussed many of these issues before, and the memo was a record of some major tasks to be done after President Johnson got the report. We had to provide for careful review of the exhibits before they were published to ensure that all classified materials had been cleared by the responsible agency before publication. I expressed concern about the manner in which the exhibits had been identified and the possibility that mistakes may have been made in their designation and description.[41]

Another substantial question related to the handling of the physical evidence that had been used by the commission. I suggested that the Justice Department might be formally requested by the commission to help deal with these questions—in particular, which items could be returned to their owners and which should be retained and, if so, by whom and where. I ended the memo by advising him that "I will be here tomorrow until the Report is completed, at which time I shall return to my responsibilities at the Department of Justice."[42]

We did not have any formal farewell meeting of the staff at the end of our work on September 22. I have the impression that each of us made our own individual departure, expressing thanks and good wishes to those around us. However fatigued we were by the intense work of the past many months, I think that we left with the sense that collectively we had undertaken a project of national importance and we had done our best to honor President Kennedy by investigating his assassination with integrity and professionalism. We knew that history would have the last word on our efforts.

■ **Presentation of the Report to the President**

On Thursday, September 24, 1964, the seven members of the commission delivered their report that told "the whole truth" about the assassination of President Kennedy to his successor at the White House. Each conclusion had the support of all seven members. According to one account, President Johnson's first comment about the report was "It's pretty heavy." The report was going to be made public at 6:30 P.M. on Sunday, September 27.[43]

After the required photographs of the commission members circling Warren and Johnson, the members left the White House. Asked whether he was glad the job was over, Warren "replied with emphasis, 'Yes!' and strode on." On behalf of the commission, Warren stated that, although federal agents would continue to trace down every new lead that might shed further light on the case, the commission would not involve itself in any follow-up or supplemental investigation. Perhaps by coincidence, Governor Connally was at the White House when the Warren Commission submitted its report. When asked by reporters whether he had recovered from his injuries, Connally reported that he was in good shape but his wrist still was "a little stiff."[44]

After receiving the report on Thursday, President Johnson gave it to his assistant Horace Busby to read and digest before reporters got hold of it on Sunday. Johnson probably felt confident that he knew the gist of the report because of his conversations with Senator Russell. Busby, a fellow Texan, had been a speechwriter and self-described "idea man" for Johnson for some time before the assassination. Johnson brought Busby to the White House and installed him as a deputy to McGeorge Bundy, but Busby was intent on leaving to go back to Texas after the November election, now only a few weeks away. Busby promptly generated all the necessary paperwork for the release and circulation of the report within the government.[45]

In a letter to Warren released after the report's delivery, President Johnson promised that he would give the report careful study and stated that he had given instructions "for the prompt publication of this report to the American people and to the world." The president said that he knew the commission "has been guided throughout by a determination to find and to tell the whole truth of these terrible events. This is our obligation to the good name of the United States of America and to all men everywhere who respect our nation—and above all to the memory of President Kennedy." He expressed his appreciation for "the readiness of outstanding Americans to respond to calls for service to their country. There has been no more striking example of this great American strength than the service of the seven extraordinary distinguished members of your commission."[46]

Johnson also signed a letter to Rankin expressing his appreciation and thanks for the work that Rankin had done in bringing the commission's work to successful completion. He stated that "there remains the task of winding up its affairs, preserving essential records, and bringing administrative matters to an orderly conclusion." Apparently Rankin had agreed to undertake the responsibility for such duties, and the president's letter thanked him for his "willingness to continue for a short period to work with the Administrator of General Services to accomplish this task and by this letter I authorize whatever help and support may be necessary for this purpose." Al Goldberg, Rankin's secretary, Julia Eide, and other secretaries and administrative personnel had agreed to help Rankin during this period. One additional chore was to oversee the production of the twenty-six volumes of testimony, exhibits, and other materials that the commission had scheduled for prompt publication.[47]

Upon release, the Warren Commission report was an immediate best seller. The Government Printing Office reported that it had sold twelve thousand copies of the report from its three local outlets within a day after its release—a total described as "phenomenal." There was virtually unanimous support for the recommendations of the commission aimed at improving the protection of American presidents. Congress was already well on the way toward approving a proposal to make the assassination of the president and certain other federal officials a crime.[48]

The initial coverage of the commission report was very favorable. The *New York Times* reported that historians and archivists described the commission's work as "the most massive, detailed and convincing piece of detective work ever undertaken." Labeling the statistical summary as "monumental," the *Times* reported that the commission's volume of testimony from 552 witnesses was "more than 100 times the roster of the 42 witnesses called before the Joint Congressional Committee on the investigation of the Pearl Harbor attack in 1945–46." The *Los Angeles Times* reported that the favorable comments about the report "ranged from general praise to agreement with specific conclusions, such as the commission's recommendation of stricter security measures for the President, and its criticism of the performance of Dallas officials and news media in the period between the assassination and Oswald's death by Jack Ruby." Senate Republican Leader Everett Dirksen of Illinois weighed in to praise the "unstinting efforts" of the commission staff, which he described "as one of the ablest and most competent groups ever assembled." The only immediate dissents to this praise came from Lee Harvey Oswald's mother and, of course, Mark Lane.[49]

Robert Kennedy, who was now the Democratic nominee for the Senate from New York, stated that he had not read the report and did not intend to do so. He issued a statement referring to his comment in Poland that Oswald "was solely responsible for what happened and that he did not have any outside help or assistance." He said he had been briefed on the commission report and that he was "completely satisfied that the commission investigated every lead and examined every piece of evidence. The commission's inquiry was thorough and conscientious."[50]

In November, the Government Printing Office published the twenty-six volumes of transcripts and exhibits.[51] Rankin, Goldberg, and other staff contributed significantly to this effort. Goldberg recalled an issue involving publication of FBI reports that identified relatives in Cuba of witnesses who had provided information to the commission. When Goldberg asked the FBI about this, the bureau authorized him to go forward and publish the reports without any deletions. Goldberg checked further with the CIA, which took a different position out of concern that some form of retaliation might result from the exposure of this information. Goldberg chose to follow the CIA advice. Unlike the commission report, these volumes were not commercially popular. The twenty-six volumes were being sold at a price of $76—about $565 in today's dollars. By the end of the first week, only eighty-six sets of the volumes had been sold over the counter at the printing office and 294 had been sent to individuals or groups that had ordered them by mail.[52]

■ Implementation by the Dillon Committee

As might have been anticipated, the embargo placed on release of the commission's report until 6:30 P.M. on Sunday was breached by the AP and UPI wire services earlier in the day. The initial stories focused on the commission's criticisms of the Secret Service and the FBI and the need for substantial improvement in protecting our presidents.

Upon hearing of these premature releases of the report shortly after noon on Sunday, McGeorge Bundy called the president and strongly urged him to take some action in response to the commission's recommendations. Bundy suggested that the president "can get ahead of the curve by announcing formation of a committee to study the Commission's recommendations." President Johnson was reluctant to take any such action without discussing it with Abe Fortas and knowing more about the commission's exact recommendations. Bundy suggested that such a committee might consist of the treasury secretary, the attorney general, and perhaps himself from the National Security Council.[53]

When the president commented that he did not understand that the report "was as drastic as you indicate," Bundy read extensively from the commission's findings on the performance of the Secret Service and the FBI. He referred specifically to the commission's recommendation of a special cabinet committee for reviewing and overseeing the protective activities of the Secret Service and other federal agencies. He made clear, however, that he was not asking that the president approve that particular approach, but instead that Johnson appoint his own committee to look at that recommendation and others made by the commission. By the end of this conversation, Johnson and Bundy were discussing possible candidates for such a committee. Bundy concluded the telephone conversation by asserting that "what I really think, myself, is that the Secret Service needs an injection of brains at the top, and that they just don't *have* it. But how to get that in a tactful, diplomatic, and effective way is very much of a different question."[54]

Later on Sunday, President Johnson created a committee to study and implement the recommendations of the Warren Commission. He appointed Dillon, Acting Attorney General Katzenbach, CIA director McCone, and Bundy. Although Johnson named no chair for the committee, it was understood that Dillon would have general supervision over the group. The "key question" on the agenda of this committee would be "whether all or part of the protective functions of the Secret Service should be turned over to some other agency."[55]

Johnson called Senator Mike Mansfield, the Senate majority leader, early Monday morning to advise him of this action. Although it was his general preference to advise congressional leaders in advance on matters that might involve them, he had acted so rapidly on Sunday that this was not possible. Johnson explained that he wanted the committee to be predominantly Republican, people who "would be fair to Kennedy but they wouldn't be vulnerable to Kennedy, and [it] wouldn't just be a Democratic National Committee document." He went on to say that for that reason he put McCone on it, "who loves Kennedy—was] very close to him, but who's [an] ultra Republican; Bundy, who also loves Kennedy, but who is a Republican, too; and Dillon, [a] Republican; and Katzenbach, [Nicholas] Katzenbach, who's not anything. I mean, he's just a good civil servant and a dean of a law school." Mansfield approved of the president's committee.[56]

The president's new committee could not meet immediately because McCone was out of the country. As soon as he was appointed, Katzenbach asked me to assist on the matter. I soon learned that Dillon had asked Robert Carswell, whom I knew from the commission's dealings with Treasury, to do likewise. Bundy appointed one of his assistants, Gordon Chase. Although I did not know it at the time, Chase was a Latin American specialist on the National Security Council staff and had been the staff member most intimately engaged in quiet efforts behind the scene since March 1963 to improve relations between Castro and Kennedy.[57]

I remember that the three principals (absent McCone) met on a few occasions at which we three staffers were also present. Pursuant to these discussions, Carswell, Chase, and I had a few chores dealing with the commission's recommendations that were not very demanding or controversial. Bundy had proposed this committee as a means of providing the president with a justifiable deferral of the date when he needed to decide whether to implement the commission's recommendations. Dillon had persuaded the Warren Commission not to move any function of the Secret Service from Treasury and wanted further support for his efforts to get increased funding for Secret Service operations. Katzenbach had a full docket of responsibilities at this time, not the least of which was persuading the new president that he could depend on Katzenbach's loyalty despite his close relationship with Robert Kennedy. Five months after Kennedy's departure from Justice, President Johnson nominated Katzenbach to be attorney general. He was easily confirmed.

Absent any controversy, the committee was able to complete its business quickly and report its conclusions in late November. The committee rejected the commission's proposals that the head of the Secret Service be elevated to a higher position in Treasury or that a new inter-cabinet group play a role in the presidential protection function. Most important, the committee decided not to move the investigative function regarding presidential protection from the Secret Service to the FBI. No one on the committee seriously considered such a move, although both Katzenbach and Bundy were aware of the limitations of the Secret Service. They were hopeful that the reorganization of the Secret Service under consideration at Treasury, supplemented by the increased funds that the department was seeking, would enable the department to address the major deficiencies identified by the Warren Commission. Johnson reportedly agreed with keeping these two functions together and was quoted as telling Dillon "that he was very pleased with the efficiency and smoothness of the present protective system as well as with plans for its expansion."[58]

With this committee assignment behind me, I concentrated on my responsibilities at the Justice Department, which seemed relatively tame and manageable compared with my duties at the commission. Like my commission colleagues, I was pleased with the initial favorable coverage of our work. But as the months and years unfolded, we were ill prepared to respond to the unexpected and severe criticism of the Warren Commission report.

CHAPTER 10

AFTERMATH

■

F ROM ITS FIRST PUBLICATION ON SEPTEMBER 27, 1964, THE WARREN COM-
mission report has generated a massive outpouring of commentary
within the United States and abroad. At this writing, more than one
thousand authors have produced book-length works, and thousands of essays
have been published in print or video form. Most of it has been critical, and in
almost all cases the critics have focused on their conviction that somewhere,
somehow, there must have been a conspiracy. Some of the theories that came
out of the criticism are incredibly imaginative—resulting in passionate debate
at the annual sessions of the conspiracy theorists as to exactly which conspiracy
theory is the most persuasive.

Much of the criticism pointed to alleged errors and omissions by those
who conducted the investigation and drafted the report. Of course, it is difficult
for me and my former colleagues not to take that personally. However, notwithstanding the views and intensity expressed by a diverse range of critics, I remain deeply satisfied that the commission and its staff got it right.

In our nine-months-long investigation, we found no credible evidence
of a conspiracy involving Oswald or Ruby and, close to fifty years later, no
one else has found any such evidence either. Over that entire span of time, not
a single person with firsthand knowledge has come forward to present any fact
that contradicts the commission's conclusions that Oswald was the assassin
and that he and Ruby each acted alone. By "firsthand knowledge," I mean facts
provided by a person who saw or heard something with his or her own eyes or
ears that is relevant to one of the issues we addressed. As a former prosecutor,
I am convinced that if there had been a conspiracy, someone would have disclosed that information since 1964.[1]

Additional information has surfaced about facts withheld from the Warren Commission by the FBI and the CIA, but none of that information contradicted or invalidated the commission's conclusions. Protecting their own
institutional interests, these agencies tarred their reputations by failing to fully

assist the commission. Full disclosure of the facts known to these agencies and mobilization of their specialized resources would undoubtedly have produced relevant information that would have extended our investigation. But these failures and their consequences have been fully explored by congressional committees since our report, and no facts have come to light that challenge our fundamental conclusions regarding the identity of the assassin and the absence of any conspiracy.

A fair evaluation of the Warren Commission after nearly fifty years needs to consider three major subjects. First, the strong and unanimous response of commission members and staff to the criticism of their work over the decades speaks volumes. The reputations of the members were well established at the time they approved the report. All of our "senior" lawyers were respected in the communities from which they came and most were nationally recognized in the profession. All of the "junior" lawyers on the staff went on to distinguished careers. Even a fervent conspiracy theorist should pause for a moment to consider the independence and accomplishments of these commission lawyers, individually and collectively, before attacking their competence or integrity.

A second essential element is recognition of the few, but important, books over the years supporting the commission's conclusions or contributing to our understanding of Lee Harvey Oswald. These include Gerald Posner's *Case Closed* (1993) and Max Holland's *The Kennedy Assassination Tapes* (2004), as well as two other books—Priscilla Johnson McMillan's *Marina and Lee* (1977) and Norman Mailer's *Oswald's Tale* (1995)—which provide important details and insights about Oswald's background and personality. Most recently, Vincent Bugliosi, one of the nation's most prominent prosecutors, reported the results of his twenty-year investigation in his 2007 book *Reclaiming History: The Assassination of President John F. Kennedy*. Bugliosi tackled all the major issues that had been raised about the commission's report and evaluated virtually every conspiracy allegation. His monumental 1,600-page book and its additional 1,000 pages of notes show in excruciating detail why none of the conspiracy theories is supported by any credible evidence.

Third, and perhaps the most important development in appraising the commission report, are the results of the four extensive "official" investigations since 1964 that touched on the Kennedy assassination—the Rockefeller Commission in 1975, the Senate "Church" Committee in 1975 and 1976, the House Select Committee on Assassinations from 1977 to 1979, and the Assassinations Records Review Board from 1992 to 1998. Although their missions varied, none of these investigations produced documents or reached conclusions challenging the essential findings of the Warren Commission. One possible exception is the separate conspiracy theory developed by the staff of the House Select Committee in 1979, which was adopted by seven of the twelve committee members and produced several strongly worded dissents. As we shall see, this contention was flawed from the beginning and was proven to be unsupportable by later scientific analysis by impartial and highly qualified experts.

■ Commission Members and Staff Respond to Critics

By the time Lee Rankin finally closed the doors at the commission's offices in November 1964, Warren and the other commission members had long since returned to their commitments on the bench, in the Congress, and in their law firms. My colleagues on the staff returned to their firms, law schools, or government agencies and in many instances began to consider new careers. I returned to the criminal division promptly because Bill Foley, the other deputy, was waiting for my return so that he could move to the Administrative Office for the US Courts as its newly designated executive director. I was promoted to his position and was the only deputy in place for a short time to assist Jack Miller in running the division.

The ink was barely dry when the FBI reacted to the report in two dramatic —and inconsistent—ways. Assistant Director Gale promptly reported to Hoover that the commission "has now set forth in a very damning manner some of the same glaring weaknesses for which we previously disciplined our personnel such as lack of vigorous investigation after we had established that Oswald visited the Soviet Embassy in Mexico." He identified several other instances where he believed that the testimony of FBI agents before the commission or its lawyers made the FBI "look ridiculous and taints its public image."[2]

Hoover's immediate response to the commission's criticism was to take additional disciplinary action on September 28 against eight of those disciplined in December 1963 and three other employees. In so doing, Hoover again rejected advice from Belmont, who suggested that Hoover was making a tactical error by taking this disciplinary action at a time when the FBI was "currently taking aggressive steps to challenge the findings of the Warren Commission insofar as they pertain to the FBI." Hoover disagreed. "We were wrong," he said, "The administrative action approved by me will stand. I do not intend to palliate actions which have resulted in forever destroying the Bureau as the top level investigative organization." A few days later, he made a handwritten notation on a memo from Assistant Director Cartha DeLoach discussing the criticism of the FBI in connection with the assassination investigation and how best to deal with it. "The FBI will never live down this smear which could have been so easily avoided if there had been proper supervision and initiative," Hoover wrote.[3]

The fact that Hoover's disciplinary actions confirmed the validity of the commission's criticism did not deter him from complaining about the commission's treatment of his agency. Twice Hoover publicly dismissed the commission's criticism as a "classic example of Monday morning quarterbacking." In a September 30 letter to the White House and Acting Attorney General Katzenbach, Hoover advised that "the Commission's report is seriously inaccurate insofar as its treatment of the FBI is concerned." Perhaps the most offensive step taken in this dishonest campaign was a telephone call to Rankin in New York by FBI Inspector James Malley, the former FBI liaison officer to the commission, on orders from "a senior Bureau official," in which Malley told Rankin that he "did the Bureau a great disservice and had out-McCarthyed McCarthy."[4]

Newspapers throughout the world treated the commission's report as a major event. Most of them "displayed the story under their biggest, blackest headlines and devoted page after page to summarizing the report's conclusions. In the major capitals, some papers began publishing full or abbreviated translations of the text." Many commentators approved the commission's report, but expressed doubt that the report would be sufficient to rebut the worldwide rumors of a conspiracy to assassinate President Kennedy.[5]

Reactions to the commission's conclusions around the world were mixed —often reflecting the political orientation of the country involved. According to one report in the *Washington Post*: "The Communist press flatly called the report a whitewash. In Western Europe and elsewhere, however, most newspaper editorials expressed satisfaction with the report and accepted [the] conclusion that Lee Harvey Oswald alone killed the President. But the reaction did not follow political [lines] uniformly. Several pro-American papers in France and elsewhere expressed continuing skepticism, saying many questions remained   unanswered."

The questions included the obvious ones: How could the security forces have failed so completely to protect the president? How did it happen "that a shabby night club owner was given the opportunity of shooting and killing Oswald while in the midst of scores of policemen"? In a summary of press comments from around the world, the US Information Agency reported that there were numerous references to charges by the distinguished philosopher

Bertrand Russell "that facts were suppressed" and that "[t]he most frequent theme is that many remain unconvinced and that history will have to provide the definitive account."[6]

Many domestic critics quickly challenged the commission's conclusion that Oswald fired the two shots that killed Kennedy and wounded Connally. That led to a proliferation of "second gunman" theories. An even larger number of critics found fault with the commission's conclusion that there was no persuasive evidence of a conspiracy of some sort. The theories regarding possible conspirators implicated organized crime, Hoffa and the Teamsters Union, the Cuban government, anti-Castro groups, pro-Castro groups, the Soviet Union, and various federal agencies and spawned a still-growing literature—with no end in sight.[7]

Although I read and heard occasional reports of these criticisms, at the time I was completely absorbed with other responsibilities at the Justice Department and the Dillon Committee. After the November 1964 election, Katzenbach summoned me and a few others to his office to help prepare a new federal program aimed at reducing crime in the United States. He told us that President Johnson, notwithstanding his overwhelming victory in the election, was concerned with the impact of the "crime in the streets" issue that got so much attention during the campaign. In a few weeks, we canvassed the alternatives for possible federal action and developed a program for Katzenbach to present to the White House. It included new legislation providing for substantial federal assistance to states and localities to improve their criminal justice systems and two presidential commissions—one to deal with national issues and the other to address crime in the District of Columbia.

While engaged in other professional responsibilities, my past service on the Warren Commission staff became a matter of public debate with the publication of three critical books in 1965–66: one by Harold Weisberg, a Washington investigator; one by Edward Epstein, a graduate student at Cornell; and another by Mark Lane.

Weisberg's book, *Whitewash,* argued that the commission's own records refuted the single-bullet theory and therefore undercut its claim that Oswald was the sole assassin. Unlike other writers, he did not adopt any particular conspiracy theory but charged: "The superficial and immature manner in which the Report deals with the possibility of a conspiracy or of a different assassin is only one of the ways in which the Commission may have crippled itself."[8]

Lane's book, *Rush to Judgment*, was, in general, a rehash of the arguments and accusations he had made during the commission's investigation. Even in this book, Lane presented no evidence to support his claims of Oswald's innocence. Lane basically stated that "the case against Oswald as the lone assassin is refuted by the very witnesses upon whom the commission relied" and that he has "no theories as to who killed the President or why it was done." He wrote many other books on the subject, including one in 2011 in which he alleged that the CIA killed the president.[9]

I read neither *Whitewash* nor *Rush to Judgment* at the time. In early August 1965, I left the Department of Justice to serve as the executive director of the President's Commission on Crime in the District of Columbia. In my opinion, no one in his or her right mind works for two presidential commissions. One is quite enough. But I was greatly indebted to the new commission chairman, Jack Miller, for the opportunities he had provided for me to learn and grow as a lawyer, and another temporary assignment for a year (or sixteen months, as it turned out) provided an excuse for delaying the decision as to whether I would return to private practice or do something else. And, as a resident of the District of Columbia, I thought this commission could definitely improve the quality of life in my community.

At some point during 1965, I did agree to be interviewed by Edward Epstein, whose book *Inquest: The Warren Commission and the Establishment of Truth*, published in 1966, was more troubling than the Weisberg and Lane books. Five commission members (Cooper, Boggs, Ford, Dulles, and McCloy) and nine other staff members (Rankin, Redlich, Goldberg, Adams, Ball, Eisenberg, Liebeler, Specter, and Stern) agreed to be interviewed by him. I was concerned about Epstein's intentions and tried to be very careful in my responses to his questions—especially when he invited me to be critical of commission members or staff colleagues.

Epstein's work was inaccurate and unfair in dealing with the commission's investigation and conclusions. After criticizing the commission members and some lawyers for lack of attention to their assignment, Epstein challenged the single-bullet theory and, therefore, that Oswald was the only assassin. He relied on the first (and incorrect) report of the FBI that a bullet had entered the president but had not exited; the mistaken statements by physicians at Parkland Hospital; Connally's conviction as to which bullet hit him; and the testimony of the autopsy doctors and others regarding the likelihood of one bullet causing both Kennedy's neck wound and all of Connally's wounds. A few days after Epstein's book was featured in the *Washington Post*, Rankin, Redlich, and Specter all defended the commission's conclusions by reference to the testimony and exhibits. Up to this point, most of the commission staff had declined to comment about the report or respond to public criticism, believing that this was the preference of Chief Justice Warren.[10]

After Epstein published his book, virtually every member of the staff who was interviewed stated that Epstein had misquoted him. I firmly rejected a quotation attributed to me criticizing some of my colleagues for periodically returning to their law firms and expressing a preference for "forty law drones, fresh out of law school, not a handful of high-priced consultants." Eisenberg recalled that he complained to the publisher about several errors in the book and that corrections were made in a subsequent edition. On the other hand, Richard Goodwin, a former aide to President Kennedy, was so impressed by Epstein's work that he proposed that Congress should establish an independent group to reevaluate the conclusions of the Warren Commission and seek new evidence, with a staff that would have more experience in digging up the facts than the commission staff possessed.[11]

An editor's note in Earl Warren's *Memoirs*, published in 1977, reported Redlich's efforts to deal with the inaccuracies in the Epstein book:

> New York attorney Norman Redlich, an assistant counsel for the Commission, wrote to Warren to advise him that he, Redlich, had provided some information which had been grossly falsified by author Edward Epstein in a book called Inquest. Inaccuracies and distortions were claimed, and Redlich then proceeded, point by point, to refute key parts of Epstein's book. He got back from the Chief Justice a letter of sympathy. It included a line that became almost a Warren theme song as the Oswald theoreticians proliferated: "We can expect much writing of this kind from charlatans and lazy writers who will not take the time to analyze all the papers to determine what the facts actually are."

Another theme characteristic of Warren's views regarding the critics was captured in his response when Joe Ball called in 1965 to complain that the "critics of the report are guilty of misrepresentation and dishonest reporting." According to Ball, Warren replied: "Be patient, history will prove that we are right."[12]

Congressman Gerald Ford and former CIA director Allen Dulles issued separate statements in early October 1966 defending the commission's conclusions. They emphasized that the critics had produced no new evidence to cast doubt on the report's conclusion that Oswald acted alone in assassinating the president. Ford suggested that using speculation of this kind "to undermine the conscientious and thorough work of the Warren Commission and members of its staff is to do a disservice to all of the American people and to the memory of the late President Kennedy." According to his aides, Ford became the first commission member to speak out in defense of the report because of the pressure from the press for comment on the commission's critics. Another reason for speaking out was the recent finding of the Louis Harris Poll, published a few days earlier, that by a ratio of three to two the American people rejected the commission's principal finding that Oswald was the lone assassin.[13]

Liebeler, then a law professor at UCLA, decided to mount his own effort to deal with the growing controversy over the commission's report. As reported in the *Los Angeles Times*, Liebeler designed a project for twenty third-year law students to examine the commission's records on seventeen specific fact issues, analyze the evidence on both sides, and suggest what the commission should have investigated more thoroughly. The article reported that Liebeler fully supported the commission's conclusions, although he was critical of some of the work done by the staff in writing the report. He described Lane's work as "dishonesty" and Epstein's as merely "incorrect." He argued that what was needed was "one piece of work which sets forth both sides objectively. Lane doesn't. Epstein doesn't." He challenged Epstein's conclusion that the commission took only ten weeks for its work; Liebeler said it actually lasted at least seven months—"and some further investigations were carried on even beyond that."[14]

The third anniversary of the assassination, in 1966, prompted extensive discussion in the press about the challenges to the Warren Commission's findings. Early in November 1966 President Johnson weighed in to support the commission's conclusions, saying that he knew of "no evidence that would in any way cause any reasonable person to have a doubt" about its findings and that the commission deserved "high marks" for its "thorough study." At about the same time, Alexander Bickel, a distinguished professor at Yale Law School, joined the chorus of doubters about the single-bullet conclusion of the commission. *Life* magazine called for a new investigation based on its analysis of the Zapruder film and Connally's testimony that he was not hit by the same bullet as hit the president. Commission members commented that there was nothing new in the magazine article and the White House referred reporters to Johnson's earlier endorsement of the commission's conclusions.[15]

Although Warren was still declining public comment, *Newsweek* magazine quoted him as telling a Johnson Administration official: "I was a district attorney in California for 12 years, and I tried a number of murder cases (an average of 15 a year). If I were still a district attorney and the Oswald case came into my jurisdiction, given the same evidence I could have gotten a conviction in two days and never heard about the case again."[16]

In late November 1966, Ball and Liebeler participated in a panel discussion in San Diego with commission critics Lane and Epstein before the Associated Press Managing Editors Convention. Epstein suggested that the X-rays and autopsy photographs turned over to the National Archives by the Kennedy family might address his principal concern—that the Warren report had failed to discuss persuasively its reasons for rejecting the initial FBI report and developing its single-bullet theory. Lane complained about the commission's failure to call several witnesses he considered critical, the secrecy of the commission's proceedings, and the likelihood that its documents would not be available for seventy-five years or more. He insisted that a new investigation was necessary.[17]

Ball pointed out Lane's many distortions of the available evidence concerning the proper identification of the assassination rifle and the source of the shots that hit Kennedy and Connally. Liebeler told the audience that he had corrected Lane's earlier assertions regarding the palm print on the rifle but that Lane persisted in his distortions of the facts. Liebeler made his views about Lane clear: "his book is a tissue of distortion and a masterwork of deceit . . . I did say to Mr. Lane's face—that which Mr. Ball was too much of a gentleman to say—and that is that Mr. Lane is going around the country telling lies for money. And Mr. Lane's response to that was to threaten to sue me for libel and I've been waiting anxiously for those papers ever since."[18]

Despite the controversy and the calls for a new investigation, none of the commission members supported such a move in the absence of any new evidence to consider. One equivocator was Russell, who began to yield somewhat in light of the ongoing debate. He declared himself "not satisfied" with some of the report's conclusions. He complained that "access to some evidence dealing with the most oft-repeated questions was barred either by the Iron Curtain or Fidel Castro, or perished with Oswald." He also made public his agreement with Connally in rejecting the theory that a single bullet struck both men. However, Russell said he saw no "hard testimony" which would produce different findings and expressed the view that any new investigating body would reach the same conclusions in the absence of additional testimony.[19]

On a Sunday television talk show, Commission member Boggs agreed with his colleagues that no new investigation was required, but suggested that the attorney general or another appropriate authority might name a group of doctors or others to examine the autopsy photographs and X-rays that had been seen only by Warren during the investigation. With the increasing focus on the autopsy, commission lawyers and others came forward with their recollections regarding the reasons why the autopsy photographs and X-rays had not been made part of the commission's records. The articles discussed the roles of Warren and the Kennedy family, but also pointed out that the testimony of the autopsy doctors precisely located the wound on the president's neck. The headline in the *Washington Post* article on this subject was "The Autopsy: The Warren Commission Did Make a Mistake. It Had Compassion."[20]

In a January 1967 speech in Los Angeles before an audience of four hundred, Ball supported Boggs's suggestion of a special panel to examine the autopsy materials. In 1968, the current attorney general, Ramsey Clark, acted on this suggestion, after soliciting my opinion and, I assume, that of other commission members and staff. After an examination of the photographs and X-rays, a panel of four independent experts confirmed the testimony of the autopsy doctors and the commission's conclusions regarding the wounds suffered by Kennedy and Connally.[21]

Also in January 1967, Chief Justice Warren learned from columnist Drew Pearson that the CIA had enlisted the assistance of organized crime in the early 1960s to assassinate Castro, which may have motivated retaliation against President Kennedy by Castro, and that he intended to make this information public. Pearson had notified President Johnson of this information three days earlier. The FBI had initially refused to pursue these allegations, notwithstanding Hoover's repeated assurances to the Warren Commission that its investigation file on the Kennedy assassination would remain "open" and that all leads would be aggressively pursued. Once President Johnson heard of these rumors, he directed the FBI to fully investigate the matter and report to him.[22]

Although Pearson had not authorized its publication and was traveling out of the country at the time, his associate Jack Anderson published the column on March 3, 1967. The column reported that "President Johnson is sitting on a political H-bomb" based on "an unconfirmed rumor that Senator Robert Kennedy may have approved an assassination plot [against Castro] which then possibly backfired against his late brother." Because of its sensational nature and lack of documentation, the column was rejected by the *Washington Post* and the *New York Post*, but was published by hundreds of other papers. Three days later, the FBI gave President Johnson its report on the subject. As summarized by Max Holland, the bureau's information was accurate on three critical issues: "The CIA did try to have Castro assassinated from 1961 to 1962 and possibly into 1963; the agency engaged members of the criminal syndicate in the United States in this effort; and Attorney General Robert Kennedy knew about the plots, and *Cosa Nostra* involvement, contemporaneously." The information leading to the Pearson column was provided by a Washington lawyer who represented one of the organized crime partici-pants in the CIA plans.[23]

A week later, President Johnson and Chief Justice Warren met at the White House to discuss this matter. Although Warren had heard about the al-legation from Pearson earlier, he did not know that it was accurate until this meeting with the president. These developments and the meeting between Johnson and Warren influenced the history of the Warren Commission report in three significant respects.

First, the chief justice had to reassess the validity of the commission report in light of this new information. When pressed for public comment on the subject, Warren for the first time publicly defended the conclusions of the commission. Second, Warren had an opportunity to educate the president about the validity of the commission's findings, including the reasons why Governor Connally was mistaken in his recollections. Third, President Johnson directed Richard Helms, now the CIA director, to give him a full report on the allega-tions in the Pearson column. In early May 1967, Helms met with President Johnson to report on the findings of the CIA inspector general about the history of CIA assassination plots directed at Castro. This information remained within the executive branch of the US government until congressional investigations in 1976 forced its public disclosure.[24]

The experience with misquotes and misrepresentations in the Epstein book led many members of the commission staff to be leery of further public discussion of the commission's report or in providing assistance to aspiring authors. Rankin and Redlich adhered to a decision not to participate in any in-terviews or public debate about their work on the commission, or to write any-thing in defense of the commission's conclusions. Eisenberg agreed with this position, but recalled that once, when he was visiting McGill University, he agreed to speak about his work at the commission.[25]

In January 1967, I joined a Washington law firm where my commission col-league Sam Stern was a partner. I practiced law there until 1995. In my first several years with the firm I assisted in representing American automobile manufacturers in complying with recent legislation imposing new safety standards on the industry and in resolving a major antitrust lawsuit instituted by the Department of Justice. In 1972, I acquired three new clients: the Ford Motor Company, the Educational Testing Service, and the Northern Mariana Islands in the Western Pacific. These clients, and several others for occasional assignments, kept me fully engaged during the 1970s and into the 1980s, leaving little time for defending the Warren Com-mission report or even communicating with my former commission colleagues.

I admired the efforts of my commission colleagues who stepped forward over the years to defend our report. Specter initially chose not to discuss the commission's work, believing that this was Warren's wish, but changed his mind after the Epstein book was published and he was challenged to respond to its criticisms. Because he was a recently elected district attorney, Specter believed he had no alternative and agreed to be interviewed for two major magazine articles in 1966. Specter joined with Belin in traveling to London in January 1967 to debate Lane on BBC, a program that lasted for almost five hours. On a much later occasion, Specter—by then a US senator—attended the annual convention of Warren Commission critics and exhibited great patience under cross-examination by the group.[26]

Griffin also participated in occasional panels to defend the commission. He recently estimated that he publicly explained the commission's work on about eighty to one hundred occasions since 1964, including two appearances at the annual meeting of critics. Griffin recalled that he was courteously received at these meetings and felt that in smaller groups he was able, at the very least, to encourage them to believe that the Warren Commission and its staff were well-intentioned and reasonably competent—a modest but still worthwhile accomplishment.[27]

Liebeler was frequently invited to debate Lane or other commission critics, and did so with characteristic vigor and enthusiasm—especially in front of the students at UCLA. Slawson joined Liebeler in one of these Los Angeles panel discussions. Slawson also recalled being so angered by Oliver Stone's *JFK* film in 1991 that he went home immediately to address its many factual errors, which resulted in an article in a University of Southern California journal. Mosk also responded on occasion to explain (and defend) the commission's key findings. Sam Stern and I on one occasion participated in a Canadian television program on the Warren Commission.[28]

Other commission and staff members wrote about our work in articles, books, or autobiographies. One issue that frequently came up was the effect of Oswald's death on the commission's procedures and conclusions. It was generally recognized that some of the evidence relied upon by the commission, such as Marina Oswald's testimony, would not have been allowed in a trial of her husband. A more difficult question is whether a public trial of Oswald, if he had lived and been found guilty, would have reduced the flow of conspiracy theories.[29]

Warren apparently thought so. In his *Memoirs*, he defended the commission's finding that there was no evidence of a conspiracy at the time.

Based on Oswald's background, Warren thought that Oswald was incapable of being the key operative in a conspiracy. He thought that a high-level government conspiracy seemed equally improbable, with no one willing to break the silence. He believed that the large number of doubters, except those deliberately profiting from the doubts, were led astray because no trial of Oswald had taken place. With such a trial, Warren believed doubts would have been defeated and purged.[30]

Perhaps the most significant staff commentary on a potential conspiracy was Goldberg's paper, *Conspiracy Interpretations of the Assassination of President Kennedy,* published in 1968, which was the result of two seminars that he gave for the Security Studies Project at UCLA. Goldberg observed that the potential consequences of international involvement in the assassination have "generally been overlooked and neglected because of the intense concentration in recent years on the domestic conspiracy aspects." Goldberg pointed out that, if the assassination had occurred a year earlier, during the Cuban missile crisis in October 1962, "the consequences for the world would have been far more fateful—plot or no plot. In November, 1963, there was time to investigate, to deliberate, and to determine that no foreign nation was responsible for the assassination of President Kennedy. This was a constructive contribution to the maintenance of stability and trust in the international order."[31]

Turning to the domestic aspects of the assassination, Goldberg sought to put the conspiracy theories into an appropriate historical context—the climate of opinion that nurtured them and the circumstances that made a whole generation receptive to these hypothetical schemes. He then commented:

And so, we must finally come to the point where we ask whether there is a conspiratorial hypothesis—any single consistently reasonable theory—that is more probable than the findings and conclusions of the Commission's Report. Do the evidence of the assassination itself and the logic of the context make it more probable that there was a conspiracy and at least two assassins or that there was no conspiracy and only a lone assassin? It is the totality of the evidence and of the context that must be considered recognizing that the individual elements are uneven in many ways—in terms of weight, significance, reliability, and probability. There are obviously elements of chance occurrence in the Commission's reconstruction of the assassination. But the perfect case is likely to be a fraudulent one. Had the Commission's purpose been to conceal the real truth and to present only a political truth, it would have hardly presented the data and the documents which are not in accord with its basic findings and conclusions. But it not only presented them—it discussed and analyzed them.[32]

Belin became the commission's most persistent defender. He often left his law practice in Des Moines to debate the merits of the commission's report with its critics. Meanwhile, he worked on a more substantial rebuttal, entitled *November 22, 1963: You Are the Jury,* published in 1973. This 504-page book relies on lengthy excerpts from the actual testimony before the commission or by deposition, and on the actual exhibits, to demonstrate how the commission evaluated conflicting testimony and reached its conclusions.

His book was favorably received by those with an interest in learning more about the commission's conclusions. Harrison E. Salisbury of the *New York Times* wrote a complimentary introduction to the book. Salisbury recognized that the Belin book "will not crush the mystique of the Kennedy assassination. But for anyone who wishes to know how the crime of this century actually occurred and why it could have occurred in no other way than that which the Warren Commission described, this work tells the story better than it has been told at any time before."[33]

I generally followed the Rankin-Redlich practice for many years, with occasional departures that served only to convince me that reasoned discussion about the Warren Commission was nearly impossible. Out in the Western Pacific, where I was working around the thirtieth anniversary of the assassination in 1993, I agreed to appear on a talk show on a Guam radio station early on a weekday morning because the interviewer was an old friend. I thought this was a location sufficiently far from Washington—8,500 miles—and a time sufficiently inconvenient for most listeners that it would not generate much interest. I was completely wrong. My wife, who was outside the studio listening with the equipment operators, saw the switchboard light up immediately with calls from listeners as soon as the host mentioned the topic of the day. Every line was jammed for the entire show. I fielded questions from people on the beach, in their offices, in their cars, and in cafes having coffee with friends. Many of them were familiar with the details of the commission's report and demanded explanations of what I regarded as quite minor points. It was an eye-opening experience.

Hundreds of books and even more articles followed the Weisberg, Lane, and Epstein arguments in the ensuing decades. Nearly all gained publication traction by rejecting one or more of the commission's principal conclusions. Web sites are available for those who wish to examine documents and testimony about the Kennedy assassination. Other sites provide opportunities for similarly inclined critics of the Warren Commission to exchange views, to hold conferences, and to raise money to support efforts to rebut the findings of the Warren Commission and, in some cases, the official findings on other assassinations as well. Lists of hundreds of JFK assassination books are available on the Internet, with recommendations from aficionados as to which five or ten conspiracy books are the most useful or persuasive. Bill O'Reilly, a popular Fox Network commentator, published his book *Killing Kennedy* in October 2012 and watched it rise immediately to the top of the best-seller list.

■ Vincent Bugliosi's Treatise Rejects All Conspiracy Theories

Vincent Bugliosi's 2007 book *Reclaiming History: The Assassination of President John F. Kennedy* reported the results of twenty years of research about the assassination. His unique contribution to the literature is his almost fanatical attention to detail in addressing each of the conspiracy theories. He concludes, in 1,600-plus pages of text and another 1,000 pages of notes delivered on a CD, that none of the conspiracy theories has any basis in fact.

Bugliosi is a career prosecutor in Los Angeles with a stunning record of 106 felony trials and 105 convictions, including convictions in all 21 murder trials. Early in his career he began to write about his most significant cases—and his book *Helter Skelter* in 1976 about the Charles Manson case became a national best seller.[34]

Bugliosi became interested in the Kennedy assassination in 1986 when he was invited to London to participate as the prosecutor in a mock trial of Oswald. Famed defense attorney Gerry Spence came to defend Oswald. Jurors flew in from Texas, as did actual witnesses to the events surrounding the assassination. Bugliosi won a guilty verdict, and the experience set him on a twenty-year mission to produce a single volume that would answer every lingering question about what happened in Dallas. His discussion, in more than four hundred pages entitled "Delusions of Conspiracy: What Did Not Happen," completely refutes the attempts to implicate organized crime, the CIA, the FBI, the Secret Service, the Soviet KGB, right-wing political fanatics in the US, President Johnson, Cuba, pro-Castro and anti-Castro exiles in the US.

In his forty-six-page introduction, Bugliosi provided the background for his undertaking this monumental effort. He did so more briefly—and more entertainingly—in his standard book-tour speech before interested audiences and prospective book buyers. In explanation of the unusual length of the book, he pointed out the "two realities" of the case, the first being that this "is a very simple case, very simple." He agreed with Chief Justice Warren's view that "if this had been a murder case in Oakland or L.A. and the victim was not the President, it'd be a two, three-day murder case. Very simple case—Oswald killed Kennedy and acted alone." But the other reality—and the main reason for the length of the book—is because of

> thousands upon thousands of assassination researchers, and conspiracy the-
> orists, who have examined every single conceivable aspect of this case for
> close to forty-four years, splitting hairs and then splitting the split hairs, mak-
> ing hundreds upon hundreds of allegations. This simple case, which remains
> simple at its core, has been transformed into its present state. . . . The Kennedy
> case is now the most complex murder case, by far, in world history.[35]

When he turned to the question of Oswald's guilt, Bugliosi set forth fifty-three separate pieces of evidence that point to Oswald's guilt. He maintained that "Only in a fantasy world can you have 53 pieces of evidence pointing towards your guilt and still be innocent." He cited the following evidence to illustrate his point: (1) Oswald owned and possessed the murder weapon; (2) he was the only employee who fled the Texas School Book Depository after the assassination; (3) forty-five minutes later, he shot and killed Officer Tip-pit—an action which Bugliosi characterized to the London jury as bearing "the signature of a man in desperate flight from some awful deed"; (4) thirty minutes later he resisted arrest and pulled a gun on the arresting officer; and (5) during his interrogation by the police immediately after his arrest, "he told one provable lie after another, all of which showed a consciousness of guilt."[36]

On the issue of conspiracy, Bugliosi told his audience that there is no *credible*—and he stresses that word—evidence that any of the suspected organizations was associated with Oswald. In simple language, he summarized his reasons for reaching this conclusion. First, after nearly forty-four years "not one single word, not one syllable, has leaked out about any conspiracy." Second, there's no evidence that Oswald ever had any connection with any of these groups believed to be behind the assassination. Third, if any of these groups had decided to kill the president, "Oswald would've been one of the last people on the face of this earth whom they would have gone to," among other reasons because he was "notoriously unreliable—extremely unstable." Fourth, if one of these groups had engaged Oswald to assassinate the president, there would have been a car waiting for him outside the depository after the shooting—either to help him escape or, more likely, "to drive him to his death."

Bugliosi concluded his San Diego Library presentation by addressing two of the main issues "that have been used very successfully by conspiracy theorists to convince Americans that there was a conspiracy in the assassination, and/or that it wasn't Oswald who fired the shots that killed President Kennedy." The two issues were the reported head snap to the rear and the so-called magic bullet supporting the commission's single bullet theory.

On the first issue, he explained that a careful examination of the two key frames on the Zapruder film refute the widely publicized claim that Kennedy's head snapped back in response to the head shot—therefore suggesting a shot from the front rather than from behind. Bugliosi made the point that only the Warren Commission report and his book contained the two important frames (312 and 313) bearing on this issue. In frame 313 after the shot to the head, the film shows the president's head pushed slightly forward—indicating a shot from the rear—and then the following frames (314–321) show the head snap to the rear, "which the pathologists say was a neuro-muscular reaction."[37]

On the subject of the "magic bullet," Bugliosi recounted his cross-examination of Dr. Cyril Wecht, the coroner of Alleghany County and Pittsburgh who was called by Oswald's defense counsel at the London trial to refute the commission's single-bullet theory and thereby raise reasonable doubt about Oswald's guilt. Bugliosi asked Wecht what he thought happened to the bullet that entered Kennedy's upper right back on a downward trajectory and then exited from the front of his throat, and specifically "how come it didn't tear up the interior of the limousine or hit the driver or anyone else? Wecht responded: "I don't know. . . . I didn't conduct the investigation in this case." Bugliosi suggested to Wecht that he had his own "magic bullet." He told Wecht: "If it did not hit Governor Connally and did not tear up the interior of the limousine, did not hit anyone . . . it must have zigzagged to the left." Wecht responded: "No, it need not have zigzagged to the left." Bugliosi asked: "Did it hop, skip, and jump over the, the car?" Wecht said: "No, it need not have performed any remarkable feat like that." Bugliosi said: "Well then tell this jury, Doctor, what, what happened to that bullet?" Wecht said: "I don't know."

Bugliosi concluded from this exchange that the conspiracy theorists apparently believe that "when this bullet exited from the President's throat it vanished into thin air without leaving a trace. Right? Now that is a magic bullet. And yet the conspiracy theorists have, have hung that magic bullet around the neck of the Warren Commission for close to forty-four years, and we find out that it was they—not the Warren Commission—with the magic bullet."[38]

■ **Subsequent Official Investigations Developed No Facts |**
   That Challenge the Commission's Conclusions

Over the thirty-four years that followed the issuance of the commission's report, four official investigations raked meticulously over the same ground—a special commission appointed by the president, a Senate committee, a House committee, and a special board created by Congress. They identified areas in which they thought perhaps the commission could have done better, but not one finding of these investigations casts any significant doubt on the commission's conclusions that Oswald was the assassin and there was no credible evidence of a conspiracy involving either Oswald or Ruby.

■ **The Rockefeller Commission (1975)**

In January 1975, President Gerald Ford created the Commission on CIA Activities within the United States. The *New York Times* in December 1974 had reported massive domestic spying by the CIA—contrary to its charter—and Ford directed this commission to determine whether any domestic CIA activities exceeded the agency's statutory authority and to propose appropriate recommendations. He asked his vice president, Nelson A. Rockefeller, to serve as chairman and appointed seven additional members. Ford appointed David Belin from the Warren Commission staff to serve as the commission's executive director.[39]

As recounted by Belin several years later, the Rockefeller Commission got off to a difficult start. After the members were appointed, the press challenged their readiness to aggressively investigate these charges against the CIA in light of their extensive government experience. Belin recommended at the commission's first meeting that it hold as many meetings as possible open to the public, and that its internal meetings be recorded by a court reporter—as had been done by the Warren Commission. Belin's new client rejected both recommendations.[40]

The Rockefeller Commission rejected four specific allegations about the CIA's involvement in the assassination of President Kennedy[41]:

> (1) Two employees of the CIA (E. Howard Hunt and Frank Sturgis), who were both convicted of burglarizing the Democratic Party headquarters at the Watergate in 1972, were supposedly in Dallas on November 22, 1963, and one of the shots that struck President Kennedy was alleged to have been fired from the grassy knoll where the two men were present. The commission concluded that Hunt had been an agency employee for many years and continued to be associated with the CIA until his retirement in 1970, but that

Sturgis had never been a CIA employee. Both men denied they were in Dallas on November 22, and their testimony was supported by other witnesses with no significant conflicting testimony.

(2) Many conspiracy theorists still believed that at least some of the shots came from the front. The Rockefeller group assembled its own five-member special panel, which concluded that both shots came from behind—as had the commission and Attorney General Clark's panel in 1968. As to the movement of Kennedy's head, "they were also unanimous in finding that the violent backward and leftward motion of the President's upper body following the head shot was not caused by the impact of a bullet coming from the front or right front."[42]

(3) A few witnesses claimed to see an assassin with a rifle in the area of the grassy knoll on the Zapruder film. After examining the specific frames alleged to show an assassin or rifle, the Rockefeller Commission concluded that "the alleged assassin's head was merely the momentary image produced by sunlight, shadows, and leaves within or beyond the foliage" and that the same was true of the "rifle" seen in another frame.[43]

(4) Oswald or Ruby have been repeatedly cast as CIA operatives, but the Rockefeller group found no credible evidence to support this allegation in either case. Addressing the contention that Hunt could have had contact with Oswald in New Orleans during the spring or summer of 1963, the Rockefeller Commission concluded that Hunt never met Oswald, was not in New Orleans in 1963, and did not have any contact with any New Orleans office of the Cuban Revolutionary Council.[44]

During this inquiry, Belin came across the CIA's efforts directed at assassinating Castro and became determined to obtain the agency's records regarding assassinations of foreign officials. The commission urged the CIA to cooperate promptly, as the presidential order creating the commission required. Belin threatened to use polygraph examinations to ensure that agency officials complied with the commission's requests. Perhaps sensing a losing battle, the CIA submitted voluminous material in early February, including the detailed results of the agency's internal investigation in 1973 ordered by director James Schlesinger.[45]

Belin was, in fact, getting far out in front of his client. Some members, including Rockefeller himself, objected to any further investigation of CIA assassination plots. But now Belin was supported by press coverage about possible American plots against foreign leaders. In early March, the commission authorized Belin to go forward with this investigation and he did so.[46]

Key CIA and other administration officials testified about the agency's plans from 1960 to 1964 to assassinate Castro. As this testimony unfolded, Belin reported "there were knowing looks from several members, who referred to the 'amnesia syndrome of much of the leadership of government during the Kennedy and Johnson years, particularly with reference to Cuba and Vietnam.'" Based on this record, Belin prepared a draft chapter for the commission's report. Although most members supported this chapter, Vice President Rockefeller was opposed.[47]

Late in May—a few weeks before the commission's deadline for finishing its work—President Ford through Secretary of State Henry Kissinger requested that the chapter not be published. The State Department had concluded it would be "inappropriate for a presidentially appointed commission" to report that the CIA had been involved in assassination plots directed at foreign leaders in peacetime. Belin was angry, especially because it was President Ford who had announced in March 1975 that the commission was investigating assassination plots. According to Belin, the commission's debate on this question was intense:

> Rockefeller made his case. I made mine. I asked the commission to ask the White House to reconsider and not bend to Kissinger. I pointed out that Dillon had already told the press we had the facts. I argued that the real issue was that the United States had engaged in shocking conduct. I argued that it would be far better to bring it out in the open now rather than to turn it over to Congress. I was joined by Peter Clapper, our press officer, who thought press reaction would be very bad. The press had already been led to believe that a final report would include a chapter on assassination plans directed against foreign leaders, he noted. But Clapper and I lost to Rockefeller and Kissinger.

A compromise solution emerged. The foreword to the commission report stated that the commission had undertaken an inquiry regarding the involvement of the CIA in assassination plans, "but time did not permit a full investigation before this report was due. The President therefore requested that the materials in the possession of the Commission which bear on these allegations be turned over to him. This has been done."[48]

Belin was "particularly upset with the decision, because it was wrong. I felt that American people should know what we found. . . . I knew the people eventually would find out, because the material we had would be delivered to the Senate Select Committee under the chairmanship of Sen. Frank Church." Belin was also "very upset that the CIA in 1964 had deliberately withheld from the Warren

Commission evidence that the CIA had been engaged in assassination plots against Fidel Castro." These developments, coupled with the increasing volume of conspiracy theories regarding the Warren Commission, persuaded Belin on the twelfth anniversary of the assassination, in 1975, to request a reopening of the Warren Commission investigation, because he believed that "it would greatly contribute toward a rebirth of confidence and trust in government."[49]

■ The Church Committee (1975–76)

The Select Committee to Study Governmental Operations with Respect to Intelligence Activities ("Church Committee") was created in early 1975. As was the case with the Rockefeller Commission, the Senate was driven to action by news reports of illegal domestic intelligence operations by the CIA. The committee was a bipartisan panel of eleven members chaired by Senate Frank Church (D-ID) and was given a broad mandate to investigate the CIA. The Church Committee published fourteen reports in 1975 and 1976 about the formation, operation, and abuses of US intelligence agencies. One of these reports examined whether and to what degree the CIA and the FBI withheld relevant information from the Warren Commission. Its conclusion was that "for different reasons, both the CIA and the FBI failed in, or avoided carrying out, certain of their responsibilities" regarding the investigation of the assassination of President Kennedy.[50]

The committee did not attempt to duplicate the work of the Warren Commission. It did not review the commission's conclusion that Oswald was the assassin. The committee pointed out that its discussion of investigative deficiencies and agency failures "does not lead to the conclusion that there was a conspiracy to assassinate President Kennedy." Rather, its detailed reports of operations directed at Castro were intended to illustrate why they were relevant to the Warren Commission's investigation. The committee cautioned "that it has seen no evidence that Fidel Castro or others in the Cuban government plotted President Kennedy's assassination in retaliation for U.S. operations against Cuba."[51]

The Church Committee summarized the extent to which the CIA and FBI were engaged in operations against Cuba in the years just before the assassination, in particular, their involvement with groups opposed to Castro— Cuban exiles in the United States, other Americans opposed to Cuba's communist regime, businesses whose property had been expropriated by the Castro government, underworld interests who had lost their profitable gambling enterprises, and virtually all the major departments of the US government. The intelligence agencies were assiduously collecting information on Cuban pro-Castro and anti-Castro activity. They were also conducting covert operations against Cuba, ranging from propaganda to paramilitary action, including the invasion at the Bay of Pigs.[52]

If both agencies had disclosed such information, the commission would have investigated whether the anti-Castro groups might have had some association with Oswald or Ruby. For example, the Church Committee traced the CIA's involvement with American organized crime figures from 1960 until early 1963, when the responsible agency official advised them that the CIA was no longer interested in assassinating Castro. It described armed attacks by Cuban exile groups in 1963 against two Soviet vessels off the northern coast of Cuba, which prompted concern within the US government and concerted efforts by federal agencies (including the FBI, CIA, Coast Guard, Customs, and Immigration and Naturalization) to reduce the risk that such efforts would lead to a confrontation with the Soviet Union.[53]

Relationship of the FBI with the Warren Commission

Hoover and other top officials at the FBI were aware that underground figures were discussing Cuba with CIA and FBI field offices in New Orleans and Miami. They were also aware of the anti-Castro armed efforts, but they did not provide any of this information to the commission, notwithstanding our specific requests to the FBI for information about the pro-Castro and anti-Castro groups in New Orleans. However, the agents and supervisors in the FBI's general investigative division, which had responsibility for investigating the assassination, were not aware of this information.[54]

The Espionage Section within the bureau's domestic intelligence division was in charge of Soviet matters and had supervised the security case on Oswald before the assassination. This division was reportedly responsible for the possible pro-Castro or anti-Castro aspects of the assassination case, but it did not conduct any meaningful investigation of a possible foreign conspiracy. Its director, William Sullivan, knew of the earlier CIA efforts to use underworld figures to assassinate Castro. But he could not recall any specific measures that his division took to explore the possibility of a foreign conspiracy to kill President Kennedy.[55]

The Nationalities Intelligence Section in this division would have been responsible for the investigation of any foreign conspiracy involving Cuba. However, the leading Cuba expert in this section was never informed of any CIA assassination attempts against Castro, had no recollection of any FBI investigation of Cuban involvement in the assassination, and was never informed of Castro's warning of retaliation. If he had been aware of this warning, this official believed that a typical reaction by FBI headquarters would have been to instruct the key field offices to alert their sources and to be particularly aware of anything that might indicate an assassination attempt. But no such notice was sent by FBI headquarters.[56]

The section expert on anti-Castro exiles within the United States was never asked to investigate whether any Cuban exile group was involved in the assassination. FBI headquarters never instructed field agents to contact informants or sources familiar with Cuban matters to determine whether they had any information concerning Cuban involvement in the assassination. The FBI explored only those Cuban issues relating solely to Oswald and Oswald's contacts, rather than the larger issue whether subversive activities of the Cuban government or Cuban exiles were relevant to the assassination. It never initiated or discussed any counterintelligence program, operation, or investigation to pursue these questions.[57]

After summarizing the respects in which the FBI failed the Warren Commission, the Church Committee stated: "Senior Bureau officials should have realized the FBI efforts were focused too narrowly to allow for a full investigation. They should have realized the significance of Oswald's Cuban contacts could not be fully analyzed without the direct involvement of FBI personnel who had expertise in such matters. Yet these senior officials permitted the investigation to take this course and viewed the Warren Commission in an adversarial light."[58]

Relationship of the CIA with the Warren Commission

The Church Committee described the sporadic contacts by the CIA with a high-level Cuban official, code-named AMLASH, who was ready to assassinate Castro, as well as the deliberations within the US government about whether, and how, Castro might retaliate against any further covert activity in Cuba. On September 7, 1963, Castro in an interview with an AP reporter warned the United States against plots directed at Cuban leaders: "We are prepared to fight them and answer in kind. United States leaders should think that if they are aiding terrorist plans to eliminate Cuban leaders, they themselves will not be safe." Although the commission was aware of Castro's threat of retaliation, the CIA did not advise the commission of its deliberations about this threat, which might have prompted some additional investigation by the commission.[58]

The Church Committee concluded that none of the CIA officials assigned to work with the commission knew of the agency's plans during 1960–63 to initiate covert actions directed at Castro, including assassination plots. The assigned officials were experts in KGB and Soviet matters and the CIA's investigation therefore concentrated on the significance of Oswald's activities in the Soviet

Union. Our commission lawyers never worked with or received information from the CIA Cuban affairs staff (the Special Affairs Staff, or SAS). According to the Church Committee, the chief of SAS Counterintelligence testified that SAS had no "direct" role in the investigation of the assassination and "there is no evidence whatsoever that SAS was asked or ever volunteered to analyze Oswald's contacts with Cuban groups." Although the CIA had considerable links to Cuba and Cuban exiles, it did not utilize these capabilities to assist the commission. The Church Committee concluded that "all the evidence suggests that the CIA investigation into any Cuban connection, whether pro-Castro or anti-Castro, was passive in nature." The committee determined: "There would seem to have been some obligation for the CIA to disclose the general nature of its operations which might affect the Commission's investigation."[60]

Although the Church Committee concluded that Ray Rocca, one of our principal CIA contacts, was not aware of any assassination plots, Deputy Director Helms knew all about them. In testimony before both the Rockefeller Commission and the Church Committee, Helms denied seeing any connection between the AMLASH operation and the investigation of the president's assassination. Helms told the Rockefeller Commission that he never perceived that Oswald's pro-Cuban activities could figure in any retaliation plans that Castro may have had. Before the Church Committee, Helms denied that he was "charged with furnishing the Warren Commission with information from the CIA, information that you thought was relevant." Instead, he was instructed only to provide information requested by the commission. Because the commission failed to ask for information about CIA assassination plots directed at Castro, he was not obligated to provide it. He added that the Warren Commission could have relied on public knowledge that the United States wanted "to get rid of Castro."[61]

The Church Committee concluded that the CIA should have investigated any Oswald involvement with pro-Castro or anti-Castro groups. It rejected the excuse that such an investigation was not warranted by the facts known at the time or that the FBI had primary responsibility for the investigation. The committee stated:

> Even if CIA investigators did not know that the CIA was plotting to kill Castro, they certainly did know that the Agency had been operating a massive covert operation against Cuba since 1960. The conspiratorial atmosphere of violence which developed over the course of three years of CIA and exile group operations, should have led CIA investigators to ask whether Lee Harvey Oswald and Jack Ruby, who were known to have at least touched the fringes

of the Cuban community were influenced by that atmosphere. Similarly that arguments [sic] that the CIA domestic jurisdiction was limited belie the fact CIA Cuban operations had created an enormous domestic apparatus, which the Agency used both to gather intelligence domestically and to run operations against Cuba.[62]

The Church Committee also concluded that "the AMLASH operation seems very relevant to the investigation of President Kennedy's assassination. It is difficult to understand why those aware of the operation did not think it relevant, and did not inform those investigating President Kennedy's assassination." The desk officer, initially in charge of the CIA's investigation, testified that knowing of the AMLASH plot "would have . . . become an absolutely vital factor in analyzing the events surrounding the Kennedy assassination." The CIA analyst who replaced him felt the same way, stating that he was not aware of the plots until 1975 and expressing "concern about the Warren Commission's findings in light of this new information."[63]

The Church Committee concluded that "[w]ith the exception of Allen Dulles, it is unlikely that anyone on the Warren Commission knew of CIA assassination efforts."[64] Senator Cooper told the committee that the subject never came up in the commission's deliberations. Rankin, Griffin, Belin, and I all advised the committee that we were not aware of the CIA assassination plans. Both Belin and Griffin told the committee that knowledge of the assassination plots was certainly relevant to the work of the Warren Commission.[65]

Most of us associated with the commission were disappointed and angered when we learned of the FBI and CIA failures to assist the commission. Several of us testified to that effect before a House Committee in 1978. Katzenbach testified that he was "appalled" that the CIA did not inform the commission about its anti-Castro activities.[66] In 1963–64, we believed that agencies would marshal their full resources to assist the commission in light of the president's mandate to do so. Such a belief—from that pre-Vietnam, pre-Watergate period—today seems hopelessly naïve. When CIA Counterintelligence chief James Angleton called David Slawson to check his reactions to the Church Committee's disclosures, Slawson frankly told Angleton how disappointed he was with his agency's failure to disclose this vital information, but assured him that Slawson would honor his commitment to preserve the confidentiality of other CIA secrets.[67]

When asked by the House committee whether such full disclosure would have changed the conclusions of the commission, Katzenbach testified:

Well, I think obviously things would have been investigated that were not investigated or investigated in more depth than they were investigated. I have no way of knowing whether what light would have been cast. I have been personally persuaded that the result was right and I do not think that it would have changed any of the evidence that they had that led to that result. But I suppose that one has to say, an investigation that did not take place, it is impossible to know what would have come out of it.[68]

I am confident that such additional investigation would not have changed the key conclusions of the commission. The commission's "ground up" approach, which focused on Oswald and Ruby and their associates, would not have been significantly different even if we had full disclosure by the two agencies. As one knowledgeable student of the commission commented: "Collectively, the Warren Commission might not have known about contemporaneous American-hatched plots to kill Castro. But it certainly examined Oswald's links to Cuba as carefully and minutely as possible—indeed, as if it *did* know."[69]

On the other hand, such additional investigation based on our knowledge of the CIA's plans might have had other important consequences. Burt Griffin has suggested, for example, that an aggressive investigative effort directed at the pro-Castro and anti-Castro groups to explore any relationships with Oswald might have altered our thinking about Oswald's motive.[70] In addition, he posits some even more significant consequences if the Warren Commission was the means by which the CIA's assassination plans became public in 1964—more than a decade before the Rockefeller Commission and the Church Committee. That would certainly have reshaped the next decade of the CIA's activities in ways that we can only speculate about. It seems to me, however, unlikely that the Warren Commission would have decided—faced with opposition by the agency and likely President Johnson– to disclose the CIA plans to assassinate Castro. President Johnson kept his knowledge of such plans secret after he learned of them from Helms in 1967 and President Ford intervened in 1975 to prevent the Rockefeller Commission from issuing its report on CIA's assassination plans. But regardless of the potential consequences of such disclosure, the CIA's deliberate failure to advise the Warren Commission fully about its assassination plots against Castro ignored the presidential mandate creating the commission and was a serious disservice to the nation.

■ The House Select Committee on Assassinations (1977–79)

The movement to reopen the investigation of President Kennedy's assassination gained momentum in the mid-1970s. In 1973, Carl Oglesby, a sometime instructor at MIT, formed the Assassination Information Bureau in Cambridge, Massachusetts. He and his associates "spoke to increasingly large audiences on hundreds of college campuses, from Maine to Hawaii and parts in between, urging a reopening of the investigation." In March 1975, a program on ABC national television showed for the first time the Zapruder film and the head snap to the rear, which created "a whole new wave of Warren Commission critics and conspiracy theorists" urging a new investigation.[71]

The disclosures by the Rockefeller Commission and the Church Committee about CIA's illegal activities, supplemented by the failures of the FBI and CIA to cooperate with the Warren Commission, fueled the demands for action. At a 1975 appearance at the University of Virginia, Robert Groden, whose pirated copy of the Zapruder film had been used by ABC, spoke to an audience that included the son of Congressman Downing, who brought it immediately to his father's attention. After he saw the film and arranged for more than fifty of his fellow congressmen to do likewise, Downing stepped forward to support the effort to get a congressional investigation of all three assassinations in the 1960s—JFK, RFK, and Martin Luther King.[72]

In September 1976, the House of Representatives established a Select Committee on Assassinations to conduct "a full and complete investigation of the circumstances surrounding the deaths of President John F. Kennedy and Dr. Martin Luther King, Jr." After its reauthorization in early 1977, the Select Committee had two years, until January 3, 1979, to complete its work. Representative Louis Stokes of Ohio was named chairman. Stokes approved the hiring of Professor G. Robert Blakey to head the staff, and Gary Cornwell, one of Blakey's deputies, directed the Kennedy investigation. Both had served several years in the organized-crime section of the Justice Department.[73]

The House Select Committee was the only government-funded investigation of the Kennedy assassination that challenged the finding of the Warren Commission that there was no credible evidence of a conspiracy. Four aspects of its 1979 report regarding Kennedy's assassination and the Warren Commission are especially significant. The Select Committee's criticisms of the commission's procedures and the scope of its investigation were mostly wrong or insubstantial and, in any event, were not shown to have affected the commission's conclusions. The Select Committee confirmed the commission's findings identifying Oswald as the person who fired three shots from the Texas School Book Depository, two of which resulted in the president's death and Connally's wounds. The Select Committee confirmed the commission's findings that the available evidence did not reveal any involvement in the assassination of the president by the Soviet Union, the Cuban government, anti-Castro Cuban groups, the national syndicate of organized crime, the Secret Service, the FBI, or the CIA.

In the final week of its work, the staff recommended a new draft conclusion about a second assassin, which was adopted by seven of twelve committee members. The Select Committee had unanimously agreed a few weeks earlier that there was no credible evidence of any conspiracy. The new conclusion stated that a second assassin fired a fourth shot at Kennedy from the grassy knoll located in front and to the right of the president's car. The staff relied solely on recently developed acoustics evidence to support its conclusion of a conspiracy—without any physical evidence or eyewitness testimony of a second shooter, a second rifle, a fourth bullet, or the identity of any conspirators.

Criticism of the Warren Commission's Methods and Investigation

In its report, the Select Committee criticized the Warren Commission for its inadequate staffing, failure to hire independent investigators, dependence on federal investigative agencies, unrealistic time deadlines, need to respond to political pressures, inadequate investigation of potential conspiracies, and the phrasing of its conclusions.

These charges have no substantial basis in fact. I have explained earlier why the commission rejected the alternative of hiring non-government investigators. We used federal agents, but we verified the facts through our own staff work in generating the record of sworn testimony on which the commission based its findings. Time after time, Select Committee counsel invited commission members or staff appearing before the committee to testify that the commission was subject to one or more of these deficiencies. All of us who testified—three commission members and eight from the staff—challenged the apparent belief of the committee staff that we worked under unrealistic time pressures and succumbed to political pressures in writing our report.

If there was grumbling by some of our lawyers about the need for more help as we finalized the report, that was par for the course. Near the end of any major project, there is always the sense that more help would be desirable. But the commission lawyers in 1964 did what lawyers always do under these circumstances—they worked harder and longer until the report was done to their satisfaction. They did not cut corners.

The committee's report identifies nine areas where, in their estimation, "the performance of the commission was less than complete."[74] Three of the areas related directly to information withheld from the commission, including the concealment of the CIA's assassination plots against Castro and the FBI's failure to disclose the disciplinary actions taken by Hoover in December 1963. There was, of course, no way that the Warren Commission could have investigated these areas without information that was deliberately withheld.

The other six areas identified by the committee included Oswald's activities and associations in New Orleans, the two and one-half years he spent in the Soviet Union, his visit to Mexico City, and Ruby's background and associations, particularly with regard to organized crime. The committee also cited the commission's failure to consider "the violent attitude of powerful organized crime figures toward the President and Attorney General Robert Kennedy, their capacity to commit murder, including assassination, and their possible access to Oswald through his associates or relatives."[75]

In many of these areas the committee staff had access to sources of information that were not available to the Warren Commission. For example, the CIA had finally concluded that Soviet defector Nosenko was a bona fide defector, so that the Select Committee was free to evaluate his credibility about the Soviet Union's interest in Oswald. In addition, the committee staff retained an organized crime expert to review the extensive material generated by the FBI's unlawful electronic surveillance of organized crime.

The Select Committee may well have conducted a more thorough investigation into some of these areas than the Warren Commission. They deserve credit for doing so. But the critical point is that the Select Committee reached the same conclusions as the Warren Commission: Oswald was the assassin and there was no credible evidence of a conspiracy in which either Oswald or Ruby was involved.

Confirmation of the Warren Commission's Findings Regarding Oswald

On the most important facts demonstrating that Oswald was the assassin, both committee and commission agreed:

- Kennedy was struck by two rifle shots fired from behind him, based principally on a unique approach developed by the committee.
- The shots that struck Kennedy were fired from the sixth floor window of the southeast corner of the depository, based on scientific analysis, witness testimony, and firearms evidence.

- Oswald owned the rifle that was used to fire these shots based on handwriting analysis and photographs.
- Oswald had access to and was present on the sixth floor of the depository building shortly before the assassination based on the testimony of depository employees and the physical evidence of his presence.
- Oswald's other actions tend to support the conclusion that he assassinated President Kennedy, in particular his murder of Officer Tippit.

Not surprisingly, Warren Commission critics were disappointed that the Select Committee had rejected virtually all of their theories in reaffirming the commission's conclusions about Oswald.[76]

The committee determined the source of the shots that hit Kennedy and Connally using a different approach than we had. The commission looked at the trajectory question from the sixth-floor window looking down, starting with the proposition that at least some shots had been fired from this window. The committee's Photographic Panel assumed nothing about the source of the shots. As Liebeler later described the panel's approach: "Using medical and photographic evidence it attempted to locate the wound paths in the President and in Governor Connally in the space of Dealey Plaza. If they could do so accurately they could then trace a trajectory backward to the point from which the shots had been fired." The panel created three trajectories—two based on the president's two wounds and the third based on the governor's wounds. Although the trajectories were not identical and did not land right in the window, each of them intercepted the southeast corner of the depository. That permitted the panel to conclude that "it is highly probable that the bullets were fired from a location within this section of the building."[77]

The Select Committee joined in the widespread criticism of the Warren Commission's failure to get access to the autopsy photographs and X-rays. The committee's Forensic Pathology Panel obtained these materials and subjected them to a full range of tests. To make certain that the photographs and X-rays were those of President Kennedy and had not been altered in any way, the panel used experts in anthropology, forensic dentistry, photographic interpretation, forensic pathology, and radiology. Based on the wounds suffered by both men, the panel concluded that the bullets causing the wounds were fired from behind. After examining Connally's back wound and the holes in his coat and shirt, the Forensic Panel agreed (with only Wecht dissenting) "that the wound in Governor Connally was probably inflicted by a missile which was not aligned with its trajectory but had yawed or tumbled prior to entry into the Governor." As is obvious, this analysis provided support for the single-bullet theory.[78]

After reviewing the medical and other testimony pertaining to the single-bullet theory, the Select Committee confirmed that both men were hit by a single bullet. As Liebeler said in 1996: "In spite of all the criticism the single-bullet theory is stronger today than it was at birth. On the basis of analytical techniques not available in 1964 and using approaches quite different from those used by the Warren Commission, the House Committee has unequivocally reaffirmed the single-bullet theory."[79]

Confirmation of the Warren Commission's Conspiracy Findings

The Select Committee agreed with the commission that, on the basis of the available evidence, none of the "usual suspects" of the conspiracy theorists was involved in the assassination of Kennedy. This included the Soviet government, the Cuban government, anti-Castro Cuban groups in the United States, the national syndicate of organized crime, the Secret Service, the Federal Bureau of Investigation, and the Central Intelligence Agency.

Elimination of all these candidates left little room for a new conspiracy theory. But the committee's staff created a narrow window of opportunity that was embraced by a majority of the committee members. While concluding that neither the anti-Castro Cuban groups, "as groups," nor the national syndicate of organized crime, "as a group," were involved in the assassination, the staff wrote "that the available evidence does not *preclude the possibility* that individual members may have been involved."[80] This sentence can only be characterized as meaningless (if not foolish) because no amount of evidence could ever preclude such a possibility. This was the same issue that I had discussed with Hubert and Griffin about our Ruby investigation in 1964.[81]

There is simply no precedent for the use of such a standard of proof in the American legal system. The courts will not find a criminal defendant guilty because "the available evidence does not preclude the possibility" that he was guilty of the crime charged. A civil plaintiff cannot prevail in a breach of contract case because "the available evidence does not preclude the possibility" that the defendant may have breached the contract. And a plaintiff in a negligence case cannot recover damages attributed to a car driven by the defendant because "the available evidence does not preclude the possibility" that the defendant was negligent. In all these instances, the prosecutor or plaintiff must meet an affirmative standard of proof—beyond a reasonable doubt in the criminal case and by a preponderance of the evidence in most civil proceedings.

The standard must be met by affirmative (and admissible) evidence presented in court by the prosecutor or plaintiff. The same is true of presidential commissions or congressional committees asked to determine what happened—or did not happen—unless the commission or committee concludes that its investigation was so limited (for any variety of factors) that it was unable to make a positive finding one way or the other.

The House Select Committee's Conspiracy Theory

On December 18, 1978, the Select Committee members unanimously approved a draft report, which concluded: "There is insufficient evidence to find that there was a conspiracy to assassinate President Kennedy."[82]

In recent months, the committee had been evaluating acoustics evidence based on a tape of police communications in Dallas with motorcycle officers in the motorcade on November 22, 1963. This particular tape contained sounds that were not conversations, apparently because the transmitter on one of the motorcycles was stuck in the "on" position on one of the two channels and was recording every sound around the motorcycle. An expert witness, Dr. James Barger, first told the committee that he could not be certain that the sound spikes on the tape were gunshots and that the differences between the spikes might represent a total of either three or four shots. To resolve these questions, Barger said he would need to pinpoint the location of the motorcycle officer with the open microphone.

After conducting some tests in Dallas, Barger appeared before the committee in September 1978. He testified that he still could not say with absolute certainty that the spikes were gunshots and that there was a fifty percent chance that the last two spikes represented either one or two shots. He also advised the committee that he had located the approximate position of the motorcycle with the open transmitter, namely, 120 feet behind the presidential vehicle.[83]

As reflected during his testimony and in news reports, the committee members were frustrated by Dr. Barger's insistence on emphasizing the limitations of his analysis of the sound spikes. He stressed the many variables involved with the testing that had been done in Dallas, including the lack of certainty as to which motorcycle radio was stuck in the open position, where it was located, and whether the muzzle of the assassin's rifle was inside or outside the window from which it was believed to have been fired. Representative Samuel L. Devine (R–OH), a member of the committee, said at one point: "I would hate to sue or to prosecute anyone on this kind of evidence.'"[84]

Cornwell and Blakey were also disappointed in Dr. Barger's testimony, hoping for a more conclusive determination that would support their view that a conspiracy existed. Up until the night before Barger's testimony, Cornwell and Blakey "were convinced the acoustics expert would report the fourth shot." Instead, Dr. Barger said under oath the he could only confirm that there was a "fifty-fifty probability" that the tape contained the noise of an additional gunshot. "I think at the last minute he realized that his whole professional career would come to be identified with this report and he wanted some corroboration for it," one committee member said.[85]

Based on the uncertainties in Barger's testimony and the novelty of the acoustics evidence, the committee members in mid-December relied on the physical and other evidence to support their finding of no conspiracy. They specifically declared in the draft report: "The committee finds that the available scientific evidence is insufficient to find that there was a conspiracy to assassinate President Kennedy."[86]

The Select Committee staff was determined to pursue the matter, even at this late date. Cornwell secured more conclusive testimony from two members of the faculty of Queens College, New York: Dr. Mark Weiss and Dr. Ernest Aschkenasy. Without adding any new data to the discussion, Weiss on December 29, 1978, testified that there was a ninety-five percent or greater degree of certainty not only that the third amplitude burst of sound on the tape constituted two separate noises but that they were in fact two shots, each from a high-powered supersonic rifle, and that the first of the two was fired from a point on the grassy knoll determined within a margin of error of only ten feet. Weiss and his colleague determined that Barger had accurately fixed the location of the motorcycle with the open transmitter in Dealey Plaza.[87]

When Barger appeared before the committee again and endorsed the ninety-five percent-certainty figure, he was questioned as to how, and why, he had changed his position from his earlier testimony that there was only a fifty-fifty probability that the third impulse was a shot. He explained that the Weiss team had narrowed the match time (between impulses on the tape and the reenactment results) and maintained a high correlation coefficient and this "resulted in our independent calculation of the expectancy that they could have achieved the match they got only 5 percent of the time by random if it had just been noise on the tape and not a gunshot from that place."[88]

Based on this reassessment of acoustics evidence only a few days before the committee's expiration on January 3, 1979, committee lawyers persuaded a majority of the members to discard their earlier findings and to conclude that

Oswald was part of a conspiracy to assassinate the president. Their report, issued with four written dissents, says:

> B. Scientific acoustical evidence establishes a high probability that two gunmen fired at President John F. Kennedy. Other scientific evidence does not preclude the possibility of two gunmen firing at the President. Scientific evidence negates some specific conspiracy allegations.
>
> C. The committee believes, on the basis of the evidence available to it, that President John F. Kennedy was probably assassinated as a result of a conspiracy. The committee is unable to identify the other gunman or the extent of the conspiracy.[89]

Several committee members were concerned by this "last-minute" effort to turn a "no conspiracy" finding into a "conspiracy" finding based solely on acoustics evidence that had been so surprisingly improved without any additional data or determining with certainty the location of the motorcycle with the open transmitter. They had invited some independent observers to hear the testimony of the acoustics experts on December 29, 1978. Two of their comments are found in the dissenting views of committee member Representative Robert Edgar (D–Pa).

In a letter dated January 2, 1979, Marvin Wolfgang, professor of sociology and law at the University of Pennsylvania, advised the committee:

> I think the works of Barger and Weiss and Aschkenasy have been exciting from a scientific perspective. I hope their studies will be published in traditional scientific journals where they will receive the usual form of scrutiny. However, I think it is premature and inappropriate for a Federal group, like your committee, to make a major policy decision on the basis of their findings[90]

Francis Davis, Dean of Science at Drexel University, advised the committee:

> Lacking something like that [a scientific report] to look at critically, I certainly think that the 95 percent confidence claim is grossly exaggerated, and it would take considerably more scientific evidence to convince me and most other scientists that their conclusions were valid. As it is, I believe that their chi-square probability test indicates a 95 percent probability that certain events on the tape could not occur by chance, but not that there is a 95 percent probability that a shot came from the grassy knoll.[91]

In a joint dissenting statement, Representatives Samuel Devine (R–OH) and Robert Edgar stressed that the experts were simply offering their opinion, which had to be weighed against other evidence, to determine whether a second assassin fired at the presidential vehicle from the grassy knoll. Most significantly, they emphasized that a key assumption underpinning the newly revised acoustics evidence was probably wrong. Reliance on the acoustics evidence depended entirely on the assumption that the motorcycle transmitter broadcasting the sounds recorded on the tape was in a very particular location—no more than 120 feet behind the president's car. The only motorcycle near that location was ridden by Dallas police officer H. B. McLain. If the transmitter that recorded the sounds was not on McLain's motorcycle, then the entire acoustics evidence analysis fell apart.[92]

Devine and Edgar's dissent pointed out that Officer McLain was not offered the opportunity to hear the tape before he testified at the hearing. He did listen to it upon returning to Dallas and asked what Devine and Edgar described as "a very simple, but important, question: 'If it was my radio on my motorcycle, why did it not record the revving up at high speed plus my siren when we immediately took off for Parkland Hospital?'"[93]

Edgar elaborated on his reasons for dissenting in a separate statement. He summarized the lack of evidence supporting the conspiracy theory based on the acoustics experts: "We found no gunmen or evidence of a gunman. We found no gun, no shells, no impact of shots from the grassy knoll. We found no entry wounds from the front into any person, including President John Kennedy and Gov. John Connally. We found no bullets or fragments of bullets that did not belong to the Oswald weapon." Reviewing the recollections of the 178 persons in Dealey Plaza who were available to the Warren Commission, Edgar pointed out that only four of these individuals believed that shots had originated from both the grassy knoll and the Texas School Book Depository. Based on this evidence, the committee had been prepared to conclude that there was no conspiracy. The staff persuaded the committee majority to reject their earlier decision and accept the "scientific evidence" of the acoustics experts by emphasizing that "Other scientific evidence does not preclude the possibility of two gunmen firing at the President," and ignoring the otherwise persuasive "nonscientific" evidence that supported a finding of no conspiracy.[94]

Edgar had no reservation in observing that the events in December 1978 "clearly demonstrate a rush to conspiratorial conclusions." Without blaming anyone in particular, he concluded: "I believe the Members of Congress did not have sufficient time or expertise to ask the tough questions. I believe the committee failed to properly consider how much weight to assign this evidence due to our own limitations of time and familiarity with the science. I believe we rushed to our conclusions and in doing so, overshadowed many important contributions which other aspects of our investigation will have on history." Edgar continued to hold these views when I spoke to him in early 2012.[95]

Representative Harold Sawyer, a Republican from Michigan, also filed a strongly worded dissent from the majority's conspiracy finding. He started with a crucial point:

> As a threshold premise, it should be noted that I believe it is important that despite the lapse of 15 years and at least two independent investigations, one by the Warren Commission and the other by this committee, which by any investigatory standards were exhaustive, no other evidence or even what might be termed a "scintilla" of evidence has been uncovered which would substantiate a conspiracy or which tends to negate the fact that Oswald operated alone.

Sawyer added that all the various conspiracy theories challenging these facts "have been, in my opinion, totally discredited or explained beyond any reasonable doubt by evidence developed by this committee."[96]

Sawyer identified several other facts that he believed raise serious and unresolved questions about the acoustics evidence.

- The tape (or Dictabelt) was fifteen years old and contained only the noise of a motorcycle, at one point the faint noise of sirens and at another the faint ringing of chimes. No expert testified that he could hear any noises suggesting gunfire. The experts maintained "that because of the 'cutoff point' of a radio transmitter, the full amplitude of loud sounds would not have been transmitted to and recorded on the dictabelt."
- Officer McLain denied that he had the motorcycle with the stuck transmitter and stated that he was receiving communications over Channel 2, the channel dedicated to the motorcade. It seemed unlikely that an officer who is part of the motorcade would have maintained an open transmitter during the entire motorcade and "remain oblivious to the fact that he was receiving constant and totally extraneous communications ... over Channel 1."
- McLain and all the other officers in the motorcade activated their sirens after the shots were fired, but there was no indication of that on the tape until "a full 2 minutes following the last of what is interpreted by the acoustical experts as the shots."

- The sounds on the tape were more consistent with a transmitter being on a motorcycle located somewhere between Dealey Plaza and Parkland Hospital. In this connection, the Dallas police monitor or dispatcher within minutes following the shots instructed a squad car to go to an area between Dealey Plaza and Parkland Hospital "and have a motorcycle officer in that vicinity turn off his transmitter which was stuck in the transmit position on Channel 1 and was interfering with central police communications on that channel."
- Although there were no chimes in Dealey Plaza, one set of chimes known to exist at the time of the assassination was located in the area beyond Dealey Plaza and toward Parkland Hospital.[97]

Sawyer found the presentation by Weiss and Aschkenasy to be "unpersuasive." He was offended by their suggestion that the committee "would not be able to find a qualified acoustics expert who would disagree with either their conclusions or the degree of certainty of these conclusions." Weiss also testified that his conclusions were based on the position of the motorcycle with the stuck transmitter as determined by Barger. But when asked whether his conclusions were dependent on the accuracy of this location, Weiss told the committee "that unless he were shown an exact replica of Dealey Plaza elsewhere in Dallas that his computations had confirmed or independently verified that correctness of Dr. Barger's motorcycle location." An experienced trial lawyer, Sawyer found this last conclusion more than he could accept without comment: "While I am acquainted with 'bootstrap' scientific analytical procedure, it would appear to me that there are far too few, if any, established or verifiable facts in this entire acoustical scenario to permit the use of bootstrap analysis to determine or sufficiently verify a given predicate to permit even reasonable reliability of the conclusions."[98]

The findings of the Select Committee were welcomed by the conspiracy theorists but treated less warmly by the press. The reversal of the committee's position in its last hours was seen by one reporter as "in keeping with the halting, often unsure nature of its two-year history.... And by the time that intriguing new lead came along, the committee was on its last financial legs and was under the stern eye of a Congress unwilling to pay for further inquiry." Many legitimate questions were raised: "Why did the testimony come only as the committee was going out of business? Why was not more than one outside expert called to corroborate it?...Why did the motorcycle patrolman contradict his own testimony last week and claim the recording couldn't have been his?" *Newsweek*'s story about the committee's "pell-mell U-turn in the Kennedy case" pointed out that the committee's conclusion of a fourth shot from the grassy knoll ignored the evidence "that Oswald fired the only shots that hit Kennedy or anything else; the fact that the supposed second gunman, gun, and bullet all evanesced without a sighting or a trace, [and] that only four of 178 known earwitnesses thought they had heard shots from *both* the Depository and the knoll." Some of the reports concentrated on the dissents filed by committee members who disagreed with the conspiracy finding and complained that relevant information had been withheld from them by the committee staff.[99]

On March 29, 1979, the divided Select Committee issued its report along with the statements of four of the five dissenters. The report acknowledged that the committee was unable to identify the second assassin who fired at the president from the grassy knoll "or the extent of the conspiracy" proved by the acoustical evidence. Blakey had no such reservations. "I am now firmly of the opinion that the Mob did it," he told the press. "It is a historical truth." Then he quickly added: "This Committee report does not say the Mob did it. *I* said it. I think the Mob did it."[100]

After an initial review by the FBI of the acoustics evidence, but before it issued any report, the Justice Department contracted with the National Academy of Sciences to examine the acoustics evidence. The National Academy established the Committee on Ballistic Acoustics, a panel of twelve scientists headed by Harvard University professor Norman F. Ramsey Jr., who was awarded the Nobel Prize in physics in 1989. The Ramsey Committee issued its report in 1982, concluding that the noise spikes (or impulses) on the tape (Dictabelt) occurred about sixty seconds *after* the assassination of the president and therefore did not result from either the three shots from the depository or a shot from any other source. The Ramsey Committee reached this conclusion after pursuing a lead provided by an outsider, Stephen Barber, who heard what he believed was "crosstalk" on Channel 1 of instructions issued on Channel 2.[101]

Even before the Ramsey Committee issued its report, Blakey reported to Chairman Stokes that Barger had seen drafts of the report. Blakey said he believed that the panel would conclude that Barger's analysis did not adequately explore "non-shot" alternatives for the four events he considered shots and that the Barber "crosstalk" demonstrates that the four events could not have been the shots of the assassination. Blakey said: "In short, Mr. Chairman, the news is not good. It appears that the Panel has set out to refute our work, not find out what happened. They have, for example, totally ignored the eye witness and ear witness testimony of shots from the knoll; they have not, moreover, considered how improbable it might be for all of our shots to be wrong and yet match the Zapruder film so well. Nevertheless, that is apparently what is going to happen." He proposed a statement that the chairman might issue upon the release of the Ramsey Committee report and call for further congressional hearings on this matter.[102]

When the panel report was issued several months later, Blakey made certain that a copy was sent to Barger. He followed up with a letter seeking Barger's technical and other comments. Blakey said: "Frankly, I am disappointed in its tone, almost deferential with the FBI, hostile with us, dogmatic in its conclusions, close-minded to the possibility of alternative views, and seemingly ignorant of contradictory evidence. I trust you are angry enough— I am—to want an opportunity to respond publicly to what has all the characteristics of a hatchet job."[103]

He urged Barger to prepare an estimate of what it would cost to undertake further analysis of the issue, complaining about the Ramsey Committee assertion that any further work on the question would not justify its cost. Referring back to Barger's change in testimony in December 1978, Blakey wrote: "Just as I believed that it was essential to move the 50-50 off dead center before, I think it is crucial to finish all analyses that can be done at reasonable costs, both to confirm (or not) what we did and to test what our new found friends have done." No further analysis was ever done under congressional sponsorship.[104]

The Ramsey Committee report conclusively demonstrated that the Select Committee's conspiracy conclusion was wrong. After examining the issue thoroughly, Vincent Bugliosi documented numerous other failures by the Select Committee that led to this unsupportable conclusion. Bugliosi concluded that "the HSCA's finding of a fourth shot from the grassy knoll has been so thoroughly discredited that it has become an indelible stain on its legacy, a very large asterisk to its otherwise excellent reinvestigation of the assassination."[105]

■ The Assassination Records Review Board (1992–98)

Congress created the Assassination Records Review Board in 1992. The law aimed at ensuring that virtually all records generated by previous investigations or held by government institutions related to President Kennedy's assassination would be turned over to the National Archives. Its enactment resulted from the continuing debate about the conclusions of the Warren Commission and other investigative bodies that gained in intensity and public acceptance with the release in 1991 of Oliver Stone's *JFK*.[106]

Congressional Hearings on the Need for Legislation

The Review Board acknowledged the significance of Oliver Stone's film in providing the impetus for the law creating the board. It reported that the film "popularized a version of President Kennedy's assassination that featured U.S. government agents from the Federal Bureau of Investigation (FBI), the Central Intelligence Agency (CIA), and the military as conspirators." Although the Review Board described the film as "largely fictional," it endorsed Stone's message in the film's closing trailer "that Americans could not trust official public conclusions when those conclusions had been made in secret." Therefore Congress passed legislation—the JFK Act—"that released the secret records that prior investigations gathered and created."[107]

The Review Board's characterization of the film as "largely fictional" was certainly correct, if understated. Members of the commission staff were offended (but not really surprised) by the liberties taken by Stone in inventing facts surrounding the assassination. Although including in his film some of the more familiar conspiracy contentions dealing with the number of shots and the "magic bullet," Stone portrayed Oswald as a "patsy" who did not fire any shots at the president. Instead, the whole scene in Dealey Plaza was staged to make it seem like he did, in order to conceal the fact that several gunmen were shooting at Kennedy from different directions—a crossfire.

David Belin spoke before the National Press Club in Washington, DC, on March 26, 1992, about the movie in a speech entitled "The Assassination of Earl Warren and the Truth." Belin began his attack on Stone's film by quoting Warren to the effect that "one person and the truth is a majority." He characterized Stone's film as an effort to impeach "the integrity of a great Chief Justice." "Earl Warren is not the only victim," he went on to say, "Stone calls the assassination a 'public execution' by elements of the CIA and the Department of Defense, while President Lyndon B. Johnson is called an accessory after the fact." Because Stone had cited the Select Committee's report as support for the "facts" dramatized in the film, Belin itemized the respects in which that report corroborated the conclusions of the Warren Commission.[108]

What angered Belin even more than Stone's lies, omissions, misrepresentations, and manufactured facts was the massive amount of money spent by Warner Brothers and Stone to rewrite history. He said: "One of the most dangerous aspects of the disinformation of *JFK* is how the television networks in their quest for ratings have helped promote the lies about Earl Warren and the Warren Commission." Belin urged the press to "expose the corporate incest between huge Hollywood empires and the television networks and the danger that this poses to our democratic society as they rewrite the truth to fit their own mold." Referring to his Rockefeller Commission experience, he said: "No one knows better than I the dangers to a free society that are posed by a CIA out of control. But from my perspective, I see an equally great, or perhaps even greater, long-range danger to our democratic institutions of government with the increasing control by the entertainment industry over our national media, particularly television."[109]

Stone's movie, Belin's speech, and the likelihood of congressional action prompted several commission lawyers to discuss how we might best respond to the movie and support legislation making assassination records public. Burt Griffin recalled that he, Liebeler, and a few others met with me in Washington, and we also communicated with Mosk in Los Angeles and Redlich in New York. In early 1992, more than a dozen staff members signed a letter to the National Archives urging release of all Warren Commission materials, emphasizing the commission's (and our) desire back in 1964 to make all of our records available for public inspection, except those with a national security classification. In an accompanying press statement, we reaffirmed our confidence in the commission's conclusions about Oswald and the lack of any credible evidence of a conspiracy.[110]

Early in January 1992, Congressman Stokes, the chairman of the former House Select Committee on Assassinations, introduced H.J. Res. 454 with forty sponsors that would mandate the release of assassination records. I appeared on April 28 representing the commission staff at the first hearing on this legislation. Building on the staff's earlier public statement, my prepared testimony expressed strong support for making public all of our commission's materials as well as those of the House Select Committee, which were being withheld from publication for fifty years. I emphasized that only two percent of our commission's records (about three thousand pages) remained undisclosed and would be subject to review by any agency created by Congress for this purpose.[dcclx]

The hearing was conducted by the Legislation and National Security Subcommittee of the House Committee on Government Operations chaired by Congressman John Conyers (D–MI), a friend of Congressman Stokes and a powerful advocate of the conclusions reached by the former House Select Committee. It was held in a large hearing room featuring a full battery of TV cameras and spectators competing for the available seats. It was clearly the congressional event of the day in Washington for one reason only—the most prominent supporter of the bill was Oliver Stone. Hoping to avoid the penetrating glare of the TV cameras, I sat down on the far end of the table for scheduled witnesses and studiously examined my prepared statement. My desire for anonymity failed with the entrance of Oliver Stone, who sat at a small table about twelve feet directly in front of me, so that the cameras immediately focused on him and I was part of the background.

The hearing began with a brief statement of its purpose by Chairman Conyers and testimony in support of the legislation by Stokes. When he welcomed Oliver Stone as the next witness, Conyers said: "Welcome, Mr. Stone. We have your prepared statement. You are probably the reason that we are all here today."[112]

In his prepared comments Stone described the two conspiracies that led to the assassination of President Kennedy and the cover-up that had prevented the members and the American public from knowing the truth. According to Stone, the second and broader conspiracy involved President Johnson, whose "appointment of the Warren Commission was a means by which to derail a serious homicide investigation which was never accomplished." As one *Washington Post* reporter described Stone's film: "Stone mixes fact and fiction at dizzying speed, stomping on presumptions of innocence, cooking up fake admissions, ignoring contrary evidence, and giving a conspiratorial tone to inconsequential facets of the tragedy that were explained long ago." His testimony did likewise.[113]

After Stone's prepared remarks, the committee members eagerly sought the opportunity to express their fascination with his presentation and their admiration for his courage in bringing these conspiracies to the committee's attention. They solicited further details regarding Stone's conspiracy theories and, needless to say, Stone was not reticent in responding to their questions. Not one committee member felt obligated to ask whether Stone had any factual support for his views or his rejection of the conclusions reached by the Warren Commission and the House Select Committee.

By the time I was called to the podium, I had decided that my staid presentation in support of the legislation had to be amended to deal with Stone's presentation and the committee's apparent lack of interest in the facts. Early in my comments, I suggested that Stone was a far better film producer than a historian. I went on to defend the conclusions of the Warren Commission. But I never had the courage to ask the committee members whether any of them had read the Warren Commission report.

When Chairman Conyers asked for my "theory of the JFK assassination," I stressed once again my view "that there are no facts, as distinct from allegations and suspicions, that undercut any of the major conclusions of the

Warren Commission." He responded: "You don't have any nagging doubts?" I mentioned the commission's emphasis on the lack of credible evidence of any conspiracy, and he repeated, "So you do have some nagging doubts." After my further defense of the commission's conclusions despite the failures of the FBI and the CIA, we had this exchange:

> MR. CONYERS: But you still have nagging doubts.
> MR. WILLENS: If you are suggesting I have nagging doubts about the conclusions –
> MR. CONYERS: No, I am asking you. I am not trying to put words into a trial counsel's mouth. You either have nagging doubts or you don't have nagging doubts. It is a free country.
> MR. WILLENS: That is why Mr. Stone could make his movie.
> MR. CONYERS: Right. And that is why you may have your nagging doubts.
> MR. WILLENS: And I have my reservations about what the future will display. But I want to reiterate there have been no facts that have come to light in the last 28 years that have undercut any of those conclusions.[114]

After Chairman Conyers and I continued this exchange to our mutual dissatisfaction, Representative Shays intervened: "Mr. Willens, I love your spirit, and I think I love your spirit more because it is not as popular to take your view. So I thank you for being true to your beliefs and expressing them so strongly." He then proceeded, very cautiously, to probe whether I might be comforted if and when more information about the assassination was released to the public. I agreed that would be useful and then said: "And to the extent that I have spoken with passion and vigor, I apologize. It is a characteristic flaw. I think that I wanted to draw a distinction between facts on the one hand and allegations, rumors, and suspicions on the other."[115]

My critical comments of Stone's movie and spirited defense of the commission led, somewhat surprisingly, to comments from the audience. When I reminded the committee that the Select Committee's reliance on acoustics evidence had been rejected by the prestigious committee appointed by the National Academy of Sciences, a voice from the audience shouted "It has been refuted!"—or something to that effect. While I was being challenged by one committee member, my young nephew from rural Western New York, attending his first congressional hearing, urged me on by shouting from the rear seats in the room, "Eat his lunch, Howard!" When I finally ended my testimony with one more declaration that not one fact had come to light since 1964 that undercut the commission's conclusions about Oswald and the lack of any conspiracy, committee members responded with quiet smiles of sympathy for my deluded state of mind.[116]

The Collection of More Records

The Review Board was successful in identifying additional records for inclusion in the JFK Collection at the National Archives. These included some preassassination CIA records regarding Oswald and a smaller number of such records at the FBI. After a review of documents from the CIA's Office of Operations and operational histories, the Review Board staff "found no evidence of contact between Oswald and [the Office of Operations] either before or after his time in the Soviet Union." The Review Board devoted several pages to describing its effort to identify previously undisclosed records regarding Oswald's trip to Mexico six weeks before the assassination. The Review Board reported that the CIA was never able to locate photographic evidence of Oswald's visit to either the Cuban or Soviet consulate. The CIA also informed the board that it did not retain any tapes of calls believed to have been made by Oswald, including one to the Soviet consulate, because the tapes had been erased in accordance with the agency's standard procedures.[117]

The board was aggressive and persistent in its pursuit of assassination records. Among its major accomplishments, the Review Board reported that it had considered and voted on more than 27,000 previously redacted assassination records and obtained agencies' consent to release an additional 33,000 plus assassination records. It also had ensured that the famous "Zapruder Film" of the assassination belonged to the American people, made public all FBI and CIA documents from previous official investigations, and permanently preserved all the autopsy photographs of President Kennedy in digitized form. The board's report stated that its legacy "lies in the more than four million pages of records now in the National Archives and available to the public with remarkably few redactions."[118]

The Review Board made a major contribution to resolving lingering doubts and criticisms about what is shown in the documentary and physical evidence relevant to the assassination. Bugliosi concluded in 2007 that among the documents released by the Records Board not one item "remotely resembling a smoking gun was found that would call into question the findings and conclusion of the Warren Commission."[119] Under the JFK Act, all assassination records not released by the board are to be opened to the public no later than 2017—twenty-five years after enactment of the law—unless the president certifies that continued postponement is necessary to prevent harm to an identified national interest and that "the identifiable harm is of such gravity that it outweighs the public interest in disclosure."[120]

Even before the law was enacted, we recognized that the extensive disclosure of information that might result would never be sufficient "to still those who want to add to the conspiracy literature."[121] That has proved to be the case.

■ A Few Final Words

The work of the Warren Commission was an extraordinary professional experience. I was fortunate to have had this opportunity to witness and shape the aftermath of what was surely a defining moment in the middle of the twentieth century. Having written this book, it no longer seems so distant.

Looking back to 1963, President Johnson made the correct decision in appointing the Warren Commission. In the absence of a trial of Lee Harvey Oswald, the American public deserved a thoughtful effort to develop the facts regarding the assassination of President Kennedy and those who were responsible. The commission conscientiously assumed this obligation and produced a report that reflected accurately the results of the most extensive criminal investigation ever conducted.

We achieved one of the other objectives motivating President Johnson—to avoid the uncertainties and conflicts that would have resulted from having multiple investigations of the assassination at the state and federal levels. Texas and Dallas officials accepted the commission's conclusions and saw no need to mount their own investigations. The commission's report also defused potential congressional investigations at the time.

But the commission did not achieve another of its objectives—to address and satisfy the endless conspiracy theories. Was there more that the commission might have done to have a greater impact on rebutting these conspiracy theories? Was this even an achievable objective? I do not think so. Consider the unending flow of books about the Lincoln assassination. Nevertheless, we had an obligation to address those theories challenging us in 1964 and we tried hard to do that effectively.

I do believe—as Chief Justice Warren predicted—that history has proved us right. The approaching fiftieth anniversary of the Kennedy assassination encouraged me to return to my journal and files and tell the story of who we were, how we worked, the problems that we faced together, the critical decisions we made along the way, and the pride that we have in our report. Yes, there were gaps unfilled and mistakes along the way, which I have acknowledged in this account. But after nearly fifty years, no one with firsthand knowledge has emerged to dispute our basic conclusions that Oswald was the assassin and that neither he nor Ruby was part of any conspiracy.

Our historian, Alfred Goldberg, offered these thoughts in support of our work:

> And what is the alternative to the Warren Commission's reconstruction of the assassination—this distressing, banal, ambiguous event that has all the earmarks of real life which are familiar to all of us, but which we often refuse to recognize or accept as true of events of great import also? The alternative is some nebulous conspiracy hypothesis seeking some sanction of fact or reality that has thus far escaped it. The element of chance in this hypothesis is confined to Oswald. All of the elements of the event that have to be supplied by the imagination—the conspirators, the other assassin or assassins, the physical circumstances of the deed, the escape of the other assassins, the keeping of the secret—all of these are presented in one-dimensional terms. There is no allowance for the chance and ambiguity of real life. There is no evidence, there are no eyewitnesses, no one talked or betrayed the conspiracy. And yet with each additional assassin and conspirator the element of chance would have been all the greater—the loose ends, inconsistencies, and contradictions. But none has come to light. To accept the mountain of improbabilities inherent in these conspiracy hypotheses required a far greater suspension of logic and judgment than does the Warren Commission with its imperfections. Indeed, it is the presence of the real life imperfections which is one of the strongest arguments for the fundamental honesty and soundness of the Report.[122]

My commission colleagues and I recognize the common human feeling that great events must have great causes. We share the sense of implausibility that someone like Oswald could have assassinated our president acting alone. Over the decades since 1963, however, we have experienced in the United States and elsewhere assassinations of public figures and wanton killings of hundreds of innocent people by single individuals motivated by hatred, political or religious conviction, racism, or unknowable personal reasons. We seem to accept readily the fact that, for the most part, these individuals acted alone, without really knowing why they did what they did. We do not routinely look for a conspiracy that might help to place the killing in some context that might better explain the killers' motives. I wonder why after several such decades so many smart and thoughtful people still insist that Oswald could not have acted alone—for one or more of the several reasons identified by the Warren Commission and elaborated upon in subsequent books by perceptive authors.

I suspect that this resistance has something to do with the unfulfilled promises of our young president in the early 1960s, before that decade became consumed by the Vietnam War and inflamed by new assassinations, racial strife, and massive urban disturbances, and by later decades that provoked increased distrust of our institutions of government. We on the commission staff lived through these years and shared these experiences. I remain convinced that we were, and those of us still here are, fair-minded persons who would have acknowledged any new evidence from any source that could withstand critical analysis. Over the past nearly fifty years, none of us has seen such evidence. I think I speak for all of my colleagues when I say that we did our work with integrity, and that work has withstood the test of time.

POSTSCRIPT: THE STAFF

■

T HIS IS WHAT THE MEMBERS OF THE COMMISSION STAFF ACCOMPLISHED AFTER 1964. I include here Nick Katzenbach, the deputy attorney general, and Jack Miller, the head of the criminal division, because they were the ones who sent me to the Warren Commission in the first place and supported me during the entire endeavor.

Frank Adams continued practicing law in New York City as a partner in the law firm Satterlee, Warfield and Stephens. One of the oldest lawyers on the commission staff, he came with a distinguished record of public service He continued to be active in state politics during the 1960s and in 1970 left the Democratic party to support a fourth term for Republican governor Nelson A. Rockefeller. He retired in about 1970 and died in 1990.

Joe Ball returned to his criminal law practice in Los Angeles and continued a courtroom career that extended over more than fifty years. During that time he represented such well-known clients as Watergate figure John D. Ehrlichman, auto maker John DeLorean, and Saudi Arabian financier Adnan Khashoggi. During the 1960s and 1970s he served on the US Judicial Conference Advisory Committee on Federal Rules of Criminal Procedure and the Committee to Revise the California Constitution. He also was a member of the California Law Revision Commission, which produced the Evidence Code of California and the Tort Claims Act of California. According to the commission's executive secretary, Ball was "one of those who worked hardest at it." Ball also served as the president of the American College of Trial Lawyers and the State Bar of California. At his death in 2000 at the age of ninety-seven, he was hailed as "the best trial lawyer in California in the 20th century."[1]

David Belin returned to his practice in Des Moines, Iowa, where he specialized in corporate law, litigation, and estate law. Later he established a second office, in New York City. He was on the board of directors of several corporations and was active on behalf of nonprofit and religious organizations. Belin returned to public service in 1975 when President Ford appointed him to serve as executive director of Vice President Rockefeller's Commission on CIA Activities within the United States. In this capacity Belin learned of extensive US government plots to kill Fidel Castro, information that had not been provided to the Warren Commission. Belin wrote two books about the Warren Commission—*November 22, 1963: You Are the Jury* (1973), and *Final Disclosure: The Full Truth about the Assassination of President Kennedy* (1988). At his death in 1999 at the age of seventy, Belin was a co-owner of *The Tribune* in Des Moines, which described him in an editorial as "a moderate Republican who had no use for the far right of his party or the far left of the Democratic Party."[2]

Bill Coleman published his autobiography, *Counsel for the Situation: Shaping the Law to Realize America's Promise* (2010), at the age of ninety. After his service on the Warren Commission, Coleman returned to the practice of law in Philadelphia. In 1975, President Ford asked him to serve as secretary of transportation. During his two years in this position, Coleman oversaw the opening of the National Highway Traffic Safety Administration's car testing center in Ohio and the enactment of regulations covering the safety of pipelines and hazardous-materials shipment. In 1977, he joined the Washington office of the Los Angeles firm of O'Melveny and Meyers, where he advised clients on litigation matters in the corporate, antitrust, natural gas, and constitutional law fields; foreign trade and other international matters; and the handling of corporate acquisitions and divestitures. He continued to be active in public matters and served in several leadership positions in the NAACP. In 1982, he successfully argued before the Supreme Court in favor of upholding a ban on tax exemptions for private schools that refused to admit black students. President Clinton awarded Coleman the Presidential Medal of Freedom in 1996.

Mel Eisenberg returned to his law firm in New York after his assignment with the Warren Commission. He then reunited with Lee Rankin and Norman Redlich at the office of the New York Corporation Counsel for a short period before accepting an invitation in 1966 to join the faculty of the University of California Law School in Berkeley, California. Eisenberg is the author of *The Nature of the Common Law* (1991) and *The Structure of the Corporation* (1976) and has published casebooks on the subjects of contracts and corporations. He has been a visiting professor at Harvard University, a Guggenheim fellow, and a Fulbright Senior Scholar. He was chief reporter for the American Law Institute's *Principles of Corporate Governance*. The ALI also turned to him as an adviser on its very prestigious publications the *Restatement (Third) of Agency* and the *Restatement (Third) of Restitution*. He was named a fellow of the American Academy of Arts and Sciences. He has delivered lectures at universities around the world, and since 1998, he has been the Justin W. D'Atri Professor of Law, Business and Society at Columbia University in New York City. Eisenberg was awarded a Distinguished Teaching Award in 1990 and maintains his professorship at Boalt Hall, the law school at the University of California at Berkeley.

John Ely began his year as law clerk to Chief Justice Warren immediately after leaving the commission staff. In 1966 he worked as a criminal defense lawyer at Defender, Inc. in San Diego before joining the Yale Law School faculty in 1968. He taught at Harvard Law School and was asked by Bill Coleman to be the general counsel at the Department of Transportation in 1975. His 1980 book, entitled *Democracy and Distrust: A Theory of Judicial Review*, discussed key problems of modern constitutional law and the role of the US Supreme Court. He was invited to become dean of the Stanford Law School in 1982 and served in that position for five years. His tenure there was marked by the introduction of loan repayment assistance programs for students choosing public interest employment, the development of clinical learning programs, and the hiring of a new generation of faculty. He subsequently published two other books: *War and Responsibility* (1993) and *On Constitutional Ground* (1996). Ely became the fourth most often cited legal scholar in history. He died in 2003 at the age of sixty-four. A former colleague at Stanford declared that Ely "was the leading constitutional law expert of his time; a superb scholar and an even more superb individual."[3]

Alfred Goldberg was the historian on loan from the Department of Defense to assist the commission. After the commission he returned to his position as historian with the US Air Force Historical Division. Goldberg then served for thirty-seven years in the Office of the Historian of the Office of the Secretary of Defense, eventually rising to be the head of that division. In that capacity Goldberg edited and produced books on the term of each secretary of defense during the last several decades, based on interviews of the persons holding that position and the military and civilian leaders that served under them. He received the Department of Defense Distinguished Civilian Service Award and the Presidential Meritorious Award. Goldberg officially retired in 2007, but remained in the Washington area and at the age of ninety-three was still working part-time, in 2012, on the editing of these volumes. He was honored in January 2012 with an award from the American Historical Society for his professional work as a historian.

Burt Griffin returned to Cleveland, where he continued to practice law for ten years. From 1966 to 1975, he served as a legal aid lawyer in various capacities, including executive director of the Cleveland Legal Aid Society and national director of the Legal Services Program in the US Office of Economic Opportunity. He was elected to serve as a judge of the Common Pleas Court of Cuyahoga County, Ohio, in 1975 and served on that court for thirty years, until his retirement in 2005. At various stages in this career, Griffin served as an adjunct professor of law at Cleveland State University, a member of the Ohio Criminal Sentencing Commission, and a member of the board of trustees of the Cleveland Psychoanalytic Center. In their periodic review of judges, Ohio lawyers generally praised Judge Griffin for his careful preparation, thoughtful opinions, and fairness in his dealing with litigants and their counsel. After retirement, he took up work as a mediator and arbitrator, and also devoted time to Cleveland community groups dedicated to the improvement of the criminal justice system.

Leon Hubert returned to his firm in New Orleans after his work on the Warren Commission. He helped draft the Code of Criminal Procedure for the Louisiana State Law Institute, which was implemented by legislation in 1966. He authored and co-authored several articles and books on Louisiana statutes and legal practice, including a pleading and practice guide. Hubert continued to teach at Tulane Law School until his death in 1977.

Bert Jenner returned to his law firm in Chicago, which became over the next two decades the prominent national firm that bears his name today. He continued to be widely recognized for his legal skills, his commitment to the profession, and his undertaking of a wide range of public assignments. In 1974, the Republicans on the House Judiciary Committee forced Jenner to resign as chief special counsel after he advocated the impeachment of President Nixon based on their inquiry into the president's role in the Watergate break-in and cover-up. During his career, Jenner received numerous awards and eight honorary degrees, was president of the Illinois Bar Association and chairman of the Judiciary Selection Committee of the American Bar Association. He helped establish the responsibility of major law firms nationwide for a continuing commitment to pro bono work of the kind undertaken by Jenner during his lifetime. Jenner died in 1988 at the age of eighty-one.

Nick Katzenbach served as attorney general under President Johnson until 1966. Although a Democrat, he cultivated the goodwill of Republican senators to help pass the landmark 1964 Civil Rights Act and the Voting Rights Act of 1965, which he also helped draft, ending a century of discrimination at the polls.[4] In 1965, he had the Justice Department seek a federal court order barring Alabama officials from interfering with the civil rights march from Selma to Montgomery, which was led by Dr. King. He resigned in 1966 because of conflict with FBI Director Hoover over that agency's illegal investigative activities and advised President Johnson that he was available to take the number-two job at the Department of State. As under secretary of state he defended the legality of US involvement in Vietnam. At the end of the Johnson administration, Katzenbach went to IBM as senior vice president and general counsel. He represented the company in a thirteen-year antitrust battle with the Department of Justice, including a trial of more than six years, which ended in 1982 when President Reagan declared that the case had no merit. After resigning from IBM in 1986, Katzenbach practiced with a New Jersey law firm and often took on special assignments in the public and private sectors. He was respected widely for reconciling differences and cooling tempers, for his unflappability under crisis, and for the loyalty and competence that he brought to every assignment. He died in 2012 at the age of ninety.

Murray Laulicht began his year's clerkship with Judge Harold Medina on the US Court of Appeals for the Second Circuit after completion of his commission assignment. He began practicing law in New York with a major firm after his clerkship and then was recruited by a New Jersey firm, where he practiced for several decades specializing in antitrust, unfair competition, and other types of business dispute resolution, including dealer and franchise issues, partnership disputes, legal malpractice cases, regulated industries, and real-estate controversies. He has been active in the American Bar Association, the New Jersey State Bar Association, and several nonprofit organizations. He has retired from the active law practice, moved from New Jersey to Florida, and conducts his own consulting practice.

Jim Liebeler chose an academic career shortly after leaving the commission and taught antitrust law and constitutional law at the University of California in Los Angeles for more than thirty years before he retired in the mid-1990s. He took a leave of absence from the law school during 1975–76 to serve as director of the Federal Trade Commission's policy planning and evaluation office in Washington, DC. With a variety of interests—including personally constructing small apartment buildings, farming, and piloting his airplane—Liebeler taught at the George Mason University School of Law in Virginia from 1999 to 2002. One of his projects during the 1980s and 1990s was an unpublished book with the working title *Thoughts on the Work of the Warren Commission and the House Select Committee on Assassi-*

nations as to the Assassination of President John F. Kennedy. Jim died in 2002 at the age of seventy-one. The dean of the George Mason University School of Law, who had learned antitrust law from Liebeler, said, "You could not have a better start than to be taught by Jim Liebeler. He was a unique combination of enthusiasm, warmth, and acute intelligence."[5]

Arthur Marmor went back to his position as Chief of the Editorial Services Branch at the Department of State. During his government career Mr. Marmor served as a historian in the Departments of Interior, Army, and the Air Force. He also taught at the American University and the University of Maryland. He died in 1968.

Jack Miller left the Department of Justice in early 1965 and created one of Washington's outstanding litigation law firms. Miller worked in Robert Kennedy's campaign for president in 1968 and later represented Senator Edward Kennedy after the Chappaquiddick episode. In August 1974, he took on former President Nixon as a client, after successfully representing several minor figures involved in the Watergate scandals.[6] Although Nixon wanted to face his challengers in court, Miller persuaded him that he could not get a fair trial and that he should accept a pardon from President Ford. He persuaded Nixon to sign a statement admitting that he had been wrong in certain respects regarding Watergate, and the pardon, granted on September 8, 1974, spared Nixon any indictment and trial. Miller represented Nixon for twenty years, asserting Nixon's ownership rights to White House tapes and documents, a hotly contested issue that took years to resolve. He handled many other politically sensitive matters over the years with a level of competence, loyalty, and discretion that won the respect of clients and adversaries. He died in 2009 at the age of eighty-five.

Richard Mosk served as a law clerk for California Supreme Court justice Mathew Tobriner for a year after his work on the commission. He then entered private practice in Los Angeles, where he specialized in litigation until 2001, when he was appointed as an associate justice on the California Court of Appeal. During his years in private practice, Mosk was a special deputy federal public defender (1975–76), served as the US appointed judge on the Iran–United States Claims Tribunal (1981–84), was a member of the Christopher Commission, which investigated the Los Angeles Police Department (1991), and was chairman and co-chairman of the Motion Picture Classification and Rating Administration. Mosk also served on many domestic and international arbitration panels, taught at the University of Southern California, and lectured at various law schools in Europe, Australia, and the United States.

Stuart Pollak completed his work as special assistant to the assistant attorney general of the Department of Justice's criminal division in 1965 and joined a law firm in San Francisco. He specialized in litigation and, on one occasion, took on a major assignment on behalf of California Rural Legal Assistance, whose federal funding had been withheld based on charges of unprofessional conduct. In the course of this assignment, which ended with a favorable ruling for the client, Pollak worked with several officials in the California state government. In another case Pollak successfully defended the California Department of Correction's use of race in an affirmative action hiring program. In 1982, he was appointed to be a judge in the San Francisco Superior Court, where he served for twenty years, until he was appointed an associate justice on the California Court of Appeal.

Lee Rankin's return to his private practice in New York was interrupted again, sooner than he expected. In 1966 Mayor Lindsay asked him to serve as New York's corporation counsel and he did so for six years. He supervised a staff of 378 lawyers, who defended New York City in a wide range of lawsuits and provided opinions on a variety of municipal problems, from the legality of a police officer's membership in the John Birch Society to the legal status of school decentralization efforts. While serving as corporation counsel, Rankin began a program under which law-school graduates worked in his office for a year or two, receiving valuable experience before moving on to law firms. He returned to his own firm in 1972 and continued in private practice until his retirement in 1978. Throughout these years he taught constitutional law at New York University Law School. After retirement Rankin and his wife moved to Connecticut and then to California. He died in 1996.

Norman Redlich returned to the New York University Law School, but took a leave of absence in 1966 to serve as Rankin's executive assistant in the corporation counsel's office. When Rankin left this position in 1972, Redlich was appointed by Mayor Lindsay to be his successor. In 1974 Redlich became dean of the NYU Law School and served in that capacity until 1988. During that period he expanded the school's library, introduced new programs, built dormitories, and "brought extraordinary faculty to this law school," according to his successor as dean. He sought to deepen the school's commitment to the training of public interest lawyers and, with this goal in mind, recruited the most renowned capital defense lawyer in the country at the time, Anthony G. Amsterdam. When Redlich died in 2011, Professor Amsterdam, referring to Redlich's lifelong, outspoken opposition to the death penalty, said, "His style in this and in every one of the important fights he fought was selfless, steadfast, unsensational."[7]

Charles Shaffer remained in the Justice Department until 1966, when he entered private practice with a small firm in Rockville, Maryland. He became widely recognized as a smart, politically savvy Washington attorney and attracted many well-known clients over the years. He represented John Dean, the White House counsel who played a critical role in the unfolding of the Watergate scandal leading to Nixon's resignation. He guided former senator George Smathers through a series of congressional inquiries related to Watergate, and also defended prominent mobsters in a case involving alleged skimming of profits from the Stardust Casino in Las Vegas. On one occasion he represented a local Maryland doctor alleged to have killed a goose on the 17th hole of a prestigious country club with his putter and who had been charged with a violation of the federal Migratory Bird Act. The details of the case, with the conflicting evidence of the behavior of both the goose and the doctor, were described by humorist Art Buchwald in a column in June 1979, entitled "Doctor's Goose May Be Cooked." As of this book's writing, Shaffer is still practicing law and hunting regularly on his thoroughbred bay gelding.

David Slawson returned to his Denver firm for a short time, but decided to pursue an academic career. He served for a year in the Department of Justice's Office of Legal Counsel before joining the faculty of the University of Southern California Law School in 1967. He remained there until his retirement in 2004. At the invitation of Bill Coleman, he took a leave of absence in 1971–72 to serve as general counsel to the Price Commission, formed as part of the Economic Stabilization Program in Washington. While at the University of Southern California, Slawson taught administrative law, agency, antitrust, contracts, and insurance. He specialized in the law of contracts and was a cofounder of the contracts doctrine of reasonable expectations. His book, *Binding Promises: The Late 20th-Century Reformation of Contract Law*, received laudatory reviews as a modern classic in the field. After his retirement, Slawson moved to Orcas Island in the San Juan chain off the coast of Washington State, and has continued to work in the field of contract law.

Arlen Specter returned to the district attorney's office in Philadelphia. He successfully ran for the position of district attorney in 1965. He stayed in that office until 1974 and then returned to private practice from 1974 to 1980. Specter won election in 1980 to the United States Senate and was reelected to four additional terms. At various times he chaired the Senate Select Committee on Intelligence, the Judiciary Subcommittee on Terrorism, and the Committee on Veteran Affairs. Whether in the majority or the minority, Specter played an especially significant role on the Senate Judiciary Committee, where his legal training and experience, combined with his considerable debating skills, won widespread respect among his colleagues. He explored a run for president in the mid-1990s, competing in the New Hampshire primary. In 2000, he published (with Charles Robbins) the story of his life and career in a book entitled *Passion for Truth: From Finding JFK's Single Bullet to Questioning Anita Hill to Impeaching Clinton*. In 2012, he wrote (with Charles Robbins) *Life Among the Cannibals*. He died in 2012 at the age of eighty-two. Upon his death, President Obama stated: "Arlen Specter was always a fighter; from his days stamping out corruption as a prosecutor in Philadelphia to his three decades of service in the Senate, Arlen was fiercely independent—never putting party or ideology ahead of the people he was chosen to serve."[8]

Sam Stern returned to his law firm on a full-time basis. He became recognized as an expert in the reform of legal infrastructure in countries moving to open-market economies. Stern has served as counsel or adviser to the governments of more than forty countries seeking advice with respect to the appropriate legal infrastructure for oil and gas, power, mining, and water. In some of these instances he was designated as a consultant from the United Nations. He has done significant work in privatization, particularly of utilities and power. Stern has lectured at conferences around the world and published in professional journals on government regulation, foreign investment/finance, project finance, and trade and risk management. He has served as an arbitrator, advocate, or expert in international commercial arbitrations. Stern is a member of the American Law Institute and has remained in the Washington, DC area.

Lloyd Weinreb served as special assistant to the assistant attorney general of the Justice Department's criminal division during 1964–65. He joined the faculty of the Harvard Law School in 1965 and became a full professor in 1968. His research interests include criminal law, criminal procedure, intellectual property, and legal and political philosophy. Weinreb has published extensively in these fields, including *Denial of Justice: Criminal Process in the United States* (1977), *Natural Law and Justice* (1987), *Oedipus at Fenway Park: What Rights Are and Why There Are Any* (1994), *Legal Reason: The Use of Analogy in Legal Argument* (2005), and *Leading Constitutional Cases on Criminal Justice* (1977 [serial]). A reviewer of one of Weinreb's books described him as "a remarkable model of competence and clarity." A law-student review of his skills as a teacher commented: "What students will find in Weinreb is a model of competence, a master of clarity, and someone who knows exactly where to put the spotlight on the issues. His mild-mannered approach also masks considerable dry wit that makes his classes enjoyable even in the earlier hours."[9]

Howard Willens. I left the Department of Justice in August 1965 to serve as executive director of the President's Commission on Crime in the District of Columbia. In a one-thousand-page report in December 1966, the commission made recommendations regarding the various institutions in the District of Columbia criminal justice system—ranging from the police function to the correctional facilities. I joined a Washington law firm in January 1967 and remained there for twenty-eight years. I represented clients in white-collar criminal work, regulatory work before federal agencies, constitutional law, and arbitration and litigation in state and federal courts. I attended the 1968 Democratic National Convention as a delegate committed to Robert Kennedy. I assisted the people of the Northern Mariana Islands in the Western Pacific during their negotiations (1972–75) with the United States that resulted in their becoming United States citizens in a commonwealth under US sovereignty and later assisted in the drafting of the commonwealth's first constitution. My relationship with the Northern Mariana Islands continued over the next four decades. I have co-written two books about the Northern Marianas—Willens and Siemer, *National Security and Self-Determination: United States Policy in Micronesia 1961–1972* (2000); Willens and Siemer, *An Honorable Accord: The Covenant between the Northern Mariana Islands and the United States* (2001);—and another book about Guam, Willens and Ballendorf, *The Secret Guam Study: How President Ford's Approval of Commonwealth Was Blocked by Federal Officials* (2005). I still live in Washington, DC, where I continue to practice law, consult, and write books.

NOTES
■

1: DECEMBER 1963: THE NATION RESPONDS

1. President's Commission on the Assassination of President John F. Kennedy, *Report of the President's Commission on the Assassination of President John F. Kennedy* (Washington DC: US Government Printing Office, 1964), 3–4 (hereafter cited as Warren Commission and Warren Report).

2. Warren Report, 5–6.

3. Ibid., 5–9.

4. Robert Caro, *The Years of Lyndon Johnson: The Passage of Power* (New York: Alfred A. Knopf, 2012), 329.

5. Warren Report, 4.

6. CIA to Warren Commission, memorandum, March 23, 1964, entitled "Rumors About Lee Harvey Oswald," 2, RIF 104-10302-10025 (hereafter cited as CIA Memorandum).

7. Warren Report, 17–18.

8. Robert H. Estabrook, "Europeans Skeptical on Kennedy's Death," *Washington Post* (December 17, 1963), p. A18; CIA Memorandum, 6–7.

9. United States Senate Select Committee to Study Governmental Operations with Respect to Intelligence Activities, *The Investigation of the Assassination of President John F. Kennedy: Performance of the Intelligence Agencies*, bk. 5 of *Final Report* (Washington, DC: US Government Printing Office, 1976), 33–34 (hereafter cited as Church Committee and Church Committee Report).

10. Ibid.

11. When the commission historian, Dr. Alfred Goldberg, recommended in February 1964 that keeping a journal would be useful, I went to my files for November, December, January, and early February to write entries in my journal for those weeks. My first entry for November 1963 reads: "For several days after November 22, 1963 none of us in the Department had any role to play in the investigation of the assassination of President Kennedy. There was, as a result, a general feeling of impotence and lethargy. Not even the Criminal Division, with all of its experienced and investigation attorneys was involved in any way in assisting the Federal Bureau of Investigation in any of the work."

12. The American Civil Liberties Union also responded quickly on November 24, 1963, to deny the published report that Oswald was a member of the organiza-

tion. See "Commission Exhibit No. 2213," Warren Commission, *Hearings before the President's Commission on the Assassination of President Kennedy*, vol. 25, Exhibits 2190 to 2651 (Washington DC: US Government Printing Office, 1964), 100 (hereafter cited as Warren Commission Hearings, with volume number).

13. Katzenbach to Bill Moyers, memorandum, November 25, 1963, in Select Committee on Assassinations of the US House of Representatives, *Investigation of the Assassination of President John F. Kennedy*, vol. 3 of *Hearings* (Washington, DC: US Government Printing Office, 1979), 567–68 (hereafter cited as HSCA and HSCA Hearings, with volume number).

14. Journal, Events of November 1963; Herbert J. Miller Jr., interview by the author, transcript, Oral History Project of the Historical Society of the District of Columbia Circuit, 1998, 105–6, available at http://www.dcchs.org/OralHistory .asp?OralHistoryID=29&Menu=Documents.

15. Ibid., 105–07.

16. Ibid., 107–08.

17. Nicholas deB. Katzenbach, *Some of It Was Fun: Working with RFK and LBJ* (New York: W. W. Norton & Company, 2008), 133; Max Holland, *The Kennedy Assassination Tapes* (New York: Alfred A. Knopf, 2004), 93; HSCA Hearings, vol. 3, 644.

18. Holland, *The Kennedy Assassination Tapes* (2004), 90.

19. Ibid., 89–96.

20. Church Committee Report, 34; Warren Commission Hearings, vol. 5, 103.

21. Exec. Order No. 11,130, 3 C.F.R.795 (1959–63).

22. Earl Warren, *The Memoirs of Earl Warren* (Garden City, NY: Doubleday, 1977), 356.

23. Ibid., 357–58.

24. Holland, *Kennedy Assassination Tapes*, 150–52, 195–206; Caro, *Passage of Power*, 443–49.

25. Caro, *Passage of Power*, 442.

26. HSCA Hearings, vol. 3, 603.

27. Roscoe Drummond, "The Assassination Probe: Doubts Raised about Makeup of Commission," *Washington Post* (December 15, 1963), E7; Walter Trohan, "Report from Washington: Wisdom of Kennedy Death Probe Policy Is Questioned," *Chicago Tribune* (December 4, 1963), 4.

28. Journal, Events of December 1963.

29. Ibid. I believe that Katzenbach, Miller, and Ed Guthman also got copies at this time. Ed Guthman was the Department's public information officer and a close confidant of Robert Kennedy. Guthman was a Pulitzer Prize–winning reporter for the *Seattle Times* who had met Kennedy for the first time in late 1956 when Kennedy was exploring the possibility of Senate hearings dealing with labor racketeering. Evan Thomas, *Robert Kennedy: His Life* (New York: Simon & Schuster, 2000), 74.

30. FBI, report, "Investigation of Assassination of President John F. Kennedy November 22, 1963," Warren Commission Documents 1 (hereafter cited as JFK

Summary Report). A similar report dealing with Jack Ruby entitled "Investigation of Killing of Lee Harvey Oswald Dallas, Texas November 24, 1963" was delivered to the department and to the Warren Commission at a later date.

31. Journal, Events of December 1963. Many years later, the transcripts of all the commission meetings were declassified in their entirety and I have read them all in the course of writing this book.

32. HSCA Hearings, vol. 3, 646–47. In interrogating Lee Rankin about this refusal by the FBI to attend the commission's first meeting, Congressman McKinney asked in desperation: "Wasn't any attempt made at that point, with this sort of dramatic refusal, to have anyone in a higher position in Government such as the Attorney General or the President of the United States, turn around to Mr. Hoover and say cooperate? In the terms of at least sending a liaison person? That is the one question here." Rankin responded: "I don't know in my experience with Government that anybody ever did that with Mr. Hoover during his lifetime." HSCA Hearings, vol. 3, 633. The memorandum that the committee had was from Belmont to Tolson, December 3, 1963. HSCA Hearings, vol. 3, 672–73.

33. Warren Commission, "Executive Session Transcript, December 5, 1963," 3–4, 26, RIF 179-10001-10000.

34. Ibid., 26–29, 33–34. Robert Storey of Dallas was the retired dean of the Southern Methodist University Law School and former president of the American Bar Association and Leon Jaworski of Houston was a former president of the Texas State Bar. This prompted some discussion of exactly what "cooperation" meant in the context of the commission's investigation; it was agreed that the commission would not release the FBI report to the Texas authorities after the commission received it. Ibid., 34.

35. Ibid., 8.

36. HSCA Hearings, vol. 3, 648.

37. DeLoach to Mohr, memorandum, December 12, 1963 in HSCA Hearings, vol. 3, 594–95; DeLoach to Mohr, memorandum , December 17, 1963 in HSCA Hearings, vol. 3, 596–98; HSCA Hearings, vol. 3, 576.

38. Included as an exhibit in HSCA Hearings, vol. 3, 677.

39. Warren Commission, "Executive Session Transcript, December 6, 1963)," 14–18, RIF 179-10001-10001.

40. Senate Joint Resolution 137, Pub. L. 88-202, 77 Stat. 362 (1963).

41. Olney's ancestry placed him firmly within the "California establishment," of which the chief justice was also a member. Olney's grandfather was a well-known lawyer who helped form the Sierra Club and served at one time as mayor of Oakland. His father, also a lawyer, served on the Supreme Court of California. The candidate himself had served in the Eisenhower administration as the assistant attorney general of the criminal division—the same job that Jack Miller currently held—and had worked with the chief justice in many different capacities over the years, including his present position as director of the Administrative Office of the Courts.

42. Warren Commission, "Executive Session Transcript, December 16, 1963," 11–12, RIF 179-10001-10002; JFK Summary Report 1, 18.

43. Ibid., 14.

44. CIA Memorandum, 11. A strong statement of the John Birch Society's position appeared in the February 1964 issue of its monthly *American Opinion*.

45. Ibid., 8.

46. Richard Warren Lewis, "The Scavengers," *New York* (the *World Journal Tribune* magazine), January 22, 1967, 5, 8.

47. CIA Memorandum, 8–9.

48. Warren Commission, "Executive Session Transcript, December 16, 1963," 21–22.

49. Ibid., 24–25.

50. Ibid., 43–44.

51. Church Committee Report, 48.

52. Ibid., 47; HSCA Hearings, vol. 3, 481, 491–92, 495.

53. Journal, Events of December 1963.

54. Ibid.

55. Ibid. This entry refers to "my files." It is almost a reflexive habit with lawyers in private practice to keep detailed files on every matter they handle. I brought this training to the department and the commission. I kept the originals or copies of virtually every piece of paper that I prepared or received, including memos "for the record" or "to the files," primarily to keep track of important discussions, events, or decisions that might not find their way into the official files of the organization or law firm where I was working. I have relied on these files and memos in writing this book. The National Archives has a vast collection of documents relating to the Warren Commission and, more generally, the Kennedy assassination. With few exceptions, I have relied on my own journal and files. I expect that most of the documents cited in this book are in the National Archives, with some exceptions that may not have ended up in the commission's official files. I have identified these as from the "author's personal files" in the endnotes to this book.

56. FBI, "Investigation of Killing of Lee Harvey Oswald Dallas, Texas November 24, 1963," Preface, vol. 5 of Warren Commission Documents 1 (hereafter cited as Ruby Summary Report).

57. Journal, Events of December 1963. Less substantive, but still important, administrative tasks included setting up procedures for handling citizen mail, handling correspondence with various government agencies, arranging for necessary secretarial services, getting extra copies of the basic reports, and arranging for a "clipping service," which would, for a fee, collect newspaper or other articles from around the country (or the world) on any subject requested. We collected this material assiduously because we believed that the commission needed to be current about what was being said and done about the assassination as reported in the press.

58. Arlen Specter and Charles Robbins, *Passion for Truth: From Finding JFK's Single Bullet to Questioning Anita Hill to Impeaching Clinton* (New York: William Morrow, 2000), 43–44.

2: JANUARY 1964: DISTRUST OF THE FBI GROWS

1. FBI, "Investigation of Assassination of President John F. Kennedy, November 22, 1963: Supplemental Report, January 13, 1964," 66–67, Warren Commission Documents 107 (hereafter cited as JFK Supplemental Report).

2. FBI, "Investigation of Killing of Lee Harvey Oswald, Texas November 24, 1963: Supplemental Report, January 13, 1964," 24, Warren Commission Documents 107.1 (hereafter cited as Ruby Supplemental Report).

3. JFK Supplemental Report, 2.

4. Warren Report, 88–89.

5. Ibid., 90-91.

6. Author to Rankin, memorandum, December 30, 1963, "Tentative Outline of the Work of the President's Commission."

7. Earl Warren for Members of the President's Commission, memorandum, January 11, 1964, "Progress Report," 4.

8. Burt Griffin, interview by the author, December 5, 2011.

9. David Slawson, interview by the author, December 15, 2011.

10. Rankin to the Staff, memorandum, January 22, 1964, "Compensation." We paid the senior lawyers $100 per day, and the junior lawyers $75 per day. In addition, they received living expenses and reimbursement for other commission-related expenses.

11. Rankin to the Staff, memorandum, January 13, 1964, 1.

12. Specter, *Passion for Truth,* 46; Slawson, interview by author, December 15, 2011.

13. Shaffer, interview by the author, November 30, 2011.

14. Ibid.

15. Ibid.

16. Author to Rankin, memorandum, December 28, 1963, "Assignments and Work Product of Commission Staff."

17. Roscoe Drummond, "The Warren Commission …: The Task is Broadened," *Washington Post* (January 4, 1964), A9.

18. Ibid.

19. Anthony Lewis, "New Look at the Chief Justice: Ten Years on the Bench […]," *New York Times* (January 19, 1964), SM9.

20. Specter, *Passion for Truth*, 55.

21. Author, memorandum for the record, January 21, 1964, "Staff Meeting of January 20, 1964," author's personal files.

22. Rankin to Staff, memorandum, January 22, 1964, "Statement of Objectives" (hereafter Rankin staff memorandum "Statement of Objectives"). In a later memorandum to the staff, Rankin indicated that the next meeting of the commission

might be as early as the following Monday, January 27. Rankin to Staff, memorandum, January 24, 1964, "Meeting of the Commission, January 21, 1964" (hereafter Rankin staff memorandum, "Meeting of the Commission, January 21, 1964").

23. Author, memorandum for the record, January 29, 1964, "Staff Meeting –January 28, 1964," author's personal files.

24. Slawson, interview by the author, December 15, 2011.

25. Eisenberg, memorandum for the record, February 13, 1964, "Second Staff Conference, January 24, 1964," author's personal files.

26. Rankin staff memorandum, "Meeting of the Commission, January 21, 1964."

27. Warren Commission, "Executive Session Transcript, January 27, 1964," 1–2.

28. Ibid., 137.

29. Ibid., 11–13.

30. Ibid., 129–32.

31. Ibid., 137–38.

32. Hoover to Rankin, January 27, 1964, quoted in HSCA Hearings, vol. 11, 41.

33. HSCA Hearings, vol. 3, 640.

34. Hoover to Rankin, February 10, 1964, concerning interview of District Attorney Wade; Hoover to Rankin, February 11, 1964, concerning interview of Lonnie Hudkins; Hoover to Rankin, February 12, 1964, enclosing ten affidavits and referring to his letter of February 6, 1964, which enclosed his own affidavit.

35. The chronology of events is set forth in a memorandum from me to Rankin dated February 10, 1964, in preparation for a staff meeting on the subject.

36. HSCA Hearings, vol. 3, 563.

37. Ibid., 602–03.

38. HSCA Hearings, vol. 11, 349.

39. Specter, *Passion for Truth*, 56.

40. Warren Commission, "Executive Session Transcript, January 27, 1964," 169.

3: FEBRUARY 1964: THE SEARCH FOR EVIDENCE BEGINS

1. "Security Tie in Oswald Quiz Hinted," *Boston Globe* (February 4, 1964), 13; Vincent Bugliosi, *Reclaiming History: The Assassination of President John F. Kennedy* (New York: W. W. Norton, 2007), *Endnotes*, 133–35 (hereafter cited as *Reclaiming History* (text) or *Endnotes* (separate endnote file)).

2. "The Whole Truth," *Baltimore Sun* (February 5, 1964), 14.

3. "Assassination Data Sought," *Christian Science Monitor* (February 20, 1964), 3; Minority of One, M. S. Arnoni, ed., "An Open Letter to Chief Justice Earl Warren, Chairman of the Presidential Commission to Investigate the Assassination of President Kennedy," *New York Times* (March 2, 1964), paid advertisement, 20; Drew Pearson, "Warren Report Won't Satisfy All: Khrushchev's Opinion." *Washington Post* (June 26, 1964), B11.

4. Journal, February 3, 1964.

5. Ibid.

6. Ibid.

7. Ibid.

8. "Security Tie in Oswald Quiz Hinted," *Boston Globe.*

9. William M. Blair, "Warren Commission Will Ask Mrs. Oswald to Identify Rifle Used in the Kennedy Assassination," *New York Times* (February 5, 1965), 19.

10. At Redlich's request, I asked the FBI to obtain their investigative reports on this subject. Journal, February 26, 1964.

11. Warren Commission, "Executive Session Transcript, February 24, 1964," 1597.

12. Journal, February 27, 1964; HSCA Hearings, vol. 11, 126–27.

13. Warren Report, 187, 406.

14. Warren Report, 406.

15. Warren to Secretary of the Treasury Dillon, December 27, 1963.

16. Author to Rankin, memorandum, January 7, 1964.

17. Ibid.; Rankin to Rowley, January 10, 1964.

18. Rankin to Rowley, January 15, 1964.

19. Dillon to Warren, January 28, 1964.

20. Ibid.; Dillon to Rowley, memorandum, December 20, 1963, "Study of Procedures for Protecting the President."

21. Warren to Dillon, draft letter prepared by Stern, February 18, 1964, author's personal files; Journal, February 27, 1964.

22. Warren Commission, "Executive Session Transcript, February 24, 1964," 1598–99; Warren to Dillon, March 2, 1964.

23. Author to Rankin, memorandum, February 25, 1964.

24. Author, memorandum for the record, February 12, 1964, "Staff Meeting February 11, 1964," author's personal files. The chronology of events is set forth in a memorandum from me to Rankin dated February 10, 1964, in preparation for a staff meeting on the subject.

25. Ibid.; Rankin to Hoover, February 20, 1964.

26. Hoover to Rankin, February 27, 1964, with enclosed affidavits of FBI agents Gemberling and Kesler; Church Committee Report, 46.

27. HSCA Hearings, vol. 11, 112.

28. HSCA Hearings, vol. 3, 625, 632–33.

29. Rankin to Lane, January 23, 1964.

30. Warren Report, xiv.

31. Author to the Deputy Attorney General, memorandum, February 12, 1964, author's personal files.

32. Warren Report, xiv; Warren Commission, "Executive Session Transcript, February 24, 1964," 1600–01.

33. Journal, February 25, 1964.

34. Author, memorandum for the record, February 25, 1964, author's personal files; Warren, *Memoirs*, 322, 325–29.

35. Author, memorandum for the record, February 25, 1964, author's personal files.

36. Bugliosi, *Reclaiming History*, 351. According to Bugliosi, Craig "could have performed the function of a responsible devil's advocate, asking key Warren Commission witnesses questions that a competent defense attorney would have, but he failed abysmally in this effort and, through no fault of the Warren Commission, turned out to be mere window dressing for the expressed goal of helping to guarantee that a deceased accused be treated fairly and objectively." Ibid.

37. Rankin to Stern, memorandum, March 6, 1964, "Treatment of Lee Harvey Oswald by Dallas Police."

38. Stern and Ely to Rankin, memorandum, March 24, 1964.

39. Author to Rankin, memorandum, March 27, 1964; Warren Report, 196–208, 231.

40. Alfred Goldberg, interview by the author, January 19, 2012.

41. Journal, February 24, 1964; Goldberg, interview by the author, January 19, 2012.

42. Richard Mosk, interview by the author, December 11, 2011.

43. Journal, February 27–28, 1964. This entry also reports that we sent a letter to Mark Lane on February 28, 1964, inviting him to testify before the commission.

44. David W. Belin, *November 22, 1973: You Are the Jury* (New York: Quadrangle, 1973), 13-16.

45. Ibid., 16-17.

46. Warren Report, 560–62.

47. This was the conclusion reached by Edward Epstein in his 1966 book, *Inquest*, and discussed by Belin in the first chapter of his book entitled "And My Husband Never Made Any Sound." Epstein ignored the contrary testimony of the other four witnesses. Belin, *November 22, 1963: You Are the Jury*, 5–8.

48. William T. Coleman (with Donald T. Bliss), *Counsel for the Situation: Shaping the Law to Realize America's Promise* (Washington: Brookings Institution Press, 2010), 175.

49. Slawson, interview by the author, December 15, 2011.

50. Journal, February 24, 1964.

51. Warren Report, 309. This letter is discussed on pages 309–10.

52. Journal, February 24, 1964.

53. Specter, *Passion for Truth*, 49–51.

54. Specter to Rankin, memorandum, February 28, 1964, "Written Material Requested in Your Memorandum of February 25, 1964."

55. Journal, February 26, 1964.

56. Burt Griffin, interview by the author, December 5, 2011.

57. Author to Ball and Belin, memorandum, March 3, 1964, author's personal files.

58. Journal, February 24, 1964.

59. Robert E. Thompson, "Warren Commission Faces 'Sidetrack' Peril," *Los Angeles Times* (February 26, 1964), A4.

60. Wesley Liebeler, *Thoughts on the Work of the Warren Commission and the House Select Committee on Assassinations as to the Assassination of President John F. Kennedy* (unpublished manuscript, 1996) (hereafter Liebeler, *Thoughts*), 110. After the House Select Committee filed its report in 1979, Liebeler wrote this manuscript comparing the findings of that committee to our commission's report. He died before he could publish the work, but his widow has provided me with a copy of the manuscript, which I have used on several occasions in this book.

61. Belin, *November 22, 1963: You Are the Jury*, 304, 306.

4: MARCH 1964: OUR INVESTIGATION EXPANDS

1. Rankin to Lane, February 28, 1964.

2. Journal, March 4, 1964.

3. Rankin to Members of the Commission, memorandum, March 6, 1964, 7–8.

4. Journal, March 5, 6, and 7, 1964.

5. Journal, March 2, 1964.

6. Ibid; Liebeler to Rankin, memorandum, March 4, 1964, "Report of Committee on Rules for the taking of testimony of the staff (sic);" Redlich to Rankin, memorandum, March 4, 1964, "Report of the Chairman of the Committee on Rules for the Taking of Testimony by the Staff."

7. Ibid.

8. Ibid.

9. Ibid.; Liebeler to Rankin, memorandum, March 4, 1964.

10. Author to Rankin, memorandum, March 5, 1964, "Proposed Rules for the Questioning of Witnesses by Members of the Commission Staff."

11. Rankin to the Staff, memorandum, March 12, 1964; Journal, March 9–10, 1964.

12. Ibid.

13. Ibid.

14. Ibid.

15. Warren Report, 315–18, 646.

16. Journal, March 9–10, 1964.

17. Warren Commission Hearings, vol. 2, 295–337.

18. Warren Report, 129–30.

19. Journal, March 11, 1964; Warren Report 130.

20. Journal, March 12, 1964; Rankin to Members of the Commission, memorandum, March 12, 1964, "Testimony before the Commission (March 16–19)"; Rankin to Members of the Commission, memorandum, March 18, 1964, "Schedule of Testimony before the Commission"; Rankin to Members of the Commission, memorandum, March 30, 1964, "Testimony before the Commission (March 31–April 3)."

21. Eisenberg to Rankin, memorandum, March 4, 1964.

22. Journal, March 13, 1964.

23. Journal, March 12, 1964.

24. Journal, March 16–20, 1964; Specter, *Passion for Truth*, 88–90.

25. Ibid., 90.

26. Author to Rankin, March 14, 1964.

27. Journal, March 16–20, 1964; Author to Rankin, memorandum, March 18, 1964; Rankin to Curry, March 18, 1964.

28. Jim Lehrer, *Dallas Times Herald*, March 19, 1964.

29. Warren Report, 41.

30. Author to Rankin, memorandum, March 23, 1964.

31. Jim Lehrer, *Dallas Times Herald*, March 20, 1964.

32. Belin to Rankin, memorandum, September 19, 1964, "Empty Cartridge Case Experiments at TSBD Building,"1.

33. Ibid. Belin reported that this experiment was repeated on two other occasions, with the result that all seven members of the commission had an opportunity personally to determine whether the depository employees could have heard the cartridge cases falling on the floor above them on November 22. Belin concluded that the commission could properly rely on the March 20 experiment, as well as the others, for two reasons. First, the similarity in sound between the falling of the empty cartridge cases and the live ammunition supported the validity of the March 20 experiment. Second, the key witness (Norman) told Belin that at the time of the March 20 experiment there was a train going over the triple overpass and also trucks going along the street which, Norman advised him, created greater outside noise than existed on November 22. Ibid., 2.

34. Journal, March 23, 1964.

35. Journal, March 24–26, 1964.

36. Griffin to Rankin, memorandum, undated, "Memorandum for the Record of Interview with Dean."

37. In that connection, he wrote that "I took considerable pains to explain to Dean that I felt that I understood why he was coloring his testimony and that I believed him to be a basically honest and truthful person and I thought that he was probably an excellent police officer." Griffin to Rankin, memorandum, April 1, 1964, "Letter of Henry Wade dated March 25, 1964 Concerning Sgt. P. T. Dean," 1–2.

38. Bugliosi, *Endnotes*, 941.

39. Griffin to Rankin, memorandum, March 31, 1964, "Off the Record Conversation with P. T. Dean," 2.

40. Warren Commission Hearings, vol. 5, 258; Griffin later told me that he decided not to take any further depositions in Dallas in order to avoid any further controversy. Burt Griffin, interview by the author, November 28, 2012.

41. Bugliosi, *Reclaiming History*, 1077.

42. Goldberg to Rankin, memorandum, undated but probably around March 13, 1964, "Proposed Outline of Report of the Commission"; Rankin to Staff, memorandum, March 24, 1964; Journal, March 30 and 31, 1964.

43. Ibid.

44. Journal, March 24, 25, and 26, 1964; this decision was reflected in Rankin's memorandum to the staff of April 7, 1964, entitled "Depositions and Testimony before the Commission."

45. Author to Rankin, memorandum, January 15, 1964, "Meeting with Representatives of C.I.A. January 14, 1964."

46. Ibid.

47. Helms to Rankin, January 31, 1964; Helms to Rankin, memorandum, February 21, 1964.

48. Rankin to McCone, February 12, 1964.

49. Coleman and Slawson to Rankin, memorandum, January 24, 1964, "Oswald's Foreign Activities—Statement of Objectives and Problems Based on Review to Date of the Relevant Materials."

50. Coleman and Slawson to Rankin, memorandum, February 24, 1964, "Oswald's Foreign Activities: Oswald's Trip to the Soviet Union and His Contacts with the State Department."

51. Author to Rankin, memorandum, February 25, 1964; Guthrie to Rankin, March 7, 1964. John C. Guthrie was the director, Office of Soviet Union Affairs, Department of State.

52. Rankin to Chayes, March 23, 1964. Chayes was the legal adviser at State.

53. Hoover to Rankin, February 28, 1964, enclosing a four-page interview of Nosenko; FBI Memorandum of Nosenko Interview, February 28, 1964.

54. Ibid. He did testify before the House Select Committee on Assassinations in 1977–78. See chapter 10.

55. Author to Rankin, memorandum, March 3, 1964.

56. Slawson, memorandum, undated, "Conference with CIA on March 12, 1964."

57. Ibid.

58. Journal, March 12, 1964.

59. The congressional investigations that disclosed this information in the 1970s are discussed in chapter 10; Slawson, interview by the author, December 15, 2011.

60. Journal, March 27, 1964.

61. Stern to Rankin, memorandum, March 27, 1964, "CIA File on Oswald."

62. Journal, March 5, 6, and 7, 1964; Author, memorandum for the record, undated, probably March 7 or 8, 1964, "Area of Security Precautions," author's personal files.

63. Ibid. Treasury's Belin was unrelated to the commission's David Belin.

64. Ibid.

65. Journal, March 9–10, 1964.

66. Ibid.

67. Ibid.

68. Ibid.

69. Journal, March 11, 1964.

70. Ibid.

71. Ibid; author, memorandum for the record, March 13, 1964, "Memorandum of Conference."

72. Journal, March 11, 1964.

73. Rankin to Rowley, March 24, 1964.

74. Journal, March 24, 25, and 26, 1964; Rankin to Hoover, March 26, 1964.

75. Church Committee Report, 49; Warren Commission, "Executive Session Transcript, December 16, 1963," 24.

76. Hoover to Rankin, April 6, 1064.

77. Ibid.

78. Church Committee Report, 50.

79. Ibid.

80. Ibid.

81. Ibid., 51.

82. Ibid.

83. "Warren Report Believed Ready to Start on Report," *New York Times* (March 30, 1964), 26; "One 'Irrational' Person Killed Kennedy, Warren Group Believes," *Washington Post* (March 30, 1964), A3.

5: APRIL 1964: MEXICO AND THE CUBAN CONNECTION

1. Church Committee Report, 24–25, 27. This briefing did not include the agency's plans to assassinate Castro because McCone did not know about those plans at the time. President Johnson did not learn of these assassination efforts until 1967. Holland, *Kennedy Assassination Tapes*, 418–19.

2. Church Committee Report, 27–29.

3. Ibid., 31.

4. David Slawson prepared a comprehensive memo on the Mexican trip and I have relied on that memo in my discussion of this trip. Slawson, memorandum for the record, April 22, 1964, "Trip to Mexico City," (hereafter cited as Slawson Mexico Memorandum), 2–3; Church Committee Report, 29.

5. Slawson Mexico Memorandum, 5–6.

6. Ibid.

7. Ibid., 6–7.

8. Ibid., 8–9

9. Ibid., 10–11.

10. Ibid., 11–12.

11. Warren Report, 307–08.

12. Ibid., 301–04.

13. Slawson Mexico Memorandum, 19–20.

14. Ibid., 20–21.

15. Ibid., 23–24. The CIA identified the KGB agent with whom Oswald discussed his interest in a Soviet visa as Valeriy Vladimirovich Kostikov. Warren Report, 734.

16. Slawson Mexico Memorandum, 7.

17. Ibid., 26, 28.

18. Ibid., 26.

19. Ibid., 30–32.

20. Ibid., 33–35.

21. Ibid., 37–38.

22. Ibid., 38–39.

23. Ibid., 40–42.

24. Ibid., 40.

25. Ibid., 44–48.

26. Ibid., 58; Church Committee Report, 40–42.

27. Warren Report, 305; Warren Commission Hearings, vol. 16, 52.

28. Slawson Mexico Memorandum, 64–65.

29. Church Committee Report, 40 n102; 40–42.

30. Slawson Mexico Memorandum, 66.

31. Ibid., 67–68.

32. Journal, April 14–17, 1964. Later that week we sent a letter following up on the CIA's investigation of the Alvarado allegation and asking for a detailed report from the expert who conducted his polygraph examination. Rankin to Helms, April 21, 1964.

33. Slawson, interview by the author, December 15, 2011; Slawson to author, January 9, 2013.

34. Journal, Week of April 20, 1964; Author, memorandum for the record with attached draft letter, April 28, 1964, author's personal files.

35. Coleman and Slawson to Rankin, memorandum, undated, "Oswald's Foreign Activities," 107.

36. Ibid.

37. Warren Report, 410–12, 729.

38. Slawson, interview by the author, December 15, 2011.

39. Rankin to Hoover, April 23, 1964.

40. Rankin to Staff, memorandum, April 16, 1964.

41. Specter to Rankin, memorandum, April 16, 1964, "Remaining Work in Area 1."

42. Hubert and Griffin to Rankin, memorandum, April 21, 1964, "re April 13 request."

43. Journal, Week of April 20, 1964.

44. Ibid.

45. Journal, April 30, 1964.

46. Ibid.

47. Caro, *Passage to Power,* 537–45.

48. Journal, May 1, 1964.

49. Ibid.

50. Rankin to Connally, April 16, 1964.

51. Specter, *Passion for Truth*, 62.

52. Hubert to Rankin, memorandum, April 3, 1964, "Report on Depositions taken in Dallas."

53. Ibid., 1–2.

54. Ibid., 2–3.

55. Hubert and Griffin to Members of the Commission, memorandum, April 1, 1964, "Possible Cuban Associations of Jack Ruby." Although addressed to the commission members, I am certain that it went to Rankin instead.

56. Rankin to IRS, April 3, 1964; Rankin to Hubert and Griffin, memoranda, April 7, 1964 and April 8, 1964.

57. Rankin to Ball, memorandum, April 8, 1964; Rankin to Jenner and Liebeler, memorandum, April 14, 1964; Conroy and O'Brien to Rankin, memorandum, April 14, 1964, "Estimated Completion of Chronology."

58. Rankin to Lane, April 30, 1964.

59. Rankin to FBI, Secret Service, CIA, State, and Justice, April 22, 1964. I sent a copy of the Robert Kennedy letter to Miller. Author to Miller, note, April 22, 1964, author's personal files.

60. Ely to Jenner and Liebeler, memorandum, April 29, 1964, "Lee Harvey Oswald's Marine Career Further Investigation"; Mosk to Stern, memorandum, April 7, 1964, "Legislation Making the Assaulting or Murdering of the President and Others a Federal Crime"; see, for example, Norman Mailer, *Oswald's Tale: An American Mystery* (New York: Random House, 1995); Pollak, interview by the author, December 12, 2011.

61. Rankin to Hoover, April 22, 1964; Journal, April 27–29, 1964. This entry provides considerable detail about the FBI's facilities and procedures.

62. Ibid.

63. Journal, April 30, 1964.

64. Warren Commission, "Executive Session Transcript, April 30, 1964," 5853–57, 5862–63, 5879.

65. Ibid., 5880–84.

66. "Paper Reports F.B.I. Knew Oswald Peril," *New York Times* (April 24, 1964), 16; "Asserts FBI Knew Oswald Posed Danger," *Chicago Tribune* (April 25, 1964), 16; "Hoover Denies FBI Men Labeled Oswald Killer," *Hartford Courant* (April 25, 1964), 13B.

67. Warren Commission Hearings, vol.4, 194, 196; Bugliosi, *Reclaiming History*, 134, 154–55, 192, 210, 221.

6: MAY 1964: CRITICAL DECISIONS

1. Warren Commission Hearings, vol. 4, 441–47.

2. Ibid., 447–48.

3. Ibid., 449–52.

4. Ibid., 450–51. The commission concluded that Marina Oswald, at her husband's instruction, had copied down Hosty's license number and surmised that the FBI office address could have been found in many public sources. Warren Report, 327.

5. Warren Commission Hearings, vol. 4, 453–54, 458–59. In general, the Trotskyites (adherents of theories of Leon Trotsky) believed that there would be a revolution in the Western capitalist countries led by the working class and that the international aspects of the revolution, not limited to the Soviet Union, would be of key importance.

6. Ibid., 459.

7. Ibid., 461–62.

8. Ibid., 463–64.

9. Ibid., 464–67.

10. Ibid., 473.

11. Journal, May 5, 1964; Warren Commission Hearings, vol. 5, 33–35.

12. Warren Commission Hearings, vol. 5, 39.

13. Ibid., 39–43.

14. Ibid., 43–44.

15. Rankin to Curry, May 22, 1964. The letter noted that the Revill report was apparently filed on April 27, 1964, rather than early in December 1963 as stated by Revill. Warren Report, 440–42.

16. Warren Commission Hearings, vol. 5, 112.

17. Church Committee Report, "The FBI and the Oswald Security Case," Appendix A, 87–94. Fain also failed to "report Oswald's refusal to be polygraphed when he testified before the Warren Commission on May 6, 1964, despite detailed questioning by Commission members Ford and Dulles as to the discrepancies in Oswald's statements and Fain's reactions to them." Ibid., 88 n. 8.

18. Ibid., 96; Bugliosi, *Reclaiming History*, 124–25, 158–59, 302–03, 936, 967.

19. Church Committee Report, 96–97; Bugliosi, *Reclaiming History*, 1336.

20. The commentary on the applicable federal evidence rule states: "The theory of Exception [paragraph] (2) is simply that circumstances may produce a condition of excitement which temporarily stills the capacity of reflection and produces utterances free of conscious fabrication."

21. Griffin, unpublished manuscript about the Warren Commission, chapter 2, 23. Bugliosi makes the same point. Bugliosi, *Reclaiming History*, 936.

22. Journal, May 4, 1964.

23. Goldberg to Rankin, memorandum, May 4, 1964, "Historical Context of the Report." 1.

24. Ibid., 1–2.

25. Journal, May 6, 1964; Rankin to Goldberg, memorandum, May 7, 1964; Journal, May 7–8, 1964.

26. Author to Rankin, memorandum, May 4, 1964, "Right Wing Associations of Jack Ruby."

27. Ibid., 2.

28. Journal, May 18, 1964.

29. Warren Commission, "Executive Session Transcript, May 19, 1964," 6601–03.

30. Journal, February 27–28, 1964. At this time Rankin suggested to me that Redlich might wish to withdraw from the activities of some of the organizations identified by the congressional and other critics.

31. Wikipedia, "House Un-American Activities Committee."

32. Warren Commission, "Executive Session Transcript, May 19, 1964," 6605.

33. Ibid., 6606–12.

34. Ibid., 6614.

35. Ibid., 6615.

36. Ibid., 6617, 6630.

37. Specter, *Passion for Truth*, 48.

38. Liebeler, *Thoughts*, 102.

39. Journal, April 27–29, 1964.

40. Redlich to Rankin, memorandum, April 27, 1964.

41. Journal, April 27–29, 1964.

42. Journal, May 5 and 6, 1964.

43. Rankin to Hoover, May 7, 1964.

44. Ibid., 3.

45. Warren Report, 97.

46. Ibid., 106.

47. Ibid., 105.

48. Ibid., 106–07.

49. Ibid., 107–09.

50. Ibid., 98–105.

51. "New Theory on How Shots Hit Kennedy," *Boston Globe* (May 30, 1964), 3; "New Evidence Reported in Kennedy Death," *Chicago Tribune* (May 30, 1964), 2.

52. Warren Commission Hearings, vol. 4, 295–300, 302, 304.

53. Ibid., 312–14.

54. Warren Report, 31–32; Warren Commission Hearings, vol. 4, 318, 321, 324–27.

55. Ibid., 321–22.

56. Ibid., 328.

57. Ibid., 329.

58. Rankin to Dillon, May 5, 1964. Rankin hoped to persuade the commission to let Stern assist him in reviewing these studies. Journal, May 5, 1964.

59. Rankin to the Commission, memorandum, May 14, 1964, "Review of Secret Service Protective Measures," 5–8, (hereafter Rankin memorandum, "Review of Secret Service Protective Measures").

60. Rankin memorandum, "Review of Secret Service Protective Measures," 3.

61. Ibid., 3–4.

62. Ibid., 9.

63 Rankin to Staff, memorandum, April 1, 1964, "Depositions"; Journal, May 7–8, 1964.

64. Rankin to Commission, memorandum, May 12, 1964.

65. Ibid.; Stern to Rankin, memorandum, March 25, 1964, "Obtaining Television Tapes of Assassination Events,"

66. Goldberg to Rankin, memorandum, May 25, 1964, "TV Tapes and Films."

67. Rankin to Commission, memorandum, May 13, 1964, "Additional Testimony before the Commission and by Deposition," 2.

68. Ibid., 2–3.

69. Kashner, "A Clash of Camelots," *Vanity Fair*, October 2009, 1.

70. Journal, Week of May 18, 1964.

71. Ibid.

72. Kashner, "A Clash of Camelots," 1, 8.

73. Rankin to Chayes, May 1, 1964.

74. Rankin to Chayes, May 14, 1964.

75. Rankin to Hoover, May 19, 1964.

76. Slawson to Rankin, memorandum, May 20, 1964, "Personal Check on State Department Files."

77. Journal, Week of May 18, 1964.

78. Slawson, interview by the author, December 15, 2011; Slawson HSCA Testimony, vol. 11, 183–84.

79. My journal entry states: "I took violent issue with Mr. Griffin in the morning and with Mr. Hubert in the afternoon and enjoyed myself thoroughly in the process." My use of the words "violent" and "enjoyed myself" may be misleading. We had a vigorous argument along the lines summarized here, but we recognized the need for such a discussion and were pleased when we found common ground for moving forward with the investigation. Journal, Week of May 11, 1964.

80. Hubert and Griffin to Rankin, memorandum, May 14, 1964, "Adequacy of Ruby Investigation." [Version 1]; author to Rankin, note, February 26, 1964; Shaffer to Rankin and author, memorandum, March 5, 1964; author to Rankin, note, March 24, 1964. By the end of March, Shaffer had returned full-time to the Justice Department.

81. Hubert and Griffin to Rankin, memorandum, May 14, 1964, "Adequacy of Ruby Investigation." [Version 2]

82. Hubert and Griffin, May 14 memorandum [Version 1], 8.

83. The "twist board" was a piece of exercise equipment that consisted of a platform on ball bearings that spun back and forth as the user rotated his or her midsection while standing on the board. The device never sold during Ruby's time, but decades later, well-known fitness equipment manufacturers would market and sell a product based on the same concept.

84. Hubert and Griffin, May 14 memorandum [Version 2], 2–4.

85. Ibid., 4.

86. Ibid., 5.

87. Rankin to Hoover, May 29, 1964; Rankin to Hoover, May 26, 1864.

88. Hubert to Sorrels, May 23, 1964; Rankin to these individuals, May 28, 1964.

7: JUNE 1964: CRUCIAL WITNESSES

1. Anthony Lewis, "Panel to Reject Theories of Plot in Kennedy Death: Warren Inquiry Is Expected to Dispel Doubts in Europe that Oswald Acted Alone," *New York Times* (June 1, 1964), 1.

2. Warren Commission, "Executive Session Transcript, June 4, 1964," 652–62.

3. PhilipWarden, "Report Move to Rig Assassination Study," *Chicago Tribune* (June 6, 1964), 6.

4. Journal, June 4, 1964.

5. Author, draft statement for R. Kennedy, undated but either June 1 or 2, 1964, author's personal files.

6. Author to R. Kennedy, memorandum, June 2, 1964, "Interview of Mrs. John F. Kennedy by Representatives of the President's Commission on the Assassination of President Kennedy," author's personal files.

7. Specter, memorandum, undated but filed in early June 1964, "Outline of Proposed Questions for Mrs. Jacqueline Kennedy," author's personal files.

8. Journal, June 4, 1964.

9. Ibid.

10. Author, draft letter to R. Kennedy from Warren, June 2, 1964, author's personal files.

11. Author, draft letter from R. Kennedy to Warren, June 2, 1964, 1, author's personal files. In the final version of the letter, signed on August 4, 1964, Kennedy stated: "In response to your specific inquiry, I would like to state definitely that I know of no credible evidence to support the allegations that the assassination of President Kennedy was caused by a domestic or foreign conspiracy." I had no personal knowledge then or now of what Robert Kennedy knew, or did not know, of the CIA's plans for covert activity against Castro, including his assassination. This subject was explored by the Church Committee in 1975–76 and is discussed in chapter 10.

12. Journal, June 4, 1964.

13. Ibid.

14. Journal, Week of June 8, 1964; author to Katzenbach, memorandum, June 12, 1964, "Proposed letter to the President's Commission," author's personal files.

15. Specter, *Passion for Truth*, 106–08.

16. Ibid., 106.

17. Ibid., 107.

18. Warren Commission Hearings, vol. 5, 178–81.

19. Ibid., 180.

20. Ibid.

21. Ibid.

22. Ibid., 181.

23. Ibid.

24. Specter, *Passion for Trust*, 107.

25. Journal, June 17, 1964.

26. Specter to Rankin, memorandum, April 30, 1964, "Autopsy Photographs and X-rays of President John F. Kennedy," in HSCA Hearings, vol. 11, 92-93.

27. Specter to Rankin, memorandum, May 12, 1964, "Examination of Autopsy photographs and X-rays of President Kennedy," in HSCA Hearings, vol. 11, 93.

28. Journal, June 17, 1964.

29. Belin, *November 22, 1963: You Are the Jury*, 345–47.

30. Specter, *Passion for Truth*, 86–88.

31. HSCA Hearings, vol. 11, 140.

32. HSCA Hearings, vol. 3, 618.

33. Warren Commission Hearings, vol. 5, 213–54. Both Goldberg and Griffin prepared questions for Rankin to use with Wade. Goldberg to Rankin, memorandum, June 5, 1964, "Questions for District Attorney Wade." Griffin to Rankin, memorandum, June 7, 1964. "Questions for Henry Wade."

34. Warren Commission Hearings, vol. 5, 213–17.

35. Ibid., 220–23.

36. Ibid., 232, 235.

37. Ibid., 254–58.

38. Ibid., 258.

39. Ibid., 266.

40. Ibid., 267–71, 273–76.

41. Ibid., 274, 276–78, 282–86.

42. Ibid., 291.

43. Ibid., 300–04.

44. Ibid., 319–22.

45. Ibid., 306, 319–322.

46. Ibid., 354, 356–58.

47. Ibid., 372–73, 378. Knight described the massive files at her office and identified some categories of people who might not be granted a passport. For example, she testified that individuals may be classified under category "R" as "individuals whose actions do not reflect credit to the United States abroad," but this category "is very narrowly construed in view of the hundreds of American citizen bad-check artists, the drunks, the con men, the psychotics who travel worldwide, and so forth."

48. Ibid,, 307–11, 328–29, 342–43.

49. Ibid., 333.

50. Ibid,, 364.

51. Ibid., 364–65. Secretary Rusk dismissed speculations that any dissident elements in the Soviet Union could have been responsible for the assassination, expressing doubt that they could have achieved their objectives through such an action and observing that such elements are under rather strict scrutiny in the Soviet Union. Ibid., 365.

52. Ibid.

53. Ibid., 367.

54. Ibid., 388.

55. Ibid., 387–88.

56. Ibid., 389–90.

57. Ibid., 391–92.

58. Ibid., 393–94.

59. Ibid., 396.

60. Ibid., 401–02.

61. Ibid., 405–07.

62. Ibid., 414–16.

63. Hubert and Griffin to author, memorandum, April 4, 1964.

64. Author to Rankin, note, April 6, 1964, author's personal files.

65. Hubert and Griffin to Rankin, memorandum, April 23, 1964, "Considerations re Polygraph Tests."

66. Belin, *November 22, 1963: You Are the Jury*, 431–33.

67. Warren Commission, "Executive Session Transcript April 30, 1964," 5879; Rankin to Tonahill, May 5, 1964.

68. Hubert to Rankin, memorandum, June 1, 1964, "Conversation with Phil Burleson, attorney for Jack Ruby"; Hubert to Rankin, memorandum, June 1, 1964, "Deposition of Tom Howard." Burleson and Tonahill decided for similar reasons that they could not ethically provide some of their original notes of conversations with Ruby to the commission. Hubert to Rankin, memorandum, June 1, 1964, "Statements made by Ruby to Burleson."

69. Specter, *Passion for Truth*, 108–10.

70. Ibid., 111–12.

71. Ibid., 112–13.

72. Warren Report, 807.

73. Warren Commission Hearings, vol. 5, 198–200.

74. Specter, *Passion for Truth*, 115–16.

75. Laulicht, interview by the author, February 6, 2012.

76. Hubert to Rankin, memorandum, June 1, 1964; Hubert to Staff, memorandum, June 5, 1964; Rankin to Hubert, memorandum, June 22, 1964.

77. Author to Hubert and Griffin, memorandum, June 1, 1964; Hubert and Griffin to author, memorandum, June 1, 1964; Rankin to Hoover, June 1, 1964; Rankin to Hoover, June 11, 1964.

78. For example, Richard Mosk asked the National Security Agency to examine materials relating to Oswald's activities in Russia and Mexico to ascertain if they served some surreptitious purpose, such as the use of microdots. After examining the materials, the NSA reported that no such methods of deception had been used on those documents. Mosk to Slawson and author, June 5, 1964.

79. Journal, Week of June 8, 1964.

80. Ibid.

81. Redlich to Dulles, memorandum, June 12, 1964.

82. Author to Warren, memorandum, June 15, 1964, "Draft portions of the Report."

83. Ibid.

84. Journal, June 16, 1964.

85. Journal, June 8, 1964.

86. Journal, June 16, 1064.

87. Ibid. "Dutch uncle" is a term for a person "who issues frank, harsh, and severe comments and criticism to educate, encourage, or admonish someone." Wikipedia, "Dutch Uncle."

88. Slawson to Coleman, memorandum, June 4, 1964, "Appendix on Lee Harvey Oswald in Mexico: Comments on First Draft," 10; Rankin to Helms, June 19, 1964; Journal, June 16, 1964.

89. Church Committee Report, 63.

90. Ibid., 65.

91. Ibid., 64–65.

92. Ibid., 35–36.

93. Journal, June 16, 1964.

94. Ibid.

95. Warren Report, 293–97.

96. Warren Commission Hearings, vol. 5, 449–50.

97. Ibid., 451–53; Warren Report, 449–50.

98. Warren Commission Hearings, vol. 5, 458.

99. Ibid., 459.

100. Ibid., 462–64.

101. Ibid., 464–65.

102. Ibid.

103. Ibid., 466–67, 469–70.

104. Ibid., 480–81.

105. I sent Warren at Rankin's request two drafts prepared by Coleman and Slawson—one on Oswald's life in Russia and the other relating to his and his wife's contacts with the State Department. Author to Warren, memorandum, June 19, 1964. Redlich sent Ford drafts of the proposed foreword, Chapters 2 and 3, a section on Oswald's life through his military service, and a section on his life in the Soviet Union. Redlich to Ford, memorandum, June 19, 1964.

106. Should be "Surrey."

107. Journal, June 20, 1964.

108. As for the other matters mentioned, we later arranged for the depositions of Mayor Cabell and his wife in July. Robert Surrey invoked the Fifth Amendment during his appearance before the commission on questions relating to the printing and distribution of a "Wanted for Treason" handbill on the streets of Dallas one or two days before President Kennedy's visit. Warren Commission Hearings, vol. 5, 420–49. The handbill contained a photograph of the president "and set forth a series of inflammatory charges against him." Warren Report, 298. Because the

commission had obtained the testimony of Robert Klause, who actually printed the handbills, Surrey's refusal to testify did not obstruct the commission's investigation. Ibid., 298–99. I have discussed the Irving Sports Shop matter previously.

109. McCloy to Rankin, memorandum, June 24, 1964, enclosing eight pages of notes regarding draft chapters two and three. We learned at some point that he had an associate in his law firm, Patrick Burns, assisting him in reviewing commission drafts. Burns officially joined the commission staff later in the summer and helped us complete our work

110. These included the need for a letter to the FBI about the polygraph examination of Ruby, the service of a subpoena on Weissman, letters to various TV stations, the need to call Mayor and Mrs. Cabell, and Hubert's willingness to take additional depositions in Dallas later in the week. Journal, June 22, 1964; Journal, June 24–26, 1964.

111. Ibid.

112. Ibid.

113. Ibid.

114. Ibid.

115. Ibid.

116. Ibid.

117. Author to Cooper, June 24, 1064, "Report of Commission"; author to Russell, June 24, 1964, "Report of Commission"; author to Boggs, June 24, 1964, "Report of Commission."

118. Journal, June 24–26, 1964.

119. Journal, June 29, 1964.

120. Ibid.

121. Ibid. Rankin made notes of the meeting reflecting the decisions made, which he had transcribed and gave to Redlich and me. Ibid.

122. Ibid.

123. Bugliosi, *Reclaiming History*, 937.

124. Rankin to Hoover, June 30, 1964; "Commission Asks FBI to Probe Publication of Oswald Diary," *Hartford Courant* (June 30, 1964), 6.

125. Ibid.

8: July–August 1964: A Tale of Tragic Truth

1. Journal, July 1, 1964.

2. Rankin to Lane, June 19, 1964; Journal, July 2, 1964.

3. The pertinent portions of Markham's testimony are set forth in Belin, *November 22, 1963: You Are the Jury,* 69–77.

4. Rankin to Lane, July 9, 1964.

5. Rankin to Hoover, July 16, 1964; Belin, *November 22, 1963: You Are the Jury*, 81.

6. Bartlett to Rankin, July 2, 1964; Journal, July 7, 1964.

7. Journal, July 14, 1964.

8. Ibid.

9. Robert S. Allen and Paul Scott, "Kennedy Death Report Split Told," *Los Angeles Times* (July 23, 1964), A5.

10. Journal, July 15–21, 1964.

11. Ibid.

12. Journal, July 22, 1964.

13. Journal, August 14, 1964. Redlich and I did not initially regard this as good news, believing "it just seemed absurd for the Commission to state that they did not have time after 8 months to perform their responsibilities." It seems evident in retrospect that we both overreacted to this development. Ibid.

14. Journal, August 21, 1964.

15. Journal, August 4, 1964. Redlich and I did not agree with Rankin that this was a particularly difficult assignment for the commissioners since they had an outline of the entire report and should be able to figure out where the particular chapter would eventually go. When we pursued this argument further with Rankin and took issue with his proposed use of our historians to edit draft chapters, Rankin "made the unfortunate slip of the tongue to the effect that if Mr. Redlich and I had our way we would produce the report 'at our leisure.'" We were a little upset by this comment, which Rankin regretted soon after. Ibid.

16. Journal, July 3, 1964; Rankin to author, note, July 7, 1964, with attached five pages of comments; Goldberg to Rankin, memorandum, July 6, 1964, "Comments on Chapter 1." Arthur Marmor, Goldberg's fellow historian on the staff, also commented. Marmor to Rankin, memorandum, July 6, 1964.

17. Journal, August 11, 1964.

18. Belin to Rankin, memorandum, July 10, 1964, "Comments and Suggestions—Chapter 2—6/25/64 Draft."

19. Journal, August 20, 1964.

20. I do not know why the commission preferred the term "Triple Overpass" rather than "Triple Underpass." The latter was the more common usage in Dallas and is used in the commission's report.

21. Rankin to Reynolds, Tague, Rackley, Altgens, and Zapruder, July 9, 1964.

22. Mosk to author, memorandum, July 17, 1964; Marmor to Redlich, memorandum, July 22, 1964, "Deputy Sheriff Eddie Raymond 'Buddy' Walthers"; Redlich to Liebeler, July 22, 1964. Specter, whose area of investigation had included both the medical testimony and trajectory of the shots, continued to be responsible for portions of this chapter. Specter to author, memorandum, July, 24, 1964, "Footnotes on Chapters 2 and 3."

23. Journal, August 12, 1964; Warren Report, 112, 116. I was unable to complete the chapter on August 14 and it was scheduled for consideration by the commission during the next week. Journal, August 14 and 21, 1964.

24. Warren Report, 110–11.

25. Ibid., 110–17

26. As discussed in chapter 10, the acoustics evidence relied on by the House

Select Committee on Assassinations in 1979 did not support the existence of a fourth shot fired from the grassy knoll.

27. The commission concluded that two small cartons marked "Rolling Readers" had been moved by Oswald to create "a convenient gun rest." Instead of books, these boxes contained "light blocks used as reading aids." Warren Report, 140.

28. Belin to Rankin, July 7, 1964, 2. He sent a copy of the letter to me with a short note indicating that he would review the materials that he had been sent, draft chapters 1, 2, 3, and 4, and be prepared to present his detailed comments when he arrived in Washington. Belin to author, July 7, 1964.

29. Belin to Rankin, July 7, 1964.

30. Ibid.

31. Rankin to Secret Service, July 11, 1964.

32. Rankin to Chief Curry, August 5, 1964 (requesting an affidavit clarifying whether a witness to the Tippit shooting had identified Oswald as the shooter); Rankin to Hoover, August 6, 1964 (requesting interviews of witnesses about the possibility that Oswald had a telescopic sight mounted on a rifle at the Irving Sports Shop); Rankin to Hoover, August 11, 1964 (requesting FBI experts to review several documents to determine if they were written by Oswald); Rankin to Hoover, August 21, 1964 (requesting the FBI to obtain affidavits from two witnesses who saw Oswald flee from the scene of the Tippit shooting); Rankin to Hoover, August 28, 1964 (requesting reinterview of Dallas rifle range operator where Oswald was alleged to have practiced); Rankin to Hoover, August 31, 1964 (requesting further investigation to resolve an apparent conflict between the testimony of an FBI agent and the Dallas policeman who had lifted a palm print from the barrel of the assassination weapon on November 22, 1963).

33. Author to Rankin, memorandum, August 8, 1964, "Chapter IV—draft dated 7/21/64"; Journal, August 17, 1964. Regarding Oswald's fingerprints on the cartons near the sixth-floor depository window, I proposed that we evaluate other explanations for these fingerprints that would be consistent with Oswald's innocence.

34. Because of his initial failure to make a positive identification, the commission decided not to base "its conclusion regarding the identity of the assassin on Brennan's subsequent certain identification of Lee Harvey Oswald as the man he saw fire the rifle." Warren Report, 146.

35. Goldberg to Rankin and Redlich, memorandum, August 7, 1964, "Chapter IV." At my request, Stuart Pollak also commented on this draft. He thought that several sections were too long and that the lineups conducted by the Dallas Police Department should be discussed in more detail. Pollak to author, memorandum, August 11, 1964, "Comments on Chapter IV." I passed his comments on to Redlich.

36. Journal, August 21, 1964. After the commission approved Chapter 4, David Belin responded to my earlier invitation to comment on this draft. Belin to author, August 26, 1964. In light of the previous controversy, I was very relieved to see that he thought the draft was "an excellent job" and proceeded to make thirty-four specific editing suggestions. I incorporated most of them into the chapter.

37. Rankin to Hoover, June 25, 1964.

38. Appendix XVII to the Warren Commission report describes the proceedings on July 18, 1964, the questions addressed to Ruby and his answers, and the interpretation of the results. Warren Report, 807–16. Specter to Rankin, memorandum, July 21, 1964, "Polygraph Examination of Jack Ruby on July 18, 1964."

39. Ibid.

40. Ibid.

41. Ibid.; *Dallas Times Herald* (July 22, 1964); *Washington Post* (July 23, 1964), A3. Herndon advised Specter that there were numerous differences between the questions that he asked and those that appeared in the press. The source of the leak was never identified.

42. Warren Report, 809–14.

43. Warren Report, 815.

44. Specter, *Passion for Truth*, 117–18. Hoover had provided a more nuanced view of polygraph examinations in his testimony earlier before the commission. Then he referred to the allegation that a witness had seen money given to Oswald at the Cuban consulate in Mexico City, but that the witness agreed to take a polygraph examination and "[t]he lie detector test showed that he was telling a lie." Hoover described the technique as "a contribution in an investigation, a more or less psychological contribution." Warren Commission Hearings, vol. 5, 103.

45. Belin, *November 22, 1963: You Are the Jury*, 443 (italics in original).

46. I have listed these investigative requests in a separate document.

47. Rankin to Hubert, memorandum, July 8, 1964; Griffin to author, memorandum, July 9, 1964; Rankin to Hubert and Griffin, memorandum, July 18, 1964; Rankin to Specter, memorandum, July 31, 1964.

48. Goldberg to Rankin, memorandum, July 10, 1964; Rankin to Niederlehner, July 8, 1964. Niederlehner was acting general counsel of the Defense Department.

49. Goldberg to Rankin, memorandum, July 13, 1964, "Showing of TV Tapes and Films"; Rankin to Hoover, July 14, 1964. Pierce was assigned to drive the "lead car," which was to be followed by the armored truck containing Oswald. Chief Curry approved a change of plans at the last moment, deciding that the armored truck would serve as a decoy and Oswald would be moved instead in an unmarked police car driven by a police officer. Warren Report, 215.

50. Warren Commission, "Executive Session Transcript, June 23, 1964."

51. Ibid., 7641–44.

52. Ibid., 7644–46.

53. Ibid., 7647–49.

54. Journal, July 13, 1964.

55. Griffin to Rankin, memorandum, September 21, 1964.

56. Journal, August 17, 1964.

57. Journal, August 20, 1964.

58. Warren Report, 322.

59. Rankin to Hoover, August 28, 1964. Rankin sent a follow-up letter seek-

ing further information about available bus service between New Orleans and Houston as of September 24–25, 1963. Rankin to Hoover, September 5, 1964. Warren Report, 321–25.

60. Warren Report, 323–24. In his examination of this matter, Bugliosi acknowledged the logic and evidentiary support for the commission's conclusion, but went on to reason that the "very *absence* of any witness or record that Oswald used commercial transportation out of New Orleans is itself at least some circumstantial evidence that he did not do so and goes in the direction of supporting the conclusion that Oswald left New Orleans with the two Latins, and was at Odio's door on the evening of September 24 or 25, 1963." Bugliosi, *Reclaiming History*, 1312.

61. Griffin to author, memorandum, August 14, 1964, "Memo on Ruby Conspiracy Portion of Chapter VI," 4.

62. Pollak to Redlich, memorandum, August 22, 1964; Slawson to Rankin, memorandum, August 28, 1964, "Questioning of Marina Oswald by Senators Russell and Cooper and Yourself." Griffin to author, memorandum, August 20, 1964, "Oswald Portions of the Foreign Conspiracy Chapter." He also thought we had devoted too much space to the possible involvement of the Soviet Union and Cuba in a conspiracy with Oswald, rather than focusing on individuals whom Oswald may have met after his return to the United States.

63. Warren Report, 274.

64. Warren Report, 309.

65. Warren Commission Hearings, vol. 5, 365; Slawson, interview by the author, December 15, 2011. Neither Slawson nor Coleman was shown or told about any transcripts, although they were told that the CIA had information indicating that Castro was genuinely shocked and surprised when he heard of President Kennedy's assassination. Slawson to author, January 9, 2013.

66. Walter Pincus and George Lardner, "The Trust Was Secondary: The Warren Commission's Real Mission Was to Avert Public Hysteria," *Washington Post* (November 22–28, 1993), National Weekly Edition, 6. The article is also indexed as Walter Pincus and George Lardner, "Warren Commission Born Out of Fear; Washington Wanted to Stop Speculation," *Washington Post* (November 14, 1993), A1. I disagree, of course, with their contentions regarding the creation of the commission or its "real mission."

67. Ibid.

68. Liebeler to author and Redlich, memorandum, August 27, 1964, "Conspiracy."

69. Warren Report, 376. See also Warren Commission Hearings, vol. 1, 22.

70. Warren Commission Staff, outline, "Oswald's Life for Discussion with Psychiatric Consultants on July 9, 1964."

71. Warren Commission Staff Member (Unnamed), memorandum, July 9, 1964, "Thoughts and Questions for Discussion with Psychiatric Consultants on July 9, 1964," which included a summary of the observations of the consultants during the discussion.

72. Early in August, Pollak, at my request, looked at Liebeler's current draft. Pollak to author, memorandum, August 3, 1964. He commented on the challenge of determining how best to discuss Oswald's personal characteristics and his political views in a way that would help a reader understand the range of possible motives. He proposed a reorganization of the chapter, which Liebeler used in subsequent drafts.

73. Journal, August 21, 1964.

74. Warren Commission Hearings, vol. 5, 104.

75. Ibid., 110, 113.

76. Church Committee Report, 51.

77. Warren Report, 24.

78. McCloy to Rankin, July 8, 1964.

79. Journal, July 2, 1964.

80. Dulles to Rankin, July 13, 1964. He recognized that the staff draft had proposed a new body at the cabinet level to oversee presidential protection but suggested that using the established NSC structure and staff would be preferable.

81. Journal, August 17, 1964.

82. Weinreb to author, memorandum, August 12, 1964, "Chapter 8"; Journal, August 20, 1964.

83. Journal, August 19, 1964.

84. Ibid; Warren Report, 455–56.

85. Author, memorandum for the record, August 24, 1964, "Meeting with the Chairman," 2.

86. Journal, August 20 and 21, 1964.

87. Warren Commission Staff, "Outline of the Report of the President's Commission on the Assassination of President Kennedy," July 21, 1964.

88. Goldberg to Rankin, memorandum, July 21, 1964, "Appendix on Allegations, Theories and Rumors"; Rankin to Hoover, July 24, 1964.

89. Goldberg to Staff, memorandum, July 24, 1964, "Allegations." I made two general suggestions and nine specific comments about particular allegations. Author to Goldberg, memorandum, July 27, 1964, "Appendix on Allegations." Alfredda Scobey, who helped Senator Russell with his commission duties, responded with a memo in which she politely pointed out several areas where the proposed answer did not accurately reflect the evidence. Scobey to Goldberg, memorandum, July 27, 1964, "Your Memorandum Concerning Allegations."

90. Laulicht, interview by the author, February 6, 2012.

91. Journal, August 19, 1964. We were advised, for example, that the National Archives would not release any FBI investigative reports in its possession without the bureau's consent. Ibid.

92. Journal, August 21, 1964.

93. In 1992 Congress enacted a law providing for further disclosure of the commission's records and those of the House Select Committee on Assassinations.

President John F. Kennedy Assassination Records Collection Act of 1992, Pub. Law No. 102–526 (1992).

94. HSCA Hearings, vol. 3, 564, 560, 599–600.

95. Ibid., 601.

96. HSCA Hearings, vol. 3, 615; HSCA Hearings, vol. 11, 141.

97. HSCA Hearings, vol. 3, 615; HSCA Hearings, vol. 11, 81–82. All of us on the staff who were asked these questions gave the same answers.

9: SEPTEMBER 1964: THE LAST DEBATES

1. Warren Report., 19.

2. Holland, *The Kennedy Assassination Tapes*, 248–51 (italics in the original).

3. Rankin to Hoover, September 3, 1964; Liebeler to author, memorandum, September 2, 1964,"Relevant Property Remaining in the Possession of Marina Oswald as of August 26, 1964."

4. Liebeler. memorandum, September 6, 1964, "Galley Proofs of Chapter IV of the Report." No recipients are indicated on the memorandum in my possession, but I am certain that it went to Rankin, Redlich, and myself.

5. HSCA Hearings, vol. 11, 212–56.

6. Jenner to Henry, US attorney, Denver, CO, September 3, 1964; Jenner to George, US marshall, Eastern District of Illinois, September 5, 1964, 1; Warren Commission Hearings, vol. 15, 709–44. The article was in *American Opinion*, published by the John Birch Society.

7. Ibid., 710; Jenner to Unger, counsel for Oliver, September 21, 1964.

8. Liebeler to Rankin, memorandum, September 4, 1964; Warren Commission Hearings, vol. 5, 588–620.

9. Ibid., 589–90.

10. Ibid., 590.

11. Ibid., 591–92.

12. Ibid., 593, 595.

13. Ibid., 594, 596–97.

14. Ibid., 601–02.

15. Ibid., 605–08, 611; Warren Report, 387–88.

16. Warren Commission Hearings, vol. 5, 614–15.

17. Rankin to Commission members, memorandum, September 1, 1964; author to Jenner, Liebeler, Coleman, Slawson, Griffin, and Laulicht, memorandum, September 4, 1964, "Chapter VI: Investigation of Possible Conspiracy."

18. Liebeler to author, memorandum, September 14, 1964.

19. In five cases, I cannot now check whether I made the change he proposed because I do not have the galley proofs containing his suggestions.

20. Warren Report, 328; Liebeler to author, memorandum, September 1, 1964, 8. This citation is to the original memorandum and not to the single-spaced version of this (and other) Liebeler memoranda that have been circulated among interested parties. HSCA Hearings, vol. 11, 258.

21. Liebeler to author, memorandum, September 15, 1964, "Chapter VI."

22. Liebeler's memorandum contained fifty-five numbered paragraphs on the draft chapter, but some of the paragraphs contained more than one suggestion. The paragraph numbered fifty-five did not comment on the chapter but reflected his intention to send the memo to Pollak.

23. Liebeler to author, memorandum, September 15, 1964, "Chapter VI." A few of Liebeler's proposals in this memorandum were rejected for reasons that are not readily apparent. These included a few proposed minor editing suggestions, such as the substitution of the word "or" for "nor" (¶ 22) or the use of the abbreviation "C" (¶ 9). It also included a few suggestions for changes in language that probably should have been made, eg. clarification of Marina Oswald's testimony regarding her husband's job in the Soviet Union to make clear that she was testifying based on what her husband had told her rather than based on her firsthand knowledge. Ibid., ¶ 26.

24. Liebeler to author, memorandum, September 16, 1964, "Chapter VI."

25. HSCA Hearings, vol. 3, 590; Warren Report, 374. In the "Conclusions" section of chapter one, the commission stated that "the commission has found no evidence that either Lee Harvey Oswald or Jack Ruby was part of any conspiracy, domestic or foreign, to assassinate President Kennedy." Ibid., 21. I believe that the absence of the word "credible" was inadvertent and that the commission would have added it if this inconsistency had been brought to its attention in a timely manner.

26. Warren Report, 22, 374.

27. Kennedy to Warren, August 4, 1964.

28. Warren Commission Hearings, vol. 5, 99–100.

29. HSCA Report, 164–65.

30. HSCA Hearings, vol. 11, 371–72.

31. Ibid.

32. Cameron to Liebeler, September 9, 1964, 1.

33. Liebeler to author, memorandum, September 15, 1964.

34. Warren Report, 381.

35. Ibid., 391.

36. Liebeler to author, memorandum, September 15, 1964, "Letter of Dr. Howard P. Rome, dated September 13, 1964"; Warren Report, 383.

37. Warren Report, 463-69; Warren to Dillon, September 9, 1964; Dillon to Warren, undated but filed as though September 9, 1964.

38. Warren Report, 467–68.

39. Although the commission heard ninety-four witnesses, the commission usually heard more than one witness at a hearing. The figures show that Russell heard only six witnesses, Boggs heard twenty, and Cooper heard fifty. Warren heard all the witnesses; Ford heard seventy, and Dulles heard sixty. According to Bugliosi, McCloy heard thirty-five, which was less than Cooper. Bugliosi, *Reclaiming History*, 455, note.

40. Rankin to Commission Staff, memorandum, September 21, 1962, "Final Responsibilities."

41. Author to Rankin, memorandum, September 21, 1964, "Miscellaneous Affairs."

42. Ibid., 3.

43. Edward T. Folliard, "LBJ Gets Warren Report," *Boston Globe* (September 25, 1964), 1.

44. "Warren Hands President Report on Assassination," *Hartford Courant* (September 25, 1964), 17D; Folliard, "LBJ Gets Warren Report," 1.

45. Holland, *Assassination Tapes*, 254.

46. Johnson to Warren, September 24, 1964.

47. Johnson to Rankin, September 24, 1964.

48. Anthony Lewis, "New Panel Plans to Act Speedily on Warren Data," *New York Times* (September 29, 1964), 1.

49. "Detective Effort Termed 'Massive,'" *New York Times* (September 28, 1964), 17; Associated Press, "Comment Favors Report with Few Exceptions," *Los Angeles Times* (September 28, 1964), 6; Jerry Kluttz, "The Federal Diary: Praise Is Voiced for Staff Engaged on Warren Report," *Washington Post* (September 29, 1964), B1; Chris Perry, "Attorney Mark Lane Blasts Warren Commission Report: Feels That Group Has Answered Few Questions and No Doubts," *Philadelphia Tribune* (September 29, 1964), 1; "Mrs. Oswald Spurns Finding on Her Son," *Chicago Tribune* (September 28, 1964), 14.

50. "Robert Kennedy Says He Won't Read Report," *New York Times* (September 28, 1964), 17.

51. "All Tips Run Down by Warren Panel: Doubts May Remain Despite Checking of Plot Theories," *New York Times* (November 25, 1964), 19.

52. Ibid.; "Collectors Shun Warren Volumes," *New York Times* (November 29, 1964), 63; Goldberg, interview by the author, January 19, 2012.

53. Holland, *Assassination Tapes*, 254–55.

54. Ibid., 256–57, 259.

55. "Associated Press, "Johnson Names 4 to Act on Report," *New York Times* (September 28, 1964).

56. Holland, *Assassination Tapes*, 259–61. Katzenbach had never been dean of a law school.

57. Lewis, "New Panel Plans to Act Speedily on Warren Data"; The National Security Archive, "Kennedy Sought Dialogue with Cuba" (posted November 24, 2003).

58. Robert B. Semple Jr., "Secret Service Is Reorganized: Changes Result from Study by Warren Commission," *New York Times* (November 11, 1964), 1; Felix Belair Jr., "Panel Opposes New F.B.I. Role in Johnson Guard," *New York Times* (November 22, 1964), 1.

10: AFTERMATH

1. The saying "Three persons can keep a secret, but only if two are dead" is

originally attributed to Benjamin Franklin in the July 1735 issue of *Poor Richard's Almanac. Bartlett's Familiar Quotations*, 16th ed., 309. Bugliosi subscribes to this belief as well. Bugliosi, *Reclaiming History*, xxx.

2. Church Committee Report, 53–54.

3. Ibid., 52–53, 55, 57.

4. Mary Pakenham, "Hoover Calls Rev. King Liar: Hits Warren Report and Soft Judges," *Chicago Tribune* (November 19, 1964), 1; "Warren Report Unfair to FBI, Hoover Quoted," *Hartford Courant* (November 19, 1964), 38. Hoover included these comments in an interview with eighteen female reporters where he also criticized Supreme Court justices as "bleeding-heart judges" for their recent rulings and called Dr. Martin Luther King "the most notorious liar in the country." President Johnson was reportedly very disturbed by Hoover's comments, in particular those about Dr. King which coincided with a previously scheduled meeting on civil rights matters between the president and a group of black leaders. David Kraslow, "Johnson Reported Upset at FBI Chief's Remarks: President Said to Have Reacted Sharply to Criticism of Dr. King, Supreme Court," *Los Angeles Times* (November 20, 1964), 5; Church Committee Report, 55– 56.

5. Associated Press, "Comment Favors Report with Few Exceptions," *Los Angeles Times* (September 28, 1964), 6; "Report Dominates World's Press as Comments Differ," *Washington Post* (September 29, 1964), A15.

6. Ibid.; "Warren Data Stir Europe: Newspapers Split on Proof Furnished by Report," *Baltimore Sun* (September 29, 1964), 5; Max Frankel, "Oswald Findings Doubted Abroad: U.S. Reports Many Papers Reject the Conclusion That Assassin Acted Alone," *New York Times* (October 3, 1964), 1. One of England's most distinguished historians, Hugh Trevor-Roper, claimed that the commission had not found any "positive evidence' that Oswald was the assassin and that the report was a "smokescreen." He was "severely taken to task by a number of critics in both the United States and Britain" but adhered to his views after admitting to one slight mistake in his analysis. "Warren Findings Again Questioned: But Trevor-Roper Concedes an Error on One Point," *New York Times* (January 4, 1965), 30; "The Warren Report Stands as Written: Danger of Infestion," *Washington Post* (January 17, 1965), 92.

7. "Study Says 2 Men Shot At Kennedy: 51 Witnesses Linked Firing to Knoll, Writer Finds," *New York Times* (March 1, 1965), 17. This conclusion was offered by Harold Feldman, writing in *The Minority of One*, which called itself an "independent monthly for an American alternative."

8. Richard Harwood, "An Inquest: Skeptical Postscript to Warren Group's Report on Assassination," *Washington Post* (May 29, 1966), A1.

9. Claudia Casssidy, "On the Aisle: Preview of Mark Lane's 'Rush to Judgment,' an Inquiry into the Evidence's Other Side," *Chicago Tribune* (May 23, 1966), C5; Mark Lane, *Last Word: My Indictment of the CIA in the Murder of JFK* (New York: Skyhorse, 2011).

10. Harwood, "An Inquest"; "Warren Report on Assassination Challenged Again," *New York Times* (June 5, 1966), 42. Several forensic scientists by this time

had publicly criticized the autopsy conducted on the president and the absence in the commission's records of the full set of autopsy X-rays and photographs. Ronald Kotulak, "Hits Autopsy On Slain J.F.K. as Inadequate: Doctor Assails Those Who Conducted It," *Chicago Tribune* (February 26, 1966), C7; "Experts Find Gaps in Warren Report," *New York Times* (February 26, 1966), 9.

11. Epstein, *Inquest*, 79; Eisenberg, interview by the author, December 13, 2011; Asbury, "Former Kennedy Aide Suggests Panel to Check Warren Report," *New York Times* (July 24, 1966), 25.

12. C. J. Earl Warren, *The Memoirs of Earl Warren* (1977), 363; Eric Pace, "J. A. Ball, 97, Counsel to Warren Commission," *New York Times* (September 30, 2000), A18.

13. Robert J. Donovan, "Kennedy Death Report Backed by 2 Panelists," *Los Angeles Times* (October 6, 1966). 1.

14. Gene Blake, "Warren Report under the Microscope at UCLA: Professor Directs Massive Analysis of Challenged Findings on Assassination," *Los Angeles Times* (October 21, 1966), A1.

15. "Johnson Backs Warren Report as Thorough and Reasonable," *New York Times* (November 5, 1964), 11; John Atticks, "Yale Law Professor Picks Flaws in Warren Commission Finding," *Hartford Courant* (November 6, 1966), 29A; Peter Kihss, "Warren Panel, under Attacks, Stands Firm on Its Findings in Kennedy Death 3 Years Ago," *New York Times* (November 22, 1966), 22.

16. Ibid.

17. "The Warren Report: A Panel Discussion," *Los Angeles Times* (November 27, 1966), F1.

18. Ibid.

19. "Commissioner Says New Probe Useless without New Evidence," *Boston Globe* (November 23, 1966), 24. Four years later, in a series of taped television interviews, Senator Russell reiterated his belief that that Oswald did not act alone in the assassination. Due to his doubts, he stated that he insisted on a disclaimer in the Commission's report emphasizing the difficulties of proving a negative proposition to a certainty and stating that, if there was any such evidence of a conspiracy, "it has been beyond the reach of all the investigative agencies and resources of the United States and has not come to the attention of this commission." Don Oberdorfer, "Russell Says He Never Believed Oswald Alone Planned Killing," *Washington Post* (January 19, 1970), A3.

20. Peter Kihss, "Warren Panel Member Suggests Independent Group Study Kennedy X-rays," *New York Times* (November 28, 1966), 29; "Heartsick Atmosphere Led to Some Warren Report Omissions," *Boston Globe* (June 27, 1967), 46; "The Autopsy: The Warren Commission Did Make a Mistake. It had Compassion.," *Washington Post* (June 25, 1967), C3.

21. "A Warren Lawyer Says Ruby's Death Can't Alter Report," *New York Times* (January 4, 1967), 20; "1968 Panel Review of Photographs, X-Rays, Films,

Documents and Other Evidence Pertaining to the Fatal Wounding of President John F. Kennedy on November 22, 1963 in Dallas, Texas," available as Assassination Records Review Board Medical Document 59. This panel is commonly known as the "Clark Panel."

22. This development and its consequences are discussed in Holland, *Assassination Tapes*, 414–28.

23. Ibid., 414, 416.

24. Ibid., 415, 417–18.

25. Eisenberg, interview by the author, December 13, 2011.

26. Specter, *Passion for Truth* (2000), 124.

27. Griffin, interview by the author, December 5, 2011.

28. Slawson, interview by the author, December 15, 2011.

29. See, for example, Richard M. Mosk, "The Warren Commission and the Legal Process," *Case and Comment* 72 (May–June 1967): 13–20; and, Alfredda Scobey, "A Lawyer's Notes on the Warren Commission Report," *American Bar Association Journal* 51, no. 1 (January 1965): 39–43.

30. C. J. Warren, *Memoirs* (1977), 364–67.

31. Alfred Goldberg, "Conspiracy Interpretations of the Assassination of President Kennedy: International and Domestic" *Security Studies Paper* no. 16 (University of California, Los Angeles, 1968), 15.

32. Ibid., 28–29.

33. Belin, *You Are the Jury*, xiii.

34. He tried the *Stockton–Palliko* case, in which Judy Palliko's husband killed Henry Stockton and Stockton's wife killed Judy Palliko, leaving only wisps of evidence that there was any connection between the two homicides. Bugliosi prosecuted the case successfully on mostly circumstantial evidence and then wrote *Till Death Us Do Part* in 1978.

35. This discussion is based on his talk at the San Diego Library on August 9, 2007, which can be heard at the following site: http://www.americanbooktour.com/.

36. Ibid.

37. Ibid.

38. Ibid.

39. The members were: John T. Connor (former secretary of Commerce), C. Douglas Dillon (former secretary of the treasury), Erwin N. Griswold (former solicitor general and dean of the Harvard Law School), Lane Kirkland (secretary-treasurer of the AFL-CIO), Lyman L. Lemnitzer (former chairman of the Joint Chiefs of Staff), Ronald Reagan (former governor of California), and Edgar F. Shannon (professor and former president of the University of Virginia). Commission on CIA Activities within the United States, *Report to the President by the Commission on CIA Activities within the United States* (Washington, DC: US Government Printing Office, 1975), x.

40. Belin, *Final Disclosure: The Full Truth about the Assassination of President Kennedy* (New York: Charles Scribner's Sons, 1988), 80–82.

41. Belin did not participate in the investigation of these allegations because of his previous position with the Warren Commission. Ibid., 178.

42. Rockefeller Commission Report, 262. The three doctors on the panel "reported that such a motion would be caused by a violent straightening and stiffening of the entire body as a result of a seizure-like neuromuscular reaction to major damage inflicted to nerve centers in the brain." Ibid. The commission discussed these conclusions in more detail at pages 262–64.

43. Ibid., 265.

44. Ibid., 267–68.

45. Belin, *Final Disclosure*, 86–91.

46. Ibid., 91–100. Belin reported that his inquiry was handicapped in two important respects. First, his commission did not have the power of subpoena and Congress rejected its request for such authority, in part because there was no member of Congress on the commission, as had been the case with the Warren Commission. Second, Congress was beginning its own investigation of the intelligence agencies and difficulties arose as to which committee should have the documents and decide whether to provide them to the commission. Belin did obtain the materials in March after meeting with the newly appointed staff of the Senate Select Committee on Intelligence chaired by Senator Church of Idaho. Ibid., 96–102.

47. The CIA officials interviewed included McCone and Helms, as well as lower-level officials (Edwards and Harvey) personally engaged in the planning of such efforts. The high-level executive branch officials in the Kennedy and Johnson administrations interviewed included Secretary of Defense Robert McNamara, National Security Adviser McGeorge Bundy, General Maxwell Taylor, and General Edward Lansdale. The two generals participated in a Special Group (Augmented) that was supposed to work with Attorney General Kennedy to implement a memorandum from President Kennedy to Secretary of State Rusk dated November 30, 1961, directing that the United States "use our available assets ... to help Cuba overthrow the Communist regime." Ibid., 124–26, 162.

48. Ibid., 163–65.

49. Ibid., 165, 173, 185.

50. The Church Committee report entitled *Alleged Assassination Plots Involving Foreign Leaders* incorporated the work of the Rockefeller Commission and produced a detailed recital of the various plans of the CIA (supported by other agencies) during the 1960–63 period directed at Castro, including his assassination. Select Committee to Study Governmental Operations with Respect to Intelligence Activities, *The Investigation of the Assassination of President J.F.K.: Performance of the Intelligence Agencies* (1976) (hereafter Church Committee Report), 2.

51. Ibid. In evaluating the relationship between the Warren Commission and the two intelligence agencies, the Church Committee did not accurately portray the commission's overall approach and its investigative capabilities. First, it incorrectly attributed to the Warren Commission a desire to complete the investigation promptly and to dispel all rumors regarding a conspiracy. Second, it erroneously concluded

that the commission relied almost exclusively on the FBI and ignored the commission's own investigation producing the testimony of 552 witnesses.

52. Ibid., 9–10.

53. Ibid., 11.

54. Ibid., 12–13.

55. Ibid., 36 and n 85.

56. Ibid., 37–38.

57. Ibid., 38–40.

58. Ibid., 7.

59. Ibid., 14. This interview appeared in the *Miami Herald* of September 9, 1963, 1A.

60. One witness before the Church Committee described the SAS as "sort of a microcosm of the Agency with emphasis on Cuban matters," which had its own counterintelligence staff that coordinated with Angleton's but was not subordinate to it. Ibid., 57–58, 60.

61. Ibid., 70–71.

62. Ibid., 59.

63. Ibid., 72, 74.

64. Ibid., 67. Although it is probable that Dulles knew of such efforts during his tenure at the agency, the record is unclear whether he knew of the plans, including AMLASH, that developed during the 1961–63 period. Bugliosi, *Reclaiming History*, 1343. As discussed earlier, Dulles's successor as CIA director was not aware of these assassination plots until the Pearson story in early 1967and the internal CIA report that was used to brief President Johnson.

65. Church Committee Report, 67–68, 72–73. Whether Robert Kennedy knew about the CIA's assassination plots in 1963 has been the subject of considerable, but inconclusive, examination. See, for example, Evan Thomas, *Robert Kennedy*, 145–59; Bugliosi, *Reclaiming History*, 1344; Bugliosi, *Endnotes*, 779–98. He and I never discussed the subject. Based on what I have read and been told, I believe the following: (1) Kennedy did not know of the CIA plot utilizing major criminal figures until the Justice Department was asked by the agency in April–May 1962 to dismiss the pending wiretap prosecution in Las Vegas; (2) memoranda of the May meeting prepared by the FBI and the CIA indicate that the attorney general told the agency to stop such activities; (3) notwithstanding Kennedy's direction, the CIA continued to pursue other assassination plots (including AMLASH) until early 1963 without informing senior CIA officials or Kennedy; (4) after the Pearson story in March 1967, Kennedy told his staff that he had stopped such CIA plots; and (5) Jack Miller, who met with CIA General Counsel Houston in April 1962 on this subject, told me several decades later that, after reviewing extensive FBI reports, he believed that Kennedy had not authorized the CIA assassination plots. Herbert J. Miller Jr., interview by the author, transcript, Oral History Project of the Historical Society of the District of Columbia Circuit, 1998, 109–10, available at http://www.dechs.org/OralHistoryID=29&Menu=Documents.

66. HSCA Hearings, vol. 3, 648;

67. HSCA Hearings, vol. 3, 648; Slawson, interview by author, December 15, 2011.

68. HSCA Hearings, vol. 3, 649–50.

69. Holland, *Kennedy Assassination Tapes*, 428.

70. Griffin, interview by the author, November 28, 2012.

71. Bugliosi, *Reclaiming History*, 996.

72. Ibid., 371.

73. House Report No. 95-1828, *Report of the Select Committee on Assassinations*, US House of Representatives, 95th Cong., 2d Sess. (1979) (hereafter "HSCA Report"), 9.

74. HSCA Report., 260–61.

75. Ibid., 261.

76. "Lone Assassin Theory Buttressed," *Hartford Courant*, (September 10, 1978), 9A; "New Evidence reported as Backing Warren probe of Kennedy slaying," *Chicago Tribune* (September 8, 1978), 2; Curt Matthews, "Warren Unit Findings Get New Support." *Baltimore Sun* (September 9, 1978), A1.

77. Liebeler, *Thoughts,* 45; HSCA Hearings, vol. 6, 35.

78. HSCA Hearings, vol. 7, 39, 41, 144.

79. Liebeler, *Thoughts*, 102.

80. HSCA Report, 129, 147 (emphasis added).

81. Chapter Six.

82. HSCA Report 501.

83. Ibid., 506.

84. Curt Matthews, "Acoustics Tests in Dallas Fail to Resolve How Many Shots Were Fired at Kennedy," *Baltimore Sun* (September 12, 1978), 1.

85. Nicholas M. Horrock, "Tracing Any Kennedy Conspirator Is Given Little Chance by Officials," *New York Times* (January 1, 1979), 1.

86. Ibid., 495.

87. HSCA Hearings, vol. 5, 587.

88. Ibid., 674.

89, HSCA Report, 1.

90. Ibid., 497.

91. Ibid.

92. Ibid., 492—93.

93. Ibid., 493.

94. Ibid., 93, 496.

95. Ibid., 498; Edgar, interview by the author, February 3, 2012. Edgar was then the chief executive officer of Common Cause in Washington, DC. He died in April 2013.

96. HSCA Report, 504.

97. Ibid., 505–06.

98. Ibid., 507.

99. Rogers Worthington, "16 Years after JFK's Death, Probers Agree—But What Next?" *Chicago Tribune* (July 26, 1979), A1; Marjorie Hunter, "House Panel Reports a Conspiracy 'Probable' in the Kennedy Slaying," *New York Times* (December 31, 1978), 1; John Herbers, "After 15 Years, Plot Theories Still Thicken," *New York Times* (January 7, 1979), E5; *Newsweek*, quoted in Bugliosi, *Endnotes*, 174; Jerry Cohen and Mike Goodman, "Contrary Data Withheld From Assassinations Panel," *Los Angeles Times* (January 27, 1979), A1.

100. Bugliosi, *Reclaiming History*, 377. Blakey elaborated on his personal conclusion in the book, *The Plot to Kill the President* (1981), which he and Billings wrote together.

101. The Ramsey report was delayed because of the desire of the committee's members to consult informally with Barger about his work before reaching their own conclusions. According to Professor Ramsey, Barger was "quite defensive about his report" and did not wish to discuss his work with new committee. Ramsey to Belin, May 20, 1992.

102. Blakey to Stokes, November 24, 1981.

103. Blakey to Barger, May 17, 1982.

104. Ibid.

105. Bugliosi, *Reclaiming History*, 380–81; Bugliosi, *Endnotes*, 153–218. The Select Committee's reliance on the acoustics evidence had been previously criticized in Belin, *Final Disclosure: The Full Truth about the Assassination of President Kennedy* (New York: Charles Scribner's Sons, 1988), 190–97; Posner, *Case Closed: Lee Harvey Oswald and the Assassination of JFK* (New York: Doubleday, 1993), 235–40; and Liebeler, *Thoughts*, 193–254.

106. The law was entitled the President John F. Kennedy Records Collection Act of 1992.

107. Assassination Records Review Board, *Final Report of the Assassination Records Review Board* (Washington, DC: US Government Printing Office,1998), 1–2 (hereafter "ARRB Report").

108. Belin, "The Assassination of Earl Warren and the Truth," address before the National Press Club, Washington, DC (March 26, 1992), 2–3.

109. Ibid.

110. Griffin, interview by author, November 28, 2012. The letter and statement are attached to my written statement before the Subcommittee of the House Committee on Government Operations on April 28, 1992.

111. 138 Cong. Rec. H1984 (March 26, 1992); ARRB Report, 2.

112. Legislation and National Security Subcommittee of the House Committee on Government Operations, *Hearings before the Legislation and National Security Subcommittee of the House Committee on Government Operations* (Washington, DC: US Government Printing Office, 1993), 89 (hereafter "Assassination Materials Disclosure Hearings").

113. Ibid., 100; George Lardner, "The Way It Wasn't; In 'JFK' Stone Assassinates the Truth," *Washington Post* (December 20, 1991), D2.

114. Assassination Materials Disclosure Hearings, 159.

115. Ibid., 164.

116. When Belin testified before the Conyers subcommittee on July 22, he repeated the major points of his National Press Club speech about Stone's film. In a characteristic show of bravado, he challenged the members of the subcommittee to ask him any question whatsoever about the Warren Commission's findings and expressed his confidence that he could answer any such query. Belin took a position on the proposed legislation far beyond what I had advocated on behalf of the commission staff; he recommended that Congress mandate release of all—repeat all—assassination records regardless of any national security classification that they might have. Statement of David W. Belin, Former Counsel, Warren Commission, and Former Executive Director, Rockefeller Commission, before the Legislation and National Security Subcommittee of the House Committee on Government Operations (July 22, 1992).

117. AARB Report, 86–91.

118. Ibid., xxv–xxvii.

119. Bugliosi, *Reclaiming History*, 379.

120. ARRB Report, 8.

121. Assassination Materials Disclosure Hearings, 164.

122. Goldberg, "Conspiracy Interpretations of the Assassination of President Kennedy: International and Domestic" (Security Studies Paper Number 16, University of California, Los Angeles, 1968), 29.

POSTSCRIPT

1. *Los Angeles Times* (September 23, 2000).

2. *New York Times* (January 18, 1999), B8.

3. Lisa Trei, "Influential Law Scholar Dies at 64" *Stanford Report* (October 29, 2003)

4. Martin, "Nicholas Katzenbach 90, Dies; Policy Maker at '60s Turning Points," *New York Times* (May 9, 2012).

5. *Washington Post* (September 29, 2002), C6.

6. Grimes, "Herbert J. Miller Jr., Justice Dept. Leader, Dies at 85," *New York Times* (November 21, 2009).

7. *New York Times* (June 11, 2011), D8.

8. Statement of President Obama, October 14, 2012.

9. *Harvard Law Record,* "Ten Professors to Take" (April 10, 2003), 2; http;//www.gvpt.umd.edu/lpbr/subpages/reviews/weinreb805.htm.

ACKNOWLEDGMENTS

■

M Y BOOK IMPROVED EACH STEP OF THE WAY FROM FIRST DRAFT TO FIN-
ished manuscript with the generous and successful help from many
people whom I acknowledge here.

I have been consistently encouraged by my colleagues on the Warren
Commission staff to undertake this effort to report on our shared experience.
In late 2011 and early 2012, I discussed this project with retired Judge Burt
Griffin (Cleveland), Associate Justice Richard Mosk (Los Angeles), UC Professor Mel Eisenberg (Berkeley), Associate Justice Stuart Pollak (San Francisco), retired USC Professor David Slawson (Orcas Island, WA), retired
Defense Department historian Al Goldberg (Virginia), former Senator Arlen
Specter (Philadelphia), retired New Jersey lawyer Murray Laulicht (Miami),
former Secretary of Transportation Bill Coleman (Washington DC), Maryland
lawyer Charles Shaffer, and Washington DC lawyer Sam Stern. Jack Rosenthal,
a close associate of both Robert Kennedy and Nick Katzenbach in the 1960s,
also urged me to tell my story.

Many readers of early drafts brought me closer to my audience and
showed me how to organize better what I had to say. My alpha readers went
through the book in its first draft and pointed out the larger conceptual problems. They are Barry Sidman, Charles Robbins, Gail Ross, Larry Barrett, Lee
Marks, Susan Liebeler, and Tom Hill. My beta readers went through my semi-
final draft looking for portions that were not clear or consistent and offering
editing suggestions. They are Alan Barak, Bill Willen, Jennifer Kelly, Jonathan
Willens, Karen and David Burnett, Maya Kara, Steve Pollak, and Stan Weinberger. After considering the comments from these readers, I enlisted the assistance of Michael Ollove, an experienced journalist who painstakingly
critiqued the manuscript.

I depended on two researchers to do the necessary research and cite
checking to make the book factually accurate: Susan Macek, both a law student
and doctoral candidate at the University of Maryland, provided research assistance for more than a year. She undertook the task with competence, profes-

sionalism, and enthusiasm and made a very significant contribution. In more recent months, Jacob Kass, a recent college graduate, assisted with research, cite checking, and the use of social media.

Several publishing professionals applied their talent and experience in bringing the book to the public. Carole Sargent, from the Georgetown University Office of Publications and a talented author in her own right, assisted me in finding an agent, Don Fehr from the Trident Media Group. In late 2012 most publishers had already decided which Kennedy-related books would be included in their Fall 2013 catalogs. Don persevered and, finally in February 2013, brought my book to Overlook Press, where Peter Mayer and his colleagues accepted it. Dan Crissman, my editor at Overlook, exhibited great patience and insight in persuading me to shorten the length of the book and to sharpen its voice. David Vyorst, an expert in social media, has skillfully introduced me to all the ways in the online world in which to communicate with people about my book. Meryl Zegarek, my publicist, brought her experience and enthusiasm to marketing the book. Facing a very competitive market in 2013, Meryl reached out to a wide range of potential reviewers and media outlets to provide me with opportunities to discuss the book around the country.

Several friends have advocated on my behalf to find venues in which to talk about my book: Burt Griffin in Cleveland, Howard Nemerovski and Stuart Pollak in San Francisco, Marc Winkelman in Austin, Scott Berrie in New York City, Stan Weinberger in Chicago, and Steven Stone in Washington, DC.

Finally, a short appreciation to my wife. Deanne and I have worked together on projects for more than forty years, including two books which we co-authored. Notwithstanding her many commitments during the past two years, she brought her considerable talent and judgment to bear as I struggled to tell the story of my Warren Commission experience in a way that might interest the reading public. When my attention flagged, she reemphasized the importance of this book to the historical record of the JFK assassination. When I got frustrated or disappointed, she showered me with optimism and positive suggestions. When the occasion arose, she edited with her usual vigorous pen. Deanne's support and wisdom were crucial in bringing this book to publication.

INDEX

■